Healing the Soul
in the Age of the Brain

Elio Frattaroli, M. D.

Healing the Soul
in the Age of the Brain

Becoming Conscious in an

Unconscious World

VIKING

VIKING

Published by the Penguin Group
Penguin Putnam Inc., 375 Hudson Street, New York, New York 10014, U.S.A.
Penguin Books Ltd, 27 Wrights Lane, London W8 5TZ, England
Penguin Books Australia Ltd, Ringwood, Victoria, Australia
Penguin Books Canada Ltd, 10 Alcorn Avenue, Toronto, Ontario, Canada M4V 3B2
Penguin Books (N.Z.) Ltd, 182–190 Wairau Road, Auckland 10, New Zealand

Penguin Books Ltd, Registered Offices:
Harmondsworth, Middlesex, England

First published in 2001 by Viking Penguin,
a member of Penguin Putnam Inc.

10   9   8   7   6   5   4   3   2   1

Grateful acknowledgment is made for permission to reprint excerpts from the following
copyrighted works:
    Listening to Prozac by Peter D. Kramer. Copyright © Peter D. Kramer, 1993.
Used by permission of Viking Penguin, a division of Penguin Putnam Inc.
    "Teach Your Children" by Graham Nash. Copyright © 1970 Nash Notes
(renewed). All rights administered by Sony/ATV Music Publishing, 8 Music
Square West, Nashville, TN 37203. All rights reserved. Used by permission.

LIBRARY OF CONGRESS CATALOGING-IN-PUBLICATION DATA
Frattaroli, Elio.
    Healing the soul in the age of the brain : becoming conscious
in an unconscious world / Elio Frattaroli.
        p. cm.
    Includes index.
    ISBN 0–670–86189–8 (hardcover : alk. paper)
    1. Psychoanalysis.   2. Psychotherapy.   3. Consciousness.   4. Soul—Psychological aspects.
    I. Title
    RC506 .F67 2001
    616.89'17—dc21   2001023996

This book is printed on acid-free paper.

Printed in the United States of America
Set in Adobe Garamond
Designed by Francesca Belanger

For my parents
and
for my children

Acknowledgements

Although I was the only person typing the words, I feel strongly that I was not the only author of this book. I am grateful to my analyst, Homer Curtis, for helping me in a long process of inspiration, perspiration and integration through which both I and the book evolved and matured. I am grateful to my patients—those who are in the book and those who are not—for teaching me about the healing power that is within us all and for helping me grow as a therapist and as a person.

I give special thanks to my mother, Yolanda, for always believing in me without reservation; to my late father, Elio, for believing in me with specific useful reservations; to my brother, Paul, and my sister, Rosemary, for believing that I really would one day finish this book; to my wife, Dianne, for her much needed love and support, for her helpful reading and rereading of the book, and for her willingness to tolerate my entitlement and make me sandwiches; and to my wonderful children, Gregory and Nicole, for inspiring me and teaching me the meaning of life.

I want to thank Polly Young-Eisendrath for her friendship, for her encouragement and for introducing me to her extraordinary agent, Beth Vesel, who has been so important to this book.

I thank Beth for valuing my ideas enough to nurse me through a painful year of writing the book proposal (after which she sold the book in a week!), and then for contributing important ideas of her own at crucial junctures during the writing of the book when I needed help.

I also want to thank Beth for guiding me toward Viking Penguin. If I wasn't already happy as a psychiatrist and psychoanalyst, I would love to work for Viking. They are a great group of people who definitely have soul. I am particularly grateful for—and a bit awed by—the skill of my fabulous editors,

Pam Dorman and Beena Kamlani, who always saw the baby hidden in the reams of dirty bath water (and mixed metaphors) I sent them and who gently but firmly made me keep doing it until I got it right. Beena appears in Chapter 10 and both Pam and Beena are featured in the last chapter. I also want to give special thanks to Susan Petersen Kennedy, the Chairman of Viking Penguin for her vitalizing enthusiasm and support.

Three study groups have contributed greatly to the book. Harvey Horowitz's weekly seminar was an amazing grace in my life for many years. It provoked me to think more clearly about the psychotherapeutic process, the philosophy of science, and the mind-body problem. In fact, it was a source of endless provocation, frustration, creativity, friendship, great meals and even a Friday night poker game. I know everyone from the seminar—Harvey, Bill Overton, Howard and Maggie Baker, Diana Rosenstein, Neil Schecker, Polly Young-Eisendrath, and Lisa Guttuso Klenk—will smile when they read my confessions in the last chapter. Then there is my psychoanalytic study group—Sterrett Mayson, Faith Cohen, Ralph and Lana Fishkin, Mike Kowitt, Betsy Webb—who have helped me grow as a therapist and who gave me much needed validation on the first version of Mary's story (Part Four). Finally, Lynne Robinson's study group on spirituality and healing has been a source of inspiration, grounding, and sustenance. Lynne, Marcy Vaughn and Peg Van Vyven have read more of the book and spent more time discussing it with me than anyone else except my wife and my editors. They have really been there for—and with—me.

Finally, I want to thank a number of special friends and colleagues who have contributed to the book in important ways that I will always remember: Jim Cox, Glen Gabbard, Laurel Lipshutz, Sheila Judge, Ron Kwon, Gabriel Rocco, June Strickland, Dick Wertime.

Sections of Chapters 5 and 13 were adapted from an article I published in the *Psychiatric Times*: "Psychotherapy and Medication: The Mind–Body Problem and the Choice of Intervention," November, 1991, p.73ff. Sections of Chapter 6 were adapted from an article I published in the *Psychoanalytic Review*: "Bruno Bettelheim's Unrecognized Contribution to Psychoanalytic Thought." vol. 81, pp.379–409, 1994.

Contents

I. The Importance of Being Conscious

*The perception of one's fellow man as a whole, as a unity, and as unique—
even if his wholeness, unity, and uniqueness are only partly developed, as is
usually the case—is opposed in our time by almost everything that is
commonly understood as specifically modern. In our time there
predominates an analytical, reductive, and deriving look between man
and man. This look is analytical, or rather pseudoanalytical, since it treats
the whole being as put together and therefore able to be taken apart. . . .
An effort is being made today radically to destroy the mystery
between man and man. The personal life, the ever-near
mystery, once the source of the stillest enthusiasms, is
leveled down.*
—Martin Buber, *William Alanson White Memorial Lectures*

*Dumb yearnings, hidden appetites, are ours,
And they* must *have their food.*
   —William Wordsworth, *Prelude: Book Fifth*

I. A Brief Introduction to the Soul

Now there are some things we all know, but we don't take'm out and look at'm very often. We all know that something is eternal. And it ain't houses and it ain't names, and it ain't earth, and it ain't even the stars . . . everybody knows in their bones that something is eternal, and that something has to do with human beings. All the greatest people ever lived have been telling us that for five thousand years and yet you'd be surprised how people are always losing hold of it.

—Thornton Wilder, *Our Town*

Being There

The first game of the 1993 National League playoffs between the Philadelphia Phillies and the Atlanta Braves was about to begin. My son Gregory and I were sitting high up in the center field grandstands of Philadelphia's Veterans Stadium—two specks of foam in an ocean of restlessly excited fans, swelling against the shores of the AstroTurf playing field. Rooting for the Phillies, we naturally expected to lose, especially against the notorious Atlanta pitching staff, one of the greatest ever assembled.

I don't remember whether we were standing for every pitch as Curt Schilling, the ace pitcher of our own team, struck out the first Atlanta batter. However, I do remember sitting down afterward and calling out loudly, "Okay, Curt, let's get twenty-six more of those!"

"Daaad!" moaned an embarrassed Greg, as seven or eight of the fans who were seated just below us turned around, chuckling. Perhaps they were wondering whether it was the voice of optimism or cynicism they were hearing. I wasn't sure myself.

The first two pitches to the second batter were strikes, each punctuated by a thunderous cheer that subsided and then rose again like a huge wave cresting. When the batter swung and missed for strike three, the wave crashed and exploded into a roar that seemed to lift the stadium with it.

"Okay, Curt, just twenty-five more!" I yelled, sitting down once again on the edge of my seat as batter number three walked up to the plate. This time Greg almost smiled, and I caught the amused eyes of a middle-aged couple seated down the aisle a few seats to our right. I felt an immediate bond with them and, by extension, with everyone in the stadium.

With each pitch to the third batter the level of excitement rose even higher, until finally Curt nailed his third straight strikeout and the stadium was transformed. The sea of restlessly excited fans became as one—sixty-three thousand specks of foam vaporizing and coalescing into a single triumphant sound, which seemed to continue unabated through the fourth strikeout, and then the fifth. I know the Phillies had to have batted somewhere in there, but I have no recollection of it.

What I do remember is screaming out, "Hey, Curt! Only twenty-two more!" and literally not being able to hear the sound of my own voice. My words were swallowed up even as they left my lips, vanishing into a joyful, clamorous tidal wave of sound. But, paradoxically, in that very moment of vanishing I had a sudden, vivid experience of inner presence. I experienced myself as a soundless eddy of consciousness, merging into a roaring unconscious sea. In that moment, I was the very sound of one hand clapping.

The Place Where Experiencing Happens

If I have told this story at all well, then readers who have had the same kind of experience will know the quality of awareness I have just tried to put into words, because they will be able to recognize it from within themselves. But what of readers who have never had such an experience? They may understand what happened as an external event, but can they ever really know what it was like as an inner awareness? To these readers I might say, "Ya hadda be there!" implying that certain experiences cannot be adequately understood unless they are shared. But then, where exactly would a person have to be in order to share my inner experience, to know what it was really like? An interesting question.

Could a person understand my experience, for instance, from having had a similar one at Baltimore's Camden Yards, which holds a mere forty thousand fans? How about at a football or basketball game? Could a person have the same sort of experience while listening to a concert at a symphony hall? How about while doing a circle dance at a wedding, or chanting in unison at a meditation retreat, or walking alone on a deserted beach? Could a person who had never shouted out at a ball game or cried "Bravo!" at a concert understand my experience? Could my son understand it, or the middle-aged couple with whom I felt bonded?

What I am trying to suggest with these questions is that the place you gotta be to understand another person's inner experience is not a particular geographic locale, or cultural institution, or social setting, or even a particular physical body, but rather an indefinable inner place—the place where experiencing happens. This is a metaphorical place, like the Ithaca of Homer's *Odyssey*, or the Rome that all roads lead to. It is a place we must struggle to get to, only to discover that we have been there all along. Even if you have never had an experience quite like mine, you might get to the place where I had it without ever getting up from your chair, and you might understand the experience much better from reading my account of it than the guy in the Braves cap could, who was sitting just three seats away from me at the game.

From Baseball to Psychiatry

As a psychiatrist dedicated to the practice of psychoanalytic psychotherapy, I often feel like a Phillies fan marooned in Atlanta's old Fulton County Stadium, trying to describe to the Braves fans there just what those five straight strikeouts were like. It seems that the psychotherapy I know and love happens in a completely different ballpark from the one where most of my colleagues hold their season tickets. Try asking a psychiatrist, "What do you call the place where experiencing happens?" and nine times out of ten you will get a quizzical look and an automatic answer: "Why, the brain, of course."

I disagree. I think of the brain as a place much like a stadium, where publicly observable, measurable, material events happen—the shouting of phonemes, the throwing and hitting of baseballs, the running of bases, the electrochemical transmission of nerve impulses. The mind, too, may be likened to a stadium, a kind of virtual "field of dreams" where private, unmeasurable, immaterial events happen—thoughts, feelings, images, sensations. But the *experiencing* of all these events happens in a place utterly different from any stadium. That's what I noticed at the Phillies game, when I couldn't hear the sound of my own voice screaming "Only twenty-two more!" As my words vanished into the din, I found myself listening to something beyond the words, beyond even the thought and the elated emotion—to a soundless voice, an inner movement, springing from the still center where all experiencing happens. In the utter privacy of that boisterous public moment, I recognized that I was listening to the soul.

Let me be clear about what I am suggesting here. I believe that humans possess a spiritual as well as a physical dimension, and that there are very real differences between brain, mind, and soul. I think of the soul as the experiencing self, the "I," an ineffable whole that integrates processes happening at four different levels of experience—body, brain, mind, and spirit. In this I disagree radically with the vast majority of psychiatrists today, who are so entranced with the powers of modern medication that they concern themselves with symptoms rather than souls, treating the chemically imbalanced brain but ignoring the experiencing self.

The Age of the Brain

I believe it should be of great concern to us—as individuals, as a society, and as a culture—that our psychiatrists conceive of personal experiencing as happening in the brain and not in the mind or soul. Current fashions in psychiatry, as in the scientific community generally, tend quickly to become current fashions in our popular thinking—"seep[ing] into popular culture like the dye from a red shirt in hot water" (T. M. Luhrmann).[1] The fashion nowadays is to use the word mind instead of soul (to avoid any spiritual connotations) and to believe that either *mind* or *soul* is really just another word for *brain*. This belief—that anything we might call mental or spiritual is really only a by-product of brain activity—is the hallmark of our current "Age of the Brain." It helps us answer academic or scientific questions about the mind and mental illness. But it doesn't provide much of an answer for the questions we really care about: Who am I? and What is the meaning of my unique experience as a human being?

To see how our official philosophy answers these ultimate personal questions, consider a few representative pronouncements by an assortment of internationally recognized experts: psychiatrist/neuroscientist Eric Kandel, philosopher John Searle, Nobel laureate biochemist Francis Crick, neurologist/brain researcher Antonio Damasio, former NIMH director Lewis Judd, and surgeon general David Satcher:[2]

> All mental processes, even the most complex psychological processes, derive from operations of the brain. The central tenet of this view is that what we commonly call mind is a range of functions carried out by the brain. (Kandel, 1998)

> [E]verything in our conscious life, from feeling pains, tickles, and itches to—pick your favorite—feeling the angst of postindustrial man under late capitalism or experiencing the ecstasy of skiing in deep powder—is caused by brain processes. (Searle, 1995)

> "You," your joys and your sorrows, your memories and your ambitions, your sense of personal identity and free will, are in fact no more than the behavior of a vast assembly of nerve cells and their associated molecules. As Lewis Carroll's Alice might have phrased it: "You're nothing but a pack of neurons." (Crick, 1994)

> To say that mind comes from brain is indisputable, but I prefer to qualify the statement and consider the reasons why the brain's neurons behave in such a thoughtful manner. (Damasio, 1994)

> [T]he understanding of mental disorders and their treatment requires a new awareness of how the brain functions, how it creates "mind," and . . . how disordered brain creates disordered mind. (Judd, 1990)

> [S]cience . . . says that the bases of mental illness are chemical changes in the brain and, therefore physical changes, changes in the basic cells of the brain. That's why I hold that there's no longer any justification for the distinction that we've made between "mind and body" or "mental and physical illnesses." Mental illnesses are physical illnesses. They're related to physical changes in the brain. (Satcher, 1999)

In the pages that follow, I will be arguing that this received psychiatric philosophy of ours suffers from two serious problems that make it hazardous to the health of our culture. First, it is *dehumanizing*, having a narrowly neurobiological focus that discounts the uniqueness of the individual and the meaning of inner personal experience. Second, it is *incoherent,* being based on a general misunderstanding of the nature of science and on a more specific misinterpretation of what psychiatric medications actually do.

Missing the Trees for the Soil

Perhaps the most interesting and surprising thing about the six unequivocal assertions listed above is that there is no evidence whatsoever to support them! They are not statements of scientific fact but rather articles of quasi-religious faith cloaked in the language of science. No philosopher, scientist, or psychiatrist even pretends to have any idea *how* brain processes could possibly produce the mysterious and ineffable experience of human consciousness. Yet the belief that "brain . . . creates 'mind' "—and the general philosophy of "scientific materialism" it reflects[3]—is so strongly held by so many scientists nowadays that it is considered unscientific even to question it. Nevertheless, it is a seriously misguided belief, and I want to emphasize that the reasoning generally used to justify it—captured especially well in the above quote from David Satcher—does not stand up to careful scrutiny.

The reasoning goes that, because the symptoms of mental illness can be alleviated by changing brain chemistry, mental illnesses must really be disorders of brain chemistry and therefore mind (and soul) must really be brain. This line of "neurophilosophical" reasoning is taken so much for granted nowadays that it can be quite startling to realize how little sense it actually makes. We could with equal logic argue that if a tree disease can be cured by changing the chemistry of the soil, then tree diseases must really be soil disorders and therefore trees must really be soil!

In fact, there is no logical or scientific reason *not* to assume that the soul is a distinct entity, rooted in the brain and dependent on it for consciousness just as a tree is rooted in the soil and dependent on it for life. If we think of the soul as the place where experiencing happens, then brain processes would be a necessary condition (like soil for a tree), but not a sufficient cause, for that experiencing. For mental illness, this would mean that what goes on at the level of the brain can never account fully for the illness as it is experienced at the level of the person; and that even though medication is often quite helpful, *it is never a sufficient treatment* for an inner crisis of the soul.

If we take this commonsense logic seriously—and I challenge anyone to refute it[4]—then we must conclude that modern psychiatric opinion is simply wrong. Mental illness cannot be just a chemical imbalance in the brain. Rather, it is a *disharmony* of body, brain, mind, and spirit within the whole person: an inner conflict of the soul. Such a disharmony may include a chemical imbalance in the brain as one of its elements, but the chemical imbalance itself is not the mental illness, nor does it cause the mental illness.

Unfortunately, entrenched beliefs tend to be impervious to logic, and so our blind cultural faith in scientific materialism has now brought us to the point where we are willing to accept extravagant and potentially dangerous uses of medication that could never be justified on the basis of scientific evidence alone. The burgeoning use of antidepressants in children is the most glaring example. Very little research has been done in this area,[5] and what research has been done has almost always shown antidepressants to be no more effective than placebos in the pediatric age group.[6] Moreover, at least one antidepressant has been associated with an increased risk of sudden death in children.[7] Most importantly, we know almost *nothing* about longer-term consequences of modifying the biochemistry of an immature growing brain.[8] And yet the *Philadelphia Inquirer* reported in 1998 that in the previous year 207,000 children between the ages of six and twelve had been prescribed antidepressants—a 43 percent increase from the year before. Also in 1998 a psychiatric journal reported that the prescription of selective sertonin inhibitor antidepressants for children *five years old and younger* had increased tenfold in four years.[9]

For adults, the trend is equally alarming. As reported in *Newsweek* on January 26, 1998, the concept of chemical imbalance is now being applied indiscriminately, not only to cases of clear-cut mental illness but to objectionable personality traits as well.[10] The fault is not in ourselves, we are told, but in our neurotransmitters! Any qualities or tendencies we might have reason to dislike in ourselves—anything from shyness to ill-temperedness to scrupulosity to simple irresponsibility—we are now being taught to think of as subtle neurochemical malfunctions that can and should be corrected with medication.

Who Do You Think You Are?

It was psychiatrist Peter Kramer who first popularized the idea of using medication to modify undesirable personality traits. In his 1993 book, *Listening to Prozac*, Kramer coined the rather chilling term "cosmetic psychopharmacology" to describe how Prozac and other medications can be used to make people feel "better than well"—"to give social confidence to the habitually timid, to make the sensitive brash, to lend the introvert the social skills of a salesman."[11] This apparent endorsement of the idea of "better personalities through chemistry" came alarmingly close to fulfilling the prophecy of *Brave New World*, Aldous Huxley's 1932 novel about a future utopia in which human individuality has been completely eliminated through biotechnology, behavior modification, and a drug called soma. Soma was designed to keep the populace psychologically mellow and emotionally bland. It was said to have "All the advantages of Christianity and alcohol; none of their defects." "One cubic centimetre cures ten gloomy sentiments," so the slogan went.

In sanctioning the cosmetic use of Prozac to make people better than well, Kramer seemed to have forgotten the lesson of *Brave New World*. Although he acknowledged the possibility of moral or ethical concerns about Prozac similar to those Huxley envisioned with soma, Kramer in the end dismissed all such concerns as irrelevant or trivial in the face of what he claimed to be one raw fact:

> The capacity of modern medication to allow a person to experience, on a stable and continuous basis, the feelings of someone with a different temperament and history is among the most extraordinary accomplishments of modern science.[12]

This fantastical assertion reminded me of a retort I once received from an eight-year-old autistic girl, a student in my classroom at Bruno Bettelheim's Orthogenic School who had been disrupting the English lesson I was trying to teach. After many attempts to deal gracefully with what I felt to be her relentlessly willful misbehavior, I finally lost my temper, stood up glowering indignantly at her, and yelled loudly: "Who do you think you are?"

Instantly the meek reply came back: "Somebody else."

According to Peter Kramer, it would seem that I could have achieved the same result—made her feel like somebody else—with far less *agita,* simply by prescribing Prozac.

Who Do You Want to Be?

I suggest that the desire to become "somebody else" is not something to be encouraged and pandered to, but something we should recognize for what it is: a sickness of the soul, a refusal or inability to accept ourselves as we really are that keeps us ultimately from becoming the person we have it in us to become. Cosmetic psychopharmacology, like cosmetic surgery and cosmetics in general, is based on the popular delusion that it is actually possible to be somebody else, that the soul's sickness can be healed through a quick, superficial "fix." More generally, the entire modern biological approach to mental illness—the so-called Medical Model—fosters the same delusory hope, equating sickness of the soul with a neurological glitch, and promising patients an easy chemical normalization without their ever having to confront the existential crisis that is at the center of their pain. It is time we all recognized this delusion for what it is. There is no quick fix for the soul, no easy procedure for becoming somebody else through a cosmetic alteration in brain chemistry. And it doesn't matter how many scientists and psychiatrists want to tell us otherwise. The science they are preaching is a religion just as unprovable as any other.

A Psychotherapeutic Model of Psychiatry

Lest I be misunderstood, let me emphasize at the outset that I am not at all opposed to using psychiatric medications. In fact, I have found them quite useful and am currently prescribing a wide variety of them, including Prozac, for about half the patients I am treating. However, I am willing to prescribe these medications only for patients I am *also* seeing in ongoing psychotherapy. Only through a psychotherapeutic process can I get to know the inner lives of my patients well enough to understand in depth not only their symptoms but also the effects that medication is and is not having on them as people. Only through a psychotherapeutic process can I attend to the personal and existential meanings that my patients' illnesses have for them, and discover how these illnesses reflect the disowned needs of the soul.

I take seriously the root meaning of the word *psychiatry*—from the Greek words *psyche* and *iatreia*—as a timely reminder of the larger purpose my profession is meant to serve, a purpose we have sadly lost track of in recent years:

> **psyche** [Greek *psychē* life, spirit, soul, self; akin to Greek *psychein* to breathe, blow] **1a:** the vital principle of corporeal matter that is a distinct mental or spiritual entity coextensive with but independent of body or soma: SOUL, SELF, PERSONALITY . . . **1b:** the specialized cognitive, conative and affective aspects of a psychosomatic unity: MIND; *specif*: the totality of the id, ego, and superego including both conscious and unconscious components

> **-iatry** [from the Greek *iatreia* art or action of healing, from *iatros* physician]: medical treatment: healing[13]

Etymologically, culturally, and ethically, *psychiatry* means "healing the soul." This is a calling, and a need, that can never be answered simply by prescribing an alteration in brain chemistry. Healing the soul requires a growth-enhancing personal encounter with another human being in a *psychotherapeutic process*. It requires what philosopher Martin Buber called an I–Thou relationship—a "personal making present," in which one person recognizes the unique individuality of another, and the other flourishes in being so recognized. Unfortunately, with the advent of cosmetic psychopharmacology and managed care, too few psychiatrists remember, if they ever knew, what a psychotherapeutic process is, and too few patients realize that healing the soul through an I–Thou relationship with their physician is a potential treatment option that is no longer being offered them. In the Age of the Brain, psychiatric treatment has been reduced to an exclusively I–It relationship, in which patients are objectified, diagnosed as "cases," equated with their brains (and genes), and treated according to standards of statistical science rather than of personal knowledge.

One of my primary purposes in writing this book is to show that this politically sanctioned, neurological vision of Medical Model psychiatry is no more than a shallow philosophical prejudice, without scientific foundation or merit, and to propose an alternative, a Psychotherapeutic Model in which the soul—not the brain—is considered the proper focus of psychiatric attention. I want to reclaim the psychotherapeutic process as the heart and soul of psychiatry, putting psychopharmacology in its proper place as only one of psychiatry's helping hands. More generally, I want to reclaim the soul itself as the most important element of our existence as individuals, as a society, and as a culture.

Whom Do You Trust?

For many of us, our first ideas about the soul came from parents or religious teachers who told us about it when we were children. They may have told us that the soul is the part of us that lives on after death, or that it is what distinguishes us from animals and makes us human, or that it is the seat of reason and moral judgment, or the part of us capable of free will. Common to all these traditional ideas about the soul is the belief that it is something spiritual—nonphysical—in human nature. Most of us grew up with some form of this belief in the soul as spirit because, instinctively, unreflectively, we trusted those who taught us to believe in it.

As adults, however, we have a greater need to think for ourselves. Rather than automatically and unthinkingly accepting authority, we aspire to form our own opinions and beliefs, based on standards of truth that are personally convincing to us. Yet childish patterns of deference to authority are surprisingly difficult to overcome, so we may find it confusing when the powerful authority of Big Science, speaking through psychiatry's Medical Model, tells us that *soul* is merely another word for *brain*. This puts us in the position of trying to form our own opinion while caught between two conflicting authorities. What we had previously thought of as the spiritual essence of our humanity we are now told is merely the echo of neurons firing, with no independent existence or functioning of its own. According to this modern scientific dogma, all our conscious experiences, the way we think and feel— even who we are—are simply a by-product of the way our brains are wired. The idea of personal autonomy, or free will, or forming opinions that are genuinely our own opinions (all these being functions of the soul, as traditionally conceived), must therefore be an illusion, a kind of trick our brain plays on our consciousness.

Yet, ironically, in rejecting the traditional religious idea of a spiritual soul for the modern scientific idea of a neurological soul, scientists and psychiatrists must inevitably appeal to the very higher faculties whose relevance they deny. Their argument depends on our ability somehow to discern that scientific facts are inherently and objectively different—more valid—than religious beliefs. But if, as they insist, all ideas are nothing more than electrochemical impulses in the neurons of the brain, determined only by other such electrochemical impulses, then how could we possibly tell whether one impulse was more valid than another? Imagine, for instance, a brain researcher who proved that the impulses that produce scientific-fact ideas happen in a different part of the brain or have a different electrical pattern from those that produce religious-belief ideas. How could he then tell which kind of impulse was better? Each would be merely an automatic response to a series of other impulses, dictated by a pattern of brain wiring and a set of electrochemical inputs that would vary from person to person. Whether you believed in science or in religion or in genocide, or whether you changed your belief from one to the other, would be a matter of meaningless neurological reflex, not of free personal and existential choice. It would have nothing to do with what is objectively true.

If, however, you believe that you are indeed somehow able to recognize ideas as true or false *objectively*—the way many scientists seem to think they can recognize mathematical equations as true and religious beliefs as false—then there has to be something autonomous in you (independent of the way your brain is wired) that is able to do the recognizing. Whatever that something is, it cannot be just another electrochemical impulse. Borrowing from Thornton Wilder, we might say that it ain't genes and it ain't culture, and it ain't even brain wiring and neurological reflex, but there is *something* about human beings that "everybody knows in their bones . . . is eternal."

By this reasoning, all scientific arguments against the idea of an autonomous spiritual soul appear to be logically incoherent—based not on scientific fact but on blind faith in the dogma of scientific materialism. So it makes little sense, if we are going to take our beliefs on faith, to have more faith in the authority of science than in the authority of religion or of our parents. *But what if we are no longer content to take our beliefs on faith in anyone else's authority? How, then, do we go about deciding what to believe?* Ultimately we cannot do better than to have faith in our own authority, and base our beliefs on what makes the most sense, and feels most deeply right, to us. Interestingly enough, this was precisely the method advocated 350 years ago by a man who has been called the father of modern science, French philosopher René Descartes.

Descartes's Truth

Descartes's philosophy began with his decision that he would trust no authority but his own experience and would believe only those things for which he could find within himself not even the remotest possibility of doubt. He resolved to systematically call into question every proposition he had ever been taught, or had heard in church, or had read in a book. He would assume to be false everything that was generally accepted as true, until he found a proposition that was, as he put it, "presented to my mind so clearly and distinctly that I could have no occasion to doubt it."[14] Through this method of systematic doubting, Descartes discovered that the only thing he could know beyond all doubt was that he doubted. In his inner experience of himself doubting, he discovered his own soul—the place from which his doubting, and all his experiencing, originated. He captured this profound self-awareness in the famous words *Cogito, ergo sum:* "I think [in this case, 'I doubt'], therefore I am."

Unfortunately, Descartes's aphorism has been almost universally misunderstood as a kind of "content-thinking"—a logical sequence of thoughts (mental contents) along the lines of the (rather strained) syllogism "It is a fact that I think; facts exist; therefore I exist." On the contrary, I believe that Descartes's words signaled his liberation from content-thinking, representing not a syllogism but an epiphany, an epochal moment of illumination. I like to imagine that it happened something like this: Descartes did indeed start out with a program of content-thinking—the systematic attempt to find a factual proposition (a mental content) that he could know to be true beyond any possibility of doubt. As he relentlessly pursued this program, however, it became increasingly clear to him that there could be no such proposition, that all content-propositions of objective fact were open to doubt. Finally, as he banged his head again and again against his self-constructed wall of doubting, the wall suddenly opened and became a window of awareness, through which he could "see" himself doubting. His attention shifted—a kind of quantum shift of consciousness—from content to process, from the endless series of questionable facts to the questioning act itself. With a shock of recognition, Descartes caught himself in the act and existential moment of questioning. In the immediacy of that distilled awareness of himself as *consciousness in process,* he recognized that he was listening to the soul, the still center and spiritual essence of his personal experiencing. It was this awareness that he summed up in the famous *Cogito, ergo sum.*

Descartes then proceeded to develop his epiphany into a formal philosophy, which we now call *Cartesian dualism.* He was so impressed with the difference between his inner awareness of the soul and his sensory awareness of the physical world that he concluded that human nature must consist of two distinct essences: the thinking mind *(res cogitans),* which is the center of consciousness and is spiritual, not subject to the laws of physics; and the physical body *(res extensa),* which operates according to the same mechanical laws that govern machines and animals.

Cartesian Dualism and the Mind–Body Problem

Descartes was by no means the first to articulate a dualistic philosophy—one that conceives the soul (or mind) as an essence fundamentally different from the brain. Dualism has a venerable tradition in Western philosophy going back clearly to Plato, with more obscure origins long before him. Of particular importance for psychotherapy, dualistic philosophy reflects the universal human experience of *inner conflict*—a tension between opposing needs and tendencies within the self that triggers anxiety, shame, or guilt. This existential condition of inner conflict has been recognized and described by virtually every known religion as an opposition between the Flesh and the Spirit: between the "lower" passions (our bodily appetites and emotional needs for pleasure and power) and the higher desires (our spiritual yearning toward truth, love, and virtue). In this way, dualistic philosophy had been linked with the religious problem of good and evil. The dualism of the Flesh and the Spirit was a way of talking about our inner sense of moral choice between our temptation toward sin and our aspirations toward virtue.

What was truly revolutionary in Descartes's thinking was that he divorced dualism from the religious problem of good and evil, and for the first time treated it in a way that can properly be called scientific—through a carefully described systematic observation of his own conscious experience. Unlike Plato and the many religious teachers who had located the soul in our innate sense of morality, Descartes discovered it in the simple but profound experiencing of self-awareness. We now take as self-evident the distinction between the private inner world of introspective awareness and the public outer world of sensory awareness (including the awareness of our own bodies), but in fact it is only since Descartes that we have become able to recognize this distinction. Descartes shifted the terms in which we think about dualism so that instead of an inner moral conflict between higher and lower passions, we now understand it as a complementarity of inner awareness and outer perception, self and other, subject and object. This shift has been profoundly important for the evolution of Western culture. It promoted the development of individualism—as a natural extension of Descartes's inward focus on the private self—and it established the modern scientific worldview, as an extension of his outward focus on the body and the objective physical world.

However, this progress that we owe to Cartesian dualism has come at a price. In shifting the focus of self-reflective awareness from the conflicting passions of the soul to the distilled consciousness of the mind, it seems that Descartes inadvertently reinforced a somewhat schizophrenic tendency in our human nature—a tendency to avoid the unsettling awareness of inner conflict by divorcing our mental life from our experience of the body. We began to shift our interest and attention from the soul to the mind, using the Cartesian dichotomy as a way of distancing ourselves from our emotional experience, thinking of the emotions as belonging to the body but identifying the self with the mind. In reflecting on the self we began to ignore the passions of the soul and to focus more and more on the dispassionate ideas of the mind. We defined ourselves no longer in terms of what we felt but in terms of what we thought and perceived.

The result of this self-alienating trend is apparent today in every major university psychology department, where course offerings are limited almost exclusively to cognitive science and neuroscience—studying the functions of a detached intellectual mind (learning, language, memory, perception, and reasoning), and the operations of a disembodied electrochemical brain. Rarely is there even a single course that deals in a meaningful way with the human emotions, still less with the experience of inner conflict. More disturbingly, what's missing from our psychology departments is also missing from our collective cultural consciousness. As individuals and as a society, we have lost the moral compass that used to be provided by our awareness of inner conflict. We no longer recognize the "existential emotions" of anxiety, shame, and guilt as signals of moral conflict, central to the life of the soul. Indeed, it now seems that we have lost touch with our emotions, and with our sense of the soul altogether.

Of course Descartes cannot be held responsible for what we have made of his philosophy. Cartesian dualism has perhaps made it easier for us to detach ourselves from our emotions, but it certainly did not create our need to do so. Nor did Cartesian dualism create the so-called mind–body problem. Rather, it simply changed the way we experience the mind–body problem. Before Descartes, we experienced it as an inner moral conflict between the Spirit and the Flesh—the problem of good and evil. Since Descartes, we have come to experience it as the problem of self-alienation—our difficulty being in touch with our feelings and bringing body, mind, and spirit together in a fully emotional experience of ourselves.

Nevertheless, there is a widespread current opinion that the mind–body problem was actually Descartes's invention—*Descartes' Error* as one book called it[15]—an unfortunate and unnecessary split he imposed on our way of thinking about ourselves. I disagree. Based on my experience of the psychotherapeutic process, I am convinced that the mind–body problem is inherent in human nature. We may experience it either as an inner moral conflict or as self-alienation, but both elements are always present to some degree. In fact they are closely related. *Self-alienation results from a defensive need to detach oneself from the disturbing awareness of inner conflict.* This link between moral conflict and self-alienation was actually quite well known to Western culture long before Descartes. It is poignantly represented, for instance, in the story of Oedipus, who tried to detach himself both geographically and emotionally from the disturbing prophecy of his forbidden passions, and then gouged out his own eyes when he was finally forced to "see" himself as he really was. Shakespeare's Hamlet, too, expressed the need to detach himself from the torment of his conflicting passions in his suicidal soliloquy (written forty years before Descartes's *Cogito*): "Oh that this too, too solid flesh would melt."

Listening to the Soul

We might say, then, that in equating the soul with a detached self-reflective consciousness, Descartes encouraged our already universal tendency to split ourselves off from the disturbing experience of inner conflict. Yet in doing so he also pointed the way to resolving this inner split, by teaching us how to use that self-reflective consciousness to pay attention to our inner lives. This is the great achievement of Descartes's method and the basis for the psychotherapeutic process of healing the soul. The idea is to focus our self-reflective Cartesian consciousness not on our thought processes but on our emotions—especially on anxiety, shame, and guilt. By allowing ourselves to have a full conscious experience of these painful emotions, we can discover for ourselves, beyond any possibility of doubt, that they always point to an experience of inner moral conflict. If we then examine this conflict further, experiencing both sides of it more fully, we discover that it always involves some degree of self-alienation, a need to disown, repudiate, or otherwise push out of awareness important elements of our emotional lives—precisely those emotions that, when we begin to feel them, will provoke anxiety, shame, or guilt in us. As we become more conscious of these previously repudiated emotions, we also become more accepting, less alienated from ourselves, because we discover that however disturbing our passions may be, and however destructive they may feel, there is always something in them that is life-affirming and growth-enhancing—a baby with the bathwater.

This entire process of self-reflection—paying careful attention to one's conscious experiences of anxiety, shame, and guilt, and then to the deeper layers of disowned, less conscious emotions they point to—is the heart of the psychotherapeutic process. I believe it is the heart of a fully human life as well. It is what I call *listening to the soul* in its most complete form: not the detached awareness of the soul as pure consciousness that Descartes emphasized, but a richer, more engaged awareness of the soul as authentic self—an ineffable mixture of pure consciousness and personal passion—captured in the full experiencing of conflicted emotion.

What Are We Really Experiencing When We Experience Ourselves?

The psychotherapeutic practice of listening to the soul reflects the principle that *it is primarily in our awareness of feeling, not thinking, that we can discover who we really are.* From this perspective, the value of Cartesian dualism has been to promote awareness of the inner life. Its weakness has been in missing the importance of the inner experience of emotion.[16] If we distinguish, as Descartes did, only between the mind as a center of detached awareness and the body as a center of mechanical physiological activity, then we cannot account for the kind of complex states of inner moral and emotional conflict that are experienced in a psychotherapeutic process. To do this, we need to expand the simple Cartesian dichotomy of body and mind—in which mind is considered synonymous with soul—by considering the soul as a complex entity, the center of the whole person, the experiencing self. We can then think of the experience of felt emotion as one in which mind and body, spirit and flesh, come together in a more or less integrated experience of the soul. We can understand the experiences of inner conflict and self-alienation as *dis*-integrated experiences of the soul in which our capacity to feel is restricted.

This is essentially the understanding that Sigmund Freud proposed in his model of the soul as a three-way interaction—either harmonious or discordant—between the id, ego, and superego. Actually, Freud's meaning is better conveyed by translating his original German terms *(das Es, das Ich, das Überich)* into their proper English equivalents: the *It,* the *I,* and the *I that stands above,* referring to processes of the body, the soul, and the detached, self-reflective mind. As Bruno Bettelheim has pointed out, the more familiar Latinate terms are really mistranslations that have reinforced a mechanistic caricature of psychoanalysis in the English-speaking world.[17] They have obscured the way Freud's ideas are grounded in personal, emotional experience, and have fostered a false impression of the psychotherapeutic process as a kind of intellectual game, a putting together of misplaced mental contents into a cognitive map, like a jigsaw puzzle. In this way Freud's method, like Descartes's, has come to be misunderstood as an application of content-thinking. On the contrary, as I will illustrate in Part Three, Freudian psychotherapy is a formal method of listening to the soul, aimed at catching oneself—the *I*—in process.

The Danger of Scientific Materialism

Considering that the mind–body problem is ultimately the problem of inner conflict, it is hardly surprising that Freudian psychotherapy and Cartesian dualism should be misunderstood and discredited nowadays in much the same way. The pervasive doctrine of scientific materialism—the assumption that mind and soul are merely by-products of brain activity—makes it all too easy to persuade ourselves that there is no mind–body problem, no inner conflict or self-alienation, and therefore no need to examine the inner life of the soul in psychotherapy. I believe that the unchecked influence of this materialist philosophy is destructive to Western culture. By discounting the inherent dualism of our inner experience, it fosters and provides a rationalization for a dangerous tendency to denial—not only the denial of inner conflict but potentially the denial of our inner life altogether. As Martin Buber has put it, "The personal life, the ever-near mystery, once the source of the stillest enthusiasms, is leveled down." What this has led to in the Age of the Brain has been a politically endorsed, corporately sponsored psychiatric drug culture that now threatens to destroy the practice of psychotherapy altogether. The rationalization (explicitly or implicitly) goes like this: "Descartes was wrong. There is no mind–body problem. Mind, soul, and brain are really all the same thing. Therefore, why spend years focusing on your inner life and trying to heal the soul in psychotherapy when medication can get you there so much faster and better?"

Our Spirits, Our Selves

If we were to look without the blinders of materialism at the current craze for psychiatric drugs, we could see it easily enough as a symptom of a sick culture seeking to anesthetize itself from the inherent pain of human existence any which way it can: through cosmetic psychopharmacology or cosmetic surgery; through alcohol, drugs, or gambling; through promiscuity or violence; through mindless television or mindless cults. The menu of choices is extensive, but instead of anesthetizing us from our pain, each choice in the end leaves us feeling emptier and more uneasy.

This uneasiness we feel, in our culture and in ourselves, is a manifestation of the mind–body problem, the impulses of the Flesh in conflict with the needs of the Spirit. Yet in the Age of the Brain, our official philosophy tells us there can be no such problem because there really is no Spirit. Believing this makes it easier for us to ignore the pain of our sickness, by eliminating the very concepts that would allow us to name it. But in thus denying the soul a forum for expression, we are left with the persistent aching of the soul's unnamed and unmet needs. These needs embarrass us, so we prefer to keep wearing the philosophical blinders that allow us to pretend the needs aren't there. We could take off our blinders if we chose to, and in fact the cure for our sickness requires that we do so, but something stops us.

Fear of Consciousness

To understand this predicament, it is useful to go back to the beginning—not the historical but the emotional beginning, the inner source of our uneasiness and embarrassment about the soul. There is a story about this beginning in the Bible—just where we would expect it, in the book of Genesis.

Consider the story of Adam and Eve's expulsion from paradise not as divine revelation but as one of those universal myths that express the deepest truths of the human condition. Seen in this way, the story tells of the birth of human consciousness. Before the Fall, Adam and Eve were conscious, but not self-conscious. There was no sense of alienation, no inner conflict to disrupt their primal state of oneness and harmony. They lived in the place of Descartes's epiphany, but without the shock of recognition. They then ate from the tree of the knowledge of good and evil and became *self*-conscious; that is, aware of themselves as separate individuals, alienated from each other, from God, and from the world around them. They had lost their state of primal oneness and had thereby attained a state of separate individuality, only it was an individuality in a world of dualism and discord, a world of both good and evil. In the language of the poet William Blake, they had left the world of childhood innocence and been launched into the fearful world of adult experience. And how did this new adult self-consciousness first dawn in them? Through shame and anxiety, the hallmarks of inner conflict: "Then the eyes of both were opened, and they knew that they were naked; and they sewed fig leaves together and made loincloths for themselves" (Genesis 3:7).[18]

They were ashamed; that is, they were aware of being alienated, not only from each other but, more important, from themselves. Their eyes had been opened to a new knowledge, a feeling-awareness of good and evil within themselves, crystallized in their experience of sexual desire. They were now in a state of inner conflict over this new self-conscious sexuality. They needed to hide from it and from themselves, covering it up. And then they became anxious, afraid of what God might see in them: "They heard the sound of the Lord God walking in the garden at the time of the evening breeze, and the man and his wife hid themselves from the presence of the Lord God among the trees of the garden" (Genesis 3:8).

So the myth of the Fall tells us that the dawning consciousness that makes us human is the awareness of inner conflict, the knowledge of good and evil within ourselves. This "fall" into consciousness occurs through an act of willfulness (eating the forbidden fruit), an assertion of self. Significantly, it can occur only after Adam is aware of a separate "other," in the person of Eve. Thus, the shame and anxiety of inner conflict involve an awareness of an internally alienated, willful self in sexual relation to an externally alienated (separate) other. Another way of putting it is that the emerging awareness of self—the dawning of human consciousness—contains both the painful awareness of selfishness and the painful envy of otherness, *each experienced as a driving force in sexual desire.*

No wonder we fear consciousness! In the light of consciousness we can see that our sexual desire involves both an envy of our partner's otherness (man's envy of the feminine, woman's envy of the masculine—universal elements of the desire to be somebody else) and a selfish need to control, punish, impose, or intrude on that otherness. This we would prefer not to see (to have the God within us—the *I that stands above*—see) in ourselves. We would rather think that our sexual desire is an expression of love, as of course it is. Yet there are times when we cannot help but notice that our desire is not only loving (perhaps not even *primarily* so) but envious and selfish as well. Then we become like Adam and Eve, ashamed and anxious because we recognize that selfishness and envy subvert the full possibilities of love, the I–Thou relation (represented by God in the story). This is the knowledge of good and evil, the shameful awareness of the soul in its ineluctable state of inner conflict.

We Do Have a Choice

I realize that my highly condensed interpretation of the story of Adam and Eve is likely to raise more questions than it answers. I do not mean it to imply that sexual desire is the only emotion that can evoke an experience of inner conflict. As Freud suggested, sexual conflicts are universal, and they operate at the deepest, most intimately personal level of the soul. But as I will describe in numerous clinical examples throughout this book, inner conflict can also revolve around anger, sadness, dependency, pride, or any other emotion that triggers anxiety, shame, or guilt in us—any emotion that threatens to make us more conscious of something we would rather not know about ourselves.

The fact that consciousness is such a threat—that each one of us has crucial aspects of our inner life we would rather not know about—should give us pause. The reason Socrates and the Delphic oracle had to admonish us to "Know thyself" is that they realized we would all, in a way, prefer *not* to. Personal consciousness is a burden and a responsibility that human beings have always been greatly tempted to avoid. Nevertheless, as Genesis tells us, this burden of consciousness is part of the human condition from which we can run but cannot hide. The more we try to deny our experience of inner conflict, the more it tends to assert itself in the form of psychiatric symptoms.

The Medical Model of psychiatry contributes greatly to this problem by catering to our fear of consciousness. It teaches us to think of anxiety, shame, and guilt as meaningless neurological glitches, and not as urgent calls to self-reflection. It denies the relevance, and even the existence, of inner conflict and discounts the usefulness of psychotherapy as a process of healing self-awareness. Instead, it promotes the pharmacological quick fix, neglecting the deepest long-term needs of the soul. The price of this neglect is one that neither psychiatry nor society can any longer afford to pay.

Fortunately, there is an alternative: a Psychotherapeutic Model of psychiatry, whose primary purpose is healing the soul. Where the Medical Model is driven by the fear of consciousness, the Psychotherapeutic Model takes this fear as the central focus of therapeutic attention. Where the Medical Model thinks of mental illness as a chemical imbalance in the brain, the Psychotherapeutic Model understands it as a *limitation of consciousness,* resulting from an inner conflict of the soul. This difference between the Medical Model and the Psychotherapeutic Model is of fateful consequence, not only for the mental health of psychiatric patients but for the spiritual health of our culture as a whole; not only for the scientific standards by which mental illness is defined and treated, but for the ideals and values by which we all find meaning in our lives. To illustrate what I mean by this, and to suggest what is at stake in the choice that confronts us, perhaps the best way to begin is with a story.

2. The Technocrat and the Cowboy

Homo sum: humani nil a me alienum puto.
(I am a man: nothing human is foreign to me.)

—Terence, *The Self-Torturer*

Bill

A young reporter for a small community newspaper was brought to the emergency room at 3 a.m. by his fiancée, after she had awakened to find him standing over her, pointing a shotgun directly at her head. Too stunned to scream, Janet had simply spoken Bill's name. Appearing confused, Bill had then lowered the shotgun and, in a kind of a daze, agreed to come with her to the hospital. He claimed that Janet was the devil and that God had told him to kill her.

Following the advice of the emergency room psychiatrist, Janet filed papers to have Bill involuntarily committed to the psychiatric unit of a community hospital for twenty days. Once hospitalized, Bill admitted that he had actually pulled the trigger, but the gun had jammed. He had been scarcely sleeping at all for the previous two weeks, while working on a story about a local election. The story had started as a routine assignment, but he had gradually come to believe it could change the course of world history, and that his being chosen to write it meant he was Jesus Christ. His thinking about the story had then further evolved into the conviction that Janet was the devil and that nuclear war could be averted only if he killed her.

In the hospital Bill was treated with the antipsychotic drug haloperidol and within a few days seemed much calmer. After two weeks he was scheduled for a court hearing to extend his involuntary commitment. At that time he said that he no longer believed Janet was the devil but also that he knew he had a problem and wanted to stay in the hospital voluntarily to continue his treatment. He was then transferred to my care as a voluntary inpatient, with the idea that he might need extended inpatient treatment and would certainly need intensive psychotherapy. In my very first meeting with him, however, he told me that he felt much better and was anxious to leave the hospital as soon as possible. He attributed his former "mistaken" ideas about Janet's being the devil to sleep deprivation. He said he was comfortable with Janet now and planned to return to her apartment. When I asked him how he felt about having almost killed her, he replied that, actually, he had known the gun was jammed because he had tested it earlier in the day, but that he had believed God would make the gun fire anyway. Not feeling reassured by this peculiar answer, I persisted: "But doesn't it worry you to think of going back to live with the woman you so recently tried to kill?"

"Doctor, there's something you have to understand," Bill answered. "I never *wanted* to kill Janet. In fact I was planning to kill myself afterward, I felt so horrible about having to kill her. It's just that it was necessary for the safety of the world."

"It sounds like you're saying you still feel that way now."

"No, no, I mean that's how I felt then. I don't believe Janet is the devil now."[1]

Bill was quite certain that his delusional attempt on Janet's life had nothing to do with any long-standing or recent tensions between them. They had been getting along quite well, he assured me. Yet he seemed guarded, as if he were being careful not to reveal too much. He showed no obvious indications of psychotic thinking now, but it occurred to me that the haloperidol might be helping him just enough that he could hide his paranoid ideas without really diminishing them. If you are paranoid enough to believe that your fiancée is the devil, you are also paranoid enough to want to hide your paranoia from the psychiatrist who might have the power to keep you locked up. If he did still believe that Janet was the devil, Bill could easily have taken my questions as indicating that I was on her side. But maybe it was I who was being paranoid now.

I realized in the hours after that first interview that I was walking around with a very uneasy feeling in the pit of my stomach. It had to do with a certain sense of urgency in Bill's unexpected request to be discharged. In the interview I had dealt with this urgency by temporizing, adopting a tone of professional formality that belied my unsettled feelings. "Well, actually," I said, "I had thought from what Dr. Smith told me that you were expecting to be here for a while, so I'm a little surprised to find that you are so anxious to get out of here so fast. Before making any decision, I would want to understand what your sense of urgency is about, and in any case it will take some time to get to know you before I could make a reasonable assessment of when you would be ready for discharge."

I was somewhat relieved by Bill's response. "Oh, I'm not feeling urgent about leaving," he said. "It's just that I feel so much better now than when I discussed this with Dr. Smith. I think the medication really did the trick. And I am still willing to see you in outpatient therapy for as long as you think it's necessary."

Yet in every therapy session for the next week, Bill renewed his request for discharge and would discuss the details of his delusions only reluctantly and superficially, reassuring me that he no longer believed such things now that the medication had allowed him to sleep again. "And by the way," he added, "I don't think I need the haloperidol anymore. I'm sleeping fine now, but the side effects are getting pretty uncomfortable, so I'd really like to stop the medication as soon as possible." He was talking calmly, but he inspired anything but calm in me.

I told Bill that I disagreed with him about how and why the medication had helped. As he said, it had cured him of sleep deprivation, but I believed it had done so primarily by damping down the overwhelming psychotic anxiety he was feeling about the imminence of World War III and about Janet's role in it. If I was right, and the haloperidol was suppressing a psychotic process that was still active within him, then it could be dangerous for him to stop taking it. Bill dismissed this idea, saying he was quite sure it was simply lack of sleep that had caused his psychosis. He added, however, that if he had to take the haloperidol in order for me to feel comfortable discharging him, then he was willing to do so.

At this point, I was beginning to feel alarmed. Bill just didn't seem sufficiently bothered by what he had done. He was too sanguine about returning to live with the woman he had so recently believed would destroy the world if he didn't kill her. And he was too unconcerned about the potential danger of discontinuing the medication that had apparently brought him back to reality. He was, in effect, telling me, "I don't have a problem. If you think it's a problem that I tried to kill Janet, I'll do whatever you say I have to do to satisfy you that it isn't a problem anymore. But I certainly hope it won't take too long." Yet there was a part of me—and perhaps this was what alarmed me most—that was worried about appearing unreasonable and was inclined simply to take Bill at his word and go along with his request for discharge. After all, he was willing to see me as an outpatient. He was prepared to continue taking the medication even though he clearly didn't like it. Furthermore, I knew that he had spoken quite openly about his delusional ideas with Dr. Smith during the early part of his stay in the community hospital, so why should I think he was trying to hide them from me now? Even so, I didn't trust him. Unreasonable or not, I knew that something felt wrong, though I couldn't tell what. In hopes of finding out, I agreed to discontinue Bill's haloperidol. I thought there was a good chance he would stop taking it anyway once I discharged him, despite his promise to the contrary. If he was going to become psychotic again, I reasoned, better he should do it while he was still safe in the hospital. Then at least it would be obvious to everyone—especially him—that there was an ongoing danger lurking inside him that needed to be taken more seriously.

It was by no means a relief to me that Bill did not become psychotic again, at least not in any way that I could detect. He remained superficially cooperative, and intent on convincing me that he was ready for discharge. The only reason I had to doubt him, it seemed, was the continued uneasy feeling in the pit of my stomach, a constant reminder of the heavy responsibility I now carried for this man who had almost killed his fiancée but wasn't particularly worried about it because he didn't feel like doing it again right now. I wondered how Janet was feeling about Bill's plan to return to her apartment as if nothing had changed. Might she not want to get out of the relationship at this point? I told Bill I needed to talk with Janet, that since she had been such an important part of his problem, I needed to get a sense of how she felt about what had happened and how she was feeling about Bill's plan to live with her again. He assured me she was feeling perfectly fine about it, but I explained that, given how dangerously psychotic he had been only a few weeks before, I had a responsibility to assess how realistically he was thinking now, and talking to Janet would help me do that. I explained to both Bill and Janet that, because of the importance of confidentiality and trust, I would not tell Janet anything Bill had told me but would feel free to share with him what she said to me.

Janet

What Janet told me was that Bill had talked to her about coming back to the apartment, and that she did think he was doing better now but really couldn't tell whether he was back to normal. She didn't say so, but I sensed that she was afraid of him and perhaps reluctant to express that fear because it might hurt or anger him. I asked what she thought had been going on with Bill during the months and weeks leading up to the incident with the gun. She told me that she had had no idea he was becoming psychotic. She'd noticed that he hadn't been sleeping much for a week or two, and that he was kind of obsessed with the story he was writing, but he hadn't talked much with her about it. In fact, he had been gradually talking less and less with her over the past several months. They had been living together for a couple of years, during which he had always been a private person and a workaholic, but in retrospect she realized that Bill really "hadn't been himself" since they had become engaged six months ago. The Bill she knew and loved was a wonderful man who cared about people, thought deeply about things, and liked to share his ideas with her. But since their engagement he had changed, withdrawing gradually into himself and seeming more and more distant, even cold sometimes, whenever he was with her. Still, these changes had been so subtle that his psychotic breakdown had come as a complete and terrifying surprise to her.

"I realize it has to be a chemical imbalance to make a person think he is Jesus Christ," she said, "but I'm confused about when it started and why it happened. As far as Bill coming home now, I guess I'm still in a state of shock about the whole thing, so I'm a little nervous about it, but I do love Bill and I'm willing to do whatever you think is best for him, doctor."

Whatever I thought best! That customary phrase struck me with unaccustomed force. I was decidedly uncomfortable with Janet's apparent willingness to put her life in my hands. What made her so confident that I, or any doctor, would know what was best in Bill's and her predicament? Of course, as I reminded myself, people have always needed to believe that their doctor is like television's fictional Marcus Welby, capable of handling any life-and-death decision wisely and effectively. Indeed, an important function of medical training is to prepare physicians to accept this need in their patients without being overwhelmed by it. You can only be responsible to the degree that you have control, and medical training provides countless experiences of how little control anyone—even the most competent physician—has over life-and-death processes. This is as true in psychiatry as in any other branch of medicine. I had often thought that my medical training helped me become a better psychotherapist precisely because it taught me that in order to take responsibility for life-and-death decisions, I had to be able to accept the *limits* of my responsibility. But Bill posed by far the greatest challenge I had yet faced to this sense of myself and my training. The degree of responsibility I felt, with two lives at stake, seemed far out of proportion to the small degree of control I had over either one of those lives. It would have been a great relief to me to be able to trade in my M.D. and let Marcus Welby handle this one.

Nevertheless, I was glad I had decided to speak with Janet. Our conversation was unsettling, but I also found it very helpful. For one thing, it made me vividly aware of just how worried and indecisive I really felt about Bill. For another, it underlined an important question that would certainly affect Bill's treatment: How much were the causes and cures of his illness biological and how much were they psychological? In assuming that Bill's psychosis was caused by a chemical imbalance, Janet was accepting the standard view of biological psychiatry, which by then had become the standard view of almost everybody in the country, it seemed, except for me and a dwindling number of colleagues who still specialized in psychotherapy and psychoanalysis. Yet in being concerned about when Bill's illness started and why, Janet was really asking a question that had nothing to do with biology, implying (I thought) that specific psychological stresses (fear of marriage, for instance) could have caused him to break down when he did. In fact, I agreed with both the biological and the psychological assumptions Janet had made. Like most psychiatrists, I had come to believe that the delusions and hallucinations of psychosis involve a serious abnormality of brain functioning that can often be helped by medication. But unlike most psychiatrists I also believed that psychotic symptoms reflect unconscious emotional difficulties—inner conflicts—and that my primary responsibility to patients like Bill was not only to prescribe medication for them, but also to help them become more aware of their emotions. I believed that being in touch with what they really felt would not only improve their quality of life—their ability to develop loving relationships and to take satisfaction in their work—but would also help to improve their brain functioning.

If I took seriously this idea that Bill's symptoms reflected an unconscious emotional conflict, it would mean that the uncomfortable emotions I was feeling in my relationship with Bill—the heavy sense of responsibility and the pervasive uneasiness—were probably a kind of instinctive response to *his* unsettled emotions. I began to reflect on this. What exactly *was* I feeling? Bill certainly made me uncomfortable and I couldn't really say that I liked him, yet I didn't dislike him. It struck me that the only real sense of human contact I had with him was this gnawing, subtle sense of dread I felt about him. He seemed disconnected, not fully present, telling me very little about his current state of mind and reporting about his psychotic self in the past as if it were someone else he was talking about, for whom he had no feeling or sense of responsibility. Other than asking to be discharged, Bill never initiated dialogue in our therapy sessions. If I wanted to know something about him, I would have to ask him a specific question; he seemed to have no interest in talking to me otherwise. He volunteered no information about himself, brought up no problems to talk about, and in general acted as if he were there only as a courtesy to me.

Of course, this behavior in itself was not unusual, I mused. Many young patients who have to be hospitalized feel put upon and mistrustful. Their lives have not given them much reason to believe in the kindness even of friends and family, let alone strangers. They are certainly not about to trust a paid staff and a paid "shrink" to have their best interests at heart. They would like to be able to trust, to feel the genuineness of another person's concern, but to do so they need time enough to develop a relationship. I vividly remembered how crucial this time factor had been in my work with another young patient only a few months before.[2]

Anne

Anne was a college freshman whom I had hospitalized after a suicide attempt, just a few weeks after her discharge from another hospital, where she had been treated for bulimia. Although Anne told me about symptoms of depression that would have made most psychiatrists reach immediately for their prescription pads, I had hesitated to put her on an antidepressant. She did not describe her experience of these symptoms with the sense of urgent despair I was used to hearing from seriously depressed patients. She did tell me of a very unhappy childhood and adolescence, full of family problems, parental alcoholism, and self-destructive acting out on her part. But she seemed distant, not quite genuine, as if she were going through the motions of a psychotherapy session to placate me rather than because she was seeking relief from distress or believed she could help herself. I talked to her repeatedly over a period of weeks about this sense I had of her, and she acknowledged that it was the "wall" she always put up to protect herself from being hurt, a wall of superficial compliance with the expectations of others. Eventually she admitted that she spent so much time behind this wall she wasn't sure she was a real person at all. It took her two months in the hospital, meeting with me forty-five minutes a day, five days a week, to tell me she had been raped.

Nowadays Anne's hospitalization would be reviewed by an insurance company's "managed care" reviewer, who would expect me to start her immediately on an antidepressant and discharge her within a week. Scientific research on the effectiveness of psychiatric medications has given insurance companies a rationalization for insisting that five days or less in the hospital should be enough for anybody, no matter what the problem. Since there is no "scientific evidence" about how long it takes a person who has been severely wounded to trust again, this factor is conveniently ignored. Had I followed managed care guidelines with Anne, treating her depression as a biological disease rather than a psychological danger signal, I might easily have confirmed her worst suspicions ("they don't want to listen to me, they just want to shove pills down my throat") and reinforced her tendency to comply with whatever was expected of her. She might then have been "cured" of her depression without ever talking about the rape. Her listlessness, insomnia, and low spirits would have disappeared, but she would not have been touched emotionally and so would have remained vulnerable to any number of delayed ill effects—both psychological and physical—from keeping her rage and shame locked up inside herself.

As it was, Anne's depressive symptoms lifted without medication once she began to talk about the rape, confirming my view that her depression, like pain or fever or any other symptom, was an adaptive response—part of the healing process, not part of the disease. Though I had understood that Anne might ultimately need an antidepressant, I also knew that it is dangerous to try to eliminate a symptom without addressing the deeper problem to which it is pointing. Just as treating abdominal pain with morphine can easily mask the signs of a bursting appendix, so treating Anne's depression with medication might have made it easier for her to hide the emotional trauma of the rape until it was too late.

At that time I didn't know how lucky I was not to have to worry about a managed care reviewer insisting that I provide what I know to be bad treatment simply because it is cheaper.[3] I did know from experience that patient listening is well worth the time and expense, that trust doesn't happen overnight, and that *two months is about the average time it takes for a hospitalized patient to become meaningfully engaged in treatment.*

A Sense of Urgency

Unfortunately, Bill was not disposed to give me—or himself—so much time. His mistrust seemed deeper, more malignant, than Anne's. Occasionally I thought I sensed something chilling in his superficially calm, cooperative presentation of himself, which, in conjunction with the subtle sense of urgency that was a continuing undercurrent in all his interactions with me, left me wondering how dangerous Bill might be to me if I crossed him. His urgent fear of personal and global annihilation had already pushed him once to the brink of cold-blooded murder, and I was fairly certain that it was the same fear, lurking just under the surface, that was now fueling his push to get out of the hospital as fast as he could (and thereby inciting my own feeling of dread). I began to talk to him about this sense of urgency each time we met, and told him how much it worried me. I reminded him of the inconsistency between his decision to transfer to my hospital for extended treatment and his then wanting to leave the minute he got there. I explained that I needed to understand better where this pressure in him was coming from before I could feel comfortable discharging him.

There was a week of stalemate, during which Bill continued to deny any sense of urgency to leave the hospital and professed his willingness to cooperate with whatever course of treatment I recommended. Meanwhile, however, he was making numerous phone calls to Janet, his father, and his mother, asking for their assistance in getting him out of the hospital. They in turn called me, and when I asked him about these phone calls Bill finally admitted that perhaps he did feel some urgency. Now that he was feeling healthy again, he explained, the hospital had become an unnecessarily unsettling place for him. He was afraid that being in the hospital for any length of time might even make him sick again, because it reminded him of things that upset him to think about. The staff and I were constantly expecting him to talk about the events that led to his admission, but he felt strongly that it was best to forget them. How could he put the past behind him if we kept asking him to dwell on it?

This was an important, even a pivotal communication. Bill's wish to forget the past and avoid dwelling on things that upset him was a direct challenge to my philosophy of treatment—my belief in the importance of being conscious. At the same time it was the first sign of his potential engagement in treatment, an honest disagreement and an admission of feelings rather than the sham cooperativeness and denial of distress I had found so unnerving in all my previous meetings with him. I was relieved to get this confirmation of what I had sensed—that underneath his calm facade Bill was afraid.

Yet in another way Bill's admission of fear was not so reassuring. It was not the sort of fear that made him want help so that he would never do something so destructive again. He really wasn't alarmed at what he had done; he was only alarmed at the prospect of having to reflect on what he had done. This kind of fear would not protect him from doing the same thing again, because he could avoid the fear simply by acting without reflecting—the same disastrous strategy pursued by Shakespeare's Macbeth:

> LADY MACBETH. Consider it not so deeply. . . .
> These deeds must not be thought
> After these ways; so, it will make us mad.
> MACBETH. . . . I am afraid to think what I have done;
> Look on't again I dare not.

Macbeth's fear came too late, after he killed the king rather than before. In then trying to fight this fear rather than reflect on it, he was driven to kill again and again, while Lady Macbeth was driven into madness.

For Bill the risk was similar. That he had not succeeded in carrying out his murderous plan meant there was still hope for him, but only if I could find a way to use his fear as an impetus rather than an impediment to self-awareness. I hesitated, feeling the intensity of my own fear in confronting this task.

Remembering, Repeating, and Feeling

I was tempted to argue with Bill on rational grounds that his fear of dwelling on the past was misguided. I wanted to remind him that "those who cannot remember the past are condemned to repeat it." Santayana's well-known aphorism applies just as much to the history of individuals as to the history of nations. Just as wars result from not remembering the lessons of world history, so neuroses result from not remembering the lessons of personal experience. Of course, remembering is a complicated business. Even when we do remember the past, most of us have a difficult time learning from it. History too often remains a collection of unintegrated facts and impressions that do not touch us where we live. Personal experiences, surprisingly, can be much the same. Even when they are recorded in the form of conscious memories, many of our own personal experiences fail to touch us where we live. The memories remain disconnected, emotionally shallow, distant or distorted, and consequently difficult to learn from. Why does a woman divorce one alcoholic husband only to marry another? Why does a man get fired from three successive jobs for similar sorts of insubordination? Why does an abused child become an abused (or abusive) spouse?

Psychoanalysis allows us to understand why it is so difficult to learn from history and from experience. It teaches that the most important lessons of personal experience (and of history) are embedded in the unconscious and cannot be remembered except through reenactment. In one of his most important clinical papers, "Remembering, Repeating and Working Through," Freud describes neurosis as the compulsive repetition in action of a personal past that cannot be consciously recollected. This reenactment of the past is a reliving not of childhood events as they actually occurred but rather of emotionally patterned interactions learned in childhood, motivated "scenarios" that tell a story based both on actual events and on attitudes, emotions, and fantasies that were developed around those events.

Freud changed his opinion more than once over the years about whether neurosis (the compulsive reenactment of an unconscious childhood scenario) derives primarily from the impact of traumatic external events or from the internally generated *drives*—compelling but unconscious wishful fantasies that produce inner conflict. Current thinking is that while unconscious childhood scenarios are always based on actual traumatic experience (a certain degree of which is inevitable even in the best of families) they also always involve the unconscious sexual/hostile/envious/competitive fantasies belonging to the so-called Oedipus complex. Freud argued that these childhood scenarios are kept unconscious—*repressed*—because they are unacceptable to the child's parents and/or to his own conscience, but that they exert a constant emotional pressure to become conscious. This pressure toward consciousness—the drive—then provokes internal opposition by the repressive force, or *resistance,* whose task is to prevent anxiety, shame, and guilt by keeping the repressed scenario unconscious.

Inner conflict, then, involves a drive toward expanded consciousness and a resistance against it. This results in a compromise that Freud described as typical for neurosis: repeating the past (more precisely, a scenario based on the past) as a substitute for remembering it. The compulsion to repeat a behavior pattern (like divorcing one alcoholic spouse only to marry another) is a sign of the unconscious trying to become conscious, against resistance, through *enactment.* It is as if our unconscious were saying to us, "I'm going to make you keep repeating this unhappy scenario until you wake up and pay attention to where it is coming from in yourself." In most cases we can be freed from the grip of habitual enactment only when we can consciously experience in the present the repressed childhood emotional situation that the scenario represents.

Freud emphasized that the repressed scenarios of the unconscious are emotionally charged, and that repression is aimed not so much at blocking cognitive awareness of the scenario per se (a woman might be very much aware that each of her husbands has turned out to be alcoholic, like her father), but at blocking the painful, frightening, or otherwise unacceptable *feelings* associated with it (she may have forgotten how alternately excited, frightened, and ultimately devastated she was by the unpredictable doings of her father when he was drunk). Fully remembering the repressed scenario means fully experiencing—"getting in touch with"—the painful emotions embedded in it. The trend in modern psychoanalytic thought is to shift the emphasis even more from the cognitive to the emotional, from the idea that we enact (repeat) what we cannot remember to the idea that we enact what we cannot feel.

In the most general terms, then, mental illness is a limitation of consciousness due to inner conflict, in which the symptoms and disturbed behavior patterns (compulsively repeated enactments) represent unconsciously organized ways of avoiding awareness of anxiety-, shame-, and guilt-provoking emotions. The goal of "dynamic psychotherapy"—the kind that deals with the unconscious forces (dynamics) of inner conflict—is to get in touch with these repressed emotions, and thereby resolve inner conflict. The goal is not simply to figure out intellectually where your problems came from in the unremembered past (though this is part of what happens) but also to experience where they are coming from now, in the present moment— to bring into full conscious awareness the emotions that are unconsciously shaping your current attitudes and behavior. Psychotherapy provides the opportunity for this kind of experience through what is called *transference.* Transference involves the experiencing of a previously unconscious feeling about a significant childhood figure (or about oneself), now "transferred" onto the person of the therapist and becoming conscious (with help, against resistance) in the relationship with him or her. Emotions that would be too threatening to feel toward my parents, for instance, I can experience more easily—with less anxiety, shame, and guilt—toward my therapist.

So much for the theory. How was I to apply it to Bill? His buying a shot-gun and trying to kill Janet in her sleep, based on a psychotic delusion, was an enactment of emotions that were too overwhelming for him to feel. His actions and his belief that Janet was the devil indicated that there must be an unconscious part of him that hated her, yet consciously he did not feel any hatred. Rather, he felt love, combined with a sense of regret that he was forced to perform the painful but necessary task of killing her. What sort of repressed childhood pain and rage had gone into what sort of unconscious scenario to produce such an enactment? In the brief two weeks I had known Bill, he had told me very little that would help me answer that question. However, I was beginning to get some ideas about it from talking to his parents.

Bill's Parents

Bill's parents had been divorced for many years, but they had both contacted me on the day he was admitted, each independently offering to help in any way they could. I told them that I needed to get to know Bill a little before I could say what role they should play in his treatment. I promised to be in touch with them in a couple of weeks. A week later they both called again, concerned about how to respond to Bill's repeated phone calls pleading for help in getting out of the hospital. At this point, since Bill himself had already involved them in his treatment, I asked his permission to meet and talk with them individually, and he agreed.

Bill's mother, Sandra, a corporate executive, was an impressive woman who conveyed a sense of both vulnerability and strength. She had been worried about Bill for some time, she told me, especially over the last five years, during which he had become distant—even cold—toward her and had seemed to be much closer to his father. He had never shown any obvious psychological disturbance before the current episode, nor had he ever been violent. She described him as a truly gentle and good man—sensitive and introverted, a great admirer of Thoreau, but at the same time deeply concerned about global issues like the environment, AIDS, poverty and famine, and, most recently, nuclear weapons. Sandra was quite alarmed now about how different Bill seemed from the person she knew him to be as a boy and young man, and she was concerned about what could have caused this dramatic change. Bill had told her recently that he had used psychedelic mushrooms several weeks before he became ill, and she wondered whether this might have triggered the psychosis in him. She also thought there was a genetic factor. She wasn't sure about mental illness in Bill's father's family, she said, but there was definitely mental illness in her own family. Her father had been flagrantly paranoid throughout her childhood years. One of her three brothers now showed definite paranoid tendencies, and her sister was suffering from a prolonged psychotic illness, possibly schizophrenia.

Sandra herself had never been paranoid or had any kind of breakdown, but she had grown up with significant emotional problems of her own and had needed years of psychotherapy to achieve the stability and self-assurance she now possessed. She felt that those years of psychotherapy had saved her life, but she worried that she might nevertheless have contributed to Bill's problems. As a child, Bill had witnessed many angry arguments between her and his father during the years before they divorced when he was seven. Although her husband had never hit or physically threatened her in all those years, she worried that Bill had been traumatized by the yelling and the constant state of tension in the house. She felt guilt and remorse that she had helped to create this tension and had not been able to end the marriage sooner. She seemed to have taken responsibility for her own mistakes and was astute enough to realize that Bill had so far been evading responsibility for his. She was very frightened about what this could lead to, and had tried to talk to him about how important it was for him to deal with whatever was going on inside him. She was particularly troubled now about his wanting to get out of the hospital. He had told her that he knew he needed psychotherapy but felt he just couldn't open up in the hospital setting. She worried that this was his way of avoiding treatment altogether but had been afraid to tell him so for fear of alienating him further.

Bill's father, Louis, an electrical engineer, was as impressive as his mother but in a very different way. Where Sandra was reflective and had a good deal to say about Bill's problems and her own, Louis was a man of action who much preferred doing something about problems rather than talking about them. He was a dynamo, full of vitality, but I sensed there was an undercurrent of tension or anxiety that might be driving him as well. Still, even with that tension—or perhaps because of it—I found Louis immensely sympathetic, and it was quite evident that he loved his son. He empathized fully with Bill's fear that staying in the hospital could make him psychotic again. Louis was terrified that if such a thing happened, Bill might never recover and would be lost to him forever. He urged me to consider whether there wasn't some workable outpatient alternative. He guaranteed financial support for however long it took, and said he would make sure Bill cooperated fully with any outpatient program I might recommend.

It was not surprising that Bill's parents were diametrically opposed on the question of whether Bill should stay in the hospital. Their differing attitudes toward his predicament reflected the two sides of my own ambivalent response to him, and I was sure that once I got to know him I would discover that he was internally torn between them, too. For the present, however, it seemed that he was allied with his father and that I, without realizing it, had been sounding like his mother from the first minute I met him. As far as Bill was concerned, I was allied with the wrong parent, a fact that went a long way toward explaining his cold aloofness with me. It also gave me a pretty good idea of what it would take to reach him in psychotherapy.

Nuclear Warfare

Bill's coldness toward his mother, now repeated in his attitude toward me, was the tip of an iceberg of unconscious hatred that he was afraid to feel. It was almost certainly the same hatred that had made him withdraw from Janet after they became engaged, and that he had enacted—without feeling it—in trying to kill her. I had already known that the process of cure would require that he become aware of this unconscious hatred of Janet, and that in becoming aware of it in the present he would be getting closer to feeling the old childhood hatreds that had shaped his unconscious scenario. I now had an idea of what that scenario was. His paranoid idea that Janet was the devil trying to instigate nuclear war was probably the echo of an old, unremembered feeling that his mother was the one who incited nuclear-family war, with his father being the one who would unleash it and Bill the one who wanted to stop it (and perhaps prayed to God to help him stop it). I recalled that in the psychological testing done during Bill's first hospitalization he had been asked to put a series of pictures into a sequence that would tell a story. He described his sequence by saying, "This man is me, and these two boys are the United States and Russia fighting. Here I stop the fighting and they go their separate ways. I am the equalizer."

Bill's fear of World War III then, along with his delusional attempt to prevent it, must have been an expression of the unconscious childhood fear, still active in him, of being caught between his warring parents and of his father's potential violence toward his mother. Currently he was (unconsciously) identified with his father in blaming his mother (and Janet and probably all women) for this, but somewhere in him I knew there must be a powerful anger against both parents that he had never felt safe enough to express openly or probably even to feel consciously. So the nuclear war he feared was, at the deepest level, the projected image of his own rage and potential violence. Which meant that in encouraging him to stay in the hospital and become aware of his feelings, I was now taking on a role in this fatal scenario. I was becoming the mother/Janet/devil, tempting his father/self to risk unleashing the nuclear explosiveness that was contained in his own violent emotions.

Further Thoughts About the Causes of Mental Illness

Let me add here to the preceding account of how I put together my understanding of Bill's scenario. It could appear that I was ignoring the biological factor in his illness and taking a narrow-mindedly psychological view that, in effect, put all the blame on his parents. This is not at all the way I understood his situation. I did think that his parents' fighting and divorce had been traumatic for Bill, but I did not think of this trauma as the cause of his illness. Neither did I think that a chemical imbalance was the cause of his illness, but I recognized that there was a huge biological component. I believed Bill was born with a genetic predisposition that made him uniquely vulnerable to psychosis, and I thought it quite likely that the psychedelic mushrooms (on top of the ongoing psychological stress of his engagement) had pushed him over the edge into a pattern of unrealistic thinking that then grew into a full-blown psychosis. I could easily imagine that Bill might never have become ill at all if not for this genetic/biological factor. After all, thousands of children grow up with parents who fight much more viciously than Sandra and Louis did, and who are not nearly so loving and well-intentioned, but very few of those children ever become psychotic.

Nevertheless, I knew that once he became ill, Bill's illness would inevitably and necessarily be shaped (rather than caused) by the traumatic experiences of his childhood or, more specifically, by the way he reacted to those experiences and ultimately processed them into the pattern of his repetitive scenario. This applies not only to Bill but to any person with any form of mental illness, and in a more subtle way to every one of us, whether we have a diagnosable illness or not. None of us gets through childhood without experiencing some trauma in relation to the problems, failures, and limitations of our parents. In fact, it is the need to make sense of and cope with these inevitable traumas that leads *every* child to develop an unconscious emotional scenario. This scenario always involves the parents, so much so that psychoanalysts have traditionally called it the parental complex. However, the parents of the unconscious emotional scenario are not the parents as they actually were, but rather the parents as the child experienced them.

This is where a biological predisposition to mental illness comes into play. Such a predisposition frequently expresses itself psychologically in the way a child's personality develops and in the way he or she processes traumatic experiences into an unconscious scenario. In Bill's case, I knew from his mother that he had been an extremely sensitive, quiet, and introverted child, so I suspected that his biological predisposition had expressed itself in an exaggerated emotional sensitivity and reactivity, which then led to a self-protective tendency toward introversion. With this kind of vulnerable personality, Bill could have experienced his parents' angry arguments as overwhelmingly terrifying, whereas an "average" child would have been able to take them more in stride. Bill would also then have kept his fear to himself, so his parents would not have recognized any early warning signs of his distress.

The result, as I conceptualized it, was that while his parents' fighting did not cause him to become ill, the form of his unconscious scenario (and ultimately of his psychosis) did reflect his reaction to their fighting *as he had experienced it.* So, however biological his illness may have been, I knew I could not treat him effectively without addressing this psychological dimension— the repetitive childhood scenario that everyone has, and that cannot help but be central to whatever mental illness one ultimately develops.

In this connection, I should also point out the role of the *Oedipus complex.* Bill's reaction to his parents' fighting was not the only experience that shaped his unconscious scenario. In fact, the scenario of mother tempting father to violence, disregarding Bill's wishes, was highly reminiscent of the story of Eve tempting Adam to eat the forbidden fruit, disregarding God's wishes—a simple variation on the theme of the Oedipus complex. This striking parallel is typical of the way unconscious fantasy scenarios conform to universal mythic patterns, and it suggested that Bill's psychosis expressed not only his conflict over hatred and violence but, at a deeper level, the inherent and universal human conflict over sexuality as well (which he would have experienced with the same exaggerated sensitivity and reactivity that influenced his reaction to his parents). However, while I recognized this unconscious conflict over sexual feelings (and saw it as an important factor in his coldness and withdrawal from Janet and his mother), I thought that these feelings would be even more disturbing to Bill, and further removed from his awareness, than hatred. Hatred was the most obvious emotion represented by the World War III of Bill's delusion, so it had to be the most immediate focus of my thoughts about how to reach him in treatment.

The Dilemma

While I was glad to have this provisional understanding of Bill's scenario, I knew that it wouldn't do anyone any good until Bill understood it, and he wouldn't understand it until he could *feel* it—the terrifying hatred toward Janet, toward his mother, toward his father, and ultimately toward himself. And how would he become able to feel all this terrifying hatred? Through hating me! This would be the transference, and it was already beginning to happen. Bill's cold aloofness toward me, his wish to get out of the sphere of my influence (the hospital), contained within it the entire story of his illness. If I succeeded in engaging him in treatment, that story would unfold in his relationship with me. I would become the one he feared; I would become the one he hated. And then I might be able to show him the deep parallels between his feelings toward me and toward his mother, how he was identified with and at the same time terrified of his father. I would also, I hoped, be able to discover and show him what had gone wrong between Janet and him that had implicated her in the same unconscious scenario. But the unsettling question remained: If Bill had become so convinced that Janet was the enemy that he tried to kill her, what was to prevent him from having a similar reaction to me? If he was to learn anything from his feeling that I was the enemy, I would have to give him strong reason to believe that I was also his ally.

This requirement actually holds for any psychotherapeutic relationship that uses the transference. Most patients will, even in the midst of feeling intensely hostile feelings toward the therapist, be able to maintain a self-observing part of themselves—psychoanalysts call this the observing ego—that regards the therapist as an ally and wants to tell him about the hostile feelings, not in order to hurt him, but to get his help in dealing with them. In paranoia, however, as in any extreme emotional state, the patient tends to get lost in the passion of the moment, losing the perspective (and the therapeutic goal) of the observing ego. Thus, the paradoxical requirement that Bill be able to hate me as the enemy while learning to trust me as an ally threatened to put us in an impossible bind. On the one hand, if I insisted that he stay in the hospital, his fear could easily overwhelm his observing ego and lock him into a paranoid conviction that I was the enemy, which would make it very difficult for him to trust me enough to learn from the transference. On the other hand, I doubted that his transference hatred would ever come to a therapeutic head unless he was forced to stay in the hospital. He was too dedicated to evading it, and as an outpatient he could easily find ways—like skipping appointments for instance—to prevent the necessary intensity of feeling from developing.

Even if I did somehow succeed in engaging Bill in such a treatment, it would be like trying to defuse an unexploded bomb. If successful, it would take years of intensive work that would be stressful, at times frightening for me, and terrifying for Bill. There would be no guarantee of success, and failure could well mean a fatal explosion. My belief in the value of this kind of therapeutic process was based partly on my experience as a patient in psychoanalysis, and partly on what I had seen my patients accomplish through psychotherapy and psychoanalysis. But I had never had a patient who scared me the way Bill did, or with whom the risk of failure was as great.

Ruminations on Dangerousness

How strong a case should I make, indeed how strong a case *could* I make to Bill that his psychosis had roots in his history, in his unconscious conflicts and in current interpersonal tensions between him and Janet? He could easily agree with the premise that those who don't remember the past are condemned to repeat it but still argue that his psychosis was merely a neurobiological malfunction having nothing to do with an unremembered past or an unexperienced feeling. Furthermore, modern psychiatry would support him, justifying his argument with the results of scientific research. I knew that such an interpretation of the research was deeply misguided, but I would have to write a book to explain how I knew it, and I could hardly count on Bill to be one of my readers. Then too there was the troublesome fact that even if Bill agreed to an extended stay in the hospital, I couldn't promise him that his fear was groundless, that the psychotherapeutic process wouldn't reactivate his psychosis. Yet I had little doubt that if I simply let him leave the hospital as he asked, even with medication (which he would probably stop taking), the psychosis would recur sooner or later anyway.

I noticed that I was beginning to ruminate somewhat obsessionally about Bill, and that my understanding of his psychodynamics was not making it any easier for me to think clearly about how to deal with him. In the course of two weeks, the uneasy feeling in the pit of my stomach had grown to a pervasive sense of foreboding, and I was surprised at how confused and paralyzed I felt. Again I wondered whether what I was feeling might not be a reflection of what was going on inside Bill. There is a psychological mechanism, which psychoanalysts call projective identification, whereby the patient remains unaware of a disturbing emotion while unconsciously provoking the therapist to feel it. This is not a mystical process; it has to do with "affect contagion," a kind of communication through nonverbal emotional expression that is a product of evolution. In simplest terms, people are genetically programmed to show their feelings in ways (especially through facial expression) that instinctively evoke the same feelings in other people. If you smile, I will tend to smile back. If you are unaware that you are smiling, I will still smile back, but you will think I am a bit strange. Projective identification works in the same way.

Perhaps then, I was picking up Bill's unconscious dread and confusion through affect contagion and in effect feeling paralyzed by his feelings. Bill's need to keep those feelings hidden, together with his wish to forget his psychosis and what he had done during it, left me with the tasks of remembering, fearing, and ultimately taking responsibility for his murderous impulses. If I agreed to treat him as an outpatient, as he wished, I would have all of this responsibility with almost no control. No wonder I felt dread. Yet how could I justify keeping him hospitalized when I had no clear evidence on which to hold him? Even if I did insist on his staying in the hospital, he was now a voluntary patient and might refuse to stay. I could always try to commit him again but would have a tough time persuading any judge that Bill was dangerous. There were no objective signs of any violent tendencies to report during his last five weeks in two hospitals.[4] There was only my subjective, instinctive uneasiness about him—my feeling that he was cold and evasive, and that he lacked a sense of responsibility for what he had done.

Perhaps, I speculated, we psychiatrists have been so notoriously bad at predicting violence in our patients precisely because we have not felt free to rely on such instinctive reactions. It wouldn't be "scientific" to accept the feeling of dread in the pit of my stomach as valid evidence of dangerousness. It was beginning to feel like pretty good evidence to me, but clearly I needed a stronger argument. Since I was having trouble finding any objective reasons to support my subjective feelings, I decided to ask for help, in the form of a formal consultation from a colleague. My hope was that a consultant would not feel paralyzed by the frightening sense of responsibility I felt in treating Bill, and so would be able to be more objective than I about how dangerous he really was. Of course, I knew that if a consultant did offer a coherent opinion one way or the other I would probably not trust it. The same factors that would allow the consultant to be more objective would also limit his ability to appreciate the fear I felt in Bill's presence, and I was not prepared to have that fear explained away. But at least, I thought, another opinion would help me clarify my thinking, and if I ever did need to explain that thinking to a judge, a consultant's report would be a useful thing to have.

The Guru

So I turned to a colleague I will call the Guru, the most respected senior clinician at my hospital. Like the psychiatrist in Joanne Greenberg's book *I Never Promised You a Rose Garden*, the Guru had been treating schizophrenic patients with intensive psychotherapy for years before there was any

Thorazine. He had the accumulated wisdom of forty years working with the most disturbed psychotic patients. I was sure he would know how to help.

He said no, flat out no. He wanted nothing to do with assessing the dangerousness of someone who might be homicidal. He said he was too old to get involved in anything that had a chance of getting him called into court. At first I was bitter over what seemed to me a less-than-noble response, but then I stopped and thought about it. If Bill were to kill Janet soon after I discharged him, I would probably not be the only one at risk of being sued. Anyone who consulted on this case would be putting himself out on a limb. I had looked to the Guru to rescue me from my predicament but had not considered what kind of predicament I might be putting *him* in. I realized that it was I who had been less than noble in expecting the Guru to take on what was really my responsibility.

Still, I knew I needed help, so it was a great relief when I hit upon a strategy that could get me the consultant's perspective I needed while keeping the responsibility for the decision squarely on my shoulders. I would get *two* consultations, one from someone who was likely to recommend speedy discharge, the other from someone who was likely to recommend long-term hospitalization. I knew immediately whom to call, quite sure what their opposing recommendations would be, yet foggy about how each would argue his case. Noticing this fogginess, I realized I was operating once again more on instinct than on reason when I put in calls to the Technocrat and the Cowboy.

The Technocrat

The Technocrat was an expert from a nearby hospital, someone I didn't know personally but had often heard mentioned as a top-notch consultant for difficult problems of diagnosis and medication management. I chose him because I knew he wouldn't think like me. He belonged to the new breed of psychiatrists who see psychiatry as a research science, who base treatment decisions not on an emotional understanding of people but on the statistical results of double-blind, placebo-controlled treatment-outcome research. This research measures responses to treatment in large groups of patients selected according to carefully refined diagnostic criteria. The ultimate goal is to match diagnostic groups with specific treatments that have been proved effective (i.e., statistically correlated with symptom relief more often than could be accounted for by chance alone) for those diagnoses. Since it is modeled after the way other branches of medicine operate, this matching of patients with treatments by diagnosis is called the Medical Model.

Psychiatrists who believe in the Medical Model, like the Technocrat, are called descriptive/biological psychiatrists—descriptive, because diagnoses are defined through precise descriptions of the symptoms and signs; biological, because most of the treatment-outcome studies emphasize biological treatments, comparing response to a medication with response to a placebo (a sugar pill that looks identical to the active medication). What makes these studies "double-blind" is that neither the patient nor the psychiatrist who measures the effects of the treatment (using diagnostic questionnaires and rating scales) knows whether the patient is taking the active medication or the placebo. I have always felt, though, that these studies suffer from—and foster in those who rely on them—another kind of blindness as well, blindness to the uniqueness of a person. Medical Model psychiatrists ultimately treat their patients not as individuals but as members of a diagnostic group. To the extent that differences between one person and another within a diagnostic group make any difference to treatment, they leave such differences to be attended to by a case manager, a social worker, or sometimes a therapist. It is often argued that the knowledge gained through treating patients as statistics is worth the loss of human concern for the individual, but I have never believed that this loss can be adequately compensated for by delegating someone else to worry about the individual.[5] Nevertheless, the descriptive/biological approach has amassed a body of specialized knowledge and clinical experience that can be extremely useful, as long as its inadequacy as a guide for treating the whole person is recognized. It was specifically for this body of knowledge and experience that I had called on the Technocrat.

The Technocrat thought Bill was a straightforward case. After assessing him, he said he didn't know how to account for the strange anxiety I felt about Bill's potential dangerousness. He felt no such anxiety. He had found Bill to be rational, articulate, personable, and "relatively nondefensive"; he made particular note of his "positive attitude" toward me and toward therapy. In the Technocrat's view, Bill had had a manic episode, manifesting the typical symptoms of sleeplessness, racing thoughts, and grandiosity. Both his paranoid psychosis and his violent behavior were consistent with the diagnosis, though not necessarily typical of it. But Bill was clearly not manic now, hence not psychotic and not dangerous. I should put him on lithium to prevent future manic episodes; and as long as he stayed on his lithium and maintained regular psychotherapy appointments so that he could be monitored for signs of recurrent illness, there would be no reason to worry about further violence.

Although I had expected the Technocrat to think differently about Bill than I did, I was nevertheless surprised and troubled by how radically different his emotional response—his personal sense of Bill—was from mine. The Bill he had met sounded like the gentle and good man his mother had described to me from the time before he became ill. I had no doubt that Bill still had this gentleness and goodness as a core of health within him. Indeed, I was counting on being able to help him reconnect with this part of himself in the course of treatment. But I couldn't help wondering whether the Technocrat had been taken in by a facade—the image of his former self that Bill had put forward without being connected to it, in the same way that I had often felt him trying to do with me. Even if the Technocrat was open to feeling that sort of thing—to sensing the guardedness and disconnectedness of a patient's facade—I suspected that his Medical Model training would have taught him to discount such feelings as unscientific.

Even more troubling to me was the Technocrat's opinion that Bill would do best with a kind of supportive, "maintenance" psychotherapy, and had no need for intensive dynamic psychotherapy, either inpatient or outpatient. He was confident that the specific manifestations of Bill's manic episode—his psychotic delusions and the murderous purposes they entailed—had nothing to do with his personality, his life history, or any current tensions in his relationship with Janet. "Psychosis is a hurricane in the brain," explained the Technocrat, implying that there is no stable link between what one does and experiences when psychotic and who one is before and after the psychosis. According to this point of view, the symptoms of psychosis are aimless, arbitrary, and unpredictable, a direct result of what the Technocrat believed to be a kind of unrestrained randomness—the hurricane—in the underlying brain events. If this were true, then even if Bill did become psychotic again, it would not necessarily involve the risk of violence. Instead of thinking that he was Jesus Christ and that Janet was the devil he had to kill, he could just as easily decide that he was king of England and try to walk onto the Concorde without a ticket.

According to the Technocrat, Bill's fear of staying in the hospital was completely reasonable. To subject him to an insight-oriented dynamic psychotherapy aimed at understanding his psychotic manifestations as an expression of his personality, feelings, motives, and relationship patterns would be to misunderstand the nature of psychosis. I would be encouraging a gratuitous, irrelevant, and dangerous preoccupation that could only undermine Bill's sense of himself, when I should be encouraging him to reestablish the pattern of his normal life again as quickly as possible.

Hearing an opinion that I considered so plainly wrong expressed with such clarity and self-assurance by a man considered an expert in his field was surprisingly helpful, like a bracing slap in the face that prompts a "Thanks, I needed that!" It made me vividly and gratefully aware of what I really believed. I thought it would be fruitless to argue with the Technocrat about the dehumanizing implications of his scientific opinion, but I did try to challenge it on its own terms. I argued that while some of Bill's symptoms fit the pattern of a manic episode, I was equally impressed with elements that were more typical of paranoid schizophrenia. For instance, Bill seemed to me guarded, suspicious, and cold, despite his superficial attempt to appear friendly. Although as a young adult he had formed successful relationships (with Janet and two male friends), I knew from his mother that he had always been fairly introverted (suggesting more of a "schizoid" than a manic-depressive tendency), and my sense of his behavior over the first couple of weeks in the hospital was that he preferred to avoid people altogether. Furthermore, I reminded the Technocrat that while a manic episode certainly can lead to violence, it is usually the violence of an impulsive outburst rather than the kind of planned paranoid murderousness Bill had shown.

The Technocrat reiterated his opinion that in a psychosis anything is possible and reminded me that, according to the third edition of the *Diagnostic and Statistical Manual of Mental Disorders (DSM)*, a patient couldn't be diagnosed as schizophrenic if some of the symptoms were attributable to manic or depressive illness.[6] Although I knew that this exclusion rule was correct by the book, I also knew that it (like every diagnostic rule in the *DSM*) is not a fact of nature but the consensus of a committee of people looking at mental illness the way a blind man looks at an elephant. I explained that my point was not to insist that Bill was schizophrenic or to argue about the technically correct diagnosis, but to emphasize that what was frightening me— the disturbing impression I had of something ominous behind Bill's facade of normalcy—had almost nothing to do with what the Technocrat included in his account of him.

Not that I was opposed to the idea of using lithium. I had certainly been aware that Bill's psychotic episode included manic-like symptoms. I knew not only that lithium (like haloperidol) was usually effective in relieving such symptoms over the short term but also that it had been shown to reduce the long-term rate of relapse. However, I wasn't at all sure that Bill's symptoms reflected a true manic-depressive illness. Nor did I agree that his condition was caused by a hurricane in the brain, or by any other kind of neurological bad weather. Certainly there was a brain dysfunction that contributed to the symptoms of his illness—no doubt related to the biological predisposition I have described—but the illness itself had to have been produced by a *combination* of psychological and biological influences.

I therefore had no illusions that lithium or haloperidol or any other medication regimen, by itself, would be enough to protect Bill (or Janet) from the dangerous war that raged within him. But I recognized that if I did end up discharging Bill soon, it would be worth having him on lithium simply for the prophylactic effect it might have. Of course, if his psychosis was closer to the schizophrenic than to the manic type, as I suspected, then lithium would not prevent him from becoming psychotic again. But if lithium was going to have a prophylactic effect, it could take a week or more to establish the blood lithium level necessary to achieve that effect, and it would be best to start treatment now, well before any possibility of discharge. So I thanked the Technocrat and ordered the necessary laboratory tests in preparation for starting Bill on lithium. I then turned to my second consultant.

The Cowboy

The Cowboy belonged to the generation of psychiatrists between the Guru's and my own. He had trained with the Guru and was known as his brightest protégé. He worked almost exclusively with the so-called impossible patients—those who cannot function, who have failed multiple treatment attempts both with medication and with psychotherapy, and who pose a serious threat to themselves or others. These patients come with varied diagnoses, but they have one thing in common: they have all put up walls, attempting to withdraw beyond the reach of people who might want to hurt—or help—them. Their walls may take the form of psychotic hallucinations and delusions, drug addiction, extreme forms of compulsive behavior, repetitive self-mutilation and suicide attempts, or chronic refractory forms of anxiety, depression, or any of the other self-protective devices that psychiatrists call symptoms. What makes these patients so difficult to treat is that they are difficult to meet. In order to make real contact, you must first get through their walls. The Cowboy prided himself on being able to make contact where others could not. If the Technocrat tended to apply scientific reason without the support of instinct, intuition, or empathy, the Cowboy tended in the opposite direction. He preferred to trust his instinct and so tended to shoot from the hip, turning the imagery and impulses of his creative mind directly into things he would say to patients that no one else would be comfortable saying but that very often needed to be said.

I knew this because I had trained with the Cowboy or, more accurately, served an apprenticeship with him during my own psychiatric residency. This training by apprenticeship involved the two of us, master and apprentice, doing psychotherapy with the same patient, three times a week individually and twice a week together.[7] We worked in this way with two of his very difficult inpatients, each over a period of several years. Meeting alone with these patients, I was able to experiment in developing my own style of doing therapy, insulated from the full burden of responsibility. Seeing them together with the Cowboy, I would mostly watch and listen, trying to understand how his mind worked as he pursued his daily quest to sneak through cracks in the wall, relentlessly insinuating himself into the patient's world. He was absolutely determined to become important to his patients—important enough to have a real impact on them—even if he had to participate in their psychoses to achieve that end.

Afterward, he would talk about how the patient had made him feel during the session, and then ask me, "What do you think went on today? What did you see?" It took me a few weeks to catch on to the fact that he was not testing me to determine whether I had understood a particular lesson he wanted to teach. Rather, he was trying to sort out what he had done and found it helpful to hear how I would explain it. Although he was well-versed in psychodynamic theory, the Cowboy rarely used it when he was with patients. He would typically get so immersed in the immediate experience of being with a patient that he needed a kind of debriefing after a session. Hearing my theoretical formulation of what he had just done seemed to bring him back to the world of linear thought and reassure him (or so I liked to imagine) that his intuitive clinical impulse had been sound. Being expected to provide these explanations was helpful for me, too. It pushed me to learn better theories just to keep up with him and at the same time taught me the limitations of all theory, forcing me to recognize a level of nonverbal subtlety in the Cowboy's emotional interaction with his patients that easily escaped any conceptual net I could ever cast. As Pascal said, the heart has its reasons which reason knows nothing of.

What I most wanted to know from the Cowboy now was how he would feel about Bill after meeting with him. I wanted to compare his reactions to my own. If he was frightened, it would give me added confidence in the validity of my own fears about Bill. If he wasn't, I would have to do some serious reevaluation of my feelings. The Cowboy suggested that he meet with Bill and me together. I agreed, albeit somewhat reluctantly because I knew what he was thinking. He wanted not only to get a sense of Bill but also to get a sense of me and the problem I was having with Bill. After all, I was the one asking for help, the one in distress, so how could he be helpful unless he understood my distress? He also wanted to get a feel for how Bill and I interacted. I knew that this approach made perfect sense, and in fact it was because the Cowboy thought this way that I had called him in the first place. But I also knew it probably meant I wasn't going to find out what I really wanted to know. The Cowboy wanted the consultation to focus on me and how Bill made me feel. I wanted the consultation to focus on the Cowboy and how Bill made *him* feel. Perhaps I was yearning for the comfort of the apprenticeship, when I could sit back and watch, safe in the knowledge that it was the Cowboy who had the ultimate responsibility.

In the end, the consultation turned out much like a visit to the Delphic oracle. You don't find out what you want to know, but you do find out what you *need* to know, if you can figure out how to use it.

The Consultation

After the introductions, the Cowboy asked a few preliminary questions and Bill gave his usual, minimally informative canned responses. The Cowboy then asked me what I was looking for from this consultation. I explained that Bill had been eager to leave the hospital pretty much since the day he arrived. "He seems fine on the surface," I said, "but I sense a pressure in him that makes me suspect that perhaps he hasn't fully recovered from some of the frightening ideas he had when he was psychotic. I'm concerned that to discharge him before he is ready could put both him and Janet in danger, but Bill has the opposite worry—that staying in the hospital might be even more dangerous, because it might make him psychotic again." I explained that I particularly wanted the Cowboy's opinion about how much danger there was of a recurrence of Bill's violent ideas and purposes, and how best to prevent that from happening. The Cowboy turned again to Bill. "Tell me a little bit more about what happened that night," he said.

So Bill spoke. "Well, as I told you, I believed Janet was the devil and that she was stirring up the nuclear arms race to bring on World War III. I got a message from God over the radio telling me that in order to save the world from nuclear war, I had to kill her. So I waited until she was asleep and then I tried to shoot her with this shotgun I had bought. I knew it wasn't working properly, but God told me he would make the gun fire anyway."

"I understand you're pretty concerned about nuclear weapons."

"Yes, I've done a lot of research on the cold war and the nuclear arms race."

"So I take it you've seen those pictures of people who survived the bombing of Hiroshima and Nagasaki?"

"Yes . . . they're horrible. What's your point?"

There had been an uncomfortable edge to the Cowboy's question, and I could feel Bill's tension in reaction to it. I, too, wondered what the Cowboy was getting at. "How close were you standing to Janet when you pulled the trigger?"

"Right next to her."

"Where were you pointing the rifle?"

"At her head."

"How close was the barrel to her head?"

"Just a few inches."

The tension was getting thicker, and I vaguely wished I didn't have to listen to this, but at the same time I was beginning to get the point of the Cowboy's questions.

"Take me back to that moment when you pulled the trigger. What was going through your mind just then?"

"What do you mean? I already told you that. I was trying to save the world from nuclear war!"

"No, that's what you were thinking when you bought the shotgun. That was the message you heard from the radio. I'm talking about the very moment when you pulled the trigger. How did you feel about Janet at that moment? How did she look to you, lying there in the bed? Did you think she might wake up and see you about to blow her brains out? Did you want her to?"

"No! Of course I didn't want her to wake up! I didn't want to kill her. I had no choice. But I felt love for her, not hate! I was going to kill myself too. That's how bad I felt about killing her."

Bill was sounding fairly agitated now, but I felt strangely calmer. Listening to the Cowboy as he pushed Bill far beyond the limits of anything I had felt comfortable doing, I recognized that the questions he was asking Bill were exactly the questions I had really wanted to ask—that I knew had to be asked. I understood immediately that my problem with Bill from the beginning had been my own reluctance to face that existential moment of pulling the trigger.

"Yeah, I understand, but we're not just talking about killing. We're talking about an explosion. A shotgun to the head at point-blank range. The moment of death. Destroying Satan. BOOM! World War III."

"Are you crazy? What are you talking about?"

"I'm talking about an explosion, man! I'm talking about World War III in your bedroom! You must have thought about what that blast would do to her head. Didn't you think what it would be like, with her brains splattered all over the bed? Didn't you imagine her head exploding when you pulled the trigger? If she was Satan, wouldn't that be what she deserves? Or did you think it wasn't real, that as long as she was asleep it would just be a dream . . . like dropping an A-bomb from a B-52, where you can't see the people dying. . . . Maybe you didn't want her to wake up because *you* didn't want to wake up. Well, Janet needs to wake up and so do you, Bill. How do you expect to leave the hospital when you're asleep?"

I was torn between admiration and envy of what the Cowboy had done. Where I had expected advice, I got an epiphany. How had he been able to move so quickly to the heart of the problem? I looked at Bill but couldn't tell what he was feeling. His eyes looked wild, but he gave no indication of wanting to leave. Then I had misgivings. Did the Cowboy really know what he was doing with Bill? Did he think his speech would be enough to wake Bill up, that Bill could understand and learn from what he said? Did he expect that Bill could simply drop the delusional explanations and be honest with himself about his real feelings and motives? Or was he doing a kind of stress interview, hoping to expose the psychosis that he thought Bill was trying to hide? If Bill did become overtly psychotic again from the stress of the interview, how did the Cowboy know that it wouldn't lead to disaster? I suspected he would call it a blessing, and I knew how his argument would go: only if Bill became openly psychotic again would there be a chance of ever getting through his wall—the facade that had fooled the Technocrat, the image he tried to maintain of being a calm, detached reporter, a skeptical but cooperative patient. This wall protected him from the fear at the core of his being—the fear of nuclear war, the fear of Janet, and, most of all, the fear of experiencing the full force of his own childhood terror and rage. To help him, I would have to reach the terrified child in him, and I might only get access to that child if he became psychotic again.

"I know what you're trying to do. You're trying to scare me! You're trying to trick me into saying I still believe Janet is the devil! Well, it won't work. I think you're the crazy one. You haven't even asked me about not sleeping. Dr. T [the Technocrat] says that's the main thing, and that lithium will take care of that problem. He thinks I'm ready for discharge, so it doesn't really matter what you think."

Bill's reaction was unsettling, but not surprising. His wall was still up, but the Cowboy's point had definitely gotten through to me. I had been evading the real issue: what it feels like, what it would feel like *to me,* to be driven to kill somebody in cold blood. I had been far too distant with Bill, and I now understood that it was because I had been afraid to empathize with him, *afraid to know that I even had it in me* to feel what must have been going on inside him in that moment of pulling the trigger. I had forgotten the wisdom of the poet, which is also the wisdom of psychoanalysis: "nothing human is foreign to me." How could I expect Bill to trust me enough to face the darkness in himself unless I was first prepared to face the darkness in me? With this new self-awareness, I was released from my paralyzing dread and was suddenly able to think clearly about the real dangers Bill and I faced.

Treatment Planning

If successful treatment depended on my being able to confront my own fear, then I didn't need to worry so much about what might or might not make

Bill psychotic again, or whether that would be good or bad for him. If I could deal with my own fear enough to make empathic contact with Bill, I was confident that I would not push him needlessly into psychosis and that if he did become psychotic again I would eventually be able to help him through it. I had only to decide what conditions I needed in order to safely experience the darkness in myself and him. Once I had put it to myself in that way, I realized that I could not confront the existential fear unless I was free from the practical fear of what Bill might do; that is, I had to know he was safe on a locked unit in the hospital. Maybe someone else could, but I knew that I could not treat him as an outpatient without experiencing incapacitating dread.

The idea of basing my decision about Bill on what *I* needed freed me from the impossible pressure of having to be sure of what he needed. It relieved me of the worry that my insistence on long-term hospitalization might confirm him in a paranoid conviction that I was the enemy who must be destroyed. Now I would not need to insist. I would simply set the conditions under which I could be comfortable being his doctor, but leave the decision up to him. If he was able to find another doctor willing to treat him as an outpatient, he was free to do so, but I would not help him pretend that there was no danger. This approach would give Bill back some of the responsibility for his own predicament.

Yet it still didn't feel quite right. For one thing, I worried that the Technocrat had already encouraged Bill's denial by telling him that there would be no danger as long as he took his lithium. Perhaps he had not realized that offering this opinion to Bill would subvert my psychotherapeutic efforts. More likely, he had disapproved of my "unscientific" treatment approach and believed he was doing Bill a service by questioning it. I didn't know whether to be angry at the Technocrat or ashamed of myself for the cowardice I now realized had led me to consult him in the first place. But either way I had to take responsibility for having exposed Bill to a Medical Model point of view that I generally thought of as misguided. It would be irresponsible now to simply give Bill a choice—between having me treat him in the hospital and having a Medical Model psychiatrist treat him as an outpatient—without first doing everything I could to make him understand how dangerous I believed the Technocrat's approach could be, not only for him but also for anyone he might harm if he became psychotic again. My belief that if Bill decided to see a Medical Model psychiatrist—someone who would treat him exclusively with medication without addressing the underlying emotional issues—he would be endangering not only his own life but those of Janet and possibly his parents as well, gave me an added burden of responsibility to all of them. I had to find a way to give some of that responsibility back to Bill, to break through his denial of the very real danger that he could try to kill again. I was fairly certain that if he fully realized what a threat he might be to those he loved, he would not be so insistent on leaving the hospital.

The best way for Bill to realize the danger would be to become aware of his murderous feelings. But it was precisely because he could not tolerate those feelings that the danger existed in the first place. The Cowboy had invited him to feel his murderousness toward Janet, but if anything this had only pushed him further into the Technocrat's camp. Since his meeting with the Cowboy, Bill had seemed even more intent on acting as normal as possible. He took reassurance from the Technocrat's opinion and dismissed the Cowboy's questions as a misguided attempt to "scare" him. If I now tried to convince Bill that his murderous feelings made him a danger to Janet, it would further alienate him. No one wants to be told what he is feeling, especially when he is not feeling it. Bill felt love for Janet, not hatred.

Perhaps, then, although he could not take responsibility for his own murderous feelings, he might be able to take some responsibility for Janet's fear, precisely because he did love her. I was sure that Janet was terrified but had been afraid to say so. She had talked to Bill about his coming home as if she agreed with him that there was no danger, but she had talked to me as if she was somewhat hesitant about it, and looked to me for assurance that it would be safe. Bill's parents had similarly been afraid to tell him how worried they were about his explosiveness, but they were counting on me to defuse that explosiveness. When it dawned on me that I was at the hub of this network of denial, I realized that I had been in denial myself, never having told Bill directly that *I* felt afraid of him and of what he might do. I also realized that I needed to involve the whole network in the treatment decision. So I called a family meeting.

Family Meeting

Present at the meeting were Bill, Janet, Bill's mother and her fiancé (who had known Bill for several years), Bill's father and stepmother, Bill's social worker from the hospital (a family therapist), and myself. To summarize briefly what took place over an hour and a half, I told Bill that, although he seemed much improved since the time of his first admission to the community hospital, I believed that this was only a superficial improvement based on the calming effect of the medication. He had not dealt at all with the deep-seated emotional problems or with the short-term relationship conflicts with Janet that had led to his breakdown. Indeed, he denied that any such problems or conflicts existed. I acknowledged that the Technocrat viewed his breakdown as a brain disorder that had no psychological basis and could easily be treated with medication, but I emphasized that I disagreed quite strongly with that view. I explained that even when medication is effective in controlling symptoms over the short term, patients are very likely over the intermediate or long term to relapse, either while still taking their medication or because they stop taking it without telling anyone. I said that genuine security against such an outcome can come only from understanding and mastering the psychological roots of the illness. I added that Bill's refusal to consider that his illness could have a psychological basis left me with a sense of dread that had been clouding my thinking about what was best for him. There had been times when I was afraid of what he might do to me, and I was even more afraid of what he might do to Janet and to himself if he remained in such a state of denial and then were to become psychotic again. I could handle my fear and even use it to help me work with him if I knew he was safe in the hospital, I explained, but I would be too afraid to work with him at this point as an outpatient. "I know you're afraid that staying in the hospital might make you psychotic again, but even if that happens, the point is that you and Janet and your family will be safe, and you will be in a place where you can deal with the emotions that you have so far been afraid to feel. If I discharge you now, I actually think it will make it more likely that the psychosis will return— only then you won't have a safety net."

I then turned to the others in the room and made the intervention that I knew would make or break Bill's treatment. I told them that I could work successfully with Bill only if they all supported my recommendation for long-term hospitalization, a minimum of six to nine months, very possibly longer. Bill needed to hear how they all felt. I knew he had been calling them, appealing for their help in getting out of the hospital. If they had doubts about the treatment I was recommending it would reinforce Bill's doubts and interfere with his treatment, so they would probably be better off in that case helping him choose another psychiatrist they could all trust. In thus making Bill's family responsible along with him for choosing his treatment, I hoped to push them to acknowledge and discuss their own fears openly, so that Bill would see the impact his actions had had, and were continuing to have, on them.

The plan seemed to work. Because I had openly admitted that I was afraid of Bill, first Janet, then Bill's mother, and finally his stepmother began to talk about how fearful they had been since hearing that Bill wanted to leave the hospital. They pleaded with him to commit himself to understanding what had happened so that it never needed to happen again. Sandra's fiancé supported them, saying that he had been very worried about Janet's safety and felt Bill had been pushing much too hard to come home too soon. That left Bill's father. He hesitated, reiterating his strong concern that being in the hospital might make Bill worse rather than better. Given what everyone else had been saying, however, he felt there really wasn't any choice. If we were all convinced that the best way for him to support his son was to support my treatment plan, then he was willing to support the plan, although he still had serious misgivings.

Bill was silent through all of this. He had looked unsettled when Janet talked about being afraid, and he now spoke up to say he would never hurt her. I said we all understood that he loved Janet and did not want to harm her when he was himself, but I wasn't sure that this would be enough to keep him from being overtaken again with the conviction that she was the devil. To prevent such a recurrence, we needed to understand the emotional conflicts that had triggered this delusion in the first place. He looked beaten down as I was talking and replied that he knew I was wrong but that he would respect his family's wishes; he would stay in the hospital and try to give psychotherapy a chance, if that was what they felt best. I wanted to believe that I sensed some relief in him, but perhaps that was wishful thinking.

I never had the opportunity to find out, because first thing next morning I got a call from the hospital saying that Bill's father had arrived and was insisting that Bill be discharged immediately. Apparently he had felt coerced into accepting my recommendation at the family meeting but realized afterward that he could not really live with the agreement. He had already been in touch with the Technocrat, who had promised to help him find another psychiatrist for Bill. Both Bill and his father agreed that since Janet was not yet comfortable with Bill's leaving the hospital, it would be best if Bill stayed with his father for a while.

I arranged an emergency meeting with Bill, Louis, Sandra, and Janet. It became clear during the course of that meeting that Bill and his father were cemented in their shared belief that he absolutely needed to get out of the hospital. They could not really listen to any other point of view. My options then were either to discharge Bill against medical advice or to try to reinstate his involuntary commitment, being fairly certain that the request would be denied by the mental health judge and that, even if the request was approved, Bill's treatment with me would be doomed. It would only further polarize him and his father into an alliance against me. Louis would spare no expense to fight through the court system for Bill's release, and Bill would simply close himself off and bide his time until they were successful. I discussed this further with Janet and Sandra after the meeting, explaining why I thought it would be futile and probably counterproductive to try to fight Bill's decision legally. They agreed. I recommended that as long as they felt afraid they should let Bill stay with his father. I also said I took some hope from the fact that Louis was clearly insisting that Bill continue in outpatient psychotherapy. Even though I believed it was misguided, his decision to stand up for what he believed best for his son might well be an important source of support and comfort to Bill in the difficult months to come.

It turned out that the Technocrat referred Bill to a psychiatrist who was known for his expertise with medication but who was also a skillful psychotherapist and a good friend of mine. My friend called me before accepting the referral, and we agreed that though long-term hospitalization would have been far preferable, it was no longer a viable option. He therefore accepted the referral for outpatient treatment with the understanding that Bill would return to the hospital at the first sign of trouble.

Six weeks later, my friend called to tell me that Bill had been found that morning on a park bench a few blocks from his father's home. He had shot himself in the head with a shotgun and was dead. He had been keeping his weekly outpatient appointments, had shown absolutely no sign of recurring psychosis, but had seemed intent on remaining superficial, denying any internal or interpersonal distress. The lithium level in his blood had been checked recently and was in the therapeutic range. He had been taking his medication.

3. An Introduction to the Psychotherapeutic Process

MICHAEL: *Don't knock rationalization. Where would we be without it? I don't know anyone who'd get through the day without two or three juicy rationalizations. They're more important than sex.*

SAM: *Oh come on, nothing's more important than sex!*

MICHAEL: *Oh yeah? Have you ever gone a week without a rationalization?*

—from the movie *The Big Chill*

Know thyself.

—inscription at the temple of Apollo at Delphi

Rationalization Versus Listening to the Soul

It has been said that, "Explanation is a place where the mind comes to rest." I could try to explain what happened to Bill in a way that would put your mind (and mine) to rest about it. But such an explanation would merely be a rationalization, a story we agreed to tell ourselves that would make us more comfortable, at the cost of keeping us at a distance from what we really feel. We would then miss an opportunity to learn from our discomfort by listening to the soul, that is, by noticing and allowing ourselves to feel what it is about Bill's story that has made our minds so restless in the first place. In an important way, Bill's tragedy highlights what is at stake in this existential choice between rationalization and listening to the soul—a choice that we all face in more subtle ways each day. Do we want to know ourselves as we really are, as the Cowboy challenged Bill and me to do, or would we prefer to follow the Technocrat's Medical Model, telling ourselves scientific stories about the brain that allow us to deny our essential nature and make it easier to ignore what we don't want to recognize in ourselves?

For many people, probably for most people, rationalization is a way of life. It can take many forms, from the innocuous to the life-threatening, from the psychotic to the scientific. Bill used a delusional rationalization to explain his attempt on Janet's life: a message from God made him do it. The Technocrat used a scientific rationalization: a hurricane in the brain made Bill do it. Bill was a patient and the Technocrat was a doctor, but both used rationalization to hide from themselves.

I believe that the whole Medical Model approach to psychiatry, like the mental illness it seeks to explain, is afflicted by this same fearful need, to hide from the existential moment of self-awareness. By explaining psychic distress as a symptom of a brain disease, the Medical Model insulates the physician from the anxiety of his own human condition. It emphasizes the difference, and the distance, between doctor and patient, defining the doctor as the one who has the specialized esoteric knowledge (a role that allows him to feel more secure), and the patient as the one who has the disease. By thinking of the patient as having a brain defect that makes him *different,* the doctor avoids the anxiety of having to feel his common humanity with his patient, and having to recognize that the patient's illness reflects an existential dilemma to which the doctor is vulnerable as well. But, of course, Medical Model psychiatrists are not the only ones who rationalize. My idea that I needed two consultants to determine Bill's dangerousness, for instance, was, in retrospect, clearly a rationalization—a way of hiding from what I already *knew* about his dangerousness because I could feel it in my own experience of anxiety.

A cynic might suggest, with some justification, that the difference between psychosis and science, mental illness and mental health, is merely a difference in how popular or socially acceptable our rationalizations are. Clearly none of us is free from self-delusion. We all depend mightily on rationalization to get us through the day without too much existential angst. On the other hand, we wouldn't have words like rationalization and self-delusion in our vocabulary if we didn't all know what it means to tell yourself a story that in your heart of hearts you know isn't true. We all have an innate capacity for discernment, a kind of instinct that, if we know how to use it, allows us to recognize when we are rationalizing and when we are in touch with what we really feel.

An Interactive Exercise

With these ideas in mind, I would like to suggest that you now pause for a moment and reflect on what you really feel after reading Bill's story. I propose that we try to use your emotional reaction as the starting point for an interactive exercise in the psychotherapeutic process. The point of the exercise will be to give you a firsthand experience of how psychotherapy works, using the distinctive method of inner attention and discernment that I call listening to the soul.

If you would like to try the exercise, please begin by taking a few minutes to simply let yourself "be with" your response to Bill's story, not so much actively trying to make sense of it as simply noticing the felt sense of it that you already have, as you are left with it from your reading. Your attitude should be one of quiet inward listening, attuning your awareness to that restless place in you that needs an explanation. Try to identify the predominant feeling tone that you notice there, and then pick the one word that best describes it (though several may apply). Take enough time to allow all the nuances of your response to register in your awareness. Please resist the temptation to read on into the next paragraph until you have actually tried to access your inner state and have selected a word.

If you had trouble deciding on the word that best identifies your feeling, it is very likely that you were too much "in your head"—the place where rationalization happens—focusing on what you *think* about Bill's story rather than what you feel about it. Try shifting your attention away from your head to your gut and your heart. At the same time allow your mind to relax and open up to the stream of thoughts, images, impressions, fantasies, memories, and associated feelings that will come unbidden into your awareness as you simply let yourself feel whatever feeling is there. This "unfocused focusing" of inner attention is what Freud called *free association—free* because of the relaxed state of attention involved, *association* because the unfettered flow of mental contents creates a kind of web of inner experience, each content associated, as a kind of commentary or variation on a theme, to the predominant feeling of the moment. By reflecting not only on your feeling about Bill's story but also on your associations to that feeling and the further feelings they evoke in you, you can gradually refine your sense of precisely what your primary feeling is, to the point that you can name it in a word that rings true as just the right one for that particular feeling.

Beginning the Psychotherapeutic Process

There will inevitably be a variety of responses, each response reflecting to some degree the individuality of the responder. Your own feeling about Bill's story will embody important elements of who you are—the unique set of attitudes and emotional dispositions that define the way you tend to react to people and events generally, and that inform your emotional reactions to this book in particular. In trying to identify this personal theme in your own response, it might be worthwhile to write down the word you chose, along with any of your associations—other feelings, thoughts, memories, and impressions—that struck you as significant in the process of choosing it.

Yet there will also inevitably be certain common responses, reflecting something about the story itself, as well as something about the less individualized, more universal elements in the human nature of the responders. For instance, I would expect most readers of Bill's story to feel at least some degree of what I felt as a participant in the story; namely *anxiety*. Anxiety is a problematic and confusing emotion. It is disturbing enough that we will go to great lengths in order not to experience it, but ambiguous enough that we often have trouble recognizing it when we are experiencing it. It is an unsettled, agitated state that brings a sense of urgency, a need to do something about it, a sense of discord seeking resolution. If you were able to stay long enough with that restless urgency to pay attention to it, you may have noticed two important elements of the anxiety experience: first, that the anxiety points to a particular incident or emotion that evoked it, and second, that the sense of urgency tends to express itself—if we don't rationalize it away—as a need for answers to certain pressing questions.

My own anxiety about Bill, for instance, gave rise to a persistent, preoccupying, question: How dangerous is he? At first I tried to rationalize the anxiety away by taking this as an objective question to be answered by a consultant's assessment rather than recognizing my own assessment that was already implicit in the anxiety itself. Had I listened more attentively within myself, instead of looking outside myself for answers, I would have noticed that my anxiety was pointing to something about Bill that felt dangerous to me, and I might then have asked a deeper, more relevant question: What is the specific danger I feel that is so threatening to me that I can't think clearly about Bill? I might then have recognized much sooner than I did that what scared me about Bill was the terrifying moment when he had actually pulled the trigger, and knowing that I would need to go back and experience that moment with him, and within myself.

Of course, the anxiety you may have felt at the conclusion of Bill's story was probably not about Bill's dangerousness, but about the meaning *to you* of what happened to him. The questions to which you need answers will reflect something unsettling in Bill's story that resonates disturbingly with something unsettling in your own life story. The good news is that if Bill's story has unsettled you in this way, raising questions for you that are relevant to your own life experience, then you have already successfully completed the first phase of the interactive exercise. You have experienced for yourself the first two (out of six) basic elements of the psychotherapeutic process: *anxiety* and *a spirit of questioning*. Together, these are the two elements that set the psychotherapeutic process in motion, the "inner voice" that calls us to listen to the soul. If you want to pursue this process further, try putting into words the questions your anxiety raises for you. Here again, writing them down would be useful, but don't be surprised if you find this difficult to do, because in order to formulate your questions clearly enough to write them down, you must allow yourself to experience and focus on the disturbing anxiety that prompts them.

But what if Bill's story does not arouse uneasiness or raise questions in you? I would then urge you to ask yourself why not. What is the basis for your equanimity? How are you explaining to yourself Bill's illness, his treatment, his fate, and your reaction to my account of them? Try putting that explanation into words. Write it down. It may be that you have leaped prematurely to a superficial interpretation—a rationalization—of Bill's story that relieves you of anxiety and eliminates the need for questioning but precludes the possibility of a deeper understanding.

If you find yourself now rushing headlong into this paragraph without yet having written down either your feelings and questions about Bill's story, or your explanation of it, then you probably haven't formulated these as well as you imagine. We seldom realize just how ineffable and evanescent the processes of consciousness really are until we try to articulate a complicated emotional experience, either out loud (as in a psychotherapy session) or on paper. The unarticulated experience always remains to some degree inarticulate. It floats in a comfortable fuzziness, and it can sometimes require considerable effort to bring it into focus under the lens of language. *You may feel a great reluctance to make such an effort,* but then you will be missing an opportunity to experience two more of the basic elements of a psychotherapeutic process: the third element, which is *introspection;* and the fourth, which is *putting into words* the feelings, attitudes, and associations that come into awareness through introspection. These two elements are integral to the process of listening to the soul. More precisely, the kind of introspection that is necessary in order to feel one's inner experience clearly and vividly enough to put it into words *is* listening to the soul. So if you haven't already done so, give it a try. Listen inside yourself to your feelings about Bill's story. Notice the questions to which your feelings give rise. Stay with the process until you can feel your feelings and ask your questions clearly enough to put them into words and write them down.

If you are having trouble getting past that great reluctance I mentioned and find yourself still balking at the prospect of committing to words the obscure impressions that Bill's story has made on your consciousness, that's okay, too. You are simply experiencing more intensely what everyone else who tries this exercise will be experiencing to a greater or lesser degree: the fifth basic element of the psychotherapeutic process: *internal resistance.*

Internal resistance is the force within us that opposes the task of putting thoughts and feelings into words. It can produce significantly painful experiences, as anyone who has ever sat for two hours trying to write the first sentence of a term paper will recognize. In a psychotherapeutic process, however, this kind of resistance can serve a very useful purpose, because it acts as a signpost to inner conflict. Our reluctance to put an experience into words points to a standoff between an unsettling emotion that is threatening to become conscious in the experience and a negative attitude that we take toward the emotion in order to keep it unconscious. For instance, a patient of mine frequently found herself suddenly wanting to cry in the middle of a session, but when I would ask what she was feeling sad about, she would dismiss the feeling by saying, "Oh, I'm just feeling sorry for myself." This self-disparaging rejection of her own impulse to cry was an automatic reaction—a kind of psychological knee-jerk reflex—that functioned to prevent her from feeling her sadness and from knowing what she might genuinely have to feel sad about. Other common examples of this sort of resistance would be a man who cannot allow himself to acknowledge, or even to feel, anger because it would interfere with his image of himself as a nice guy, or a woman who does not allow herself any emotions at all because she considers them too childish or self-indulgent. This sort of stereotyped negative attitude toward elements of our own emotional life reflects a habitual reaction pattern that is ingrained in the personality. The reaction happens so automatically that we typically don't notice it consciously but simply take it for granted as the "normal" way to react to this or that sort of emotion.

We all have such negative reaction patterns—resistances—structured into our personalities. Their purpose is to help us maintain psychological stability by keeping our disturbing emotions out of awareness and so keeping our anxiety level at a minimum. The trouble is, we maintain this stability at the cost of remaining divided within ourselves, unable to accept ourselves as we really are. Psychotherapy provides a corrective to this self-alienated condition in that the therapist has no such resistance toward accepting the patient's emotional life. Because he does not take the patient's negative attitude for granted, he can more easily recognize it and then help the patient recognize it. Once the patient can feel himself reacting with this negative attitude, it becomes easier to notice the emotion he is reacting against, and then bring it into full consciousness. In this way, the function of the resistance is reversed. Instead of being a mechanism for remaining unconscious, the resistance becomes a path to consciousness. For this reason, some psychoanalysts have gone so far as to describe psychotherapy simply as a process of identifying resistances, and putting them into words.

So if you feel stuck on the task of putting your feelings about Bill's story into words, try putting your feeling of "stuckness" into words. What exactly is the negative attitude that makes you unable or unwilling to articulate your inner experience? Try putting that into words, and you may discover that all roads lead to Rome—the place where experiencing happens—even the road of not wanting to go there.

Resistance in the Psychotherapeutic Process

Let's say, for instance, that a reader is feeling impatient with the interactive exercise at this point. He has found nothing illuminating in it so far. He has pen and paper in hand but has written nothing. He wonders briefly whether his impatience might be a sign of resistance—an impatience with something in his feelings about Bill's story that he doesn't want to recognize—but he quickly becomes impatient with this idea, too, and in a flourish of annoyance writes down "I'm impatient. So what?" This would be a fairly elegant example of resistance: a way of dismissing the interactive exercise under the guise of *doing* the exercise, saying in effect, "There, I've put my feeling of stuckness into words, and what good has it done me?" Actually this is quite typical of a kind of resistance that happens regularly in psychotherapy. For instance, if I say to a patient, "It sounds like you're feeling pretty disappointed (bitter, sad, etc.)," the patient may respond, "Sure, but how do I get over that?" Though the patient seems to be agreeing with my comment, his response really serves to deflect any emotional impact the comment might have. It maintains the resistance by saying in effect, "I don't need you to tell me I'm bitter. What I need is to learn how *not* to be bitter!"

Both these resistances—the reader's impatient "So what?" and the patient's more subtle "How do I get over that?"—function primarily to direct attention back at me and *away from the inner life of the resister*. Nevertheless, if listened to in a spirit of introspective self-questioning, either reaction could be used to facilitate rather than resist the psychotherapeutic process. The reader might ask himself, for instance, "What is it about the interactive exercise, or perhaps about Bill's story, that I feel particularly impatient with? Does my impatience feel like irritation or is it more like the urgency of anxiety? In either case, what do these feelings point to?" The psychotherapy patient might ask, "Why do I need to 'get over' my disappointment (bitterness, sadness, etc.) at all? What is there about simply letting myself feel the feeling that seems so intolerable or unacceptable to me?"

We Have Nothing to Fear but Consciousness Itself

Two points are worth emphasizing here. First, the resistance to putting thoughts and feelings into words is motivated by the fear of consciousness. It is ultimately a resistance against self-awareness. Second, although the primary aim of resistance is internal—to keep our own emotions unconscious—the way it actually works is often by directing itself externally, deflecting attention from inside to outside. In psychotherapy what this means is that I will tend to focus my attention on the therapist instead of focusing within myself. For instance, I may be unable to relax enough to experience my feelings and put them into words because I am too worried about what my therapist would think of me if I did. Or, as in the example just cited, I may distract attention from whatever feeling I am reacting to in myself by reacting instead to the therapist—looking to him for advice, asking questions ("How do I get over that?") and otherwise engaging and interacting emotionally with him.

In the interactive exercise this externalization of the resistance could manifest itself as a state of reactivity—impatience, for instance—toward me as author that interferes with your willingness or ability to reflect on your response to Bill's story. For instance, you may not like my tone. You may blame me for being, say, too arrogant, or too self-righteous in my criticisms of the Medical Model, or too preachy. Perhaps you feel insulted or manipulated at the idea that I am trying to use your emotional reaction to Bill's story as a way of selling you on psychotherapy. Or perhaps you are already involved in psychotherapy and are angry at me because I have aggravated your misgivings about the process by describing a treatment that ends badly. Any of these reactions could inspire opposition to the task I have set you of putting your feelings and questions into words, and so constitute a resistance. On the other hand, perhaps you are so impressed by what you have read so far that you are eager to take me as an authority, to skip over the difficult task of asking your own questions, and jump directly to the answers you now expect me to provide forthwith. This, too, would be a resistance, under the guise of a "positive" reaction to me. In either case the reactivity—negative or positive— embodies a kind of "resistance through relationship," translating what is primarily an internal resistance against self-awareness into an interpersonal resistance against, or for, me. This translation of the internal to the external is what psychoanalysts call *transference*. It is the last, and in many ways the most important, of the six elements of the psychotherapeutic process.

Transference

Transference is ubiquitous, an aspect of all human experience, yet it is a surprisingly difficult phenomenon to describe adequately. It is usually understood as the tendency to react to another person as if he or she were an emotionally important figure from childhood, the idea being that feelings about a person from the past (memory of which is being resisted) are "transferred" onto a person in the present. For instance, you may object to my self-righteousness because something in my tone reminds you of your authoritarian father. In addition, and more significantly, transference is the tendency to react to another person as if he or she were an emotionally important but unconscious part of oneself. Here we attribute to the other person feelings, attitudes, and motives that are currently active but unconscious within us. We recognize in the other person something we cannot tolerate recognizing in ourselves, so that our feelings about something internal are "transferred" onto someone or something external. For instance, you may object to my self-righteousness because something in my tone reminds you of a secret, disowned arrogance within yourself. The philosopher Kierkegaard identified this latter dimension of transference (without calling it that) as "an inverted image of the internal," in which what is threatening to emerge into awareness from inside is experienced as something pressing in from outside. The technical term for this vitally important aspect of transference experience is *projection*—seeing in someone else the projected image of what we don't want to see in ourselves.

A typical example would be the father who cannot tolerate any dependency feelings in himself, who then "transfers" or "projects" his contempt for those feelings onto his son, maintaining a vigilant watch over the boy, ready to berate him for any signs of being a "weakling." By focusing his attention—and his contempt—on his son's insecurities, such a father can successfully avoid noticing his own inner feelings of weakness and self-contempt, keeping them unconscious at his son's expense. Another example would be the woman who cannot tolerate her own hostile/competitive impulses who then feels intimidated by her husband's self-assertiveness and allows him to make decisions for her because she is unable to disagree with or criticize him.

Transference and Reality

When I say that readers who experience a strong reaction to me, whether negative or positive, are experiencing transference projection, I do not deny that I may have done something to provoke such feelings. After all, I did write an intentionally disturbing chapter about Bill, and my style has perhaps bordered on the polemical or been a bit preachy in places. Even so, it is important to recognize that the emotional valence my style may have for the reader will vary from one person to the next. One reader may feel preached at while another will feel inspired by the sermon. One will feel manipulated and object angrily while another will feel stimulated and applaud. Some readers will react to my approach with curiosity, some with skepticism, and some with apprehension. Some will automatically reject it while others will automatically accept it, without in either case questioning or making a real effort to understand it. Each reaction reflects a different transference disposition toward me, an attitude that was already present as a *pre*disposition (a reactive tendency) before the reader began the chapter, probably before he or she opened the book. Such predispositions establish a *frame of mind* in which we tend to selectively notice certain aspects of a person and not others, and so react with a skewed attitude that we could never maintain if we saw all sides of the person's purposes and motives.

Of course, as a therapist, I know that it is almost always a mistake to try to "correct" a patient's transference projections by explaining to him what my purposes and motives "really" are. In fact I may not always know what my purposes and motives really are. I may be unwittingly influenced by an unconscious attitude that my patient can detect more accurately than I, precisely because his transference predisposition is to be on guard against just that sort of attitude. For this reason, I would never say to a patient, "I wasn't preaching at you. You only heard me that way because of your tendency to react to me as you do to all authority figures, as if I were the image of your father." (An alert patient might respond, "Thanks for the sermon.") Rather, I would ask the patient to tell me more about what it felt like to be preached at by me. What was it that particularly offended him about my preachiness and why? I might also ask him whether he had any thoughts about why I acted that way. Did he think I was always preachy, for instance, or that I was being especially so with him for a particular reason? In the end, I believe it should be up to the patient to decide for himself how much his feeling preached-at reflects a transference predisposition to react that way (to any authority figure, for example) and how much it is an accurate perception of my tone, content, and (perhaps unconscious) purpose.

So What?

The ability to make this sort of distinction—to discern how much our reactions are colored by emotional prejudices and predispositions and how far we can trust them as accurate reflections of whatever we are reacting to—is one of the most important results of psychotherapy, certainly the result most immediately relevant to the quality of our relationships. Although the entire psychotherapeutic process contributes toward developing this ability, we develop it primarily through experiencing and "working through" the transference. Here the therapist plays a crucial role (as you will see in Part Four), through his ability to accept the patient's transference reactions with an open, nonjudgmental attitude that invites deeper self-reflection. The fact that I cannot replicate this role with you as reader in working through your transference reactions to me as author is an unavoidable limitation of the interactive exercise. Nevertheless, you might continue the exercise and reflect further on your transference reactions by asking yourself the sort of questions I outlined in the preceding paragraph.

Putting Transference Feelings into Words

Suppose, for example, that the frustrated reader who wrote, "I'm impatient. So what?" wants to get beyond this resistance and test out my explanation of transference as it applies to his own feeling of impatience. Putting his feeling into words, the reader might write down, "I'm really irritated with all this precious talk about listening to the soul, and existential dilemmas, and knowing yourself as you really are. To me it's all just an excuse, a fancy story Frattaroli is telling himself—and trying to foist on me—to evade responsibility for his failure to save Bill's life." He then thinks, "Wow, I'm feeling angrier than I realized. It seems strange that I should be so irritated with this guy for writing about the soul when that's really what I bought the book to read about. There must be more to my reaction. What is it that is really bothering me? It's not that I disagree with his ideas about the soul. What gets to me is that he's trying to use those ideas as a kind of self-justification—to rationalize away his own failure!"

Proceeding further, he then asks himself, "What is it exactly that gets to me about that? What does Frattaroli's not taking responsibility mean to me personally that I'm so angry about it?" As he lets himself feel his reaction more deeply he then notices that he feels betrayed by me, and he is reminded of a poignantly painful childhood experience of feeling betrayed by the doctor who failed to save the life of his ailing father. Without realizing it while reading Bill's story, he had been counting on me to find a way to help Bill, just as he had counted on the doctor to help his father, and he felt betrayed in the same way by my failure. This much would be a transference of disturbing feelings originally belonging to someone from his past onto me in the present.

But now suppose my reader wants to determine whether his reaction to me also contains an element of projection—a transference onto me of disturbing feelings from his own unconscious—so he decides to stay with the feeling of betrayal and see what else comes into his awareness about it. He notices that the feeling involves a definite tone of reproach—of blaming me for failing to help Bill, just as he once blamed his father's doctor for not doing more to save his father's life. As his thoughts gravitate back to that earlier, sad time, he recalls a very old feeling: that he himself had failed his father, that *he* was to blame for his father's illness and death because of his constant misbehavior prior to that illness—certainly not an uncommon reaction for a child to have when a parent dies. He realizes then that blaming his father's doctor must have been a projection of his self-blame, an attempt to alleviate his own guilt, and he wonders whether he is now blaming me in the same way, for the same purpose. (Remember that, even if he is correct in his assessment that I am making excuses for my own failure, his need to blame me for that is personal *to him,* and in that way a transference projection.) But if so, then what current self-reproach would he be trying to assuage now through this transference blaming of me? As an adult, he understands that his father died of a cancer that was so advanced by the time it was diagnosed that no one could have done anything to save him. He should have long since let go of blaming himself for his father's death. So if there is an element of projection in his blaming me now, then *there would have to be something else, currently active but unconscious within him, that he is blaming himself for and needing to project onto me, under cover of that old self-recrimination.*

Following this logic of projection, my reader realizes that whatever he might unconsciously still be blaming himself for would be implicit in what he is consciously blaming me for. So he tries to focus in on his feeling of blaming me, as contained in his reproachful feeling of betrayal. As he lets himself feel this once again, he recognizes that it combines the old childhood anger at my failure to save Bill's (his father's) life with a much more present feeling of outrage over my not taking responsibility for my failure. He finds himself wanting to say to me, "Who the hell do you think you are to preach at me about listening to the soul, and knowing myself as I really am? Why don't you practice what you preach and admit your own failure and your own rationalizations!" But if this complaint represents a projection, wouldn't that mean he was unconsciously blaming himself for the same thing—for a tendency to be arrogantly and hypocritically preachy? That's certainly not the way he usually thinks of himself, but he reviews his important relationships, looking for evidence of such a tendency—perhaps one that he has had to fight to keep in check. His thoughts turn once again to his father, and he remembers, perhaps more clearly than he ever felt it as a child, how much he had resented and disapproved of his father's lifestyle, *how much he would have liked to preach at his father* to stop working so hard and drinking so much and start thinking about his children for a change. As he lets himself feel this reproach, it hits him that he had not only blamed the doctor (and himself) for failing to save his father's life but also blamed his father for dying, for being too busy to go to the doctor, and for anesthetizing his pains with alcohol until it was too late for a doctor, or anyone else, to help him.

Will the Real Reader Please Stand Up

I realize that my actual readers may be inclined to object to this hypothetical impatient reader of mine. You may feel that I have invented him to fit my theory. His self-analysis of transference feelings and associations may seem to unfold a little too neatly to be believable. Even if you did find yourself believing it, you might wonder whether I somehow tricked you into believing it. I will certainly admit that what I have presented is a condensed and schematized example of a process that in real life would usually be much more difficult. Most people would require years of psychotherapy to develop the introspective ability necessary to accomplish such a self-analysis. Nevertheless, as an idealization, I believe the example does present an accurate picture of the layers of feeling and memory that can unfold from a single transference reaction. Initially, this was all I intended it to do. But as it turns out, there is another dimension to my impatient reader's self-analysis, one that I discovered only upon completing it, that makes it altogether believable not only as an idealization but as a realistic example. What I discovered was that, as a product of my own imagination, the impatient reader is really *me,* responding to my own writing. The feelings and associations I imagined the reader having were at the same time my own feelings and associations to Bill's story. His imaginary psychotherapeutic process was then part of my own real process. But I recognized this only at the very last minute—as I imagined him discovering that he blamed his father for dying, and found myself unexpectedly flooded with memories of my own father's death. I then realized that in the process of trying to teach my readers how to do the interactive exercise, I had inadvertently done it for myself.

I can now confirm, after a little reflection, that my hypothetical patient's discovery is also a valid insight for me. Though my father was not a drinker, and though he thought a good deal about his children, and didn't die until I was forty-one years old, I can recognize that I did blame him—in a way that I hadn't felt consciously until now as I am writing about it—for a certain stubborn closing-himself-off during his last illness that made it impossible for me and my family to reach or help him. But if this feeling about my father is a product of my own interactive exercise, then it must be important not only in its own right but also as an association to my feeling about Bill's story. Reflecting on it in that vein, I can recognize that under cover of blaming the Technocrat, and blaming myself, I blamed Bill, too, more than I had been willing to admit, for *his* stubborn closing-himself-off—for putting himself beyond my, or anyone else's, power to reach him.

Making the Unconscious Conscious

I hope that this brief exercise has begun to give you a feel for what happens in the psychotherapeutic process. Just to summarize: Anxiety and a spirit of questioning initiate the process, by calling our attention to a disturbing emotion that is threatening to become conscious. Introspection and putting it into words carry the process forward, by enabling us to experience more fully this anxiety-provoking unconscious emotion. Resistance and transference deepen the process, by provoking us to react (within ourselves and to the therapist) in ways that bring the disturbing emotion into sharper focus. The overall goal of the process is to resolve inner conflict by bringing our unconscious emotions into full conscious awareness. This is a liberating and healing experience, because it allows us to reclaim a disowned part of ourselves, along with the increased power and responsibility that go with it.

Transference plays a particularly important role in this healing expansion of consciousness, by bringing the disowned unconscious part of ourselves into the relationship with the therapist. It propels us into an emotionally charged interaction with the therapist that allows us to have a new experience (via projection) of our conflict-producing emotional needs and tendencies—like my impatient reader's experience of my arrogant preachiness, and then of his own. To put it simply, getting in touch with our emotional reactions to our therapist is a crucial step toward getting in touch with our emotional reactions to ourselves. Ultimately, it leads to greater acceptance both of ourselves and of others, in a variation on the comic-strip character Pogo's famous theme, "We have met the enemy and they is us!"

Psychotherapy As Inward Journey

Another interesting implication of the interactive exercise that you may have noticed is that a person does not have to be in formal psychotherapy to experience all the basic elements of a psychotherapeutic process. These are elements of the "inward journey," a universal process of spiritual quest, the need for which seems to be part of the human condition. This quest has taken many different forms in different ages and cultures, but it always starts with anxiety and a spirit of questioning, proceeds through a self-reflective attitude and an attempt to put inner experience into words, and encounters internal resistance and transference (to the guide, guru, shaman, teacher, intimate friend) along the way. Well-known examples of such a quest are to be found in the writings of philosophers and spiritual teachers, from Plato's *Symposium*, to St. Augustine's *Confessions*, St. Ignatius Loyola's *Spiritual Exercises*, Descartes's *Meditations*, and Kierkegaard's *The Concept of Anxiety*; and in the works of poets, from Homer's *Odyssey* to Dante's *Divine Comedy* to Shakespeare's *Hamlet* and *King Lear*. Joseph Campbell argues that the Arthurian myth of the quest for the grail is a symbolic representation of this inward journey as a universal experience.

Martin Buber described the inward journey as a process of actualizing our innate capacity for "authentic human existence." "Every personal life," wrote Buber, "[is] engaged in such a process of actualization, [in which] the forces making for actualization are all the time involved in a microcosmic struggle with counterforces."[1] In the terminology of dynamic psychotherapy, the "forces making for actualization" are the forces of unconscious emotion, pressing toward consciousness. The "counterforces" are those of internal resistance and fear of consciousness. The resulting "microcosmic struggle" is the inner conflict of the soul, with the anxiety, shame, and guilt it produces.

The psychotherapist acts "as a helper of the actualizing forces" by helping the patient listen to the soul, allowing the unconscious to become conscious and so achieving a new level of integration.

Dynamic Psychotherapy Is an Appropriate Treatment for All Mental Illnesses

Psychiatrists adhering to the Medical Model, which lacks the language to talk about such things, will certainly object to the apparent self-indulgence of recommending an inward journey for people suffering from a psychiatric disorder. But the kind of psychotherapy I describe in this book is as effective for those with diagnosable mental illness as it is for anxious philosophers. I have found that many patients, including some of the most seriously ill patients, welcome psychotherapy, and make excellent use of it, precisely because they recognize their illness as an existential crisis that has propelled them on an inward journey whether they like it or not. Psychiatrists who think of the mind as a biological organ and of mental illness as a brain disease too often dismiss such philosophical or spiritual concerns as bordering on the delusional, symptoms of their patients' illnesses that are best suppressed in the interest of getting on with a normal life. When this happens, the best hope is that the patient will be persistent enough in his illness that he manages eventually to cure the physician.

Still, of course, relatively few of the patients who consult a psychiatrist or psychotherapist do so because they are consciously looking for an inward journey. They come for help because they are hurting, because they want some palpable relief from their urgent emotional pain or distress. Does psychotherapy work specifically for this kind of problem? The answer, simply, is yes. For those with a diagnosable mental illness, whether they are looking for self-actualization or whether they simply want to stop the pain, the psychotherapeutic process is a real treatment designed for real illness.

It is important to recognize that people need an inward journey for the same reason they tend to become mentally ill—the inner conflict of the Spirit with the Flesh. Mental illness develops when the anxiety, shame, and guilt arising from this universal conflict become too intense to handle through ordinary coping mechanisms—typically when there is a combination of past traumatic experiences and present acute stresses (which may, of course, include chemical imbalances). When that happens, the symptoms of mental illness function as a kind of emergency coping mechanism, a way of relieving the anxiety generated by the otherwise unmanageable inner conflict.

This understanding of symptoms is so fundamentally at odds with the modern psychiatric view of mental illness as a chemical imbalance that I want to reemphasize it here. *I am convinced that all psychiatric symptoms originate in the way I have just described—as adaptive mechanisms to relieve the anxiety generated by inner conflict—and that they are appropriately and effectively treated by a psychotherapeutic process (with or without medication) aimed at resolving inner conflict.* The symptoms will no longer be necessary (and chemical balance will be restored) once the unconsciously conflicted, anxiety-provoking emotions have been fully accepted into consciousness, that is, once they are no longer provoking unmanageable anxiety.

The Unique Advantage of Dynamic Psychotherapy

As a treatment, dynamic psychotherapy has a powerful advantage over all other approaches that make use of the inward journey, including meditation, vision quests, twelve-step programs, consciousness-raising groups, or self-help guides. It has the same advantage over many other treatments— cognitive therapy, behavioral therapy, interpersonal therapy, problem-focused therapies, supportive counseling—that are called psychotherapy but are missing crucial healing elements. What dynamic psychotherapy offers that all these methods lack is a unique synthesis of private inner experience and interpersonal process: a specific focus on inner conflict as the nexus of change, combined with a method that takes advantage of *transference as the vehicle for change.*

As I will discuss more extensively in Part Four, a psychotherapeutic relationship facilitates the process of change by providing a setting in which transference can develop and intensify in an atmosphere of trust, and where it can be consciously experienced, understood in perspective, and harnessed in the service of healing. The healing action—making the unconscious conscious and so becoming more fully ourselves—comes through listening to the soul, the engaged awareness of our inner state of conflicted emotion as it evolves through our engagement in an emotionally conflicted transference relationship with the therapist.

II. The Medical Model and the Psychotherapeutic Model

A Personal Commentary on Psychiatry,
Science, and the Philosophy of Life

The questions of real philosophy have a different "taste" from those of
academic philosophy, as it is officially taught. . . . These [academic]
formulations are like the tracks in the forest left by a living creature, while
the creature itself, the real question, is still alive and moving somewhere else.
To approach the living question with the mind alone is impossible. The
intellect must be coupled with feeling in order to stir a person to authentic
inquiry. Real philosophy recognizes that ideas have sensations and emotions
connected with them, and that one responds to them with the
whole of oneself.

—Jacob Needleman, *Real Philosophy*

[I]t is not the theoretical mastery of a problem which
permits its deepest understanding. It is one's inner
experiences that permit gaining a full grasp of what
is involved in the inner experiences of others, a
knowledge which then can become the basis for
theoretical studies.

—Bruno Bettelheim, *Freud's Vienna*
and Other Essays

4. A Lecture to Young Psychiatrists

The fact that serious and wise people with penetrating minds have so long sub-scribed to such rigmaroles about the nature of science can be understood only as expressing a deep, underlying urge of our modern civilization. It is due to a funda-mental reluctance to recognize our higher faculties, which our empiricist philosophy cannot account for. We dread to be caught believing—and, in fact, knowing—things which are not demonstrable by the measurement of observed variables. . . . We look carefully over our shoulders and pick our words appropriately, to avoid say-ing anything . . . metaphysical . . .—for fear of offending the ruling assumptions about the strictly mechanical origin of science.

—Michael Polanyi, "Scientific Beliefs"

It was dusk, and scattered snowflakes were beginning to fall as I pulled onto the interstate for a two-hour drive through a cold January evening to give a lecture to a group of psychiatric residents. The residents had asked me to talk to them about psychotherapy in the practice of psychiatry. Although I had been pleased to receive this special invitation, I was also disheartened by the thought that residents who want to learn how to do psychotherapy now need a guest lecturer from out of town to teach them about it. In the Age of the Brain, dynamic psychotherapy, once the cornerstone of psychiatric training, is no longer considered relevant to psychiatric practice and so is taught min-imally or not at all in most psychiatric residency programs. With this sad state of affairs in mind, I decided to focus my lecture on the vital link between what we practice and what we believe, and on the importance of distinguish-ing what we have been taught to believe from what we believe because we can feel it in our guts and hearts. If psychotherapy is to survive, I thought, then young psychiatrists are going to have to learn how to think for themselves, to question what they are being taught and to pay attention to what they really feel.

This chapter presents the same lecture I gave that night in 1995—still formally addressed to young psychiatrists but edited so that a general audience of readers can "listen in"—because I believe that the philosophical crisis in psychiatry today mirrors a deeper philosophical crisis in our culture as a whole. If the planet itself is to survive, then we are all going to have to learn to think for ourselves, to question what we are being taught and pay attention to what we really feel.

What's Left Now That We've Erased Descartes's Error?

It seemed a happy coincidence when you invited me to talk to you today about psychotherapy in the practice of psychiatry, because for the last year or so I've been writing a book on that very topic. As it turned out, however, it was quite a bit harder than I expected to pull myself out of the cloud of half-formed thoughts that constitute a book-in-progress, and choose an hour's worth of reasonably completed thoughts to share with you. Then it occurred to me that perhaps you could help. There's a research project I've been working on in connection with the book, which I thought I might ask you all to participate in tonight. But first, I should probably give you some of the background.

Probably the very first thing that started me thinking about the ideas that are now the subject of my book was an editorial written by Robert Stoller in the *American Journal of Psychiatry* in 1984. Here is what Stoller wrote:

> We psychiatrists pay a high and unacknowledged price these days for our great advances: More and more we ignore the clinical skills that detect, at all levels of awareness, what another person feels. The shift is clearly marked in our practice, research, teaching, literature, and ideal for professional identity. Brain replaces mind, miraculously erasing the great philosophic problem. . . . Sensitivity to proper drug levels . . . has pushed aside sensitivity to emotional nuances. . . . Many psychiatrists cannot decipher the subtle, pervasive, nonverbal communications that are the way humans express their interior. These colleagues were not trained to do so, were not in their training exposed to teachers who could do so, and do not feel that doing so is important. They don't know what they are missing. Are such skills too nonsci-

entific, too nonmedical, too removed from brains or synapses or molecules or reflexes . . . ? Even grimmer, are they statistically unmanageable? (p. 554)

What I found particularly striking in Stoller's commentary was the idea that the erosion of our psychotherapeutic practice was being caused by a change in our philosophical beliefs. Psychopharmacology was replacing psychotherapy because brain was replacing mind—that is, chemical imbalance was replacing inner conflict—as the philosophical basis for psychiatric explanation. When the president, the U.S. Congress, and the National Institute of Mental Health then joined in declaring the 1990s to be the Decade of the Brain, they were putting an official seal of approval on this shift in psychiatric philosophy, confirming that brain has now replaced mind not only in psychiatry but in our culture as a whole—which means that our doctors, our scientists, our philosophers, and most of our best-educated citizens now hold the following truths to be self-evident: first, that all so-called mental illnesses are really brain disorders; second, that all mental events are really by-products of brain events; and third, that there really is no mind–body problem after all, because *mind* is really just another word for *brain*. In fact, the received wisdom nowadays is that the mind–body problem was really "Descartes's error"—an unnecessary dualistic split between mind and body that he foisted on an unsuspecting world in a way that clouded the thinking of otherwise sane people for three and a half centuries but is now *known* to be invalid.

But then, what are we left with now that we have corrected Descartes's so-called error? For us in psychiatry, things are just as Stoller predicted. We no longer consider it important to trouble ourselves with the inner lives of our patients—the nuances of thought, feeling, impulse, and imagery in their minds and souls. We take a more "scientific" approach, which considers those private experiences that are of such deep concern to our patients to be merely *epiphenomena*—insubstantial shadows cast on the screen of consciousness by the ongoing stream of brain events—full of sound and fury perhaps, but in the end having no real influence on the symptoms and maladaptive behaviors that we believe are caused directly by chemical imbalances in the brain.

Privately, of course, we do continue to value our own mental, emotional, and spiritual experiences, as if they signified something more than an epiphenomenon ever could. But in the Age of the Brain, we tend to keep such feelings to ourselves, fearing that it would be politically and scientifically incorrect to be so naively dualistic in our thinking.

A Scientific Research Project

Well, I have always found this kind of homogenized, conventionalized thinking rather troubling, and I got to wondering how Descartes, unquestionably one of the smartest people who ever lived, could have made an error so egregious and yet so subtle that it misled all the other smart people for more than three centuries without anybody noticing! And how did all the smart people suddenly become free from this centuries-old Cartesian spell? How did we become so confident that we now know something Descartes didn't? How do we know, for instance, that we haven't simply fallen under somebody else's spell?

Naturally, I turned to science for an answer. I began working on that research project I mentioned earlier. The research is on the issue of social conformism and theoretical orthodoxy in psychiatry—how we actually receive our received wisdom. So if you're ready and willing, I would like to ask everyone in the audience to answer five preliminary screening questions. They require only yes-or-no responses, so you can simply raise your hand to indicate a yes, and just sit there to indicate no.

(I invite my readers to answer these same five questions. To get a feel for the exercise, you will have to imagine that a group of your peers is watching you as you raise your hand or keep it lowered in response to each question.)

Okay, first question: Before today, how many of you had heard or been taught or read anywhere that Descartes was wrong, or that Cartesian dualism has been an impediment to clear scientific thinking about the mind? Second question: How many of you believe that's true? Third question: How many in the audience have actually ever read any Descartes? Fourth question: How many believe they could explain what's supposed to be wrong with Descartes's dualistic thinking well enough for the person sitting next to you to understand the explanation? Fifth question: How many of you have felt in any way put on the spot, or uncomfortable about answering any of these questions?

(The response at the original lecture was interesting. There was a scattered, and noticeably hesitant, show of hands for questions one, two, and three; one brave hand for question four; and an audience full of hands for question five.)

Trust Your Instinct

Now, my real point in asking you these questions today is to raise a larger question about why we believe the things we do. Why, for instance, do we consider it scientific to believe that our most profound inner experiences are by-products of neurons firing—though this can never be proved—but dismiss the idea of an immaterial soul as religious prejudice precisely because it can never be proved? Why do we imagine that science, in which our culture seems to place a quasi-religious faith, is nevertheless free from religious prejudice, when we know nothing at all about the religious or antireligious convictions of scientists? Why are we so ready to trust someone else's statistics? Why are we so reluctant to trust our own instinct? For instance, I imagine that most of you felt some sense of discrepancy just now between my claim to be doing scientific research and the casual, not-very-scientific way I seemed to be going about it. Your instinct probably warned you that there was something fishy going on, that I must be pursuing some hidden agenda. But then, how do you know whether you can trust that kind of instinct?

Well, in terms of today's topic, psychotherapy, that's an important question, because it turns out that the second most important attribute of a good psychotherapist is the ability to trust your instinct. The first most important attribute is the ability simply to recognize your instinct, especially the instinct that tells you when there is a hidden agenda. That instinct is what gives you the inner sense of discrepancy I was just talking about, that warns you when there's a mismatch between what you're seeing and what you're getting—between what the patient is officially presenting and what your common sense and gut feeling about the patient tell you must be true. The reason such feelings of discrepancy are important is that they point to areas of inner conflict in the patient, conflict between what the patient feels safe to show and talk about and what's really going on in him or her emotionally, conflict between what feels socially acceptable and what feels real.

Of course, the patient isn't the only one with those sorts of conflicts. The whole issue of conformism and orthodoxy revolves around the fact that none of us feels altogether comfortable showing what's real when it conflicts with what seems acceptable. That's why I thought people might feel put on the spot by my questions, worrying whether someone might think "Geez, can you believe Agnes has never read Descartes?" or "Geez, can you believe Albert reads philosophy for fun?"

Now you may think I am making too much of this experience of hesitating to raise one's hand in a lecture. You may consider it a commonplace event, a sign of normal insecurity. True enough. Yet the very fact that such insecurity *is* normal, that we all have misgivings about our beliefs and feelings, and that we all hesitate to trust our instinct, is one of the most remarkable facts of our existence. It is a sign of our alienated, divided human condition, what Freud described as the inherent conflict between the *I* and the *It,* what the author of Genesis described as a result of eating from the tree of the knowledge of good and evil. You might say that Adam and Eve's disobedience was the primal act of nonconformity and that we human beings have been torn between our impulse toward arrogant self-assertion and our need to fit in and follow the rules—and therefore hesitant to raise our hands in lectures— ever since. The awareness of this universal form of inner conflict is the knowledge of good and evil, and we are all reminded of it each time we experience anxiety.

Physician, Heal Thyself

To put it differently, we are all hesitant to show ourselves openly, whether by raising our hands or by acknowledging what we really feel, because we all have anxiety about what hidden parts of ourselves might come out in the process. That's why psychiatrists need psychotherapy as much as their patients do. The more intimately we try to understand a mentally ill person, the more we must call on those hidden parts of ourselves and the more our own anxiety will be activated. It is inevitable that the panic, despair, rage, and self-destructiveness of psychiatric patients will stir up unresolved emotional conflicts in anyone who tries to engage them in treatment. Hence the traditional expectation that psychiatrists should get psychotherapy for themselves, especially during their training. Unfortunately, the so-called Medical Model of psychiatry now seems to have abandoned this tradition. It no longer treats anxiety as an essential aspect of the human condition, an adaptive signal of emotional conflict that needs tending to. Rather, it treats anxiety as a "disorder," a brain defect, something that leaves you branded with a five-digit code number, which high-functioning people like us psychiatrists should not have. We are no longer teaching our residents that, to be physicians, they must first heal themselves. Instead of teaching them to take their own anxiety seriously and use it constructively in a psychotherapeutic process, we are encouraging them to ignore or deny their anxiety by taking a position of scientific detachment toward their patients. Of course, we all know that this doesn't really work. Even a psychiatrist who wants to do nothing more than diagnose illnesses, write prescriptions, and manage medication would still have to avoid every temptation to understand or relate to patients on an emotional level if he or she ever hoped to avoid anxiety. Even then the psychiatrist could succeed only if the patient happened to be cooperative, nonchallenging, nonsubversive, and responsive to treatment—an unusual combination indeed. Otherwise, even the most remote, scientifically detached psychiatrist will inevitably experience anxiety in working with patients.

I propose that we should think of this anxiety that patients provoke in us as a great blessing, a gift our patients give us. When we try to deny our anxiety, it makes the patient more anxious, hence more symptomatic. This in turn makes us more anxious, initiating a vicious cycle that, if we are trying to do psychotherapy, will continue until we either get rid of the patient or acknowledge that we have problems of our own to deal with. In this way our patients force us to be honest, both with them and with ourselves. Unfortunately, the Medical Model offers us an easy way out of this disturbing but growth-enhancing existential predicament. When the patient makes us feel anxious, we can simply prescribe a pill and plan to see the patient for fifteen minutes a month. Any further signs of recalcitrance we can then blame on the patient's treatment-resistant diagnostic subtype, ignoring the fact that the real resistance to treatment is within ourselves.

Both common sense and everyday experience tell us that people do not choose a career treating mental illness unless they have a personal stake in it. We all enter the field with some awareness of problems in ourselves and in our families. We then have a choice: to acknowledge our anxiety and accept responsibility for our problems or to ignore our anxiety and deny our problems, using the Medical Model conception of the doctor role to emphasize the distance and the difference between ourselves and our patients. If we choose the path of acceptance, we will want to seek an emotional engagement with our patients and use the anxiety they generate in us as a spur to our own psychotherapeutic process. If we choose the path of denial, we will avoid engagement with our patients and view their troubled attempts to engage with us merely as symptoms of their broken brains.

Why It's Worth Reading Descartes

Given that this is the Age of the Brain and that the path of denial is politically correct, it becomes all the more difficult, and at the same time all the more urgent, that we learn how to recognize and trust our own instinct, to distinguish what feels real from what we believe simply because we have been taught it. Here again, philosophy is crucially important. The choice between facing or running away from our own anxiety entails a choice between a philosophy of mind that values and fosters self-awareness, and the so-called neurophilosophy that is currently in vogue, which ignores or denies the inner life altogether. That's why I believe Descartes still has a lot to teach us. His whole philosophy was based on self-awareness and trusting his instinct. He recognized that everything he had previously taken to be true was a prejudice, based on someone else's authority, something he had been raised or taught to believe, something he had read in a book or perhaps even heard in a lecture. He resolved to discard all such prejudices and go back to the real source of all his beliefs, namely, himself. He trusted that he would find within himself, in his own capacity for inner discernment, the most reliable indicator of what is true and what is false or dubious. Essentially, he believed that he had a deep and reliable instinct that would allow him to recognize the truth when he encountered it. To a culture like ours, which practically worships scientific evidence, Descartes's approach sounds radical, subversive, and implausible. Yet the kinds of questions Descartes was trying to answer, like many of the most important questions in life, simply cannot be answered by scientific research.

The Most Interesting Questions Are Larger Than Science

Consider for a moment the most dramatic example of a question that scientific research cannot answer: How do we actually know that scientific research is a valid way to discover or prove anything? Or some related questions: How did anyone ever come to the conclusion that the scientific method, or syllogistic reasoning, or the ability to express observations in mathematical form, gave us some kind of privileged access to the truths of nature? How do we know that science is anything more than an intellectual game? What makes us so sure that it is more trustworthy than, say, astrology? And even if we do believe in science as the path to truth, how do we ever decide whether this or that particular piece of evidence is convincing enough or whether we need to go back and recheck some of the data? How do we recognize subtle flaws in a research design, and how do we recognize that these are flaws rather than advantages? What determines our inner sense of conviction or doubt? How can anyone ever tell the difference between something that seems true and something that really is true? *Ultimately, the value of all scientific research depends on the answers to these questions, yet scientific research itself is helpless to answer them.*

Now consider a more personal set of questions: Did your parents love you? Does your lover or spouse love you? If so, is it the same kind of love you got from your parents or is it different? Either way, how can you tell? Whom do you love, and how can you tell that what you feel for them is love? How do you know whether you are loving or needing someone? Loving or using someone? Being loved or being used? Or some ineffable combination of these? When people say "Do the right thing," how do they recognize what the right thing is, and how is it to be distinguished from the wrong thing? When we are crying, how can we tell whether or not there is a secret joy or anger mixed with the sadness? How can we tell whether the sadness is genuine or something we put on for show, or to manipulate a response in someone else?

Again, none of these questions can be answered by scientific research. They all require an inner process of discernment, in which we identify and make distinctions between subtle qualities of private experience. The same faculty of inner discernment that allows us to distinguish a genuine feeling from a sham one ultimately provides the only means by which we can distinguish between research results that make sense and ones that are bogus. These private acts of discernment are outside the domain of scientific research, yet the design, the interpretation, and the validation of the research all depend on them. In other words, we judge science—in fact, we invented science in the first place—according to some inner criterion of truth that is itself beyond the reach of science. *You have to be outside the picture to paint the picture, to recognize it as a picture, and to be able to tell when there's something wrong with the picture.* From such a perspective it is evident that scientific research is only one of many frames that can be placed around human experience, only one of many religions through which human beings have sought to orient themselves in the cosmos.

In theory this may all sound obvious enough, but in practice we are generally oblivious to the frame within which we are operating at any given moment. We are all to some degree like Molière's bourgeois gentleman, speaking prose for forty years without knowing it. This oblivion of ours is a remarkable but elusive phenomenon. The best way I know to describe it is in the form of an old joke that you've probably all heard but perhaps without stopping to think about its implications.

Back to the Ballpark

It seems there's this guy sitting at a baseball game with bananas in his ears. The guy sitting just behind him notices this, and begins to feel uncomfortable about it, especially since no one else around them seems to be at all concerned, or even to notice the anomalous bananas. This second guy vacillates, first questioning his own sanity, then trying to ignore the bananas, but in the end unable to contain his curiosity. In the bottom of the fourth inning he throws caution to the winds, leans over and says, "Excuse me, sir, I couldn't help but notice that you have bananas in your ears. Why is that?" The guy turns to him somewhat blankly and replies, "Sorry, buddy, I can't hear you. I have bananas in my ears."

Now at the risk of ruining a perfectly good joke, I'm going to interpret it as a statement of the human condition. The guy with bananas in his ears is Everyman—you and me—in our normal state of superficial consciousness. The bananas in our ears are systems of rationalization, the comforting stories that we tell ourselves to evade the need for genuine self-knowledge. The guy behind us who notices the bananas represents our inner awareness, our capacity for discernment, that instinct for discrepancy that tries to alert us when we are stopping our ears to the music of our own deepest experience. By the way, it is by no means coincidental that the second guy is sitting behind the first guy the way a psychoanalyst sits behind a patient, suggesting that Everyman could use an analysis!

In fact it does make sense to think of the guy with bananas in his ears as a patient. The bananas would be his symptoms, which point to an underlying emotional conflict but at the same time interfere with his ability to recognize that conflict for what it is. This fits the traditional psychoanalytic idea that a symptom is the disguised expression of a repressed unconscious emotion. In effect, the patient says, "Sorry, I can't listen to my feelings, I have symptoms in my ear." By the same token, you could just as reasonably view the guy with bananas in his ears as a psychiatrist. The bananas would be his theories, which indicate his interest in understanding mental illness, but at the same time interfere with his ability to understand an actual patient as a person. In effect, the therapist says to the patient, "Sorry, I can't really hear you empathically. I have theories in my ear, and I can only hear what filters through them."

So basically, we are all walking around with bananas in our ears. The bananas show us there is something we need to pay attention to, but they interfere with our ability to pay proper attention. They point to something and at the same time keep it hidden. Thus, the bananas function as a compromise between our need to know and our need not to know. The idea that symptoms serve this banana function—expressing a repressed emotion that is trying to become conscious, but in a disguised way that keeps it unconscious—is one of the cornerstones of Freudian theory. But the idea that *theories* serve the same banana function—explaining people, but in a way that actually prevents our understanding them—is less well known. Those who know it have generally had to learn it the hard way, as I discovered for myself about fifteen years ago.

What's the Matter with Mind over Matter?

At that time I had become increasingly concerned about the rapidly expanding influence of biological theories of mental illness, particularly of depression. I was amazed at how quickly the vast majority of psychiatrists, psychotherapists, and the public at large had all come to accept as fact the idea that depression is a purely biological disease, when only a few years before we had taken it for granted that depression was produced by inner conflict and traumatic experience. I viewed this shift in attitude as a cultural tragedy in the making—the first step in the spread of a frightening *Brave New World* doctrine that all mental illnesses, and ultimately all mental events, are biologically caused and biologically manipulable. Why would anyone want to hold such a dehumanizing belief, I wondered, and how do they justify it?

The answer seemed clear: *because scientific research has demonstrated that antidepressants work.* Hundreds if not thousands of studies on all the available antidepressants have yielded remarkably uniform results: 60 to 70 percent of depressed patients get symptomatic relief from an antidepressant, while only 30 to 40 percent get relief from a placebo. The reasoning that leads from these data to the idea of biological depression goes as follows: since the anti-depressant is twice as effective as the placebo in alleviating depression, and since the antidepressant changes brain chemistry, then depression must be a problem of brain chemistry. Of course, any self-respecting researcher would agree, if pressed, that this reasoning is specious. Logically and scientifically, you can't conclude anything about what caused a symptom from what relieves it. For instance, the fact that drinking fluids reduces fever does not mean that dehydration is the cause of the fever. In fact, dehydration is usually a result rather than the cause of a fever. Similarly, the fact that cutting down on sugar relieves the symptoms of diabetes doesn't mean that too much sugar is the cause of diabetes. Rather, an inability to produce insulin is the cause and too much sugar is the result. By the same logic, the fact that changing the serotonin balance alleviates depression cannot be construed as evidence that a serotonin imbalance caused the depression. A serotonin imbalance may very easily be the result rather than the cause of a depression.

I'm sure the researchers must tell themselves that the evidence, though not conclusive, is highly suggestive or at least consistent with the hypothesis that depression is a biological disease. But even this would be a radical misinterpretation of the evidence. Ironically, those very antidepressant efficacy studies that are taken to validate the biological theory of depression provide an even stronger argument for a psychological explanation, by showing time and time again, in relentlessly reproducible fashion, the incredible power of the placebo effect. What the data indicate is that if you take any group of depressed patients who have the familiar biological symptoms of depression (sleep disturbance; loss of appetite; difficulty concentrating; slowing of thought, speech, and movement) and you give those patients a pill—any pill—about 35 percent of them will have the mind-over-matter response called the placebo effect. In other words, their biological symptoms will be relieved, due not to the biological action of the pill but to the psychological idea that this pill will cure them. So then, what if the pill in question happens to be an antidepressant rather than a sugar pill? There would still have to be a 35 percent placebo response, which leaves only another 35 percent out of the total 70 percent antidepressant response that could be due to the specific biological action of the pill. In fact, the placebo response to an antidepressant would almost certainly be higher than the typical 35 percent response to an inert sugar pill because the biological side effects that the patient experienced (dry mouth, drowsiness, etc.) would tend to reinforce his belief that this must be a potent medication he is taking.

In other words, the placebo effect of an antidepressant is at least as strong as its biological effect, which means that psychological influences are at least as important as biochemical influences in producing a positive response to any antidepressant. No doubt a biological change occurs in everyone who responds positively to an antidepressant, but at least half the time that biological change is the by-product of an idea, a mind-over-matter effect not of the pill itself but of what the pill means to the patient. This interpretation of the research is far more logical than the commonly accepted one. It shows clearly how much our materialistic philosophy has prejudiced and confused our thinking about mental illness, and proves that we really have no rational justification for believing that depression is a purely biological disease.

The Joke Was on Me

Well, I felt like the guy in the joke when this understanding first dawned on me. I could see that Big Science had bananas in its ears, so I looked around to see if anyone else noticed. When I tried the idea out on colleagues in the hospital cafeteria, many of them looked momentarily confused but then quickly recovered with a comment like "That couldn't be right. Otherwise they would have thought of it already!" Others were more thoughtful and came to the conclusion that there must be two populations hidden within the typical depressed cohort in these studies, that if you looked closely enough you would find a smaller group of *really* depressed patients who had the biologically antidepressant effect and then you would realize that those who have the placebo response weren't really so depressed to begin with. Maybe so, I thought, but if there really were these two distinguishable groups, then how could it be that the *DSM* and the NIMH and all our other prodigious instruments and institutions of diagnostic discrimination have thus far failed to discriminate them?

I was unable to talk myself out of the conviction that those bananas were really there, so I submitted a paper to the *American Journal of Psychiatry* arguing my case. I wasn't really surprised when the paper was rejected, but my jaw dropped when I read the editor's explanation for rejecting it. "The present state of our knowledge," he wrote, "indicates that the 'Placebo Effect' may be the result of a neurophysiologic response by way of neurotransmitters." There it was: *"Sorry buddy, I can't hear you, I have bananas in my ears. We couldn't possibly have misinterpreted the research on antidepressants, because we've misinterpreted this other research on the placebo effect in exactly the same way, and it confirms our original misinterpretation."*

Here is what the editor must have been thinking: The brain can produce neurotransmitters called endorphins (naturally produced—*end*ogenous— brain chemicals that attach to the same nerve receptor sites that m*orphine* does, with similar pain-reducing and euphoric effects). Current research suggests that a placebo response is accompanied by a release of endorphins. Therefore, it must be the increased endorphin level that "causes" the placebo response. In other words, the "neurophysiologic response by way of neurotransmitters" to which the editor referred to was one in which endorphins somehow "cause" the pleasant placebo thoughts that relieve the depression. But the fact is, you must have the pleasant thought first in order to trigger the endorphin response. What else could it be but a thought that tells the brain to release more endorphins? There is no imaginable chain of strictly neurochemical causes that could lead from swallowing a sugar pill to the release of endorphins without the intervention of a purely psychological cause—not a happy molecule but the happy thought "This pill will cure me!" That thought must come first, before any endorphins can be released, acting as an uncaused cause on the brain, generating the endorphin release that accompanies the placebo response, but not itself generated by anything neurological. After all, how could the brain by itself tell that a sugar pill's molecules are different from all other sugar molecules? If metabolizing sugar is all it takes for the brain to initiate a placebo response via endorphins, then we should all be encouraging our depressed patients to eat frosted flakes. An endorphin release may well be an important step in the placebo response, but it is a response to a meaning, not to a molecule.

The Mind-over-Matter Factor

Over the years I have been very much impressed not only with the placebo response but also with the mind-over-matter element generally in people's response to treatment. For instance, I have seen a schizophrenic patient who remained unresponsive for three years to antipsychotic drugs become suddenly medication-responsive after a breakthrough occurred in his psychotherapy. I have seen anti-anxiety agents and antidepressants that worked wonderfully when there was a positive, idealizing transference lose their effectiveness as the negative, mistrustful transference emerged.

I'm sure you all know about the research showing that cognitive-behavioral therapy produces exactly the same changes in the brains of obsessive-compulsive patients as Prozac does. Of course, old-time psychiatrists like me don't need positron-emission tomography (PET) scans to convince us that treating the mind actually changes the brain. That's what we do for a living. In the era before managed care, for example, it was common practice when hospitalizing a patient with a psychosis or major mood disorder to wait a few days before prescribing any medication. Why? Because experience showed—and I myself saw this many times—that even the most dramatic biological symptoms of mental illness often disappear quite rapidly once the patient feels he is in a safe, nonstressful, and caring environment. I recall one patient in particular who would become manic—pressured, grandiose, psychotic, unable to sleep—whenever he got involved with a woman, but then recovered completely, even without medication, within two days of being admitted to the hospital. Did this mean he wasn't really suffering from a chemical imbalance in the first place? Not at all. His symptoms were indistinguishable from those of any other manic-depressive patient. He clearly had a neurophysiological disturbance, but like all such disturbances, it occurred and had meaning within a psychological context and was triggered, at least in part, by psychological stressors.

Novelist William Styron makes this very point in *Darkness Visible,* his account of the nearly fatal depression he suffered in 1985.[1] Styron's view of depression is particularly interesting because it is derived not from any psychiatric school of thought but simply from his introspective examination of his own experience. He describes the dark and terrifying desperation of the depressed state of mind as a kind of madness, so disruptive and overwhelming that he has no doubt it must be due to a "chemically induced . . . upheaval in the brain tissues"(p. 47). Yet at the same time based on his self-reflections, he believes that such chemical upheavals in the brain have psychological meaning and are in fact caused by psychological stress in the mind. He came to understand his own depression in particular as the result of an incomplete mourning of his mother's death when he was thirteen years old, and he believes more generally that depression always originates in some profound experience of loss. "[I]n the nethermost depths of one's suicidal behavior," he writes, "one is still subconsciously dealing with immense loss while trying to surmount all the effects of its devastation" (p. 81). This understanding of depression as a psychobiological reaction to a psychological stress is very much in line with my own view. It emphasizes the mind-over-matter factor that exists in all mental illness and highlights the shallowness of the widespread popular opinion that depression is a purely biological disease.

As it turned out, the mind-over-matter factor was also crucial in the healing of Styron's depression. Having failed to respond to two different antidepressants, he had been taken off medication entirely for ten days in order to clear his system for treatment with a monoamine oxidase (MAO) inhibitor. When his psychiatrist then explained that this new antidepressant might take up to six weeks to work, would require significant dietary restrictions, and might make him impotent, Styron felt even more hopeless than he had before, and that very evening he decided to kill himself. He took several days to prepare for his suicide and was on the verge of carrying it out when he happened to hear a piece of music that reminded him of his mother. Flooded suddenly with poignant memories of his life and loved ones, he realized that killing himself would be an act of "desecration," not only on himself but on his family, whereupon he woke up his wife and told her he needed to be hospitalized.

Styron's account of how the hospitalization cured his depression—by fostering the healing action of the mind on the brain—is so contrary to what our prevailing philosophy would lead us to expect, and so antithetical to what our managed care treatment guidelines would ever allow, that it stands as an indictment of current psychiatric beliefs and practices. Here is what Styron wrote:

> Many psychiatrists, who simply do not seem to be able to comprehend the nature and depth of the anguish their patients are undergoing, maintain their stubborn allegiance to pharmaceuticals in the belief that eventually the pills will kick in, the patient will respond, and . . . the hospital will be avoided. . . . [B]ut . . . I'm convinced I should have been in the hospital weeks before. For, in fact, the hospital was my salvation, and it is something of a paradox that in this austere place with its locked and wired doors and

desolate green hallways—ambulances screeching night and day ten floors below—I found the repose, the assuagement of the tempest in my brain, that I was unable to find in my quiet farmhouse.

This is partly the result of sequestration, of safety, of being removed to a world in which the urge to pick up a knife and plunge it into one's own breast disappears in the newfound knowledge, quickly apparent even to the depressive's fuzzy brain, that the knife with which he is attempting to cut his dreadful Swiss steak is bendable plastic. But the hospital also offers the mild, oddly gratifying trauma of sudden stabilization—a transfer out of the too familiar surroundings of home, where all is anxiety and discord, into an orderly and benign detention where one's only duty is to try to get well.

The hospital was a way station, a purgatory. When I entered the place, my depression appeared so profound that . . . I was a candidate for . . . shock treatment. . . . I avoided it because I began to get well, gradually but steadily. I was amazed to discover that the fantasies of self-destruction all but disappeared within a few days testimony to the pacifying effect that the hospital can create, its immediate value as a sanctuary where peace can return to the mind. (pp. 68–70)

It is sobering to realize that this treatment that saved Styron's life *is no longer available today in any hospital in the United States.* A hospital cannot possibly serve the healing sanctuary function that Styron describes when patients know that their days are being numbered by an accountant. In 1985, Styron was able to stay in the hospital for two months, confident that he would not be discharged until he had substantially recovered. Today, under managed care, the best he could hope for would be to be admitted for two or three days, started on an antidepressant that he knew wouldn't work for four to six weeks if at all, and then asked to make a commitment not to kill himself so that his psychiatrist could still sleep at night knowing he had discharged a patient who was just as depressed as on the day he was admitted. Even if he were able to pay the $40,000 monthly cost of a longer hospitalization out of his own pocket, someone like Styron would spend most of his time simply watching other patients come and go. Given today's managed care time constraints and quick-fix mentality, the doctors and hospital staff would no longer be able—or even know how—to provide the kind of intimately personal psychotherapeutic treatment that can be truly healing.

My point here is not simply to criticize managed care, but to say that the inadequacy of psychiatric treatment under managed care guidelines is symptomatic of a much deeper problem of philosophy: the dehumanizing scientific materialism that pervades our culture, that denies the inner life of the soul and assumes that only what is physical is real. The fact is, there could be no managed care without such a philosophy to support and rationalize it. Economic pressures may explain why businesses and insurance companies would want a managed care system, but they do not explain why organized medicine has been so willing to cooperate with such a system. Nor do they explain why thousands of individual practitioners would agree to treatment restrictions that systematically force us to violate the sacred trust of the doctor–patient relationship by putting the financial interests of insurance companies before the best interests of our patients. That never could have happened if we didn't already have a philosophy that encourages us to discount the importance of the doctor–patient relationship. Starting from the belief that only the physical is real, we can all too easily convince ourselves that our only responsibility to patients is to medicate their broken brains. If we assume that the mind has no impact on healing, then we don't need to worry about whether we have our patients' best interests at heart, or about how dehumanizing our hospitals have become, because we don't really believe that such nebulous nonbiological factors make a difference anyway.

The Importance of Philosophy

The fact that depression can respond so dramatically to a placebo or to an experience of sanctuary in the hospital does not prove it is a psychological illness, any more than the fact that it can respond dramatically to Prozac proves it is a biological illness. My point is that our exclusive emphasis on biological treatments for depression and other mental disorders is in no way justified either by scientific research or by clinical experience. Rather, it is a matter of philosophy. To illustrate further what I mean by this, consider the kind of assumptions you automatically make about a depressed patient who comes into your office complaining of sleeplessness, weight loss, inability to concentrate, loss of sexual desire—all the biological symptoms of depression. Naturally, the patient also has a story to tell, with all kinds of potential emotional meanings. Which of the following two choices comes closest to the way you actually think about this patient as you first meet him? Choice 1:

The key to the patient's depression is in his broken brain. Biological depression is always caused by some sort of biochemical or neurophysiological imbalance. That would be the *Archives of General Psychiatry* position, a reflection of the Medical Model's philosophy of scientific materialism. Choice 2: The key to the patient's depression is in his story. The biological symptoms of depression are always caused by a psychological conflict, that is, by the struggle to maintain repression of painful emotions that, if they became conscious, would be unacceptable or overwhelming to the conscious self. That would be the radical awareness-of-feelings position, a reflection of the psychotherapeutic philosophy of mind–brain dualism.

Now it may well be that your instinct tells you this is a trick question and the answer I am really looking for is "both." But I hope you will go beyond thinking about which answer I want to hear and consider which answer you yourself automatically reach for when you are in the consulting room with a depressed patient. How do you actually react when your patient is complaining that he can't sleep and has never felt so horrible in his life? Is your first instinct to reach for your prescription pad, reassuring the patient that this is a fixable biological problem? Or do you start from the assumption that your patient must be in the grip of a personal and existential crisis, and therefore hold off talking to him about medication until you've formed a reasonable impression of what's going on in his life that might lead to such a crisis? If you think about it carefully, I believe you will agree that the correct answer to this question cannot be "both." Sure, you can talk to him in the course of your evaluation about both dimensions of his depression. But the point is, you can't do both at the same time, and your inclination about which one to do first says something important about the way you think—and has an important influence on how your patient will end up thinking. Even if we all agree that depression is both a biological and a psychological entity, in the moment that we intervene therapeutically we are still forced to choose between the two perspectives. What we actually say to the patient inevitably reveals which perspective we consider primary.

Light and Life

Consider a parallel question from the field of physics: Does light travel in the form of waves or in the form of particles? Here we all know that the paradoxical answer is both, yet in the experimental observation of light, physicists must choose between one way of looking at it or the other. If they use one kind of experimental arrangement, they observe electromagnetic waves. If they use a different methodology and apparatus, they find no evidence of waves but discover instead that light consists of tiny photon particles. In other words, the nature of light depends on the observational framework through which we choose to look at it. So, too, with human nature. If we look at ourselves through the lens of introspection—that is, through the conscious awareness of inner emotional experience in all its immediacy—then we discover that human nature is dualistically divided, in a perpetual state of conflict between the Flesh and the Spirit, unconscious and conscious, love and hate. But if we look at people through the external lens of the senses, we can see only that human nature is physical, a pattern of brain activity corresponding to a set of measurable, visible, audible, or palpable behaviors.

What I am getting at here is that the mind–body problem is still very much with us. It is as much a fact of nature as the wave-particle paradox. *Mind* is not just another word for *brain* any more than *wave* is just another word for *particle*. The proposition that mental illnesses are merely brain diseases is not a scientific fact but an unprovable and implausible philosophical prejudice, an attempt to evade the awareness of existential anxiety by simply defining it out of existence. Nevertheless, ever since Adam and Eve, mankind has always felt anxiety from the conflict between the Flesh and the Spirit. Denying the existence of the Spirit will not make the anxiety go away. It remains as ineradicable evidence of the mind–body problem. In fact, I would go so far as to say that anxiety *is* the mind–body problem. It is an uneasy combination of physiological response and dawning awareness; an unconscious feeling trying to become conscious, something that has existed only in physiological form in the body, now beginning to emerge painfully into a psychological form in the mind. It reminds me of the image of Michelangelo's statue of prisoners torn between the desire to break out of the inarticulate marble and the temptation to sink back into it. But saying this, I become anxious, because I imagine you all must be thinking, "Geez, first Descartes, then Adam and Eve, and now Michelangelo. How is all this ivory-tower philosophy going to help me deal with the reality of having to treat patients under managed care?"

My answer is that managed care has absolutely nothing to do with reality. We all know there can be no such thing as "managed caring." It's an oxymoron, a contradiction in terms. There is, however, such a thing as being practical, and my point is that the mind–body problem is extremely relevant to the practical problem of how to understand and treat our patients. It's the problem of how we decide what treatment to offer, and when to offer it. For example, consider a new patient who has just had his first panic attack. Will you prescribe medication during the first visit, or will you begin with a few sessions of psychotherapy alone? What if the patient has already had two panic attacks? How about three? Where will you draw the line and how do you decide where to draw it? That's the mind–body problem. What about the patient who has been unhappy but functioning during fifteen months of twice-a-week psychotherapy, who now tells you with a sense of urgency that for the last three nights in a row she has woken up at two o'clock feeling anxious and desperate? Will you think of this symptom as part of the evolving psychotherapeutic process, perhaps a sign that there is an unconscious transference conflict coming to the surface, or will you think of it as a sign of a coincidental biological depression that could interfere with the psychotherapeutic process unless you medicate it? How you think of it will determine your choice of therapeutic intervention. How you intervene will in turn have a major effect on the course of the treatment, and it is an effect you cannot control for. That's the mind–body problem. At the abstract level it is easy enough to say that mind and brain are equally important elements of the human soul. At the practical level, we can focus our awareness on only one element at a time, and every one of us—even if we recognize both perspectives as important—will consider one of them more important to focus on than the other.

Just how difficult it can be to balance these two perspectives was made vividly and painfully clear to me the second time I took the oral section of the national boards in psychiatry. I had failed the boards in my first attempt, you see, because I had arrogantly and unwisely assumed that I already knew how to interview a patient and so didn't need to prepare. In the clinical interview, I had done what I always do—tried to establish a psychotherapeutic rapport, an I–Thou relationship with the patient, who told one of the most complicated and tragic stories I have ever heard. When it came time to go through the differential diagnosis (the list of every diagnosis that might possibly apply to the patient, which is then winnowed down to one or two most probable diagnoses), my mind was still reeling from the effort to absorb both the facts and the pain of this patient's life. I commented that he probably met the criteria for every disorder in the *DSM-III*. My examiners were not amused. Too late, I understood that the empathic awareness necessary for psychotherapy is incompatible with diagnostic precision. So before taking the exam a second time, I ate humble pie, did some practice interviews, reviewed psychopharmacology manuals, boned up on the *DSM-IIIR,* and generally crafted myself into a finely honed diagnostic instrument. I was ready.

The first event of the day involved watching someone else's taped diagnostic interview and then having two examiners question me on what I had observed. The patient's presentation was that of an uncomplicated unipolar depression, with classic melancholic symptoms. I had the case cold, nailed the differential diagnosis, ran through the bio-psycho-social treatment plan, including first-line, second-line, and third-line antidepressants; side effects; drug interactions; MAO dietary precautions; indications for electroconvulsive therapy—I was ready for anything!

Except one small thing I hadn't prepared for: "What can you tell us, Dr. Frattaroli, about the patient's psychodynamics?"

"Excuse me? Psychodynamics?"

I was in trouble, stunned to find myself drawing a complete blank, as if I'd never even heard of Freud. I had thrown myself so completely into an *Archives of General Psychiatry* mind-set that I had lost track of my normal psychotherapeutic mind-set. I had been so busy running through my diagnostic and psychopharmacologic checklists as I watched the videotape that I hadn't given a thought to the patient's inner experience or unconscious conflicts. My examiner must have noticed my blank-faced chagrin and taken pity on me, because he then generously gave me a hint: "For example, how does this patient deal with anger?"

"Oh, anger!" I said, as a duck dropped down with the word "anger" around its neck and my psychoanalytic awareness came flooding back. It turned out I had been processing the whole thing in psychodynamic terms all along, only subliminally, while my conscious mind was occupied with diagnosis and psychobiology. I was then able to talk cogently about the patient's obvious conflict over repressed anger at her husband and mother and how this was implicated in the incident that had precipitated the depressive episode.

The good news in this story is that a psychotherapeutic perspective can coexist with a biological perspective, even if you can't do both at the same time. The bad news is how easy it is to forget that there are two perspectives—how easy it was for me to lose track of what I value most when faced with intimidating demands for short-term answers from third-party reviewers. If you want to avoid this bad news in your own practice, the best advice I can give you is to start by doing what Descartes did: be skeptical of everything that is generally accepted, everything that is proclaimed by authorities or imposed by third parties, everything you have been taught; listen to your feelings, and trust your instinct. If you have trouble doing that, then get some good psychotherapy or psychoanalysis for yourself until you can do it. If you are a psychiatry resident and have never had psychotherapy yourself, go get some now—not because I said so but because, when you think about how uncomfortable you sometimes are with patients, you know you could use it. Meanwhile, no matter what job you take, try to put aside at least ten hours a week to treat patients in psychotherapy outside of managed care guidelines, even if you have to see them for a very reduced fee in order to do it. Remember that the word *psychiatry* means "healing the soul," not "medicating the brain." Managed care may be spreading like a cancer now, but in its greed it will inevitably devour itself. When that happens, those of us who still know how to do psychotherapy will have something invaluable to offer both to our patients and to our profession.

5. The Swimming Pool and the Quest

You who are on the road
Must have a code that you can live by
And so become yourself
Because the past is just a good-bye
　　　　　　　　—Graham Nash, "Teach Your Children"

Man is made by his belief. As he believes, so he is.
　　　　　　　　　　　　　　—Bhagavad Gita

A Fix for the Brain Versus a Home for the Heart

When I first gave the lecture that appears in Chapter 4, I had been working on this book for about a year and a half. But it was actually almost five years earlier—in the last week of March 1990—that the book first began to take shape in my mind. It all started when an issue of *Newsweek* appeared with a Prozac capsule on its cover—just where the picture of a person should be, I thought. It was not only the cover of that issue that got my attention, though. It was also the brief note, buried in its obituary section, announcing the death of Bruno Bettelheim. "If Dr. B wasn't dead already, this would definitely kill him," I thought ruefully. I knew how much Bettelheim had always deplored what that *Newsweek* cover was so blatantly glorifying: our drug culture and its quick-fix mentality.

The ironic coincidence of Prozac's much-heralded arrival on the cultural scene together with Bettelheim's scarcely noticed departure epitomized for me the predicament of our society. It meant that everything Dr. B stood for—and everything I cared about as a psychiatrist and as a person—was being lost in our cultural frenzy for the quick fix. To me this loss felt very personal. You see, it was Bruno Bettelheim—"Dr. B" to his students—who first taught me about healing the soul and inspired me to want to become a psychiatrist.

I had worked for Dr. B in the early 1970s at the University of Chicago's Sonia Shankman Orthogenic School, the residential treatment center he created for emotionally disturbed children.[1] Under Bettelheim's guidance, the School was an extraordinarily loving and nurturing place, a place of healing and growth for the staff as well as for the children. In one of his books, Dr. B described the Orthogenic School as *a home for the heart*, and that's very much the way I experienced it. It became my model for what psychotherapy should be: a place dedicated to fostering the inner life, a place of love and respect— an I-Thou relationship—in which we can feel what we truly feel, and so become who we truly are.

The End Is in the Beginning

One of Dr. B's most memorable and useful teachings was that "the end is always in the beginning." By this he meant that the assumptions, attitudes, and expectations with which we approach a therapeutic encounter or life situation define how that encounter or situation will evolve.

Alfred Flarsheim, another of Dr. B's students, reported a wonderful illustration of this lesson, taken from ethologist George Schaller's book *Year of the Gorilla*.[2] It seems that Schaller (whose writings inspired Dian Fossey) had been able to collect far more detailed observations of the behavior of free-living gorillas than any previous scientific observer. Schaller attributed his unprecedented success to the simple fact that he had decided not to carry a rifle. This forced him to be sensitive to the gorillas' subtle behavioral signals and allowed him to get quite close to them without making them feel threatened. Earlier, less successful observers had gone into the jungle armed with rifles because they assumed (incorrectly) that gorillas were dangerously aggressive and would make unprovoked attacks. *The end is in the beginning.* Schaller ended up with different results because he started out from a different assumption. He assumed that the gorillas would not be dangerous as long as he treated them with respect. So he began without a rifle and ended up discovering that he didn't need one. In contrast, the ethologists who carried rifles found that they did need them. In other words, they found exactly what they had been expecting: that gorillas were too dangerous to observe closely, and sometimes attacked and had to be shot. But these observers had created rather than discovered this confirmation of their preconceptions. It was not the gorillas' innate aggressiveness that had prompted them to attack. Rather, the observers themselves had inadvertently provoked the gorillas to attack by their thoughtlessly intrusive behavior and bearing—influenced by the false security and sense of invulnerability they took from their rifles.

Schaller's experience is relevant for psychiatry. Just as the rifle reflects the ethologist's preconceived assumption about gorillas, so medication reflects the psychiatrist's preconceived assumption about symptoms. *The end is in the beginning.* The possibility of prescribing medication, like the availability of a rifle in the jungle, fosters the tendency to bring premature closure to an encounter. It affects the psychology of the psychiatrist in such a way that he is unlikely to get close enough to the patient to obtain an in-depth understanding of whatever symptom seems to be calling for medication. He is unlikely to learn more than what is necessary to confirm what he already assumed, that indeed this is the sort of symptom that requires medication.

Psychiatrists today are far less tolerant of the unknown (and our fear of it) than we were when we had fewer pills in our therapeutic "arsenal." We now cling to the security of the prescription pad, the white coat, and the Medical Model. We take the formal history and mental status, assign the diagnosis with its proper five-digit code number, prescribe the proper pill, describe its major side effects, and monitor blood levels, all based on the latest scientific data. This ritualized activity serves, along with its official purposes, to insulate us from our own anxiety by emphasizing the distance and the difference between us and our chemically imbalanced patients.

It is worth comparing this dehumanizing I–It attitude with the humanizing I–Thou attitude taught by Bettelheim:

Just as the patients have to learn that they possess all the necessary resources within themselves to get well, staff members must become able to comprehend that within them resides all the knowledge necessary to understand the patient. . . . [T]wo main principles . . . were the essence of many staff discussions. The first is that "The patient is always right"—that is, nonsensical as his behavior may seem to us, it makes excellent sense to him—and the second, that an understanding of what this meaning to him may be can best be approached or directly derived from our own inner experiences. What we have to do is ask ourselves the question: What conditions would induce me to engage in exactly the type of behavior which seems irrational or otherwise deviate in the patient?[3]

Psychiatry and the Philosophy of Life

Bettelheim's approach is the very heart of the Psychotherapeutic Model. It understands symptoms as meaningful expressions of the self, in marked contrast to the Medical Model, which treats symptoms as dangerous and alien to the persons who have them. The difference between these two attitudes toward symptoms reflects a deeper difference in attitudes toward people. The Psychotherapeutic Model is grounded in the similarity—the common humanity—between physician and patient. The Medical Model is grounded in scientific research, in which the doctor treats the patient as an object of detached observation.

How did psychiatry end up with two such radically different approaches to treating people and their illnesses? Because the psychiatrists who follow either approach start from radically different philosophical beliefs and values. *The end is in the beginning,* and what ends in the psychiatrist's choice of treatment begins in his choice of philosophy. I don't mean the kind of philosophy located in unreadable books written by dead intellectuals. I mean what philosopher Jacob Needleman calls "real philosophy": a living organization of experience, a set of implicit assumptions, deep, often hidden, in the grain of our personhood, that is the basis both for our way of life and for our attitude about the meaning and purpose of life.

Not that psychiatrists are generally aware of how their treatment decisions reflect their philosophy of life. In fact, most psychiatrists will tell you they simply use whatever treatment "works best." They like to think of their treatment approach as strictly pragmatic, and would rather leave philosophy out of it. But philosophy is not like an American Express card. It is impossible to leave home without it. There is philosophy implicit in everything we do, though it remains, for the most part, outside of our awareness. What looks on the surface like a pragmatic choice of the treatment that works best is, at a deeper level, a choice of philosophy. What we think works best depends on what we are trying to accomplish, which in turn depends on what we think is worth accomplishing, which depends ultimately on our all too often unconscious philosophy of life.

Philosophy and the Art of Bicycle Riding

I learned this lesson the hard way one Sunday afternoon about fifteen years ago, when I tried to pick the method that would work best for teaching my son how to ride a two-wheeler. It was a beautiful crisp fall day, and the last thing on my mind was philosophy. Standing there behind Gregory, my hands on the back of his bicycle seat, I could almost hear the theme song from the old television show *Father Knows Best* playing in the background.

"Okay, start pedaling and don't look back," I said optimistically. Famous last words. The bike kept tilting and Gregory kept looking back, complaining loudly that I wasn't holding it steady enough. I snapped back at him that I couldn't keep the bike straight if he wouldn't look ahead and pedal harder.

"But what if you let go and I fall?" he pleaded.

"I won't let go until I know you won't fall."

"But how will you be able to tell?"

"Just turn around and pedal!"

Before long, I had a backache, Gregory had a headache, and we decided to pack it in and try again the next day. We slouched back to the house, Gregory grumbling reproachfully that he would never be able to ride without training wheels and I cursing Robert Young (the dad in the TV show) under my breath.

Next evening when I returned home from work I was surprised to see Gregory happily pedaling his two-wheeler up and down the driveway. "Look, Dad, no training wheels!" He explained that Evan, an older boy who lived next door, had taught him how to ride the bike.

"How did he do that?" I protested, aware that I ought to be sounding more pleased.

"Simple! He told me that to ride a two-wheeler, the first thing you have to do is fall down a lot of times."

I knew immediately that there was something important in this little episode, but it was not until the third or fourth time I told the story that it dawned on me it was really a story about unconscious philosophy. *Those who are unaware that they have a philosophy are condemned to act it out on their children.* Gregory and I had come to grief over an unexamined and misguided philosophical assumption. When I stopped to ask myself why I had failed and Evan had succeeded, I recognized that my teaching had been guided by my anxiety—and by Gregory's—that he would fall down. Our goal (implicit in this shared anxiety) had been not simply that he learn how to ride a two-wheeler, but that he do so without ever falling down. *The end is in the beginning.* We had failed because we started from the assumption that falling down would be bad. Evan had succeeded because his philosophy involved the opposite assumption, that falling down would be good.

Perhaps most people would not ordinarily consider the assumptions "Falling down is bad" and "Falling down is good" to be philosophy, but in fact they are the central tenets of the two major philosophies of life and—not coincidentally—also the basic premises of the two major models of psychiatry.

The Swimming Pool

The first philosophy, according to which falling down is bad, I call the swimming-pool philosophy. Paul Stookey, of the folk group Peter, Paul and Mary, captured the essence of it when he said, "You know what swimming is to me? It's staying alive when you're in the water." But what really brought the meaning of this philosophy home to me was a comment made by a classmate and close friend of mine one gray December afternoon many years ago, as we stood together at the edge of our college swimming pool, contemplating the twenty-five-yard lap lanes that stretched out before us.

"You know," Ron said, "life is a lot like swimming laps. You put your head down, you dive in, and you go back and forth and back and forth and back and forth. Every once in a while you bump into someone, and you say 'Excuse me.' Then you put your head down again and go back and forth and back and forth and back and forth."

According to the swimming-pool philosophy, the purpose of life is to stay afloat, to function smoothly, maintaining the equilibrium of the status quo. Bumping into other swimmers is to be avoided as much as possible. In other words, falling down is bad.

The Quest

The second philosophy, according to which falling down is good, I call the quest philosophy. Also known as the perennial philosophy, it is symbolized by the Arthurian myth of the quest for the grail.[4] The quest is an adventurous seeking of a higher or better state. According to the quest philosophy, the purpose of life is to pursue this higher state—enlightenment, wisdom, self-actualization—by progressing through a series of difficult, dangerous trials. The successful mastery of each trial brings the seeker to the next level in his or her gradual ascent toward the ultimate goal, which, though it may be unattainable, is inherently worth pursuing. But the process of undergoing a trial inevitably involves some error. You can't find your way to a higher level without learning from your missteps. Falling down is therefore good.

The Swimming Pool and the Quest in Psychiatry

From a child falling down while learning to ride a bicycle to a patient having a "breakdown" while learning to navigate the life cycle is but a short metaphorical step. Just as different attitudes toward falling down lead to different methods of teaching a child to ride a bike, different attitudes toward psychiatric symptoms lead to different models of treating a patient with mental illness. The Medical Model exemplifies the swimming-pool philosophy that falling down (disequilibrium) is bad. It views psychiatric symptoms as "chemical imbalances"—disruptions of neurophysiological equilibrium—that should be "fixed" quickly with medication lest they cause further disruptions of psychosocial "stability" and "adjustment" (i.e., bumping into people). In other words, the Medical Model considers symptoms as a kind of falling down that is bad: unfortunate and unnecessary spills from the cycle of life.

The Psychotherapeutic Model, in contrast, exemplifies the quest philosophy's premise that falling down is good. It views psychiatric symptoms as manifestations of inner conflict—unconscious emotions trying to become conscious against the internal forces of resistance—presenting opportunities for growth that should be facilitated in a psychotherapeutic process that respects the need to bump into other people (and thereby become more conscious) through transference. In other words, the Psychotherapeutic Model views symptoms as a kind of falling down that is good—necessary trials in our quest for self-actualization.

Falling Down Is a Way of Growing Up

Just as a father who believes that falling down is bad will try too hard to control his son's equilibrium on a bicycle, and thereby interfere with the boy's learning, so a psychiatrist who believes that symptoms are bad will try too hard to control his patient's chemical and emotional balance, and thereby interfere with the patient's growth. As Alfred Flarsheim put it, "In order to operate without trying to control a patient we must have confidence in his potential for spontaneous maturation and development." Medical Model psychiatrists try to take control with medication because they do not have this confidence. They are aiming not to facilitate maturation and development, but simply to return the patient to his previous level of functioning. They view the patient as someone having trouble swimming laps, not as someone facing an important trial in his quest. You bump into somebody, you say excuse me, then you put your head down again and get back into the swim. Given this philosophy, it makes sense to try to remove the symptom as quickly as possible because it did derail the patient from his previous level of functioning and it interferes with his regaining that level again. But the end is in the beginning. If we start with a different philosophy, then we will end up with different treatment methods, and different results.

Psychotherapeutic Model psychiatrists start from the assumption that symptoms are the very embodiment of the patient's potential for spontaneous maturation and development. Their goal is to facilitate the maturational process that is already inherent in the symptom. They view disequilibrium, whether manifest in obvious symptoms or not, as a natural and inevitable result of the inner conflict that is intrinsic to human nature. Developing a symptom is a necessary step toward integrating that conflict, a way of focusing the disequilibrium and calling our attention to it, and thereby initiating or furthering a psychotherapeutic process. Seen from this point of view, symptoms are the place where growth happens, human nature's way of waking us up and stopping the world so that we can get out of the pool and climb into the quest. Disequilibrium, falling down, and bumping into people are good. Indeed, from this psychotherapeutic perspective, they are not merely good but essential to a fully human existence.

To Be Human, the First Thing You Have to Do Is Fall Down

In describing this important difference between the swimming pool and the quest in psychiatry, I am writing in the belief that if psychiatrists and patients really understood that they were making swimming-pool choices and neglecting the very real alternative of the quest, many of them would want to reconsider their assumptions. But I am also writing as a person who believes that most of us, most of the time, live our lives in the swimming pool without quite realizing it. I consider the choice between the swimming pool and the quest in psychiatry therefore to be a special case of a much larger choice that each one of us must make about how consciously we want to live our lives.

Here again, it is instructive to think about the story of Genesis, which tells of how consciousness was born in the very first falling down. From the perspective of a swimming-pool philosophy, Adam and Eve's existence before the Fall was the ultimate ideal, an endless floating in the unconscious equilibrium of eternity. There was no disruption, no change, no desire, no choices to make, and no death, because there was no time. The impulse toward a higher consciousness—the desire for knowledge of good and evil—was disruptive to this blissful condition and therefore considered bad.

From the perspective of a quest philosophy, on the other hand, life before the Fall, however blissful, was not a fully human life. Adam and Eve were in a state of limited, infant consciousness, without the freedom to choose, without responsibility for their actions, and without self-awareness. Their forbidden desire for the knowledge of good and evil then transformed their existence into a quest. It propelled them out of eternity into a world of time, marked by a new adult awareness of the restless, ever-changing dialectic of inner conflict: the uneasy conjunction between their joyful experiences of love and creativity and their exciting but disruptive experiences of lustful desire and self-aggrandizing ambition.

If we think of this falling down and this quest as something Adam and Eve could have avoided by making a different choice, we have misunderstood the point of the myth. The Fall is not itself a choice, but rather the beginning of the possibility of choice—what Kierkegaard called "the possibility of possibility." Adam is Everyman. Eating the forbidden fruit is growing up and becoming conscious. We all begin to do it sometime during our "terrible twos," when by saying "No!" we reject the infant paradise of undifferentiated communion with mother. This "original sin," our first act of defiance, is also our first act of self-definition and the beginning of our self-awareness as separate individuals. But it is only the beginning, because our first and enduring reaction to this "possibility" of self-awareness is to try to cover it up and then hide from it, as Adam and Eve tried to cover up and hide from God. To grow into full human consciousness requires not only the defiant awareness that we are willfully alienated from others but also the shameful awareness, and ultimately an acceptance of the fact, that we are naked—alienated from ourselves in a state of inner conflict. To achieve this level of self-awareness we need the repeated trials of the quest, falling down again and again until we overcome our need to hide from ourselves and learn to recognize, and so become, who we really are.

Symptoms and Self-Actualization

Under the Medical Model, then, symptoms are seen as a kind of fall from grace, unwelcome, destructive intrusions on the smooth course of day-to-day life. Under the Psychotherapeutic Model, symptoms are seen as necessary shocks that lead to recognition, important trials in a painful but rewarding quest for self-actualization that begins with our first "no" and continues through the entire course of human development. In this view, symptoms are manifestations of inner conflict: disguised expressions of forbidden unconscious emotions, uneasy compromises between our conflicting needs to hide from ourselves *and* to become ourselves. In that sense they represent an attempt, only partially successful, to integrate the conflict between the swimming pool and the quest—between our need to maintain stability by keeping ourselves unconscious, as if we had never desired the forbidden fruit, and our need to reap the rewards and punishments of Adam's fall, as we grow into a more fully human consciousness.

These very different attitudes toward symptoms imply correspondingly different ideals of mental health. The Medical Model's attitude that symptoms and disturbing emotions are bad implies an ideal of mental health as a "steady state": the capacity to be stable, to maintain chemical (and emotional) balance and social adjustment. The Psychotherapeutic Model's attitude that symptoms and disturbing emotions are good implies an ideal of mental health as an evolving process: a capacity for growth, a lifelong progression of emotional and moral development, expanding consciousness through enriching new experiences of emotions that were previously forbidden (repressed).

How Did Psychiatry End Up in This Muddle? It's Freud's Fault!

This deep split in psychiatric attitudes toward illness and health has very real and potentially dangerous practical consequences—like the seemingly unbridgeable gulf between the Technocrat's and the Cowboy's approaches to Bill. It reflects psychiatry's ongoing failure to resolve its own inner conflict, to integrate the opposing values of the swimming pool and the quest. It also illustrates quite vividly how those who do not remember the past are condemned to repeat it. For, you see, the rift between the Medical Model and the Psychotherapeutic Model is by no means a new one. Surprisingly enough, both models originated more than a century ago in the theories of one man, Sigmund Freud.

Freud's clinical understanding of mental illness was always that of the Psychotherapeutic Model, informed by a quest philosophy and framed in terms of inner conflict, but there was always a strong Medical Model current in his thinking as well—a need to explain his clinical observations in biological terms. In fact, his primary theoretical model during the first half of his career (1890–1915)—the so-called libido theory—was actually the original psychiatric theory of chemical imbalance. Like the Medical Model today, it pictured the soul or mind *(Seele)* as equivalent to the brain, and tried to explain anxiety and the symptoms of mental illness in swimming-pool terms as a disruption of neurochemical equilibrium.

Freud's Swimming-Pool Philosophy: The Libido Theory and the Constancy Principle

Freud defined *libido* as a specific form of neurological energy belonging to the sexual drive. He hypothesized that increasing the amount or "charge" of libido in the neurons of the brain produced pain, whereas decreasing—"*dis*charging"—it produced pleasure. Discharge could be interfered with in two ways: by inner conflict or by simple sexual frustration. In either case, when the quantity of undischarged libido reached a certain critical level—producing a chemical imbalance—it would either "spill over" in a toxic physiological process that was experienced as anxiety or be diverted into the formation of a neurotic symptom. In other words, anxiety and/or symptoms were by-products of a libidinal imbalance—an excess of libido in the neurons that could not be discharged normally.

Freud's neurophysiology was wrong, of course, because he developed his theory in 1897, long before anything was known about how neurons actually work. We now have a more refined picture of chemical imbalance as a disproportion between "transmitter" molecules (serotonin, for instance) and "receptor" molecules in the synapses where nerve impulses are transmitted from one cell to another. But this great advance in scientific knowledge has told us nothing at all about how a chemical imbalance in the brain could possibly produce a disturbing experience in the mind or soul. In fact, the idea that chemical imbalances cause mental illness is no more scientific today than it was in 1897.

In that sense, Freud's theory had a distinct advantage over current neurological theories of the mind, in that he was well aware of his philosophical assumptions and never mistook them for scientific facts. He referred to the libido theory as a *meta*psychology precisely in order to indicate that it was a philosophy rather than a science. He explicitly defined its swimming-pool assumptions in the form of a hypothesis he called the *constancy principle*. According to the constancy principle, all psychological processes are designed (by evolution) to maintain a low-level steady state of energy (libido) in the neurons. The point of this evolutionary design—and implicitly the purpose of life and the goal of mental health—was to avoid pain and seek pleasure by maintaining a comfortable low-energy state of libidinal equilibrium. This meant avoiding external stimulation (which produced an unpleasurable increase in libido) and quickly discharging any internal excitation that arose directly from the sexual drive. In other words, "Keep swimming, but only hard enough to stay afloat. Try to stay in your lane and not bump into other swimmers, but when the inevitable collision does occur, make it a quickie and get back into the swim. Falling down (libidinal imbalance) is bad, so keep pedaling (discharging libido) and don't look back."

Freud's Quest Philosophy: The Principle of Eros

The problem with the constancy principle—or *pleasure principle,* as Freud soon began to call it—was that the purpose of life it defined boiled down to the pursuit of the most immediate gratification. Freud's mind could never come to rest in the amoral hedonism of such a philosophy. He began to ask himself, why, if the soul is really operating solely on the premise that falling down (unpleasure) is bad, did his patients have such an apparently perverse need to trip themselves up. Where did they get their relentless compulsion to punish themselves and otherwise subvert their own hedonistic purposes, to unnecessarily deny themselves pleasure and put themselves into painful high-energy states of inner tension? Then, too, why weren't all states of inner tension experienced as painful? Why were they so often experienced as pleasurably stimulating and exciting? Why did people so regularly prefer the complex, high-energy state of love, for example, to the simple discharges of lust? Indeed, if it were not for the increased excitement involved, why would a person ever want to dive into a swimming pool or take the training wheels off his bicycle in the first place?

Ultimately, just as Gregory and I discovered that the premise "Falling down is bad" was a misleading guide for learning to ride a bike, so Freud eventually realized that his libido theory was an inadequate foundation for a science of human nature. In order to explain all those motivations that violated the constancy principle, Freud had to introduce a second principle of motivation, the principle of *Eros,* which he borrowed from Plato's *Symposium.* Freud described Eros as a kind of life force, essentially the opposite of the constancy principle: stimulus-seeking rather than stimulus-avoiding, tending toward higher rather than lower levels of energy and complexity. Where the aim of the constancy principle was to reduce libidinal tension through discharge, the aim of Eros was to resolve tension through integration. Where the constancy principle was a principle of stability, Eros was a principle of growth.

Close but No Cigar

As you might imagine, the path that took Freud's thinking from the constancy principle to Eros was more convoluted than the brief outline I have just given would suggest. He found it difficult to give up the materialistic assumptions of the constancy principle and to embrace the spiritual implications of Eros. What he needed, *and what psychiatry still needs today,* was an integrated theory that includes both sides of human nature: the Flesh and the Spirit, the physiological needs of the swimming pool and the soul's need for the quest. As I will discuss in Chapters 14 and 15, Freud spent his entire career trying to develop such a theory, and in the end came very close to achieving it. But the almost-integrated theory he ended up with gradually fell apart after his death, as different groups of his followers each began to emphasize a different aspect of his theory and almost everyone missed the overall point of what he had been working toward.

Erik Erikson and the Eight Stages of Life

Probably the closest anyone came to developing the kind of integrated theory to which Freud aspired was psychoanalyst Erik Erikson, whose model of human development is still the clearest, most comprehensive and accessible statement we have of the Psychotherapeutic Model's overall quest philosophy.[5] The one limitation of Erikson's theory is that it doesn't explicitly address the mind–body question—how the neurological and the spiritual are integrated in human nature. The great strength of the theory is that it does explain how our swimming-pool need for emotional equilibrium and social adjustment is integrated within our larger need for self-actualization through the struggles of the quest.

Building on Freud's mature theory of inner conflict (between the *It* and the *I that stands above*), Erikson pictured life as a progressive struggle to integrate the conflicting needs of the swimming pool and the quest—the need for stability versus the need for growth, the need to remain unconscious versus the need for consciousness. These needs remain with us throughout the course of development, says Erikson, but the quality of our integration changes as we grow toward self-actualization. We may never fully become ourselves, but we do tend to get better at it as we progress through the eight stages of the life cycle. Here's how it happens: As we move from infancy to old age, we face a series of "stage-specific" conflicts between what we aspire to—the goals of the quest—and what pulls us back—the swimming-pool fear of falling down or bumping into people. During the first year of life, the basic conflict is trust versus mistrust. During the toilet-training period it is autonomy versus shame and doubt. Then follow initiative versus guilt during the so-called Oedipal period (ages four through seven); industry versus inferiority during the grade-school years; identity versus diffusion during adolescence; intimacy versus isolation in young adulthood; generativity versus stagnation in the middle years of adulthood; and, finally, integrity versus despair in the years of maturity and old age.

All these Eriksonian conflicts revolve around the common theme of desire versus inhibition—an ambivalence based on our (incipient) shameful awareness that good and evil are inherent in our own desire. Each of Erikson's "goods" can become evil if the desire for it is carried too far. Each of his "evils" can in turn serve the good by protecting us from the danger of carrying our desire too far. But the danger is different at every stage. It changes as we grow, as does the level of consciousness required for mastering the danger. That is why, as Erikson observed, people tend to have different sorts of breakdowns—and different sorts of healing experiences—at different stages, depending on which of the eight stage-specific conflicts they are struggling with at the time and on how successfully they have mastered the previous ones. Even though a person might have superficially similar symptoms as a teenager and again as a forty-five-year-old, for instance, the symptoms will likely have a very different meaning in terms of the person's quest. The symptom-producing conflict in each case will be different, reflecting the unique issues and emotions that belong to that particular stage of the person's life.

I have not yet had the opportunity in my career to see the same patient both as a teenager and as a forty-five-year-old, but I have seen the same symptom, with different Eriksonian meaning, in a nineteen-year-old daughter and a few years later in her forty-five-year-old father. My work with these two patients illustrates how symptoms serve to crystallize the conflicts of particular developmental stages, and how the Psychotherapeutic Model understands and treats these symptom-producing conflicts as trials in the patient's quest.

Example 1: Identity Crisis

Anne was the young woman I described briefly in Chapter 2, who became suicidally depressed after being raped while in her first year of college. As you may recall, Anne did not tell me about the rape during the first two months of her hospitalization. Instead, she tried to keep up an image—what Jung would have called her *persona,* and psychoanalyst D. W. Winnicott would have called her *False Self*—essentially the image of herself as her parents would have wanted to see her. This in itself was not unusual. Each one of us has such a False Self, a mask we wear in our dealings with other people (and too often with ourselves) that reflects a tendency to comply with the needs and expectations of others—to live according to someone else's idea of how we should live, the way a child lives according to his parents' rules and needs.

This orientation is sometimes called *extrinsic motivation*. To the extent that we are extrinsically motivated—as we all are to some degree—we are dominated by a swimming-pool need to hide in a superficial Eden of conformity, taking care not to bump into people, and not to make waves. But Anne's need to hide in such a False Self conformity was extreme, to the point that she felt herself to be unreal, as if there was nothing to her except her False Self image. She felt this way especially after the rape. Her parents would never be able to accept her now, she believed, and she doubted that I would be able to accept her, either. Although she tried valiantly to present herself as she always had (and as she believed her parents would have wanted), she could not escape the devastating feeling that the rape had destroyed her image, and her "self" along with it, forever.

Anne's depression thus represented a failure or loss of identity, a feeling that she was nothing—and had never been anything—but an image, a mask now shattered beyond any possibility of repair. But that was only the swimming-pool meaning of her depression, and the identity she had lost was only her "conformist" identity. In terms of the quest, her depression was not only a loss of that old identity (a falling down that was bad) but also an attempt to find a new identity (a falling down that was good). After all, the inner person who actually felt Anne's depression, who could be aware of herself as nothing but a false image and could feel depressed about that, must herself be more than that false image. No mere image can be aware of itself, or notice that it is missing something. In that sense, Anne's depression was a new and genuine experience of her True Self—an inner self, born out of the ashes of her old image, that could discern the difference between image and substance. This True Self was intrinsically rather than extrinsically motivated, needing to live for herself rather than for her parents. She still felt the devastating pain of her depression—the mixture of anxiety, shame, and sadness over losing her familiar self-image—but in that pain she could recognize the sound of her innermost being crying out for something more real, more genuinely hers, to care about and live for.

Anne became able to let herself feel and talk about both meanings of her depression as she began to experience the hospital, and her relationship with me, as a safe haven where she was free to feel whatever she felt and be whoever she was. This happened gradually once I told her (probably a week or two into her hospitalization) that I kept getting the feeling in our sessions that she was far away—emotionally disconnected—and seemed to be going through the motions of psychotherapy mostly to please me, rather than talking about anything that felt really important to her.

In Eriksonian terms, Anne's depression was a symptom of a classic adolescent "identity crisis." It embodied the conflict between her swimming-pool need to lose herself in living to please her parents and her quest need to find herself by rebelling against them. In terms of the first need, Anne's depression meant that her life was no longer worth living, because her parents could never again be pleased with her. In terms of the second need, it meant that she would have to change, because her life was no longer worth living *as she had been living it*. The first meaning belonged to her unconscious swimming-pool philosophy, the second to her unconscious quest philosophy. In deciding to tell me about the rape, then, she was not only taking a great personal risk but also making an important philosophical choice: to take her pain more seriously than her image, to think of her depression not as a sign of her failure to be the person she should have been, but as a sign that she needed to become who she really was.

Depression As Rebellion

Erikson's concept of identity crisis has become so much a part of our cultural idiom that we now take it for granted that adolescents will need to rebel against their parents in order to find themselves. That such a rebellion can take the form of a clinical depression is less obvious, and seldom recognized when it happens, even by psychiatrists. What could depression have to do with rebellion, after all? If anything, it seems quite the opposite of rebellion. But to a psychoanalyst, that is precisely the point: depression seems the opposite of rebellion because it is a rebellion turned inward, a symptom of inner conflict between the impulse to rebel and the need to conform. We are nowadays so used to thinking of depression as a biological illness without psychological meaning (or, if we do think about it psychologically, as a problem of low self-esteem), that we have forgotten this older, wiser view of depression as *anger turned against the self*. Whether or not it is a disorder in the brain, in the soul depression is always an expression of unconscious anger toward someone else, repressed and turned inward against the self, creating a state of inner conflict that is experienced as self-hatred (which certainly does lower self-esteem). But in the process the depression provides an indirect outlet for that repressed anger, as a disguised, unconscious rebellion—a refusal to participate (disguised as an inability to participate) in the life that makes us so angry.

People who are living with a depressed person, or trying to treat one, can often feel this disguised rebellion in the form of a subtle nonverbal reproach, an implicit complaint leveled against anyone who wants to help the patient "get over" the depression. I got a distinct impression of such a nonverbal message from Anne during the early weeks of her hospitalization. It was an emotional undercurrent that I could feel as part of my sense that she was far away and going through the motions. Trying to engage with this faraway person each day in our psychotherapy sessions, I would get the sense that, by staying depressed and distant, she was fighting me off. It was as if she felt my efforts to help her were intrusive and her depression was a way of saying, "I won't go along with this. Don't even try to get into my head. I won't let you therapize me!"

The Rage to Cure

I realized that I could have been misreading Anne. My sense of her depression as a rebellion could have been a projection of my own subtle therapeutic frustration—my unconscious "rebellion" against her depression. Whenever a psychotherapist or psychiatrist has too great a need to cure his patients—in order to prove his own worth, for instance, rather than out of concern for what the patient needs—he will tend to become easily frustrated and intolerant of patients who don't get better quickly. Freud called this tendency *furor sanandi*—"the rage to cure." It is both an essential ingredient and a universal problem in the motivation of all who are drawn to the helping professions, and one of the primary reasons why all psychotherapists and psychiatrists need psychotherapy for themselves. Until they learn to recognize and come to terms with this rage to cure, therapists generally have trouble distinguishing their own needs from their patients' needs. In this case, however, I was aware of the danger and was fairly confident that I was reading Anne correctly—that it was her repressed rebelliousness I sensed in her depression and not a projection of my own frustrated need to "therapize" her. Any doubts I had on this score were quickly settled once I began to see Anne with her parents in weekly family therapy sessions.

Unconscious Adolescent Rebellion

In working with adolescent patients in the hospital, I have found that meeting regularly with the family—the patient together with the parents and sometimes siblings—is essential. It gives me a firsthand experience of the emotional atmosphere in which my patient has been living and allows me to identify and intervene in dysfunctional patterns of interaction that may be contributing to my patient's illness. In my meetings with Anne and her parents, this definitely proved to be the case. What particularly struck me—and what convinced me that Anne's depression was indeed an unconscious adolescent rebellion—was the great difficulty her parents had accepting that their daughter was sick. Simply put, Anne's father and mother did not believe in mental illness, especially not for someone in their own family. As they saw it, being depressed was simply an excuse for being weak. They had both had very difficult lives themselves, they told me, and had always managed to cope. They prided themselves on being able to suppress or ignore all painful emotions, and to tough it out in the face of any problem life could throw at them. But their daughter's unyielding depression and her inability to cope with it were now posing a formidable challenge to their whole way of life. When Anne was first hospitalized, their urgent mission was to get her back on her feet and back to college as quickly as possible. When this didn't happen, they became frustrated, embarrassed, and increasingly angry—victims of a parental version of *furor sanandi.* In the family meetings they began to blame Anne for not pulling herself out of her depression, and became openly skeptical of my "talk therapy," which to them seemed nothing more than another excuse for her to wallow in her problems. But when Anne finally told them that she had been raped (shortly after she told me), they were jolted out of this disapproving attitude and suddenly felt horrible—anguished for their daughter and furious at her attacker. They could now understand that she had been traumatized and were able, for a while at least, to stop blaming her and show their love by supporting her decision to go to the police and press charges against the man who had raped her.

Initially, it was a great relief to Anne that her parents did not blame her for the rape as she had feared they would. She gradually came to realize, though, that their unexpected support did not really represent a change of heart for them. As loving as it was, their support remained predicated on their need for Anne to be strong—a fighter, not a quitter—and on their intolerance of what they perceived as weakness. They seemed surprised and dismayed when her decision to take action against the rapist was not enough by itself to relieve her depression. I explained to them that the rape was not Anne's only problem; that the most important source of her depression was a deeper and older unhappiness within herself. I warned them that she might need several more months of intensive treatment in the hospital and that if she didn't deal with this unhappiness now, she would remain vulnerable to repeated depressions and possibly another suicide attempt in the future. I told them, quite simply, that her life was at stake.

Anne's parents grudgingly accepted that she needed to stay longer in the hospital—I hadn't left them much room to do anything else—but it went against the grain of everything they believed. Her father soon began to preach again to Anne about the necessity of being tough. "I know you feel like you can't handle going back to college after what you've been through," he would say, "but you have to try. Giving up is absolutely the worst thing you could do. Sure it's hard to be depressed, but that's the way life is, and the only way to deal with it is to tough it out. Hell, your mother and I are depressed every day of our lives. Do you think it's easy for me to get up and go to work every day? Three out of four days I wake up in the morning and think I'll never be able to put on a suit again, or look at another tax form in my life. But then I wash my face, have a cup of coffee, ask your mother to give me a good kick in the pants, and I'm out the door and on my way through another day. Do I like it? No. Is it necessary? Absolutely."

Conscious Adolescent Rebellion

For weeks, Anne would listen to these exhortations and feel horrible about herself, unable to respond to her father. "He's being so polite in our meetings with you," she would tell me privately, "but I know what he's really thinking—that I'm a worthless wimp. He has no clue that being honest about what I really feel—the way I'm learning to do with you—takes more strength than anything he's ever done in his life! Oh God, I know that's a terrible thing to say, and I have no right to say it, but it really is how I feel sometimes."

Being able to use her sessions with me in this way, to articulate the differences between her father's opinions and feelings and her own, without fear of disapproval from me, was immensely helpful to Anne. It eventually led to her being able to risk her father's disapproval by objecting out loud to the way he was lecturing her. She explained to him that the kind of depression she was struggling with was not something she could overcome with a cup of coffee and a kick in the pants. Nor was it simply a reaction to the rape. "You say I'm not being tough, but to me, what I'm doing is a lot harder than what you want me to do. I'm trying to face the fact that something has felt wrong in my life for a long time. It just doesn't make sense to try to force myself back into a life that wasn't working to begin with. Why do you think I became bulimic two years ago? It was because I couldn't stand my life!"

In thus confronting her father, Anne was able for the first time to feel the rebelliousness that had previously been unconscious in her depression. This was a tremendous sign of progress, but it also made Anne feel so anxious and guilty that she had a recurrence of her old symptoms of bulimia. Such a regression into an old pattern of illness is not an uncommon reaction to the danger of too much progress and is all part of an overall growth process—two steps forward, one step backward. In fact, it occurred to me that Anne's "eating disorder" had itself been an early expression of the same impulse for growth that was now much more obviously embodied in her identity crisis. The alternation of binge eating and vomiting was a kind of bodily metaphor for an ambivalence that she was not yet ready to be aware of at a psychological level. The binge eating symbolically reflected her need to remain dependent by taking in all her parents' goals and values as her own. The vomiting reflected the opposite need, to reject—spit out—her parents' image and expectations of her and so begin the difficult task of becoming herself.

This is the sort of inner struggle that every adolescent must go through in order to grow up. The struggle doesn't always produce psychiatric symptoms as it did in Anne, but when symptoms do occur, it is important to remember that they are part of the solution rather than part of the problem. In Anne's case, her bulimia had been the first thing that forced her to notice, at least briefly, how unhappy she really was. She had tried to ignore this warning, however, and to keep it hidden from her parents. She had even managed to suppress her bulimic behavior when her parents did discover it. But when the rape then shattered her already tenuous balance, instead of falling back into her bulimia she fell forward into a new symptom—depression—that actually represented an advance in her development. In becoming overtly depressed, Anne began to feel her unhappiness in a way that she could no longer ignore. In becoming incapacitated she forced her parents to pay attention, too. Thus, the shift from bulimia to depression brought the conflicts, both within herself and between herself and her parents, more clearly into consciousness. This was a sign of growth, a shift from acting out her conflicts toward experiencing them emotionally and so being able to talk about them in a way that her parents could begin to understand.

As you would expect, the eventual result for Anne was by no means a complete rejection of her parents' values, but rather an integration of what she had genuinely learned from them with what came more uniquely from her. This integration did not happen easily. In fact, once Anne began to disagree openly with her father in our weekly family meetings, not only did her bulimic symptoms return but there followed several unsettling months of sometimes bitter arguments, during which it seemed that neither of Anne's parents might ever be able to appreciate what she was trying to tell them. But as she gradually became more effective at articulating and arguing for her own goals and values (around issues like how she dressed, who her friends were, when she would go back to college, whether she would live at home or on campus, what she majored in), her parents could not help but respect her for the strength of her convictions. Nor could they fail to notice that in standing up for herself with them, she was also gradually coming out of her depression. Although they continued to view her need to remain in the hospital as a weakness, they gradually discovered that they could amicably agree to disagree about this, with a sense of mutual respect and acceptance. Anne was then able to leave the hospital (after eight months altogether) and get on with her life. In fact, she blossomed. I did continue to work with her for another year of outpatient psychotherapy, but her growth very quickly became a self-perpetuating process in which I was no longer needed.

Symptoms Are Part of the Solution, Not Part of the Problem

It was an awe-inspiring privilege to be able to witness Anne's healing and growth from such an intimate vantage point. I would like to think that I was important for a while in facilitating her inner process, but I suspect that the most important thing I did for her was simply to allow her human nature to take its own course, along a path that I knew had to pass through her depression. In thus recognizing the growth potential contained within her symptom, I was following another important precept I had learned from Bruno Bettelheim: *Respect the symptom.* Bettelheim taught that symptoms are adaptive, creative achievements, the best solution a patient has so far been able to come up with to the otherwise unmanageable problems of his or her existence. However painful or disruptive a symptom might be, Bettelheim assumed that the patient would not have gone to the (unconscious) trouble of creating that symptom unless she needed it. To respect the symptom, then, meant to recognize that it was serving an important purpose, and it meant also to respect the person who had (unconsciously) created the symptom to serve just that purpose.

In this formulation, Bettelheim was himself following a much older teaching, part of the most ancient tradition of medicine. From Hippocrates to Freud, the wisest physicians have taught that *symptoms are a manifestation not of a disease but of a healing process*—what the ancients called the *vis medicatrix naturae,* or "healing power of nature." In the Hippocratic view (about which I will have more to say in Chapter 13), disease was a disharmony of conflicting humors and elements, and symptoms were the organism's attempt to establish a new harmony. Freud expressed the same idea by saying that symptoms are unconscious attempts to resolve inner conflict—the product of a "compromise" between the unconscious emotion trying to become conscious and the internal resistance that seeks to keep it out of awareness. In other words, as with Anne's depression, all symptoms are attempts to harmonize the conflicting needs of the swimming pool and the quest—the False Self's need for stability and conformity versus the True Self's need for self-awareness and autonomy—in the overall service of growth.

Unfortunately, in the Age of the Brain, psychiatrists try to cure patients by removing their symptoms, not realizing that those symptoms may be acting unconsciously to *heal* the patient. Most psychiatrists today would start Anne immediately on an antidepressant and discharge her quickly from the hospital, hoping to get her back on her feet. In so doing they would be unwittingly supporting her False Self, reinforcing her parents' message that depression is a sign of moral weakness, and discouraging her from taking seriously her own inner life. She might never mention the rape, and would probably never become aware of the nature of her differences with her parents. Not only would she miss the opportunity to learn and grow from her illness, but her parents would miss an opportunity to learn and grow from it too.

Example 2: Midlife Crisis

Three years after I had last seen Anne, I got a call from her father, Joe. Anne was doing wonderfully, he assured me, but he now had a problem of his own that he needed to see me about. He had been having an increasingly difficult time at work for the last few months, he said, and on that morning something had snapped. He woke up feeling worse than he had ever felt in his life. The effort it had taken just to force himself out the front door had left him shaking, drenched in a cold sweat. He could not bring himself to get into the car and drive to work. In fact, he felt as if he might never be able to return to work again. So he came to see me.

"It suddenly occurred to me that maybe my situation was not so different from Anne's," he told me. "I've never forgotten what you said back then about how sometimes having a breakdown is the best thing that can happen to you if it helps you recognize that your life is on the wrong course and that you need to change it. At the time—I guess you remember—I thought that was a pile of bull, but it certainly turned out to be true for Anne. . . . Well, I guess I'm not too proud to learn something from my daughter. You know she's been on me for a while now about my drinking. She says if I'm drinking this much, then there must be something I'm not dealing with. Well, today I think I realized what that is. I hate my work. I've always hated it. All those lectures I used to give Anne about how important it is to keep functioning— I know I was really trying to fight my own temptation to give up. For years I've been trying to convince myself that things will get better, that the problem is this client or that client, or maybe my boss. But my clients have changed and my boss has changed and it's never gotten any better. The fact is, I never really wanted to be an accountant in the first place. I don't think I'm even very good at it. The problem is, I don't feel as if I've ever been any good at anything, or that I ever will be."

It turned out that Joe did have a significant clinical depression, severe enough that it was not only impossible for him to work but difficult to motivate himself to do anything else, either. Just the process of getting to my office seemed to exhaust him. He wanted to try psychotherapy because he had seen it work so well for Anne, but it soon became clear to both of us that his depression, unlike Anne's, was interfering with his ability to concentrate, so that he couldn't focus his attention enough to make good use of psychotherapy. We therefore agreed to try an antidepressant, and within a few weeks he felt more at ease, was able to eat and sleep better, think more clearly, and make better use of his psychotherapy. But the antidepressant did nothing to change how much he hated his job, or to alleviate the sense of dread he felt whenever he tried to imagine himself going back to work. He continued to feel generally demoralized and down on himself a good deal of the time, and it was unclear to what extent this was an ongoing depression, not fully relieved by medication, or to what extent it was a natural psychological reaction to being existentially lost. Either way, Joe was still too depressed to work, so he took a temporary disability leave from his job and resolved to spend the next several months using his psychotherapy sessions to figure out what he really wanted to do with the rest of his life.

Nel Mezzo del Cammin di Nostra Vita . . .

As Dante first described it almost eight hundred years ago, midlife crisis is like a "dark forest," encountered "halfway through our journey of life," in which we lose our sense of direction—the "straight path" that up until then we have followed. Something goes wrong that overwhelms us for a time, bringing us to a halt and forcing us to reevaluate our position. For most people, the jolt comes from such common calamities as the loss of a job, a sudden disability, the death of a parent, an extramarital affair, marital discord or divorce, the biological clock running down, or an empty nest. Or it may come simply from the dawning awareness of aging and mortality. In any case, the combination of the stressful event and our reaction to it—usually an episode of depression or anxiety disorder—makes us feel that we can't go on any longer as we have been. We are forced to stop and ask ourselves whether the life we have been living is the life we truly want to live.

And so it was that Joe, halfway through the journey of his life, was now forced to stop and consider the frightening question of whether he should change his career. Up until then he had always thought of his work simply as a job, a way of making a living, in which his all-important purpose was to achieve social and economic security and stability for his family. In this he had been following an unconscious swimming-pool philosophy, seeking primarily to maintain the equilibrium of a conformist, extrinsically motivated False Self. But Joe's depression now forced him to consider the possibility that work could and perhaps should be an intrinsically motivated choice of his

True Self. From the perspective of a quest philosophy, a career is not a job but a "vocation"—a life work to which we are called by our deepest needs, aspirations, and values, a way of actualizing our full human potential. In that sense, Joe's depression and midlife crisis crystallized for him the universal conflict between the swimming pool and the quest. He felt torn between his need to maintain stability by returning to the security of the job he hated at the accounting firm and his need to grow by following his inner calling.

This picture was further complicated by the fact that Joe had recently been promoted to a supervisory position, and in fact it was just at that point that his work had begun to feel especially intolerable. "Maybe I'm just being a coward," he worried. "Or maybe I just don't have what it takes to be a supervisor. I hate being in a position where I'm expected to criticize other people's performances and then have to deal with all their flak when they don't like being criticized." It occurred to me that Joe might be suffering from a classic "success neurosis," that the sudden increase in power and prestige of his new position had provoked unmanageable anxiety from which he then had to retreat by becoming depressed. If so, then his inner calling might actually be in the direction of being a supervisor, where he would have to face the fear of his own power and become more of a leader, learning to deal more effectively with people; whereas his psychological stability might be best served by returning to his previous accounting job, with its more manageable, predictable problems. As it turned out, neither of these alternatives really matched the way Joe felt. When he thought about it, he realized that even the responsibility of being a regular accountant—trying to satisfy the Internal Revenue Service, the clients, and the firm—had always felt quite oppressive and demoralizing to him. It reminded him of the way he had felt as a child, trying to satisfy the unreasonable and inconsistent demands of his parents. Being expected then to take on additional responsibilities as a supervisor had simply pushed an already intolerable situation past the breaking point.

Joe realized further that most of the activities he had really enjoyed in his life involved using his hands—doing carpentry, plumbing, and painting around the house, for instance, and developing his own photographs. He liked working alone and he especially liked being his own boss—feeling responsible only to himself. He recalled that much earlier in his life he had dreamed of going into business for himself but had never permitted himself to take the dream seriously. He had been too afraid of failure. Unconsciously, he equated the idea of being his own boss—and becoming his own person— with repudiating the demands of his parents and so becoming a failure in their eyes. He had thus remained stuck in the mind-set of his adolescence, too afraid of displeasing his parents (for whom he then substituted the IRS, his clients, and the firm) to take the risk of doing what he needed to please himself. In that sense his depression was a kind of delayed but necessary adolescent rebellion, the beginning of a crucial developmental shift from the swimming pool to the quest, from the extrinsic motivation of living for his parents to the intrinsic motivation of living for himself.

In terms of Joe's old swimming-pool philosophy, his depression had meant that his worst fear had come true—he was a failure. But he now discovered that, in terms of his newly emerging quest philosophy, this failure felt strangely liberating. Having hit bottom, with nowhere to go but up, Joe no longer found it so frightening to think about starting his own business. He didn't need to make much money at this point in his life, because Anne was about to graduate college and begin working, and his wife was doing well at her own job. So after weeks of deliberation and several false starts, Joe decided to follow his vocation. He put ads in all the local papers and set up shop as a handyman/jack-of-all-trades, hoping eventually to be able to specialize in cabinetmaking. Once he began to get his first small jobs, he discovered that he loved the work every bit as much as he had thought he would and that his customers were eager to refer their friends to him. With that, the last traces of his depression faded and he was able to discontinue the antidepressant.

The Purpose of Symptoms Is Healing the Soul

My work with Anne and Joe was informed by my Psychotherapeutic Model belief that falling down is good—that the crises of mental illness are like the trials of a quest, important opportunities for personal and spiritual growth. The idea is that there is a psychotherapeutic process inherent in the life cycle, a series of stresses that force us to reexperience and reintegrate our inner conflicts, sometimes in a way that produces symptoms of mental illness, always in a way that challenges us to confront ourselves as we really are. It is only in suffering and struggling with these challenges that the soul can heal itself and grow. As we reintegrate our conflicts at successively deeper levels, we become stronger, wiser, and in fact better people—better in the sense that we are more conscious of our own emotions, and therefore less driven by automatic reflexive (unconscious) personality tendencies (aimed at maintaining our swimming-pool equilibrium) and freer to react to other people with the empathy of the Golden Rule. For Anne this meant (among other things) overcoming her automatic mistrustful tendency to put a distancing wall between herself and other people and discovering the satisfaction of talking to people about (and trusting them to understand) what she really felt. For Joe it meant overcoming his automatic tendency to lecture Anne about the proper way to live and discovering that he actually had something to learn from her about the quest.

From this point of view, both Anne's and Joe's depressions were necessary growing pains—crises of identity and of vocation that were integral to their struggles toward self-actualization. If, as I believe, *all* psychiatric symptoms are in the same way part of the healing/growing process, then the question of whether a psychiatrist should use medication or psychotherapy or both becomes secondary to the much more important question of what philosophy is guiding his overall approach to the patient. With Joe I had no hesitation in using an antidepressant. With Anne, following the same philosophy, I thought it was particularly important *not* to use one. However, if Anne were to have another episode of depression at some point in the future, I would be open to the possibility that her circumstances might be different and that an antidepressant might be helpful. In each case, I try to think about medication and the patient's need for swimming-pool stability within the larger context of the quest—what the patient needs at this particular moment in his or her life to further his or her growth as a person.

6. The End Is in the Beginning: A Tribute to Bruno Bettelheim

[A]t the heart of our work is not any particular knowledge or any procedure as such, but an inner attitude to life and to those caught up in its struggle, even as we are.
—Bruno Bettelheim, *The Empty Fortress*

Dr. B

The first thing I learned about Bruno Bettelheim when I began working as a student teacher at the Orthogenic School was that the cafeteria got suddenly quiet when he walked into the room. In that palpable hush, I recognized something like a collective expression of awe, testimony to the power of an extraordinary man. That's pretty much all I knew about Bettelheim (except also that he was a famous psychologist, notorious among University of Chicago students for calling campus radicals emotionally disturbed) when he stopped me in the hallway on my third day at the Orthogenic School and, without preamble, offered me a permanent teaching position. I was simultaneously thrilled, confused, heartsick, and embarrassed. I had just passed the New York City teachers' exam and was planning to move there to teach in the public schools the following fall. I had only taken the student teaching position at the Orthogenic School to fulfill a requirement for my master's degree program in elementary education. I had thought it might be an opportunity to broaden my horizons—and perhaps even to meet the great man—but an immediate job offer from him was the last thing in the world I was expecting. Yet, from my very first hour at the school, I had come to feel that I was somehow home. I could not have articulated at the time what had so quickly captivated me about the place, but I know now that it was the atmosphere of love and acceptance, and the prevailing belief that, for children and staff alike, there was absolutely nothing in the world more important to do than attend to our inner lives.

Flustered, I stammered out, "Oh . . . I, uh, didn't know there were any openings for teachers." Bettelheim responded in his thick Viennese accent, "Well, if there wouldn't be any openings, I wouldn't offer you a job!" Vintage Dr. B—no nonsense, no evasions, common sense. What I heard was "You know why you are here. I just offered you a chance to change your life. That *is* what you were looking for, isn't it?" Bettelheim's directness had transformed a simple job offer into an intimate personal invitation to a mentoring relationship that he knew I wanted but was hesitant about wanting. Of course, you might think that this is only a wish-fulfilling story I like to tell myself, that most of what I heard in Dr. B's words and experienced in our interaction came from me rather than from him.

"Exactly," I can hear him saying, with a mischievous twinkle in his eye. "But that is precisely the point! The last thing I am looking for in a staff member is a parrot who cannot think for himself!"

"Helping Others in Their Becoming"

Perhaps because he worked with children, Bettelheim was vividly aware of psychotherapy as a growth process. He viewed the task of the psychotherapist as very much like that of parent, child care worker, and teacher. He called this task "helping others in their becoming" and compared it to the work of a midwife—Socrates' metaphor for the art of true teaching—or to the function of Virgil as the guide and muse of Dante's inward journey in *The Divine Comedy*. In this process Bettelheim thought of the therapist's goal as not to cure the patient but simply to *accompany* him, facilitating and participating in the patient's own inherently self-healing growth process:

> [W]e have to become like Virgil. We must take by the hand those who have lost their way in the darkest of woods, and hence lost all hope. They will take courage from our willingness to guide them through hell and back into life, as we explain at every step taken together the infinite variety of human emotions we encountered on this journey. But to embark on this journey at all every one of us, like Dante, must first encounter himself in his own darkness where his straight way was lost.[1]

A Physician of the Soul

When people ask me what it was like to work with Bettelheim, I tell them that he was by far the greatest teacher I have ever met and that the most wonderful thing about his teaching was that it was entirely a matter of common sense. He used to say that he knew only three things, but those of us who counted remember four clinical maxims that were the constant themes of Dr. B's teaching:

1. The end is in the beginning.
2. Respect the symptom.
3. The patient is always right.
4. When you don't understand what a patient is doing, ask yourself under just what circumstances you would act in just the same way.

In trying to explain these ideas to students, I often refer them to a scene from Akira Kurosawa's *Red Beard*, a film that I first saw when I was working at the Orthogenic School and that will always be linked in my mind with the memory of Dr. B. Red Beard is a man much like Bettelheim, a master physician whose life is devoted to running a small hospital and clinic for the poor. The film tells the story of his relationship with Yasumoto, a young doctor assigned to him as an apprentice. When Yasumoto first arrives at the clinic, he is an arrogant young hotshot, full of himself and of the latest medical knowledge. At first he looks down his nose at Red Beard and refuses to obey his orders, but through his education he learns to recognize his own arrogance and grows, as a doctor and as a man, until he becomes, like Red Beard, a true physician of the soul.

Yasumoto's education begins when Red Beard assigns him his first patient, Otoyo, a twelve-year-old orphan girl whom they have just rescued from a brothel where she was being kept as a slave. Otoyo is sick with a high fever, and in addition appears to be emotionally disturbed. She is mute, and repeatedly goes through compulsive pantomime motions of scrubbing the floor (her job at the brothel), with an expression on her face that is at once vacant and terrified. Red Beard warns Yasumoto that Otoyo's mind is sicker than her body, and then leaves him to care for her as best he can. For two days she rejects all of Yasumoto's efforts to help her. She refuses to take water from him, refuses to let him examine her, refuses even to speak, but simply stares at him with eyes he describes in his journal as "suspicious, insolent, and very lonely." In the pivotal scene, Yasumoto tries to give Otoyo a spoonful of medicine and she abruptly slaps the spoon away, splattering him in the face. Wounded, he turns away from her in an angry, dejected sulk. At that moment, Red Beard comes into the room and Yasumoto tells him, with bowed head, that he has given up. Otoyo is simply impossible to treat, he says bitterly.

Red Beard then sits down at the bedside, pours out a spoonful of medicine and offers it to Otoyo. With a quick backhanded movement she splashes it in his face, just as she had done with Yasumoto. Red Beard raises his eyebrows and calmly pours out another spoonful of medicine and offers it to her. Again she slaps it rudely into his face. With a look of resignation and perhaps a hint of amusement, Red Beard then slowly pours out another spoonful of medicine and once again politely offers it to her. Again she slaps it defiantly back at him, but now there is also fear and confusion in her face. Red Beard patiently repeats the procedure once more, and this time Otoyo hesitates, hitting the spoon almost reluctantly, just hard enough to spill the medicine but without splashing him. It is beginning to dawn on her that perhaps this man really isn't going to get angry—that perhaps, unlike any other adult she has ever dealt with, he wants to help her, not use her. As this realization dawns, she opens her mouth, as if in bewilderment, and Red Beard gently inserts the spoonful of medicine. A few hours later she begins to talk, for the first time in the film, asking Yasumoto, "Why didn't he slap me?"

Corrective Emotional Experience

Kurosawa's *Red Beard* portrays a physicianly ideal that I take also as a moral ideal for human life generally. In particular, the scene I have described depicts an attitude of the physician—Red Beard's caring patience in the face of Otoyo's provocative behavior—that is at the heart of the psychotherapeutic process. This attitude, an unintimidated but nonretaliatory acceptance of the patient's hostile negative transference (her expectation of being mistreated), gently commands the patient's attention by offering her a new and unexpected experience of love, very different from the negative responses she is used to from many previous painful experiences. Such an attitude of acceptance in the therapist creates an atmosphere of safety and trust, and gives the patient a model for a new way of being in the world.

Of course, the need to repeat old patterns through the transference relationship is such that the patient will not change easily but will need to test the therapist's acceptance repeatedly to make sure it is trustworthy. When the therapist is able consistently to subordinate his personal emotional reactions (the "*counter*transference") to his understanding and concern for the patient, then a deep process of learning and growth can occur for the patient. This process has been termed corrective emotional experience. What happens is that the unexpected experience of being accepted by the therapist forces the patient to stop and question his or her own transference attitude. This leads to a new self-awareness—a recognition that the source of the problem is not in the therapist but in the patient's own emotions.

In *Red Beard*, it is not only Otoyo but Yasumoto who has such a corrective emotional experience. Through witnessing and feeling the impact of Red Beard's intimate healing encounter with Otoyo, Yasumoto is forced to recognize his own childish impatience and arrogance—both toward Otoyo and toward Red Beard himself. The defiant treatment-rejecting attitude that had so frustrated Yasumoto when he encountered it in Otoyo was, after all, not much different from his own defiant teaching-rejecting attitude toward Red Beard. Recognizing this, Yasumoto felt shame, and understood that in his uncooperative young patient he had met the enemy and she was him.

Staff Meetings

Yasumoto's experience with Otoyo illustrates how, by persisting in her illness, the patient can ultimately cure her physician. In this case, Otoyo frustrates Yasumoto to the point where he has to recognize (with an assist from Red Beard) that his frustration is *his* problem—an intolerance of what he sees in her that he hasn't wanted to see in himself. In this way, just as a patient can discover his or her disowned, unconscious "dark side" through the transference relationship with the therapist, so too the therapist can (and must, for therapy to be effective) learn about his own dark side through the countertransference relationship with his patient. This, more than anything else, is what I learned from Bruno Bettelheim.

In daily staff meetings, for instance, Dr. B's teaching was always geared toward helping his staff understand how our own unconscious difficulties were contributing to our patients' difficulties. At each meeting, he would ask one of us to present a problem we were having with one of the children. Rarely would we have a chance to speak more than a sentence or two before Dr. B would grasp the nature and source of the problem. He would then interrupt us with a pointed question that effectively undercut the story as we were about to tell it—and as we had been telling it to ourselves—and forced us to listen within to what we were feeling at that moment. The emotional attitude with which we were about to tell the story always reflected something important about the emotional attitude with which we had been approaching the child. Each answer we gave to Bettelheim would then prompt another challenging question from him, in a Socratic dialogue that ended only when we had understood how the problem we were describing was in fact one of our own creation.

To give the reader a better sense of this process, I would now like to retell the story of Yasumoto's education, imagining Bettelheim as his teacher. My point will be to highlight the relevance of Bettelheim's ideas to the larger themes of this book. In particular, I envision a teaching dialogue between Yasumoto and Bettelheim that is emblematic of the cultural dialogue we so sorely need between the Medical Model and the Psychotherapeutic Model.

Act One

Let me set the scene for this imaginary dialogue: Yasumoto is a bright, arrogant young psychiatry resident fresh out of medical school. He has just been called to evaluate Otoyo, who was brought to the emergency room, dehydrated, feverish, and mute. He spends fifteen frustrating minutes trying to get her to drink, to talk, and to let him examine her so that he can discover the source of her fever, but he gets nothing for his efforts except a face full of liquid Tylenol. He looks at his watch and realizes he is late for his first meeting with an ongoing seminar on the psychotherapeutic process, taught by Bettelheim and open to all the psychiatry residents. Not knowing what else to do, he signs Otoyo out to one of the medical residents, promising to return soon, and rushes off to attend the seminar. He walks into the seminar room, preoccupied with worry about his patient's untreated fever, angry about the sticky stuff still on his shirt, and wondering why he ever chose psychiatry in the first place. He is trying to look inconspicuous, but Bettelheim interrupts the class to greet the latecomer.

BB: Welcome. You are Yasumoto?

YAS: Oh, hi. Yes, Dr. Bettelheim, I'm Yasumoto. And I'm sorry for being late.

BB: You look troubled. What's the matter?

YAS: Oh . . . I guess I'm frustrated. I've only just started here and already I feel like quitting! I've just been in the emergency room trying to evaluate an impossible patient!

BB: Perhaps you could tell us more what is impossible about this patient.

YAS: Well, she's twelve years old and lives in a brothel where she works as a slave. She was brought in with a high fever and they called me because she wouldn't talk or let anyone examine her, and no one from the brothel was able or willing to provide any useful information about her. She's dehydrated and probably has some kind of an infection, potentially a serious one, but she wouldn't let me examine her, either. I couldn't get her to talk, not a single word, and she absolutely would not drink or take any medicine. The most important thing right now is to get some fluids in her and start her on an antibiotic for the infection, but of course we can't do that properly until we know what the infection is. I'm thinking that maybe if I give her some Thorazine it will calm her down enough to let me examine her. But it would have to be by injection. I tried to give her some liquid Tylenol by mouth, because I thought the fever might be impairing her mental state, but she just threw it in my face. She is totally noncompliant and just won't take any medicine voluntarily.

BB: Well, and why should she?

YAS: What do you mean?

BB: I mean, you seem upset that she doesn't take medication, apparently because you believe strongly that she should take it. I ask you simply to examine that belief: Why should she take medication?

YAS: Well, I guess I thought it was pretty much understood that when you are sick you should take medicine. How else are you going to get better?

BB: So then she should want to get better?

YAS: Yes, of course!

BB: And why is that?

YAS: So that she can live. And I can already guess your next question. Yes, as a doctor, I do believe that she should live!

BB: And how will she be able to live, do you think, once she gets better?

YAS: Well, I'm not sure I know exactly what you mean—the same as anyone else, I suppose, just as she did before she got sick.

BB: You mean she should live in the brothel, then, and that you will have her sent back there once her fever is treated?

YAS: Hmm. I hadn't really gotten around to thinking about that. I was more concerned about her dehydration and fever as the immediate problem. But now that you mention it, probably it was having to live in such an environment that made her sick in the first place.

BB: That's right. So then I repeat my previous question: Why should she take medication?

YAS: Okay, I see what you mean, she has no reason to get better if it means going back to the place that made her sick in the first place. She probably expects that I will be sending her back there, so it would make sense to her that she should refuse to take her medicine.

BB: Exactly! The patient is always right, as I keep telling you; not you personally, Yasumoto, because you are new to the class and haven't yet had the opportunity to make the same mistake ten times, but your more experienced colleagues, who cannot stop thinking that their patients should be doing something different from what they are doing. You see, it is not the patient who is impossible, but the psychiatrist who thinks he knows what would be better for his patient. Patients may be crazy, but they ain't stupid. If they could do something different that would be better for them, they would already be doing it! The patient is always right, and you are in trouble when you find yourself believing otherwise. Your responsibility is not to know what your patients should be doing differently, whether it be taking their medicine, feeling less depressed, or not hearing voices anymore. Your responsibility is simply to understand how what they are doing makes sense. You must assume that if Otoyo doesn't take her medicine, or doesn't talk, she must have good reasons for it, which it is your job to appreciate. You must *respect the symptom.* Remember that each symptom is an accomplishment, the best solution your patient has so far been able to find to the problems that beset her, given the inner resources at her disposal.

Intermission

At such a juncture in an Orthogenic School staff meeting, Bettelheim would typically pause, giving everyone, and especially the staff member who had been on the spot, a chance to absorb the lesson. When he got an indication that we were open to it, he would continue his questioning further, with the goal of helping us recognize more specifically what it was in us that had been interfering with our ability to empathize with the child's predicament. The idea was that even if the child had been expressing herself in a confusing or provocative manner, there was a real human need behind the distorted communication, that we would have been able to identify and respond to appropriately were it not for our own anxiety. However unruly the child's behavior, it had only become a problem when it pressed a neurotic button in us. This was certainly true for the Yasumoto of my revisionist movie, whom we may now imagine silently reflecting on Bettelheim's words for a few moments, then looking up with an expression of puzzlement, as if trying to formulate a question.

Act Two

BB: So now, what do you want to know?

YAS: I think I understand where I went wrong. It was easier for me to focus on diagnosing and treating Otoyo's infection than to imagine what it must be like for her to grow up scrubbing floors in a brothel, knowing that soon she will be expected to perform as a prostitute. A bacterial infection I knew I could do something about, but I didn't want to face the larger question of whether I could really do anything meaningful about Otoyo's life.

BB: That's right. So when Otoyo prevented you from doing what you already knew how to do, you felt helpless, full of the painful awareness of what you do not yet know how to do. Inwardly you blamed her for making you feel helpless and inadequate, so you started to think about forcibly injecting medication into her body. Again, it is something you know how to do, but if you consider the larger picture you will probably not be so eager to do it. Would she not experience such an injection as a kind of rape, exactly the sort of abuse she has been given every reason to expect will be her lot in life?

YAS: Yes, I can see that now. It was my frustration and anger that made me want to force Thorazine on her, yet if I don't do that, she's so uncooperative that I don't know what I can do for her!

BB: Well, what do you want to do for her?

YAS: *(Hesitating)* Well, this is embarrassing. I know it goes directly against what you've just been telling me, but the fact is, I really am very preoccupied with her fever. I don't think I can just turn that off. I know it's not what you wanted me to say, but the truth is, what I really want to do for her is diagnose her infection and give her medication for it.

BB: Yasumoto, it is hardly a sign of respect for me that you are so concerned to give me the answer you think I want to hear. In any case I am glad you did not do so. It is sometimes necessary to risk the embarrassment of taking seriously one's own inner promptings! Yet there should be no embarrassment in wanting to practice a skill you know you are good at in order to help a person who sorely needs it. It would be malpractice to do anything less. Otoyo may be in real danger if her infection goes untreated, and it is only natural that you should want to provide her with the medication that you know will help her.

YAS: Yes, except for the slight problem that she throws it in my face!

BB: And from this you conclude what?

YAS: That she won't take any medicine voluntarily.

BB: Perhaps. And what else do you conclude?

YAS: *(Again hesitating, but much longer this time)* I guess I'm back to trying to give you the answer you're looking for. . . . *(Frustrated)* I really don't know. She threw the medicine in my face. She won't talk to me. I can't read her mind. I conclude that she refuses to take the medicine. What else can I possibly conclude?

BB: Excellent question. In fact, it's the same question I have just asked you: What else can you conclude from the fact that Otoyo throws the medicine in your face? It seems that you now throw something back in my face. Should I therefore conclude that you don't want to answer my question or that you refuse to take the medicine I have to offer?

YAS: No. I'm sure you realize that it is quite the opposite. I really tried to answer your question, and I want to answer your question. I'm just not able to, because I'm not thinking very clearly right now.

BB: And what is it that clouds your thinking? What are you feeling?

YAS: Anxious, self-conscious, on the spot . . . intimidated.

BB: I see. Then perhaps you could also conclude that Otoyo was feeling anxious and intimidated. Probably she, too, was not thinking very clearly when she threw the medicine back in your face. Perhaps she was afraid of you and your medicine.

YAS: I guess I hadn't really thought about that. She seemed a lot more angry and defiant to me than scared.

BB: Certainly, but what makes someone like Otoyo angry and defiant?

YAS: Well, I'm sure it must have something to do with how she was brought up in that horrible environment, but more specifically than that, I don't know.

BB: That's right—you can't read Otoyo's mind. Yet perhaps you already know more than you realize, or could do so, by reading your own mind. What makes someone like you angry and defiant? For instance, just now when you threw the medicine back in my face.

YAS: I guess that was kind of defiant, but it was because I was feeling confused and defensive. I felt as if you were trying to make me look stupid. Or at least I was afraid I would look stupid if I didn't come up with the right answer.

BB: In the same way, I suspect you were afraid you would look stupid or incompetent if Otoyo didn't take her medicine, as if that meant you had failed to come up with the right answer.

YAS: You know that's really true. I did feel I had to prove something, and not only to myself, but to those medical residents in the emergency room. I wanted to show them I could succeed with her where they couldn't. They usually don't have much respect for psychiatrists, you know.

BB: And so you took it personally when Otoyo so rudely rejected your efforts, as if she, too, was trying to make you look stupid.

YAS: Yes, I suppose I did. I certainly came in here feeling stupid.

BB: There is a lesson here that you would all do well to learn. It is so simple that it is practically impossible for intelligent people to understand it: *The end is always in the beginning.* You see, Yasumoto, you began, at the moment you first met Otoyo, already feeling intimidated, worried that you would look stupid. You then proceeded to interpret everything she did according to your own fear, focusing only on what threatened to make you look stupid. As a result, you were exquisitely sensitive to Otoyo's anger and defiance but oblivious to the fear that lay behind it. And so you ended exactly where you began, feeling stupid. The end is in the beginning. What you ended up seeing in Otoyo was just what you started out expecting to see—a patient who wanted to make you look stupid.

YAS: Yeah, now that you explain it I can see how I did that. But then, how do I overcome it? I still don't have a clue about what to do with Otoyo.

BB: Patience, Yasumoto. You young psychiatrists are always in such a rush to fix everything that you never stop to ask yourselves whether what you fix is really broken. That the end is always in the beginning is a truth, not an obstacle to overcome. To deal with Otoyo effectively in the end, you don't need to fix or overcome anything but only to understand the attitude with which you approach her in the beginning.

YAS: I'm not sure I follow you.

BB: Look. You start out with Otoyo afraid to look stupid. You try to overcome this feeling in yourself by overcoming *her,* using all the doctoring techniques you know. This doesn't work, and in the end you feel stupid anyway. So now you want to figure out what to do differently, to get a different result. But you are feeling stupid, and can't seem to believe that anything you can think of will work. So you are back where you started, approaching Otoyo in fear of looking stupid again. That's fine, only this time, don't try so hard to overcome this fear but simply allow yourself to feel it. Pay attention to your inner attitude. What do you notice about this feeling of yours, this being afraid to look stupid?

YAS: I notice I'm feeling it right now with you. I don't seem to do very well at answering your questions.

BB: Yes, but again you try to *overcome* your fear, by producing the correct answer. If you really want to learn how to answer my questions correctly, remember that the end is in the beginning. How you are able to answer my question will depend on the attitude with which you approach the question. So go back to the beginning. Notice first how you are listening to me.

YAS: You mean besides the fact that I'm scared to death of you?

BB: Well, if you are scared to death of me, I hardly think that is besides the fact! The problem is precisely that you want to make your fear besides the fact, to skip over it or push it aside. If you do not take your own fear seriously, how will you be able to understand, or even notice, when your patients are afraid?

YAS: You mean like Otoyo.

BB: That's right. . . . So what does your own fear tell you about Otoyo?

YAS: That she must have been afraid too. I know you already said that before, only I didn't quite get it. . . . In fact, I guess she must have been a lot more scared of me even than I am of you. You know, she would *have* to be. It's really so obvious that I'm embarrassed I didn't see it when I was with her. Here she is in a completely unfamiliar setting, with a strange man in a strange white coat trying to poke at her with stethoscopes and reflex hammers and bottles of medicine. How could she be anything but very confused and frightened?

BB: Exactly! It is almost as bad as being in an unfamiliar classroom and having a psychologist with very thick glasses and a foreign accent prodding you with endless questions! Yet you have been able to handle it, Yasumoto—with the help of your anger and defiance, I might add. So even though Otoyo may be more frightened than you, it would probably be safe to assume that what helps you to take your medicine will also help her to take hers.

YAS: Well, it helped that you haven't gotten totally fed up with me the way I did with her, even though I guess I have been fighting you. It's really been more in self-defense than anything else. . . . Okay, I get it, so I have to remember that when Otoyo threw the medicine in my face it was in self-defense as well.

BB: Exactly!

YAS: I also appreciate it that you've spent so much time with me, focusing just on my problem. I know there are a lot of other residents here, and I'm sure they have issues they would have liked to discuss, too.

BB: And how can you use this to help you with Otoyo?

YAS: Well, let's see. It gives me the sense that you thought I was worth spending time on, that you don't think I'm so stupid, just that I need a little medicine, I suppose. Hmm. So Otoyo was probably worried about what I would think of her, too. Maybe she was afraid I would think she was some kind of whore or something, given where she came from, or maybe she assumed I would be like the men who visit the brothel.

BB: Very likely. And one way that she might try to find out who you really are and what you really think of her would be to act as badly as possible from the outset, so that you will reveal your true colors and she can know where she stands.

A Tableau for Psychiatry

I have conceived this imaginary dialogue as an extended commentary on the state of psychiatry as it is today and as it should be. The particular scene I have enlarged upon from Kurosawa's *Red Beard* I take as a kind of tableau representing two alternatives for how a psychiatrist (or any physician) might think about illness and the use of medication. Yasumoto, like a Medical Model psychiatrist, starts out thinking exclusively of the physical dimension of illness and so equates treatment with medication. He proceeds in arrogance, ignorant of his patient's real condition and driven by an unconscious anxiety over just how much his own real condition resembles hers. As a result, he tends to see in her only what threatens him—her difficult symptoms and negativistic behavior—and he reacts to these as problems he must "attack" (with *furor sanandi*) and overcome so that he can feel secure about himself as a doctor. By viewing his patient in this way, he distances and alienates himself from her, in what Martin Buber would call an I–It mode of relationship: a "setting at a distance" of the other person, treating the other as an object, a set of symptoms, a problem case, an It. Red Beard/Bettelheim, in contrast, like a Psychotherapeutic Model psychiatrist, thinks of his patient as a whole person. He understands that while medicine may be necessary for her body, genuine healing can take place only in her soul, and only through the psychotherapeutic impact of her relationship with her physician. He recognizes that his patient's existential condition is not fundamentally different from his own; he can accept her negativistic behavior because he respects and empathizes with the fear and mistrust behind it. He treats his patient as he would want to be treated, in what Buber would call an I–Thou mode of relationship:

> not a looking at the other, but a bold swinging, demanding the most intensive stirring of one's being, into the life of the other . . . the particular real person who confronts me, whom I can attempt to make present to myself . . . in his wholeness, unity, and uniqueness.[2]

Participating Observations

This way of framing the difference between the Medical Model and the Psychotherapeutic Model highlights the meaning of Bettelheim's maxim "The end is in the beginning." The attitudes and expectations with which a psychiatrist approaches a patient are self-fulfilling prophecies. They affect the way he views the patient, which in turn affects the way he relates to the patient, which in turn changes the patient's reactions to him in a way that conforms to what he expected in the first place. Central to this teaching is the idea that a psychiatrist or psychotherapist is a *participant-observer*, always contributing—for good and for ill—to the ongoing, evolving state of his patient, even in the attempt to look at the patient objectively.

Yasumoto's attitude when he meets Otoyo, for example—feeling insecure behind a facade of arrogance, overly concerned with his own success or failure—leads him to take it as a personal defeat when she resists his efforts to help her. He doesn't notice her mistrustfulness but only her negativism, which he takes as evidence of her unyieldingly defiant attitude toward *his* treatment. In this situation Otoyo might easily have become the "impossible" patient Yasumoto considered her, because his own negativistic reaction to her negativism would have given her more reason to be mistrustful and so solidified her resistance to treatment. Red Beard's intervention produces a different result because Red Beard starts with a different attitude—one that allows him actually to see a different patient. He experiences the same symptomatic behavior and defiant attitude that Yasumoto did, but instead of reacting to this as an insult to him, he accepts it as a defensive symptom that is necessary for her. Approaching Otoyo with this different attitude (respecting the symptom) allows Red Beard to see—and, more important, allows Otoyo to become—a different patient: a frightened little girl who is mistrustful and challenging, but open to treatment.

One Otoyo, two patients. The different frames of mind (and spirit) with which the two doctors observe and interact with Otoyo bring out different potentialities within her. The difference in what they are able to see in her, and how they react to what they see, profoundly influences the way she in turn is able to see and react to them. Otoyo herself, like any patient, is an ineffable mystery. It is only through her encounters with doctors that she becomes either a hopeless case or an evolving person.

Participant-Observation and the Principle of Complementarity

The concept of participant-observation is indispensable for psychiatry: how a psychiatrist views a patient (observation) is linked to his manner of relating to the patient (participation) in a way that inevitably changes the patient. As it turns out, this same basic idea is generalizable, and applies as a model of scientific observation not only in psychiatry and psychotherapy but in every other field of science as well. In fact, the premise of participant-observation was formally defined by physicist Niels Bohr as a general scientific principle that many consider to be the single most important idea of the twentieth century: the principle of complementarity. According to Bohr's principle (which I will discuss at length in the next two chapters), every scientific observation is really a participant-observation—an interaction between the observer and the observed that changes the state of the observed in the very act of observing it. *The end is in the beginning.* What we end up seeing is a function of how we choose to look at it.

Let me remind you of two examples I have already touched on. The first is the wave–particle paradox in physics: whether we observe particles or waves when we look at light depends on how we choose to measure (interact with) it experimentally. *One light, two phenomena.* Light in itself is an ineffable mystery. Only through its encounters with physicists does it become either particles or waves. The second is George Schaller's story of the ethologists and the gorillas: whether we discover dangerous or peaceful gorillas in the jungle depends on how we choose to observe (interact with) them—armed or unarmed. *One gorilla, two phenomena.* The gorilla itself is an ineffable mystery. Only through its encounters with ethologists does it become either a dangerous wild animal or an intelligent fellow primate.

The Responsibility to Choose

The end is in the beginning. What makes Bettelheim's principle especially valuable is that it amplifies the idea of participant-observation to make it not only a principle of scientific observation but one of moral engagement as well. If the way we see the world actually changes the world, then to consciously choose the way we want to see the world becomes a serious moral responsibility. As the Bhagavad Gita says, "Man is made by his belief. As he believes, so he is."

We cannot have it both ways. In psychiatry and in life generally, the way we view each other—with an I–Thou or an I–It attitude—is inextricably linked to the way we treat each other, whether seeking to meet in the intimacy of a genuine personal relationship or treating each other merely as need-satisfying objects. As human beings we are capable of both ways of seeing and relating, and we are making choices between them—whether consciously or unconsciously—at every moment. *The end is in the beginning.* Which model of psychiatry we end up with will be determined by the way we choose to see and treat each other as human beings. The choice between the Medical Model and the Psychotherapeutic Model, then, is not only a choice between different philosophies or between different attitudes and prejudices about mental illness or about human nature generally. It is also a moral choice of what kind of world we want to live in—what kind of world we want to create. This is a choice that falls not only to psychiatrists but to all of us.

One human condition, two human natures. We ourselves remain an ineffable mystery. Only through our encounters with each other, and with ourselves, do we become either embodied souls engaged together in a quest or highly intelligent primates swimming laps by instinct in the great pool of life.

III. Science:
The Untold Story

The great physicist Niels Bohr, father of the quantum theory of the atom, has suggested that his "principle of complementarity," according to which the same phenomena have to be described in two mutually exclusive models, may be a universal principle rather than merely a principle of atomic physics. He would . . . have us look upon determinism and freedom as both true, each in its own frame of reference. . . . This view is apparently in line with the following statement attributed to Bohr: "There are the trivial truths and the great truths. The opposite of a trivial truth is plainly false. The opposite of a great truth is also true."
—Robert Waelder, "Psychic Determinism and
the Possibility of Predictions"

7. Two Kinds of Truth: The Principle of Complementarity

The verified necessity for us to accept two very different views of natural events, mutually irreducible one to the other, a necessity which has been given the name of complementarity, *is one great gift of physics in our epoch to the thinking of all humanity.*

—Merle A. Tuve, "Physics and the Humanities"

Analysis and Synthesis

There is an apparent inconsistency in my discussion of the two models of psychiatry that needs to be clarified. On the one hand, I reject the Medical Model with its swimming-pool belief that symptoms are bad, because it is based on a false conception of science and caters to a dehumanizing tendency in ourselves and in our culture. As an alternative, I advocate the Psychotherapeutic Model because it respects the symptom and the needs of the soul. On the other hand, I am quite ready to accept the Medical Model as a useful and even a necessary perspective on people and their symptoms. It addresses the need for stability—for chemical and emotional balance and for social adjustment—that is a very real element in our human nature. That's why, with many patients (as with Joe), I use medication to provide enough stability so that they can better use their psychotherapy to help them grow. In fact, as I stated in Chapter 5, I believe that what psychiatry needs most today is not to reject the Medical Model, but rather to integrate it within a more comprehensive Psychotherapeutic Model that respects the needs of the Flesh *and* the Spirit, the swimming pool *and* the quest.

So why do I present the Medical Model and the Psychotherapeutic

Model as either–or philosophical choices when my ultimate goal is to integrate them? The answer requires a closer look at Niels Bohr's principle of complementarity.

Bohr's basic idea, you will recall from Chapter 6, is that every scientific observation is really a participant-observation. A scientific observer does not merely look at something or someone but looks in a particular way that actually influences ("participates in") what he ends up seeing. In fact, Bohr was more specific. He stated that every science has precisely two particular ways of looking—*analytic* and *synthetic*—that produce two very different types of observation. In physics, for example, the analytic perspective sees simple particles where the synthetic perspective sees complex waves. In ethology, the analytic perspective sees instinctively aggressive gorillas where the synthetic perspective sees instinctively peaceful gorillas who may also become instinctively aggressive when threatened. In psychiatry, the analytic perspective sees impossible treatment-resistant cases where the synthetic perspective sees mistrustful persons who put forward a defensive facade of resistance but deep down are open to treatment. More generally, the analytic perspective sees a chemical imbalance in the brain where the synthetic perspective sees an inner conflict of the soul.

Mutually Exclusive but Complementary

In all these examples, the analytic perspective is clearly the more limited one. It "misses the forest for the trees"—loses sight of the big picture (the synthetic perspective) by focusing exclusively on one element of that picture. You can't see waves while focused on particles, nor can you see the innate peacefulness of gorillas while mentally prepared to shoot them at any moment. You can't see the mixture of mistrustfulness and hope in a patient while intent on overcoming her resistance, nor can you listen to the soul while trying to figure out what prescription to write.

Now here's where my apparent inconsistency comes in. In a way, it does make sense to reject the analytic perspective. Considered *by itself,* it is oversimplified and misleading. By focusing on one element of a much more complex picture, it takes that element out of context and so misses the essential meaning of the picture. In the case of the Medical Model this is a serious problem. By focusing diagnostically (rather than empathically) on the patient's brain, behavior, and symptoms (rather than on his inner life) the

Medical Model psychiatrist sees and treats the patient as an object (a case, a disorder) and ignores his or her essential humanity.

Bohr recognized this problem but said that it was not so much a problem with the analytic perspective per se as with the analytic perspective considered *by itself,* as if it were the whole truth. He pointed out that the serious limitation of the analytic perspective was also its great advantage. By ignoring the forest, it was able to see the trees much more distinctly, and could then go even further—focusing first on the functional elements of a tree (roots, trunk, branches, leaves, seeds), then on progressively deeper levels down to cells, molecules, and atoms, and finally all the way down to the finest grain of its elementary particles. This is the kind of detailed information we could never get while we were busy looking at the big picture—for example, considering the forest and its role in a global ecosystem.

Bohr summed this up by saying that the two ways of looking—analytic and synthetic perspectives—were mutually exclusive. It is just as inevitable that we miss the trees by focusing on the forest as it is that we miss the forest by focusing on the trees. Either way, we miss something important. This being the case, Bohr formulated the principle of complementarity to stipulate that *the analytic and synthetic perspectives are mutually exclusive but also complementary,* in that every science requires both of them. Each perspective provides a kind of knowledge that the other perspective cannot, and both kinds of knowledge are indispensable to a complete scientific explanation (of anything).

What Would an Integrated Model of Psychiatry Look Like?

According to the principle of complementarity, then, a complete science of mental illness—and, more ambitiously, a complete science of human nature that includes mental illness—would require both the Medical Model and the Psychotherapeutic Model as equally valid perspectives. If psychiatrists could understand this much, it would certainly be an important step toward integration. At the very least, it would help correct two widespread but dangerous misconceptions: that all mental illnesses (and all mental activity) will eventually be explainable in terms of brain chemistry, and that medication can (and has already begun to) replace psychotherapy as the treatment of choice for mental illness.

But the integration I have in mind would go further. It would start from the idea that, *scientifically*, the Medical Model and the Psychotherapeutic Model represent equally valid analytic and synthetic perspectives. But it would then go on to recognize that, *philosophically*, psychiatry must inevitably choose between the two perspectives, giving priority to one or the other in the way we prefer to look at and treat our patients (and each other) at any moment. In that sense, while the two perspectives may be equally valid, a true integration would have to account for the fact that they are by no means equally valuable.

The Mona Lisa and You

To get a sense of this difference in value between the two models of psychiatry (and between the analytic and synthetic perspectives generally), consider a jigsaw puzzle of the Mona Lisa. From an analytic perspective, the individual pieces of the puzzle, put together, add up to the whole picture. In this perspective we are focusing attention on how the physical parts fit together topographically. If we were studying the actual painting instead of a jigsaw puzzle, our analytic perspective would focus on how the paint pigments are mixed and layered to produce the overall color patterns. If we were studying a computer image of the painting, it would focus on how the software program translates bits of digital information from an electronic file on disk to a pattern of pixels on the screen. In each case, we would be seeing the whole as equal to the sum of its physical parts—a useful perspective as far as it goes, but one that fails to capture what most people would consider the essential qualities of da Vinci's painting. To do that we would need to look at "the big picture" from a synthetic perspective—an aesthetic experience of the Mona Lisa as an artistic representation. Here the whole on which we are focusing is clearly greater than, and at a different level of experience from, the sum of its physical parts. The fitting together of puzzle pieces or the layering of paint pigments or the translation of bits to pixels is a necessary condition for the aesthetic experience, but is utterly insufficient by itself to account for that experience.

Bringing the metaphor home now, consider your own idea—your thoughts and mental image—of the Mona Lisa. From an analytic perspective, your idea is the product of many interrelated neurochemical events. From a synthetic perspective, it is an immediate personal experience—an inner sense of what the painting means to you and how you feel about it. Then consider the actual woman, Mona Lisa herself, as she sits posing for the artist. From an analytic perspective she can be explained as a kind of computerized sum (or product) of her biological pieces working together, her smile caused by a complicated sequence of neurological and muscular events and a history of behavioral conditioning. But to understand her would require a larger synthetic perspective, in which she is seen as a person, a unique individual whose smile is motivated by complex feelings about her situation and, more important, by an eternally mysterious act of self-consciousness. If there is any doubt about which of these two equally valid perspectives is the more valuable, you need only ask yourself how you would feel about it if *you* were Mona Lisa.

Scientific Observation: A Matter of Perspective and a Matter of Values

The complementary analytic and synthetic pictures I have just painted of Mona Lisa—as a mechanistic biological "object" and as a motivated self-reflective person—are typical of the Medical Model's I–It diagnostic perspective versus the Psychotherapeutic Model's I–Thou empathic perspective. These are not just alternative kinds of data we can collect about human beings. They are alternative views of what really matters about a human being and what matters in life generally. At that level—the level of values—our need to choose between the two perspectives is a moral obligation, as it was in the case of the alternative pictures of Otoyo as seen by Yasumoto and by Red Beard, and of the alternative pictures of gorillas as seen by gun-toting ethologists and by George Schaller. We know which perspective Otoyo found more valuable—and was the higher moral choice—and there can be little doubt about which was more valuable (and moral) for the gorillas.

I hope this makes it clear why I consider the Medical Model, like the analytic perspective generally, to be an unacceptable philosophical choice. At the level of science, there is no doubt that it provides valid and useful information. But at the level of values it is, quite literally, dehumanizing. In fact, the very goal of an analytic perspective is to remove the human element from scientific observation by treating the observed as an "It," a thing or event "out there," completely separate and different from the observer. The goal of the synthetic perspective is just the opposite: to incorporate the human element by taking into account the observer's participation in the observed, treating the observed as a "Thou," an entity that we can "identify" with because it is defined in terms of its relation to us.[1] This is true even in physics, where the mathematical "wave function" (the synthetic perspective) does not describe a detached object (an atomic particle) but rather a "probability wave" of experimental encounters: the range of possible instances in which the observer can define—or in effect create—the atomic particle in the very act of measuring it. Similarly in biology, the synthetic perspective entails an I–Thou relation in that it pictures an organism as a living creature, defined in terms of behaviors, functions, and purposes it has that are similar to our own. The analytic perspective conceptualizes the same organism as an electrochemical machine controlled by inorganic physical forces—an I–It attitude that ignores everything about the organism that would allow us to identify with it. Likewise in psychiatry, the synthetic perspective focuses on a person as a Thou: a self-reflective human being with thoughts, feelings, and intentions like ourselves. An analytic perspective treats the same person as an It: a biological organism like a laboratory animal, or a "case" of mental illness.

Reducing a Thou to an It: Collapsing the Wave Function

Bohr emphasized that there is a hierarchy of sciences, from physics (the simplest) through chemistry and biology to psychology/psychiatry (the most complex). Each level is characterized by an undefinable "element of wholeness," an irreducible quality of experience that uniquely typifies the phenomena of that particular science. In physics, the element of wholeness is called the *quantum of action.* In biology, it is *life* itself. In psychology, it is *consciousness.* In each case, the indivisibility of this element of wholeness is what allows the observer to identify with the observed, and in fact, to be properly understood, demands a synthetic perspective.[2]

Consider physics, for example. Modern physics began with the purely analytic perspective of Newtonian mechanics. All objects—whether atoms, billiard balls, or planets—were viewed as particles. The synthetic perspective was then established by quantum physics, which discovered that atomic particles can also be viewed as quantum waves (mathematically defined in terms of the quantum of action) and that it is actually their "wave nature" that gives shape and substance to the material world as we know it. If we removed the quantum of action—and with it the essential "waveness" of matter—from the universe, we could no longer distinguish between atoms, billiard balls, and planets. Everything would collapse into a single particle. In fact, this is just what happens (in a small way) whenever a physicist uses the analytic perspective to measure a subatomic particle at a particular place and time. Physicists actually refer to such measurements as *collapsing the wave function.*

I will explain this further in Chapter 8, but here is the basic idea: in order to show that an electron is a particle, the physicist must actually measure it, thereby reducing or "collapsing" the probability wave (the electron cloud) of its possible locations into a single dot on a photographic plate. Physicist Lawrence Bragg compares this collapsing through measurement to the way that time, in its passing, collapses an indeterminate future into an irrevocably determined past:

> Everything that has already happened is particles. Everything in the future is waves. . . . The advancing sieve of time coagulates waves into particles at the moment "Now."[2]

Bohr pointed out that a similar kind of collapsing occurs in every science when we try to observe things from an analytic perspective. In biology, for instance, there is no way to observe a living organism from a rigorously analytic perspective—that is, to determine the mechanical, chemical, and electrical details of its biological processes under controlled laboratory conditions—without killing the organism in the process. In other words, the analytic perspective collapses the organismic function, eliminating the element of wholeness—the very life—that makes the organism biological in the first place. Likewise in psychiatry. To observe a human experience analytically (i.e., in terms of its underlying neurological processes or statistical behavioral patterns), the psychiatrist must ignore the element of wholeness—the quality of consciousness—that makes it a uniquely human experience in the first place. Instead, he must treat it as if it were a nonhuman (unconscious) biological event, reducing the mystery of human awareness (collapsing the experiencing function) to a brain process or to an instinctive or conditioned behavior.

It's a Scientific Fact: The Psychotherapeutic Model Is Better Than the Medical Model

Summing it up, we might say that a particle is a collapsed wave with the quantum taken out of it; the past is the collapsed future with the possibility taken out of it; a body or biochemical system is a collapsed organism with the life taken out of it; and a human organism is a collapsed person with the consciousness taken out of him or her. In that sense, it can be said that the synthetic perspective is always better than the analytic because it captures the essential quality that makes things what they are—the element of wholeness—in a way that an analytic perspective (which by definition eliminates the element of wholeness) never can.

Consider what this implies. For any pair of complementary perspectives—wave versus particle, living organism versus electrochemical machine, self-aware human being versus behaviorally complex organism—the synthetic perspective is not only more valuable than the analytic perspective but actually includes the analytic within a more comprehensive framework—collapsing into the analytic perspective when the element of wholeness is ignored. In physics, for example, the mathematics of the quantum wave function includes the simple analytic variables that, if measured, would define a particle within the complex synthetic terms that define a wave. In biology, the theory of evolution includes the analytic concept of mutating DNA within the larger synthetic picture of an organism's adaptation to its changing environment. In psychiatry, the Psychotherapeutic Model includes the Medical Model's analytic concept of a chemical imbalance in the brain within its larger synthetic picture of an inner conflict in the soul.

What's Needed?

What modern psychiatry requires, then, is an expanded understanding of science that incorporates the analytic observation of the brain within a larger synthetic perspective on the soul. This larger perspective would have to include consciousness—the element of wholeness—in a scientific method for observing not only the symptoms, but also the private subjective experience of mental illness. In Chapter 8 I will explain how the Psychotherapeutic Model provides just this needed perspective, and how the psychotherapeutic process can be understood not only as a clinical method of treatment but also as a scientific method of observation that allows for a genuine science of subjectivity.

8. A Science of Subjectivity: Complementarity and Consciousness

The story of the ugly duckling is well known. Other ducks called him ugly and looked down on him until it turned out that he was not a misfit of a duckling but a specimen of another, beautiful kind of bird, a swan. Psychoanalysis, largely, though by no means entirely, a matter of introspection and empathy, is treated as though it were a purely physicalistic discipline, and scolded and berated for its deficiencies as such. It is time to understand that the ugly duckling is not a duckling at all.

—Robert Waelder, "Psychoanalysis, Scientific Method, and Philosophy"

The Voice of Science

One of my goals in writing this book is to help readers who have never experienced psychotherapy get a feeling for what it is really like. This would be a difficult task under any circumstances, but in the Age of the Brain it is even more so. The current climate of opinion makes it very difficult to write about psychotherapy in a way that will be taken seriously. The primary obstacle is a widespread popular prejudice that psychotherapy—especially long-term dynamic psychotherapy—is unscientific. Every major newspaper and weekly magazine in the United States has carried dozens of reports in recent years about how medication has revolutionized the practice of psychiatry, replacing long-term psychotherapy as the treatment of choice for all forms of mental illness. These reports invariably emphasize the scientifically proven effectiveness of medication and the lack of evidence for the effectiveness of long-term psychotherapy.

In fact, these reports are highly misleading. It is certainly true that in very short-term (six to twelve weeks) research studies, medication has consistently proven more effective than psychotherapy in reducing symptoms of every mental illness studied. But as Joseph Glenmullen points out in his recent book, *Prozac Backlash,*[1] there is also an important but not-much-publicized body of research proving that short-term (three to nine months) psychotherapy *alone* is actually *more* effective than short-term medication in reducing symptoms over the longer term (as measured at one- to four-year follow-up visits) for patients with depression and anxiety disorders.

Unfortunately, none of this research—even that cited by Glenmullen—bears much resemblance at all to real-life treatment situations. For one thing, it has been limited entirely to short-term treatment. For another, it has studied only cognitive-behavioral, interpersonal, and supportive forms of psychotherapy done (typically by inexperienced therapists) according to rigid protocols that must be followed rather mechanically so as to minimize the therapeutic impact of the therapist's uniquely personal qualities and talents. Finally, and perhaps most importantly, the research has examined treatment outcomes *only* with respect to the swimming-pool goal of symptom reduction. No scientific researcher has *ever,* to my knowledge, tried to compare medication with long-term (more than one year) dynamic psychotherapy done by well-trained therapists who work with transference and countertransference, or to compare treatment outcomes in terms of long-term quality of life, mutuality of relationships, and personal growth. This is hardly surprising, considering that treatment-outcome research has been funded primarily by pharmaceutical manufacturers, who naturally prefer to invest their research dollars in studies designed to show their products to best advantage. Moreover, any controlled scientific study of long-term psychotherapy would be prohibitively expensive, especially given the funding priorities of the NIMH in the Age of the Brain. But perhaps the most important reason for the absence of research on the effectiveness of long-term psychotherapy is that most people, including most researchers, are simply unaware of the crucial differences in goals and methods between the various short-term problem-focused psychotherapies, that are aimed (like medication) at symptom relief and emotional stabilization, and long-term dynamic psychotherapy, which promotes emotional growth and inner freedom—self-actualization—through an introspective focus on inner conflict and transference.

The result of all these factors has been a pervasive, scientifically endorsed cultural prejudice—reinforced by doctors, insurance companies, and the popular media—that long-term psychotherapy is obsolete and medication can now do everything psychotherapy used to do, only faster and better. This was the central message of the hugely popular best-seller *Listening to Prozac*, in which psychiatrist Peter Kramer marshaled a great mass of scientific evidence to conclude that *"[i]n doing just what psychotherapy aims to do, Prozac performs chemically what has heretofore been an intimate interpersonal function"* (my italics). My purpose in this chapter will be to show that Kramer's conclusion and the antipsychotherapeutic prejudice it embodies are based on a radical misunderstanding of the nature of scientific evidence.

The Voice of Experience

If you stop to think about it, both common sense and everyday personal experience should tell you that Kramer's message cannot possibly be correct. Chemistry may be compatible with intimacy, but it is certainly not the same "interpersonal function." As anyone who has ever been infatuated or infuriated can appreciate, chemistry is the basis for an I–It relationship, in which I react to the other person as an object—a sex object or other fantasy figure, a good guy or bad guy, an ally or opponent in a game. These I–It patterns of relationship are encoded in the brain and can be influenced by chemistry, but they are very far from intimacy. Rather, they are stereotyped emotional patterns (like our repetitive unconscious childhood scenarios)—instinctive responses to generic interpersonal triggers. Intimacy, on the contrary, is a conscious choice in relation to an individual person. It does include an element of chemistry, but it requires a more important, nonchemical element as well: the platonic love, or agape, of an I–Thou relationship, in which I experience and value the other person as a unique human being like myself.

Dynamic psychotherapy is a method specifically designed to transform chemistry into intimacy. It expands our capacity for I–Thou relatedness by freeing us from the "repetition compulsion" of our reflexive I–It interaction patterns. It does this—makes us more capable of intimacy—by making the unconscious conscious: enabling us to consciously feel the emotions that have been unconsciously generating our automatic interpersonal responses. In that sense, it is especially clear that no medication can ever do what dynamic psychotherapy aims to do, simply because no medication works by making the unconscious conscious! Medication works by adjusting brain chemistry in a way that makes us feel more comfortable and allows us to function—play the game of life—better. Making the unconscious conscious does something very different. Not only does it expand our capacity for intimacy but it allows us to become more fully ourselves.[2]

Making the Unconscious Conscious: Where's the Evidence?

Unfortunately, those who listen to the voice of modern science now dismiss the idea of "making the unconscious conscious" as a Freudian fantasy. Scholar Frederick Crews, for example—author of numerous attacks on Freud and Freudian psychotherapy—argues that there can be no such thing as making the unconscious conscious because science has proved that there is no such thing as a repressed unconscious![3] (Recall that repression is the psychological mechanism through which disturbing emotions and childhood scenarios are kept unconscious.)

This is a startling claim, which could be very damaging to psychotherapy if it were accepted as true. Yet the only scientific evidence Crews puts forward against Freud's idea of a repressed unconscious is a published review of psychological research that concludes, "there is no controlled laboratory evidence supporting the concept of repression." Even if this conclusion were true (which, as it happens, it is not),[4] the very idea that a lack of controlled laboratory evidence ever could invalidate the theory of repression is seriously misguided. It reveals a fundamental misunderstanding of what scientific evidence is and how it can properly be used. Crews himself is not responsible for this misunderstanding. He is a literary scholar with no particular expertise in science. He simply took an already popular misconception about science and used it in the service of his antipsychotherapeutic prejudice. The fact that the distinguished *New York Review of Books* then saw fit to publish Crews's unfounded anti-Freudian diatribe shows just how pervasive the misunderstanding of science in our culture really is.

The truth is, we do not need controlled laboratory evidence to be certain that repression exists. Repression is a self-evident fact of everyday life—a simple extension of something everyone has experienced: the tendency to block unpleasant thoughts and feelings out of awareness. Many of us have also experienced repression directly, in the moment of its lifting—for example, becoming suddenly aware of an unpleasant emotional tendency that other people have always seen in us but that we had never before recognized or felt within ourselves. Why should we need a laboratory experiment to convince ourselves of something we can know directly from our own inner experience? The idea that we do—that no knowledge can be considered scientific, valid, or true unless it has been proved in a controlled laboratory experiment—is a modern aberration, a radical misconception about scientific knowledge that may serve ideological prejudices (and managed care business practices) but clearly does not serve the pursuit of truth.

To appreciate just what is wrong with our common ideas about scientific evidence, consider a piece of dialogue from the movie *Contact*, where the scientist (Jodie Foster) challenges the minister (Matthew McConaughey) about his belief in God:

"How do you know you're not deluding yourself? . . . I'd need proof."
"Proof. [*Pensive pause*] Did you love your father?"
"What!?"
"Your dad. Did you love him?"
"Yes, very much."
"Prove it."

The minister knew, beyond any need for proof, that the scientist would have no answer. He knew that, in the case of love (unlike repression), it really is true that no controlled laboratory evidence exists, or can even be imagined, to support the concept. But he also knew that this is irrelevant. No one—not the most myopic of research scientists, not even Frederick Crews himself— would consider the absence of laboratory evidence to be a valid argument against the existence of love. In fact, if we want to prove that love exists—or repression, or the cold war, or racism, or anything that we know about primarily because we can feel it—then a controlled laboratory experiment is the last rather than the first place we should be looking for evidence.

In the pantheon of important questions that human beings can ask about themselves and the world around them, *only the very simplest questions can be answered in a laboratory.* Only in physics and chemistry are the relevant variables few enough that scientists can potentially know and control all of them in an experiment. For anything as complicated as a biological organism— especially a self-reflective biological organism—there will inevitably be many variables that cannot be controlled in a lab. In fact, for the study of human consciousness, it is highly unlikely that we can ever know for sure what all the relevant variables are!

Climbing the Ladder of Science: From Physics to Biology to Psychiatry

By way of illustration, imagine that you are a scientist who wants to study the behavior of elementary subatomic particles. Your experimental apparatus will be a cyclotron, or particle accelerator. You put a few atoms in the apparatus, fire it up, and wait for the results to appear on your readout screen. After you have accumulated enough results, you will look for a repeated pattern that can be described in a mathematical formula and used to make precise predictions of subatomic particle behavior in general. (This is admittedly an oversimplification, but you get the idea.)

Now suppose you become bored with elementary particles and decide you want to study something more complex—say the mating habits of chimpanzees—only you aren't sure how to go about this scientifically. If you put a pair of chimpanzees in your particle accelerator and fire it up, you will end up with two dead chimpanzees on your hands and nothing on your readout screen. Does this mean it is impossible to say anything scientifically valid about the mating behavior of chimpanzees? Of course not. It simply means there are far too many variables influencing chimpanzee behavior for you to be able to study it with the methods of physics. The first rule of science is that *the method of observation must be appropriate to the phenomena being observed.* That is why the science of animal behavior—ethology—doesn't use particle accelerators or try to express its findings in mathematical form. Instead, it uses detailed naturalistic observations of animals in the wild over long periods of time, looking for repeated patterns of behavior that can be described precisely enough in words to permit accurate predictions—for instance about how chimpanzees will mate or not mate under specified conditions.

Now suppose you get bored again and want to move on from chimpanzees to study human behavior instead. You will need yet another method of observation. Human beings living in society are far too complex and diverse to be amenable to the kind of naturalistic observation that works for chimpanzees living in the wild. Unlike the stereotyped, instinctive behavior of animals, human behavior varies so much from individual to individual that very few patterns can be identified precisely enough for us to be able to predict who will do what under which conditions. In psychiatry, for instance, it is impossible even to define depression exactly. There are no depressive behavior patterns that apply in the same way to every patient who might be considered depressed, because each patient experiences and reacts to his particular version of depression somewhat differently. For this reason, psychiatrists have traditionally relied on detailed individual case reports—like the stories of Bill, Anne, and Joe—in their efforts to study mental illness.

Unfortunately, such reports are nowadays considered merely "anecdotal" evidence and therefore unscientific. As narrative descriptions of individual patients' private experience, case reports are inevitably colored by the subjectivity of both the patient and the psychiatrist-narrator. This is thought to be at odds with the proper scientific goal of objectivity—defining generalities and regularities that apply to all members of a class, or to every occurrence of a particular kind of event, so that we can then use these well-defined regularities to make reliable predictions.

Can There Be a Science of Subjectivity?

Now you might think that, since we all share the same human nature (however varied its individual manifestations may be), an adequately detailed study of one patient's subjective experience could easily reveal generalities and regularities that would apply to all people. It is fairly likely, for instance, that all people in all ages and all cultures have experienced the same basic human emotions, so it stands to reason that we should be able to identify common patterns in our emotional experience that, if true for one person, must be true for all people. In fact, this was exactly Freud's reasoning a hundred years ago when he developed psychoanalysis as a scientific method for observing the inner life of individual patients. In applying this method to his patients and to himself, he discovered that there is indeed a general pattern in the emotional life of all people, a universal emotional scenario, reflected in the mythical story of Oedipus Rex, that involves an inner prohibition against anxiety-provoking sexual desire. In elaborating on this discovery of the so-called Oedipus complex, Freud identified three major elements of what ultimately became his general theory of inner conflict: first, the *dynamic unconscious,* the disturbing unconscious emotions pressing toward consciousness; second, *repression,* the unconscious mechanism that prohibits these emotions from becoming conscious; and third, *signal anxiety,* the inner alarm that warns us when a prohibited emotion is threatening to become conscious and activates the mechanism of repression.

To some readers it may be surprising that I write about Freudian psycho-analysis as if it were a legitimate scientific method, considering how regularly Freud is vilified nowadays as the perpetrator of everything unscientific in the field of human psychology. In fact, I believe that Freud's psychoanalytic method is the only legitimate scientific method for the study of human subjectivity—the systematic attempt to find generalities and regularities in human emotional experience. Of course, as some of his critics have rightly pointed out, Freud himself did not always properly adhere to his own method.[5] Moreover, the method has been refined considerably since he first developed it. The current "state of the science" is pretty much what I summarized in Chapter 3 as the six steps of the psychotherapeutic process. This too may come as a surprise. Since I have described the psychotherapeutic process in such poetic terms as "the inward journey" and "listening to the soul," how, you might ask, can I claim it as a scientific method of observation? For that matter, how can a process of healing also be a method of observation? The answer to these questions requires a closer look at what is involved in the psychotherapeutic process of "making the unconscious conscious" and a reexamination of what is required for an observation to be considered legitimately scientific.

The Psychotherapeutic "Laboratory"

Consider first the interpersonal setting in which the psychotherapeutic process takes place. The formal psychotherapy session is a kind of virtual laboratory for observing subjective experience. The structure of regular meetings and the technical rules for conducting the interaction (which the therapist learns from his training and the patient learns from the therapist) make a psychotherapy session uniquely different from the conversations of everyday life. It is designed to focus exclusively on the inner life of only one of the participants in the interaction. More specifically, it is designed to promote the process of unconscious emotion becoming conscious through the transference, under controlled conditions that facilitate its observation. The act of observation itself is the introspective equivalent of a laboratory measurement in quantum physics. It brings an indistinct, previously unrecognized emotion into the focus of immediate awareness as a clearly identifiable feeling. In so doing it actually changes the state of the observed—makes the unconscious conscious—even in the moment of observing it. It is in producing this change of state that the act of observation also becomes a healing event—a consciousness-expanding, self-actualizing experience of the resolution of inner conflict.

But Is It Really Scientific?

Still, however healing it may be, this transformation of the unconscious into consciousness in the act of listening to the soul, in the context of a therapeutic relationship, will no doubt strike most people as anything but scientific. It is a uniquely subjective experience, after all, the product of a personal interaction between patient and therapist and, more important, of a private, invisible, internal interaction between the patient (the observer) and his own inner state (the observed). This is certainly not the kind of objective, measurable, reproducible laboratory observation that would be considered scientific by current standards. But the point I am trying to establish in this chapter is that those standards are quite unreasonable. In fact, as it turns out, they are based on an outmoded nineteenth-century model of scientific objectivity that was made obsolete three-quarters of a century ago by the discoveries of quantum physics.

Here we come back to the principle of complementarity. To put it simply—in terms of basic concepts introduced in Chapter 7—the problem with our current scientific standards is that they are based entirely on the analytic perspective and so always miss the forest for the trees. This is a very general statement, of course, but for readers who appreciated the point of the Mona Lisa example from Chapter 7 and of the dialogue from *Contact* quoted above, it will be enough for you to understand exactly what I mean. For many readers, though, and especially for those scientifically minded readers whose basic assumptions I am here challenging, I know that a more detailed explanation is necessary.

Science Is in the Mind of the Observer

The outmoded nineteenth-century model of scientific objectivity on which our current standards are based is known as *positivism* or *empiricism*. According to this model, scientific objectivity requires an absolute separation between the observing subject and the observed object. The object and its behavior are assumed to exist "out there," independent of any act of observation. The underlying belief is that our knowledge of the world comes only through sensory experience, and that scientific (i.e., objective) knowledge can come only through sensory experience that is measurable, quantifiable, and ultimately visible, either to the naked eye or to scientific instruments that provide visual readouts.

Although not formalized until the nineteenth century, positivism had been the prevailing philosophy of the natural sciences from the time of René Descartes and Isaac Newton. Classical physics—Newtonian "mechanics"— represented the positivist ideal of objectivity because its mathematical equations could describe the behavior of "objects" without any reference to the observing "subject" or his measuring instruments. But by the third decade of the twentieth century, physicists began to realize that this model of objectivity was inadequate. It worked only for relatively slow-moving, massive, "mechanical" objects (like bullets and billiard balls), and even then only as an approximation. First Einstein's theory of relativity and then the new theory of quantum mechanics showed that, for very fast-moving nonmechanical "objects" (like light) and for very small ones (like subatomic particles), a crucial element of nonpositivistic subjectivity—a dependence of the observed on the perspective of the observer—enters inevitably into the process of observation.

In the famous wave–particle paradox of light, for instance, it was found that when light is observed using one experimental apparatus it appears in the form of electromagnetic waves, but when observed with a different apparatus it appears as discrete "particles," or *quanta,* of energy called photons. No apparatus could be constructed, or even imagined (Einstein tried in vain for thirty years), in which both forms of light could be demonstrated in one experiment. Similarly, in the uncertainty relation developed by physicist Werner Heisenberg, it was discovered that one apparatus allows us to measure the position of an atomic object and another its energy, but that measuring either variable makes it impossible to measure the other, so either the energy or the position of the object remains necessarily uncertain.

This unavoidable dualism in the observations of quantum physics implied an intrinsic subjectivity in the process of scientific observation, in which what we observe depends on how we observe it, and what we end up defining as reality is determined by the lens through which we choose to look at reality. In fact, this element of subjectivity even entered into the mathematics. The defining equation of quantum physics—the "wave function"—did not refer to the behavior of actual objects "out there" but only to the possible measurements that could be made of *states of a system* (i.e., states of interaction between a nonmechanical, invisible, quantum object and the mechanical measuring instrument on which that object leaves a visible mark or trace). In other words, the wave function referred not to the object itself but to the subject's interaction with the object—the measured "impression" of the observed on the observer. As Heisenberg explained it,

> [W]e can no longer talk of the behavior of the particle apart from the process of observation. . . . The question whether these particles exist in space and time "in themselves" can thus no longer be posed in this form. We can only talk about the processes that occur when, through the interaction of the particle with . . . a measuring instrument, the behavior of the particle is to be disclosed. The conception of the objective reality of the elementary particles has thus evaporated in a curious way, not into the fog of some new, obscure, or not yet understood reality concept, but into the transparent clarity of a mathematics that represents no longer the behavior of the elementary particles but rather our knowledge of this behavior.[6]

The Principle of Complementarity Revisited

It was Heisenberg's mentor, Niels Bohr, who first recognized that the quantum wave function was a clear mathematical refutation of the core assumption of positivism—that an object can be observed as it "really" is, "out there," independently of the subject observing it. Bohr pointed out that a physicist observing electrons is not really looking at electrons but rather at a pattern of scattered dots or circles on a photographic plate, which he then interprets as the impression either of electron particles or electron waves. It is these "impressions" that the wave function describes as states of the system—records of the interaction between observed and observer, whose configuration (dots or circles) will depend both on the objective nature of electrons (whatever that is) and on the subjective choice of experimental setup. Bohr's genius was to realize that the resulting dualism of particles and waves reflects not two mutually exclusive objective states of electron nature, but two mutually exclusive subjective states of *human* nature. The two fundamentally different "ways of knowing" electrons point to an irreducible dualism in the way the human mind gains knowledge through experiencing, whether it be the experiencing of electrons, of light, of life, or of the mind itself.

Bohr proposed that the mathematics of the wave function constituted a new paradigm of scientific objectivity. In this paradigm, every observation is understood as a partly subjective event, not a direct perception of an object "out there," but an *experience* involving some kind of *interaction* between a subject and an object of the experience. The object that is observed will inevitably reflect the subject's way of observing it—the analytic or synthetic framework or "lens" through which he chooses to interact with the object.

The problem with positivism, Bohr pointed out, is that it allows for only one of these lenses—the analytic—and therefore leaves scientists with a decidedly myopic view of the world, valid as far as it goes but in the end doing for science just what blinders do for a horse. By limiting the observational data to quantifiable sense perceptions, it helps scientists focus on a narrow goal in front of their nose, but it keeps them from noticing the big picture as it presents itself in their own consciousness.

Science and Consciousness

As you might expect, this positivist obliviousness to the big picture is most apparent precisely in the (so-called) scientific study of consciousness, about which we hear so much nowadays. Scientists like Francis Crick, for instance, who believe that we are "nothing but a pack of neurons," have fostered a widespread but misconceived assumption that the scientific study of consciousness means the study of brain processes that (supposedly) produce consciousness. This assumption violates the principle of complementarity. It confuses the neurological *conditions* of consciousness (the analytic perspective) with the actual experiencing of consciousness (the synthetic perspective).

It should be self-evident that the only way we can possibly know anything—scientific or otherwise—about conscious experience is through observing someone's conscious experiencing of it! That's why it makes eminently good sense to think of the psychotherapeutic process as a scientific method of observation and of individual case reports as a valid form of scientific knowledge. The positivist objection that psychotherapy cannot be scientific because it depends on a subjective interaction between the observer and the observed is clearly untenable, given that it was just this sort of interaction in the observations of quantum physics that disproved positivism in the first place. In fact, the similarity between the observational interaction in psychotherapy and in quantum physics was fundamental to Bohr's understanding of complementarity.[7] He pointed out that, just as we can have no direct sensory perception of subatomic particles (contrary to the requirements of positivism) but only of the visible impressions they make on our measuring instruments, so too we can have no direct awareness of unconscious mental processes but only of the discernible (and rememberable) impressions they make on our observing consciousness. Furthermore, just as the experimental measurement of an atomic object changes the state of the object (into a particle at a certain location or a wave with a certain energy) in the very act of measuring it, so too the psychotherapeutic observation of inner experience changes the state of the experience—makes the unconscious conscious (as a thought or a feeling)—even in the process of experiencing it.

Bohr then went on to propose that since all scientific observations involve this sort of subjective influence of the observer on the observed, the proper task of any science should be not to eliminate the element of subjectivity but rather to recognize it and describe it objectively—"unambiguously" as he put it—in words of the common language. In fact, Bohr defined science generally as nothing more, or less, than this: *the unambiguous description of human experience in words of the common language.*

Science and Language

Bohr rejected the positivist notion that a scientific description had to be a mathematical one. All knowledge consists ultimately of verbal descriptions, he insisted, even the mathematical laws of physics, whose terms are merely symbols for words of the common language (mass, velocity, acceleration, force, energy, distance, time, etc.). In fact, the reason physics can be described in mathematical terms at all is that the phenomena it deals with are fairly simple. Yet even in quantum physics, Bohr pointed out, the mathematics alone is not enough to describe observed phenomena unambiguously but must be supplemented by a common-language description of the experiment. Recall that the mathematical terms of the wave function do not refer to a visible object but rather to mutually exclusive interactions of an invisible object and a visible measuring instrument. Accordingly, a clear verbal description of that measuring instrument and what appears on it is essential to a complete description of quantum phenomena.[8]

Bohr emphasized this requirement of a nonmathematical, common-language description in quantum physics because he saw it as the key to objectivity in all areas of human experience:

> The fact that in atomic physics, where we are concerned with regularities of unsurpassed exactness, objective description can be achieved only by including in the account of the phenomena explicit reference to the experimental conditions, emphasizes in a novel manner the inseparability of knowledge and our possibilities of inquiry. We are here concerned with a general epistemological lesson illuminating our position in many other fields of human interest.[9]

Bohr's point was that the objectivity of a description does not depend on its terms being mathematical, but on their being used *unambiguously.* This was a crucial concept. An unambiguous (i.e., objective) description is one framed in words of the common language that are defined and used clearly enough that everyone (in principle at least) can understand the described object of experience in the same way and can thus be in a position to repeat and validate the observation.

Although Bohr never spelled it out, I believe he viewed objectivity as inherent in the common language itself. What makes it common, after all, is that everyone understands its terms in more or less the same way, because these terms capture something objective or universal or absolute in experience. But of course "more or less" is not enough for an unambiguous description, so this inherent objectivity of language must be supplemented by carefully describing not only what is observed (the object) but how it is observed (the subject). In other words, an unambiguous objective description must include a description of the observer's frame of reference (way of knowing), not just in quantum physics but in every area of human experience. This would enable a reader to identify with the subjectivity of the observer and see the same object because he sees it in effect through the same eyes (or measuring instruments). Such an observation would be objective in the sense that it could be consensually validated, independent of the subjectivity of any individual observer.

A Complete Scientific Description Is a Complementary Description

Bohr's general solution to the problem of scientific objectivity, then, was as follows: Given that all knowledge consists of verbal descriptions of experience, and given that every experience entails an interaction between a subject and an object, then an objective (i.e., unambiguous) description must be one that describes an observational interaction from both sides, the *subjec*tive and the *objec*tive. In quantum physics, this means describing an atomic object both in the mathematical terms of the wave function and in plain English as a visible mark left at a particular place on a particular measuring device. In biology, it means (for example) describing animal behavior both as a social pattern of courtship and also as a series of biochemical events. In psychiatry it would mean describing a patient's emotion both as an inner experience that is known through listening to the soul and as a measurable biochemical event or an external behavior that is visible in the patient's facial expression and body language.

In claiming that the psychotherapeutic process is a legitimate scientific method, then, I am arguing for the principle of complementarity as a comprehensive paradigm of science that allows not only for the study of the objective physical world but for the study of subjective human experience as well. In this paradigm, individual case reports are an absolutely essential form of scientific knowledge, whose validity depends on the observations (individual experiences) being described unambiguously in words of the common language, in a way that takes explicitly into account the inevitable subjective interaction of the observer and the observed.

Unfortunately, few psychiatrists today—indeed few scientists outside of quantum physics—understand the principle of complementarity. Medical Model psychiatry in particular, and the biological sciences generally, are still operating on the obsolete standards of positivism, taking seriously only the analytic, reductionistic framework of what can be seen and measured. Sociobiologist E. O. Wilson is a well-known spokesman for this pervasive "scientistic" attitude, most notably in his recent best-seller *Consilience: The Unity of*

Knowledge.[10] Unlike Bohr, who argues that the unity of knowledge lies ultimately in the mind of the observer, with its intrinsically dualistic perspective, Wilson argues that all forms of knowledge, including the natural sciences, the social sciences, psychology, and the humanities, can ultimately be boiled down (with the help of neural science) to one simplistic framework of observation and explanation:

> The central idea of the consilience world view is that all tangible phenomena, from the birth of stars to the workings of social institutions, are based on material processes that are ultimately reducible, however long and tortuous the sequences, to the laws of physics.

I consider it nothing short of alarming that such a narrow and misleading view of science continues to be accepted as the gold standard of truth in our culture almost three-quarters of a century after it was decisively invalidated by quantum physics. Of particular concern to me is that positivism supports the widespread prejudice against psychotherapy. It panders to our fear of consciousness, by providing a scientifically endorsed rationalization for either ignoring inner experience altogether or reducing it to the simplistic terms of laboratory science. Common sense alone should tell us that this approach misses what is most important in human life.

Subjective Experiences and "Objective" Tests

At this point, I'm sure some readers must be finding it hard to believe my claim that Medical Model psychiatry ignores inner experience altogether. After all, even psychiatrists who do nothing but prescribe medication must talk to their patients first! Doesn't that imply that they have to be taking the patient's subjective experience into account? Well, not really. My point is that both the questions these psychiatrists think to ask and the answers they are then able to hear from their patients are dictated by the very narrow assumptions of positivist science. This means that when a Medical Model psychiatrist does talk to a patient, he is not participating in an open-ended conversation in which he is trying to *understand* that patient's inner experience as an individual. Rather he is conducting a highly focused interview in which he is trying to *categorize* the patient's experience to match a diagnosis and treatment strategy. According to the Medical Model, the most proper scientific way to do this is through the use of standardized questionnaires known as *rating scales*.

Rating scales seek to eliminate the subjectivity of inner experience by "objectifying" and quantifying it. They translate subjective experiences into objective test questions, treating them not as conscious experiences of individual patients but as a statistical distribution of numerical scores across a large population of patients. The best-known scales of this type are those used in the study of depression: Beck's Depression Inventory (BDI), a simple questionnaire that a patient can fill out in the waiting room; and the Hamilton Rating Scale for Depression (HAM-D), a more elaborate questionnaire that the psychiatrist fills out, based on a structured, standardized, diagnostic interview. Both questionnaires measure the severity of depressive symptoms (suicidal thoughts, sleep disturbance, loss of appetite, feelings of hopelessness, helplessness, mistrust, anxiety, low self-esteem, etc.) according to the format "very much__ somewhat__ not very__ not at all__." These checked-off responses are then translated into numbers, added up, and used to determine whether the type and level of distress "counts" as a clinical depression—in other words, whether it is far enough above the median score of the general population to be statistically "abnormal." If it is, then the patient is eligible to be studied in double-blind, placebo-controlled treatment-outcome studies whose purpose is to predict the mathematical probability that any depressed patient will respond to antidepressant treatment (i.e., have a statistically significant improvement in his BDI or HAM-D score after six weeks to three months of treatment).

The organizing positivist assumption implicit in the use of rating scales is that *the best way to be objective about a person is to treat the person as an object.* Rating scales do this by defining a patient not as a person but as a collection of visible behaviors (check marks on a questionnaire), happening "out there," completely separate from the researcher who observes, interprets, and quantifies the behaviors. But, as we have seen, this way of being objective ignores the most important lesson of twentieth-century science—that the process of observation always involves an interaction between the observer and the observed. Reducing a patient's inner experience to its visible by-products may permit us to answer questions like "What are the chances that John's questionnaire response about hopelessness will change after three weeks of taking Prozac?" But it leaves us no room even to ask a question like "If John's questionnaire response does change, is it because he feels genuinely better or because his participation in a scientific study has given him a false sense of hope that will last only as long as the researcher continues to show an interest in how he feels?"[11]

I submit that a model of science that encourages us to be content with answers to the first question without offering any way even to imagine trying to answer the second has completely lost touch with the human nature it claims to be studying. It may solve the problem of how to classify people, but in doing so it creates the far more serious problem of dehumanizing people. Fortunately, there is an alternative.

A Psychotherapeutic Science of Subjectivity

Suppose that John is a patient who, after feeling hopeless and depressed for several months due to a career disappointment, begins a course of twice-a-week psychotherapy along with Prozac. In his psychotherapy he identifies a long-standing tendency to depressive reactions based on "low self-esteem." He relates this tendency to having been constantly criticized by his father as a child. He feels somewhat relieved by this explanation but when his depression then begins to improve, he isn't sure whether to attribute the improvement to his new "insight" or to the Prozac. Then his therapist goes away for a three-week vacation; within days, John's depression and hopelessness return full force.

At this point, John is in a position to ask himself the sort of question posed above: When he was feeling so much better before his therapist went away, was it a genuine feeling (i.e., a stable change in mood and self-esteem, due either to the Prozac or to the insight) or was it a temporary euphoria, based on some unconscious and unstable feeling about his relationship with the therapist (i.e., on the transference)? The answer to such a question can have important ramifications for John's treatment, but it requires the kind of judgment about private inner experience that can easily be colored by wishful thinking and/or theoretical prejudice. Philosopher of science Adolf Grünbaum, for instance, would argue that neither John nor his therapist could ever answer the question reliably, because John will always tend to produce the answer he believes the therapist wants to hear, and the therapist will always tend to produce the answer that fits his preconceived theoretical assumptions.

But now imagine the same scenario amplified with a few details from the therapist's private experience. Suppose that John's therapist has had a feeling all along that John's insight was somewhat superficial—more of a solution to an intellectual puzzle than a new awareness of previously unconscious feelings. During sessions, whenever there has been a silence of more than a few seconds, the therapist has felt a subtle pressure from John, as if John was waiting for him to speak, expecting him to say something helpful. The therapist has noticed himself responding to this pressure by trying too hard to be helpful, instead of simply waiting and allowing John to feel his own discomfort with the silences. This interactive pattern of transference and countertransference suggests that John's good feeling from his treatment has been unstable all along, predicated on the therapist's ongoing active support. Imagine, then, that the therapist offers the following interpretation: "Perhaps your state of feeling good or feeling depressed was always more dependent than we both realized on your sense of our relationship—how you were feeling about me and how you imagined I was feeling about you—and perhaps that changed when I left for vacation." The interpretation has a big impact. It opens up a whole new area of John's experience. He recalls other times, both with his mother and in his adult relationships with women, when he has had a great deal of difficulty with separations or with situations where the woman was temporarily unavailable. Over the next few days, he reviews his history of transient depressions and recognizes that almost every one of them was associated with a life situation in which he felt abandoned in some way. Eventually, he comes to realize that he tends to start feeling bad about himself whenever he is alone for any length of time, and that he has always organized his life so that he never has to spend too much time by himself.

Dr. Grünbaum might argue that John's new insight is no more reliable than his original insight, and that both insights could easily have been motivated by a need to agree with or please his therapist. But such a need could hardly explain the therapist's ongoing countertransference response—his tendency, under the pressure of John's unspoken transference need for reassurance, to try too hard to be helpful. This response suggests that John has been maintaining his good feeling only by eliciting continual reassuring support from the therapist. Such a consistently repeated response in the therapist would stand as independent evidence—something the therapist observes in his own inner experience that corroborates what John observes in himself—validating the correctness of John's new insight that his tendency to become depressed is a response to experiences of feeling abandoned. Further validation would be available if the therapist manages to change his countertransference response pattern so that he can allow silences to continue until John chooses to speak. In this case we could formulate a *testable prediction* that John will become increasingly uncomfortable—that he will begin to feel more alone, abandoned, and depressed—in reaction to the therapist's silence.

What I am proposing here is that, by putting the therapist's experience and John's together, we can achieve a reliable, objective, scientific answer to the original question of whether John's good feeling was a genuine improvement or an unstable transference euphoria. More generally, I am proposing that the psychotherapeutic process is not only a treatment method but also a scientific method for observing and validating inner experience—a way of being objective about being subjective—that conforms to Niels Bohr's nonpositivistic model of scientific objectivity. Rather than considering the patient as an object completely separate from the researcher/observer, it considers the patient as a subject *in interaction* with the therapist/observer.

What Makes It Scientific Is Also What Makes It Work

It is important to emphasize that the psychological explanation I have just presented of John's depressive tendency would be scientifically valid whether or not it "worked" to relieve his depression. In fact, I would not expect that such an insight, by itself, could possibly relieve his depression. Certainly it would benefit John to recognize that he has a pattern of becoming depressed whenever he feels abandoned, rejected, or alone. In order to change such a pattern, however, he would need to reach a deeper level of self-awareness. Assuming that his depression is a symptom of anger turned against the self, I would not expect John's depressive reactions to change until he can fully experience his anger. More specifically, he would have to be able actually to feel his anger (perhaps even rage) about experiences of abandonment and rejection in his current life situation, in his childhood, in his relationships with women, and especially in his evolving transference relationship with his therapist.

To put it differently: Gaining scientific knowledge about emotional patterns does not produce lasting psychotherapeutic change unless it is pursued far enough to make the unconscious conscious. But ultimately these two processes—gaining scientific knowledge and making the unconscious conscious—do go hand in hand. In John's case, the first stage of scientific observation—defining John's pattern of depressive reactions to abandonment/rejection—was validated by the unconscious becoming conscious *in the therapist.* The therapist became aware that John's pattern involved a subtle interpersonal pressure (unconscious transference) that evoked a corollary pattern (countertransference) in him—a tendency to protect John from feeling abandoned/rejected by trying too hard to relieve the tension whenever there was a silence. The second stage of scientific observation—the unconscious becoming conscious *in John*—would come when the therapist can then refrain from alleviating John's unconscious transference pressure (when he stops jumping to fill the silences) and so allow John to feel his transference emotions consciously (i.e. his anger over feeling abandoned/rejected by the therapist's silence).

In other words, the two stages of observation go together to create a healing psychotherapeutic process. What makes the psychotherapeutic process scientific, then, is exactly what makes it work. Recall the lessons of complementarity: (1) every scientific observation involves an interaction between observer and observed, and (2) scientific objectivity requires an unambiguous description of that interaction from both the side of the observed and that of the observer. In the psychotherapeutic process, the observational interaction is the transference. Both the efficacy of the treatment and the objectivity and validity of the science will depend on the patient and the therapist both being able to experience the patient's transference clearly and vividly enough to put their experience into words. To the extent that the transference is in the patient (experienced in his own observing consciousness) an unambiguous description requires putting into words the details (associations and feelings) of his private self-experience, as in my account of a hypothetical self-analysis in Chapter 3. To the extent that the transference is in the interaction—with the psychotherapist as observer/experiencer and the patient as observed—an unambiguous description requires a detailed account of the impressions the patient's communications make on the therapist's consciousness. The idea is that we can achieve scientific objectivity only by fully describing the conditions of observation (the observer's way of knowing) along with the observation itself. In atomic physics this means describing the experimental apparatus. *In psychiatry it means describing the observer's state of mind.*[12]

With this in mind, I now want to deepen my discussion of the psychotherapeutic process by devoting the next four chapters to a detailed case report of one patient's psychotherapy. I will tell Mary's story not as a continuous sequence of events that happened over a period of weeks, months, or years, but as a dialectical process of unfolding awareness, happening in discontinuous moments of concentrated interaction with me, her therapist. I will describe this unfolding not only as Mary experienced it but also as I experienced it. My first purpose in doing so is to give the reader a realistic sense of the kinds of emotional interactions through which the unconscious actually becomes conscious in a long-term psychotherapeutic process. My second purpose is to present a case report that is *scientific* in the fullest sense of the term.

IV. Experiencing the Psychotherapeutic Process

Change begins by not trying to change. What you imagine you must do in order to change yourself is often the very force that keeps you precisely the way you are. How else can you explain the years and decades of your own foiled plans for growth and broken resolutions? Consumed by an apparent passion to be "other" than who you are, you try to be who you are not, but in so doing succeed only in being a person who is trying to be other than who you are. Beneath all the layers of wanting to be different, self-dissatisfaction, pretense, charade, and denial is a self. This self is a living, dynamic force within everyone. And if you could remain still long enough here, now, in this very place, you would discover who you are. And by discovering who you are, you would at last be free to discover who you yet also might be.

  —Rabbi Lawrence Kushner, "Acceptance and Change"

The doctor-patient relationship remains one of the last remaining nontrivial forms of relationship possible for modern people.

  —Jacob Needleman, *The Way of the Physician*

9. Anxiety and the Spirit of Questioning

With no bird singing
The mountain is yet more still.
　　　　　　—Thomas Merton, *Zen and the Birds of Appetite*

Mary

When I first met Mary, she was thiry-nine years old and had never seen a psychiatrist or psychotherapist before. Although she had gone through several years of mild delinquency and marijuana abuse during her adolescence, she had shown no obvious signs of behavioral or psychological disturbance since that time. She was quite successful in her career as an account executive, had long-term friends, and thought of herself as capable of a full range of strong feelings. In short, she appeared to belong to that ill-defined congregation sometimes referred to as the "worried well."

Mary wanted to begin psychotherapy because she had found herself over the previous few months becoming increasingly angry with her boss, stewing for days at a time over what seemed like trivial incidents at work. She had had similar difficulties with two other bosses during the past six or seven years, she said, which she had never been able to address with them. In one case she had moved to a different company and in another had moved to a different department. She didn't want to have to keep moving, and was hoping that psychotherapy might help her identify what was really going on in these relationships, especially with her current boss, so that she could find a better way to deal with him.

Over the first two months of weekly psychotherapy sessions it became evident that Mary's problem with her boss, while very real, was only the tip of an iceberg—the part that was easiest for her to identify and talk about. It turned out that she had been unhappy, off and on and to varying degrees, for years. In fact, she had only recently emerged out of a period of deep despondency over the breakup of a two-year romantic relationship, the most recent in a long series of failed relationships with men that had included two brief marriages when she was in her twenties. Both marriages had come to grief over Mary's refusal to start a family. Although she had always attributed her reluctance to career conflicts, she now admitted to me something that she had never told anyone, and had only recently begun to admit to herself: she had never liked children and was particularly uncomfortable around infants. She was intensely embarrassed to be lacking what she thought of as the normal maternal feeling that any woman ought to have. As her fortieth birthday approached, she was also feeling increasingly tense and pressured around her mother who, Mary was sure, was impatiently waiting for her daughter to remarry while there was still time to produce a grandchild.

Psychoanalysis

As she talked about these problems over the first several weeks of treatment, Mary gradually developed a sense that all of her difficulties—with bosses, lovers, children, her mother—were somehow tied up into one knot of tension and stress, which she had managed to live with for years without paying it too much attention, but which she now wanted to be able to untie. To this end she accepted my recommendation that we begin a full-scale psychoanalysis. This is the original, classical form of psychotherapy as developed by Freud, in which the patient free-associates while lying on a couch, with the analyst seated behind and out of sight. The "fundamental rule" of free association is that the patient should try to put into words whatever comes into awareness, censoring nothing, tracking and reporting as fully as possible on the "stream of consciousness"—the thoughts, images, fantasies, and feelings that flow involuntarily through our awareness at every moment but that typically escape our notice because our attention is directed elsewhere. The idea of using the couch, with the analyst out of sight, is to facilitate an inward focusing of attention (listening to the soul) by fostering relaxation and making it more difficult to distract oneself with trying to gauge the analyst's expectations (a common form of resistance) through facial expression and body language. The use of the couch combined with the practice of free association is thus designed to shift the normal balance of interpersonal interaction in the direction of listening to oneself rather than looking to the other person.

Because full psychoanalysis requires four or five sessions a week for anywhere from five to ten years, many patients assume that if their therapist recommends analysis it must mean that they are seriously disturbed.[1] On the contrary, it usually means that the therapist considers them to possess two important personality strengths that lend themselves to psychoanalytic work: the capacity to tolerate anxiety (which tends to be stirred up as free association threatens to bring the unconscious into consciousness), and the capacity for and interest in self-reflection.

Impulse and Urgency

As we examined more fully the details of Mary's relationships with men, we noticed a clear pattern, in which she would either abruptly end relationships, or abruptly set limits (e.g., by refusing to discuss having children) on any interaction that threatened to become too intimate. Not surprisingly, this pattern was to manifest itself prominently in the psychoanalytic relationship, which is more intimate in certain ways than any other. The first time this happened was a little more than a year into Mary's treatment.

At that time, Mary was beginning to understand her pattern with men in the light of what she had come to recognize as her overly dependent relationship with her parents, especially her mother. She had noticed that, both with her lovers and with her bosses, she tended to feel torn between a compulsion to repeat that familiar pattern of overdependency and a counterbalancing need to rebel and assert her autonomy by breaking off the relationship altogether. She had expressed the hope that through working on her relationship with me she could develop a different, healthier model for how to be with a man—one that struck a more comfortable balance between dependency and autonomy. Nonetheless, she generally had trouble focusing on what went on in her interactions with me, and found it much easier to talk about her boss. She would often complain to me about how overbearing, controlling, self-centered, or manipulative he was, yet I noticed that she did so with a subtle undertone of pleading that suggested she did not feel entitled to be angry at him—as if she needed some confirmation from me that her anger was justified. The situations that had initially prompted her to seek treatment were ones in which she had felt flooded with anger almost against her will. In situations like these she felt that her anger must be wrong, and was therefore hesitant to do anything about what made her angry. But in addition she reported many other difficult, uncomfortable interactions with her boss in which her feelings were more obscure—where she thought she was probably being treated unfairly but had trouble distinguishing that the bad feeling she was having about the interaction was actually anger. As she gradually learned to recognize this pattern of dysfunctional anger management through talking about it with me, she began to feel a greater sense of permission to be angry, and was then at least some of the time able to assert herself more effectively at work. Nevertheless, she continued to report interactions—with her parents as well as with her boss—where it sounded to me is if she had good reason to be angry, but where she herself didn't seem to feel anything more than a kind of vague, tense discomfort. In fact I sometimes had the uneasy sense that she was overly dependent on me to tell her when she was angry—or when she should be.

She then came into a session one Monday morning and announced, without warning, that she had decided it was time to end her treatment. She had been thinking a lot about it, she said, and felt that she had really gotten everything she needed from the analysis. She felt much better about her boss now because she was able to tell him when she disagreed with him, and she was handling her mother better too—well enough that she felt ready to move ahead on her own.

There was a palpable tension—a brusqueness—in Mary's announcement, as if she had no wish to discuss it and was eager to move on to a different topic. I felt a sudden agitation and inward flash of anger. Mary had never so much as hinted to me that she might be thinking about quitting. Indeed, quite the opposite—she had frequently made a point of telling me that analysis was the best thing she had ever done for herself. So I felt blindsided, but I kept my reaction to myself. I reflected that, by provoking such a reaction of agitation in me, she was in effect sending me a signal, alerting me that something was agitating her that she was either unaware of or unable to put easily into words. A law of emotional interaction is that "like evokes like." A strong emotion in one person will automatically tend to evoke a similar, mirroring emotion (or resistance against it) in the person toward whom it is directed.[2] I therefore considered my own angry response as a signal, probably reflecting the fact that Mary herself was acting in anger toward me without realizing it.

I asked Mary to tell me about the process of her thinking, and the feelings she had been aware of that led her to make this decision just now, today. She answered that she had simply reviewed her reasons for wanting psychotherapy in the first place—which were to learn how to deal better with her boss and with men generally—and decided that she had now accomplished these goals. Although she wasn't currently involved with a man romantically, she felt confident that the progress she had made in being able to stand up to her boss would translate into an improvement in her relationships with men generally. As for not liking children, she had decided that this was an understandable outcome of certain experiences she had told me about with her brother and sister, and was unlikely to change enough in the next year or so that she would be able to have children of her own. In any case, she was pretty much set on a career path that left little room for children in her life.

I told Mary that I understood her reasoning but thought her conclusions were debatable enough to make me suspect that there must be more of an emotional reason why she had come to those conclusions just now. Perhaps something she had been talking about recently was upsetting to her, or perhaps I had done or said something that had hurt her or made her angry? To this, Mary responded with an edge of impatience in her voice, denying any awareness of being upset, angry, hurt, or in any way dissatisfied with her treatment. She looked at the clock, as if wishing for the session to be over so she could stop talking about this irksome subject. As for why she had come to her decision just now, she said, the only thing she could add was that recently she had "been feeling really tired from all this psychotherapy": "You know, I've mentioned more than once how difficult it is to arrange my schedule so that I can get here four times a week. I suppose what happened recently is that it just got to feeling like too much of a hassle. And besides, I really do think it's pretty clear at this point that I've accomplished everything I can expect to here."

Again I felt jolted, and had a strong urge to tell Mary that she obviously wasn't expecting very much of herself then. I felt alarmed by the judgmental hostility of this impulse and remained silent, trying to process it, allowing the feelings that were prompting the judgmental impulse to take shape in my awareness. I noticed that I was feeling hurt and, on reflection, realized more specifically that I felt insulted. What I had actually heard Mary saying was "I think it's pretty clear that I've accomplished everything I can expect to *with you.*" In other words, "Since you clearly don't have anything more to offer, it's no longer worth the hassle to see you." I was actually fairly certain, judging from her weary, impatient tone, that this was what she really meant, but I was equally certain that she didn't realize it. I believed her when she said that she wasn't *feeling* any anger at me, and I was sure she had no idea how insulting her words sounded. In any case I understood that she would not have wanted to hurt or insult me, even unconsciously, unless she herself felt hurt and insulted.

I pointed out how striking it was that Mary had said nothing in the preceding weeks to suggest that she was thinking about ending therapy or feeling that it was getting to be a hassle. The suddenness of her decision, I said, together with a sense I got that she was somewhat pressured and impatient in the way she told me about it, suggested that she was feeling a sense of urgency. I asked if she were aware of any such feeling. After a moment she smiled reflectively and said, "You know, now that you mention it, I really am feeling incredibly pressured about this, much more than I had realized!" It was both a surprise and an unexpected relief for her to recognize this disproportionate sense of urgency within herself—a need to end the analysis right away, today, that was inconsistent with any rationalization she had been able to give herself for doing so.

"How close is this pressure that you're feeling with me now to that feeling you've often talked about—the feeling you get when things start feeling too close for comfort in a relationship with a man?"

"You know, it's exactly the same feeling! Wow, that's amazing. It's the same feeling that made me break off all those relationships! . . . So what does it mean, then, that I'm feeling it now with you?"

"Well, we don't really know what it means yet, but it does make sense that sooner or later you would develop the same sort of problem with me that you've had with other important men in your life. That's what's called transference. Whatever problem people come into analysis to talk about, they end up repeating the problem in their relationship with the analyst. And that's actually good, because when we're experiencing the problem together, it puts us in a much better position to understand it than if we simply talked about how you've experienced it in the past. I suspect that the sense of pressure and urgency you were feeling comes from an anxiety being stirred up in you by something happening in our relationship right now that is similar to what pushed you to break off those earlier relationships with men."

It may strike the reader as ironic that after describing anxiety in Chapter 3 as the reason someone would want to get into a psychotherapeutic process, I am now presenting it as the reason someone wanted to get out of one. Of course it is both. There is a delicate balance between the desire to understand and deal with what arouses our anxiety and the instinctive need simply to do whatever it takes to make the anxiety go away. For Mary, that balance wasn't tipped, and the real psychotherapeutic process didn't *begin* until she first felt the impulse to *end* her treatment and then began to question herself about what sort of anxiety might be generating it.

"It makes sense that there must be an anxiety there, like you're saying," she reflected, "but I'm not aware of anything I could call anxiety, only that I feel this pressure."

Affects, Emotions, and Feelings

To understand Mary's experience, it is useful to distinguish formally between affect, emotion, and feeling as three degrees of emotional experience (though in practice I, like most people, often use *emotion* and *feeling* as synonymous). An *affect* is a purely physiological unconscious process or state—the biological component of an emotion. An *emotion* is a complex conscious experience that is based on an affect. It involves a sense of physiological arousal, an impulse or urge toward action, along with a degree of discernable *feeling*—a more subtle quality of awareness that can be introspectively distilled out from the physiological urgency of the emotional experience, and that does not impel toward action.

It is possible to have an affect without experiencing the emotion that should go with it, as when tears come to the eyes but with no accompanying sense of feeling moved by sadness; or when there are palpitations, dizziness, and sweating but no awareness of being anxious or alarmed; or when, as with Mary initially, there is an impulsive action (telling me she was quitting today) but no awareness of feeling pressured to act. It is likewise possible to have an emotion without experiencing the feeling quality that should go with it, as when a person is aware of being impelled to act but cannot identify the feeling that is implicit (and unconscious) in the action. This was Mary's situation once she became aware of feeling pressured to quit analysis. She noticed the physiological arousal—the sense of pressure—and the urge to action that are part of an emotion, but not the feeling that would have allowed her to accurately characterize what kind of an emotion it was.

Finally, it is possible to experience a feeling by itself, independent of any of the physiological indicators and impulses of emotion. Wordsworth's famous comment that poetry "takes its origin from emotion recollected in tranquillity" suggests the kind of calm, centered, highly nuanced awareness that such pure feeling involves. It is only through such a subtle awareness of feeling-tone that we are able to discriminate our own motives and values, and to understand the meaning of our emotional experience. This kind of distilled self-awareness is the ultimate goal of the psychotherapeutic process, but the early stages of the process happen primarily at the level of affect and emotion.

With this in mind, I told Mary it was certainly possible to have anxiety without being aware of it as such, but that if she could stop and fully let herself have her feeling of pressured urgency, in all its intensity, she should be able to detect the anxiety behind it. I added that she would then be in a position to work on changing her pattern of abruptly cutting off relationships. She would need first to notice the feeling of anxiety when she had it, and then to allow herself to stay with the feeling, in all of its discomfort, long enough to know what the anxiety was really about, resisting the temptation to short-circuit the experience through impulsive action.

"It seems that important areas of your life are being controlled by disturbing emotions that you are not aware of," I explained, "but once you can fully experience these emotions, you will no longer have to be controlled by them."

Mary thought about this for a minute, then replied, "So you're saying that the way to get better is first I have to feel worse, to feel all the bad feelings, as painfully as I really feel them, without trying to run away from them. I get the idea, only I'm a little concerned because I don't know how much pain I'm really capable of feeling, and that scares me. You know the time about a year before I saw you when I felt so depressed after breaking up with Tom? I had to force myself to fight through that depression, to keep busy with work, because I was terrified to think of how low I might sink if I gave in to the bad feeling. I think that's why I didn't even consider getting into therapy until after I had already started feeling better. Therapy would have been like an invitation to give in to the bad feeling, and I was afraid of where that might take me."

"So right now you're worried that those old painful feelings must still be there, deep down, and that if you start getting in touch with your anxiety, as I'm suggesting you try to do, it will be like opening up Pandora's box."

"Yes. How do I know the bad feelings won't get out of control and make me depressed again if I start focusing on them?"

"Well, I'm sure the feelings that caused your depression are still there, and it's possible they are part of what's unconsciously provoking this sudden pressure to end treatment. But I think you'll find that most of the pain of those feelings comes from having to fight so hard to control them, and that if you actually let yourself feel the feelings, they will turn out to be not as scary or painful as you imagine, and you'll actually feel more in control."

The Importance of Being Conscious

I have found that most people, like Mary, are skeptical of the idea that simply by feeling an uncomfortable feeling they can develop more of a sense of control over it. After all, it seems that you would have to give up control in order to allow yourself to feel an emotion that instinctively you would rather suppress. And once you have given up that control, wouldn't you be more likely to get carried away, overwhelmed by the emotion, than you would be to feel a greater sense of control over it? How can you get more control by giving up control?

In fact, you don't. Or rather you do, but in a paradoxical way. The paradox is related to the fact that we tend to be at our most controlling when we feel least in control, not when we feel strong but when we feel weak. We need to control things primarily because we are afraid of them. We try to control wild animals with cages; wild people with laws and prisons; unpredictable gods with prayers and rituals; and wild, unpredictable feelings with repression, suppression, rationalization, denial, and when all else fails, with a symptom. In this fearful need for control, we are a bit like Fred, the man in the old joke who developed the symptom of going to the same newsstand every day, buying his paper, and then, without reading it, proceeding to tear it up into little pieces and scatter them in the street. After watching this compulsive ritual for several weeks, the newspaper vendor finally asked Fred what the point of his performance was. Fred replied that he was trying to keep the stampeding elephants away. "But there are no stampeding elephants within three thousand miles of here!" protested the vendor. "See? It works," Fred answered.

In a sense, Fred's symptom did work—not to control the stampeding elephants, of course, but to control his anxiety over the danger of uncontrollable emotions that those elephants symbolized for him. But Fred's control was not genuine. It was a false, neurotic control, based ultimately on the fear that his emotions would actually be as dangerous as stampeding elephants. Yet clearly, if they were so, then scattering bits of paper in the street could never contain them. The real danger to Fred then was not from feeling his emotions but from the irrational action to which he was driven in order not to feel them. What made the action irrational was that it was an effort to control something that ultimately cannot and does not need to be controlled.

Nietzsche once wrote that he would "never tire of emphasizing" one "small terse fact . . . that a thought comes when 'it' wishes, and not when 'I' wish, so that it is a falsification of the facts of the case to say that the subject 'I' is the condition of the predicate 'think.' "[3] Nietzsche's insight—which certainly applies to emotions as well as to thoughts—suggests that it is an illusion to believe we are ever truly in control of our inner processes. It is fear of having to give up this illusion of control, I believe, that explains Fred's anxiety about stampeding elephants and Mary's difficulty with the idea of "allowing" her feelings to come when "they" wished, and more generally the resistance all of us have to the process of free association. We all have trouble accepting that we are to a large extent "lived" by an "it" over which we have no control, so we try to exert control just where we have it least, over the flow of our thoughts and especially our emotions. Yet, paradoxically, we are afraid to exercise the control we actually do have, in our ability simply to pay attention to this irrepressible flow of consciousness—to listen to the soul—without trying to control it.

This is the only predicate—not think, not feel, but *pay attention*—of which "I" am truly the active subject. After all, it can only have been attention to his own inner process that brought Nietzsche to his insight in the first place, just as it had once brought Descartes to his "I think, therefore I am." Each man no doubt experienced his own particular insight as the kind of Nietzschean thought that came unbidden, when *it* wanted to, and not when *he*—the ostensible author of the insight—chose. Yet there had to be, at the same time, a Cartesian consciousness—an activity of attention—in each man that could recognize the insight, when it came, as important, and could then choose when and how to articulate it. Each man might then have said, à la Descartes, "I recognize (through an act of attention), therefore I am."

The Best Way to Get Rid of a Feeling You Don't Want

This condition of Cartesian attention to one's own inner process affords the kind of genuine control that comes from giving up control. It involves being secure and flexible enough that we don't need to control what happens next but can simply experience it as it happens, with an openness to new experience and a sense of acceptance, both of other people and of our own feelings. But it is difficult to achieve such a state of openness and acceptance when you are anxious. Anxiety is a signal that something from the unconscious—something unknown and uncontrollable, like a stampeding elephant—is threatening to shatter our illusory sense of being in control, generating mistrust of other people and intolerance of our own emotions. We then have a choice: to react like Fred, feeling out of control and trying to compensate by becoming more controlling and/or more symptomatic; or to accept and respect what we cannot control, paying attention to it, in a spirit of questioning, as an important message from our own unconscious, an opportunity for a new and richer experience of ourselves and the world.

Recognizing that such considerations may not be completely convincing and don't necessarily make the prospect of feeling painful or frightening feelings any more appealing, I generally tell patients: "The best way to get rid of a feeling you don't want is to let yourself have it." Of course, this way of putting it itself demands further explanation. It's not that letting yourself have a feeling makes the feeling simply disappear. Rather, it changes the feeling from one you don't want, and need to control because you are afraid of it, into one you can comfortably accept. But how can this be? Does a wild animal become tame simply from being let out of its cage? Well, not exactly, but then letting yourself have a feeling you don't want is a lot more difficult than simply opening the door of a cage. The process of inner attention through which you let the feeling happen—the psychotherapeutic process—actually changes the way you experience the feeling. In fact, what you discover is that it wasn't really a *feeling* you were so uncomfortable with in the first place, but rather the unsettling pressure of an *emotion*. Becoming more conscious of the feeling that goes with this disturbing emotion tends to defuse the emotion— making it possible to simply have the emotion as an inner experience without being so unsettled by it, or so pressured to act on it impulsively.

The "Taming" of the Emotions

Consider more closely the analogy between an emotion and a wild animal. Just as George Schaller needed to be able to tolerate and respect his own fear in order to approach free-living gorillas without a rifle, so we must be able to tolerate and respect our own anxiety in order to approach what we imagine to be dangerous emotions without unnecessary defenses and resistances. Again, it is not the inherent destructiveness of the emotions but rather the contemptuous, dismissive, or fearful attitudes with which we keep them warded off or caged up out of awareness that make them dangerous. The inner adjustments Schaller had to make in order to maintain the open-mindedness of a scientific observer while respectfully approaching the gorillas without a rifle radically changed the way he experienced and thought about them. Similarly, the inner adjustments we must make in order to allow ourselves to feel the emotions that make us anxious, approaching them respectfully, with the idea of learning something about ourselves, actually changes the way we experience them.

To put the matter metaphorically, as long as your attitude is one of actively trying to get rid of an anxiety-provoking feeling, you are seeing only its dark emotional surface. At that level of awareness the emotion looks like dirty bathwater. You can't see through the anxiety, guilt, or shame that it stirs up. As you let yourself *have* the feeling—experience the emotion fully—your attentiveness deepens and you begin to notice the baby in the bathwater, the previously disowned awareness that has been there all along, obscured by the inner conflict it provoked. The process is a subtle but also a very natural one. Whether you prefer to think of it simply as getting in touch with a feeling or, more profoundly, as listening to the soul, you will realize once you experience it that you have always known how to do it.

Anxiety Versus the Need to Remain Unconscious

Mary's first taste of this process was noticing—and recognizing—the sense of impulsive urgency that was pushing her to cut short her relationship with me. She realized that, whatever her rationalizations might have been, she had been trying to run away from something inside herself. This insight alone brought her an unexpected sense of relief and calm that seemed to dissolve any impulse to run away! At least that's what I thought initially, when she quickly relaxed back into the analysis as if there had never been any urgency or anxiety. By the very next session, she seemed to have forgotten that she had ever wanted to leave. Not only was she comfortable continuing her treatment but she felt a renewal of her familiar grateful feeling that psychoanalysis was the best thing she had ever done for herself. Yet amazingly, she was no longer the least bit curious about what had just yesterday been making her want to terminate this wonderful experience.

Just as amazingly, neither was I! Instead of wondering how such an apparently compelling sense of urgency could evaporate so easily, I was simply relieved at Mary's change of heart, and pleased at the effectiveness of my intervention, never noticing that there was something wrong with this picture. The fact that Mary had let herself feel her sense of urgency should have led to a modulation of the urgency and thereby brought into her awareness the more nuanced feeling of anxiety behind it. But when her urgency simply evaporated without a trace of anxiety, I failed to notice that this went contrary to what my theory would have predicted. The net result was that after twenty-four hours neither one of us remembered that there had been so much as a question about Mary's feeling any anxiety in her relationship with me. In fact, we continued not remembering it right up until the next time Mary came into a session and without warning pulled the rug out from under me by calmly announcing that she had decided it was a good time to end her treatment. This happened only ten months later, but Mary acted as if she had no recollection that it had ever happened before. She did not stop to question herself but again tried to disguise her sense of urgency (from herself as well as from me) by describing her decision as a result of thoughtful deliberation.

The same scenario would ultimately play itself out four times over the first three years of a fairly lengthy treatment. Each time it happened, we would discuss it and Mary would be struck by the repeated pattern. She would decide to stay in analysis to work on changing that pattern and then would promptly forget again that it had ever happened. Eventually it struck me that she was really going from one extreme to the other, acting just as abruptly and unreflectively in deciding to stay in treatment as she had been in deciding to terminate it. She was simply shifting from a position in which she had to get away from treatment in order to avoid feeling anxiety, to one in which she had to stay in treatment to avoid feeling anxiety. (This latter tendency—to avoid anxiety by staying in a relationship—was in fact the key to Mary's overdependence on her parents, which she was thus unconsciously re-creating in her transference relationship with me.) The movement was so subtle, and happened so quickly that I had to stop and remind myself that I knew there had to be a feeling of anxiety she was skipping over. I had to remind myself that what I was asking of Mary was indeed possible—to have an urgent impulse and at the same time to feel the anxiety behind it. I knew that this was possible because I had experienced it myself. Each time Mary had pulled the rug out from under me by trying to quit the analysis, I had felt a retaliatory impulse (e.g., the urge to tell her, disdainfully, that she wasn't expecting very much of herself) and at the same time a feeling of conscious alarm over the hostility of that impulse. The problem was that Mary never seemed to feel any such alarm, either at her impulse to end treatment or at her impulse to stay in treatment. Rather, she simply surrendered to her impulses as a way of keeping any conscious feeling of alarm from surfacing.

Was it the same anxiety, I wondered, that was one moment impelling Mary to get out of treatment and the next moment impelling her to stay in, or was she caught between the Scylla and Charybdis of two clashing anxieties? Without her testimony, from her own felt experience, there could be no way of knowing for sure, but I was content to wait. I knew that neither the impulse to get out of treatment nor the counterbalancing impulse to stay could succeed indefinitely in keeping Mary's anxiety at bay. Eventually it would come into her awareness and stay there long enough for her to describe it. The rapid movement from one extreme to another was but the swing of an unconscious emotional pendulum, and the laws of emotional physics require that, sooner or later, such a pendulum has to swing back. As long as Mary remained unaware of the anxiety that accompanied her impulse to leave treatment, that impulse would inevitably return, again and again, as if to say "I'm going to make you keep doing this until you get it right!" (i.e., until you listen to your anxiety).

The Repetition Compulsion

The anxiety-driven oscillation of an unconscious emotional pendulum is one way of describing what Freud called the *repetition compulsion*—the universal tendency to act out the same unconscious scenario time after time, automatically, despite obvious indications that it leads to unhappiness. It is an impressive phenomenon. Everyone does it, but we seem to have great difficulty noticing ourselves doing it, so we tend to go on doing it indefinitely, unless and until we can somehow arrange to catch ourselves in the act, usually by getting ourselves painfully jolted into an awareness of what we are doing.

Getting into psychotherapy is probably the most efficient way to arrange for such a shock of recognition. Psychotherapy makes the swinging of the pendulum noticeable by placing it within the stable framework of the therapist's steady observation. Set within such a frame, the oscillation of the pendulum creates a subtle emotional vibration that first the therapist and then the patient can feel; a reverberation of the unconscious anxiety that keeps the pendulum in motion, which will be felt consciously only if we stop the motion and pay attention—if, instead of acting on an impulse, we stop and simply feel it, and can then also feel the anxiety that accompanies it.

The way this happened for Mary was that she became so impressed by her *resistance*—by her repeated failure to notice her own sense of urgency, and her repeated surprise when I would point it out to her again—that eventually the scenario became familiar. She began to recognize the sense of urgency without prompting when it returned, and to remember that in the past it had left her as often and as suddenly as it had come over her. In effect, by repeatedly noticing *me* noticing her inconsistency, Mary became able to notice it herself and couldn't help but be troubled and curious about it. She was then able to ask herself, "What's wrong with this picture?" She became aware that she had actually been trying to conceal her sense of urgency from me and became uneasy about the deceptiveness of the rationalizations she had been offering for wanting to end treatment. She then felt a need to explore further the discrepancy between what she actually felt and the story she had been telling herself and me about what she felt.

Often it doesn't occur to people to get into psychotherapy until life itself (with the cooperation of the unconscious) finds a way to knock them over the head with the awareness of their repetition compulsion. In Alcoholics Anonymous they refer to such an event as "hitting bottom," when the alcoholic realizes he's made such a complete mess of everything he values most that he can no longer deny or rationalize away his illness. Hitting bottom works not just for alcoholism but for any serious problem that we might be inclined to evade through denial and rationalization. But self-awareness doesn't necessarily require hitting bottom in the sense that your entire life must be lying in shards around you. It only requires that you hit up against something repeatedly and unpleasantly enough to catch your own attention.

A Personal Example

My own first painful awareness of the repetition compulsion came the night before a march on Washington in 1969. I was staying with a group of friends and fellow protesters, and naturally the conversation turned to politics. Before long, I found myself passionately railing against the evils of the military-industrial complex. Or rather I began to notice people getting seriously irritated with me for doing something that, until I saw their reaction to it, I would not have identified as railing. I can't say that I remember the details of the conversation, but, knowing myself as I now do, it probably went something like this:

BOB: You know, I still don't get it. It's so obvious that what we're doing in Vietnam is not only wrong but isn't working that it kind of makes you wonder. After all, Johnson wasn't stupid, and neither is Nixon. What do they think they've been fighting for, really?

ELIO: I'll tell you what they've been fighting for. Big business! That's what imperialism has always been about—money and power! The rich getting richer by exploiting the poor and using them for cannon fodder whenever it makes economic sense to do so . . . and then whitewashing their actions with self-righteous flag-waving rhetoric!

NANCY: Yeah, but I've never been able to figure out what our economic interest in Vietnam is. Are you really so sure we have one?

ELIO: Why the hell else would we be over there?! A good used-car salesman never lets you know what's really under the hood. They're not about to reveal what economic interests are being served—other than the obvious ones of weapons manufacturers—but you can be damn sure they're shilling for *someone.*

BOB: Yeah, well maybe you can be damn sure, but I'd prefer to have some facts to back up what I believe, and you don't seem to have any.

I was taken aback, especially because, given that we were all there for the same reason, I had expected that everyone would appreciate and endorse the points I was making. One of my friends explained to me that it wasn't so much what I was saying as the vitriolic intensity with which I was saying it that was alienating everyone, including him. In fact, he said, the way I was arguing made him want to disagree with me even when he agreed with me! Wounded and embarrassed, I rewound my mental tape recorder and listened to myself; sure enough, I could hear that I had been out of control.

More important, I was struck by an uncanny similarity between this incident and one that had occurred three years earlier in a college bull session. The topic then had been religion, and I was holding forth about the oppressive evils of Catholicism when I suddenly found myself being shouted down by three of my friends, who told me in a not very friendly way to lighten up or get some professional help quickly, preferably both. I was caught between the surprised realization that I had been spitting out much more venom against the Church than I had realized was in me and a sullen resentment of my so-called friends, whose criticism I then proceeded to blow off with the rationalization that they simply couldn't understand my feelings because they had not been raised Catholic. Three years later in Washington, that kind of rationalization wouldn't work. I still felt sullen and resentful toward the friends who had criticized me, but I could no longer deny that they had a point. I couldn't so easily blow them off or get past the unsettled feeling they had left me with until I had made some kind of sense of it.

As I stewed over the incident, I recognized suddenly, with a startling sense of inner certainty, that the feeling quality of my old righteous indignation against the oppressive Church was identical to the quality of my current righteous indignation against the exploitive U.S. government. That moment of recognition was my first taste of what I now call listening to the soul. In the identity I could feel between these two intense emotional reactions, I could also feel my *self* as the orchestrator of that mode of reacting. It then occurred to me that the real source and motive for my anger must lie deeper than the places I had so far been looking for it—that however many valid complaints I might have against church and state, they were not enough to account for the stridency of my response. "So it must be my parents I'm really angry at!" I thought.

Anxiety As Consciousness Trying to Happen

As discerning readers will have already inferred, the deep unconscious wellspring for my adolescent attacks on Catholicism and American imperialism is still active in my motivation for writing this book. My current targets for criticism are Medical Model psychiatry (another rigidly dogmatic church), and the culture of managed care and the quick fix (other manifestations of unbridled capitalist greed). My personal psychoanalysis has helped to soften the stridency of my righteous indignation, by allowing me to recognize a piece of myself in the persons and institutions against which I protest. However, it has by no means removed my valid reasons for protesting.

But my purpose in telling this story about my own personal encounter with the repetition compulsion is not simply to explain my polemical tendencies. It is to provide an objective, unambiguous account of my own attitudes and way of thinking—the observational lens through which I was seeing and trying to understand Mary. It is also to convey a more vivid sense of the shock of self-recognition I have so often felt in the simple experience of listening to the soul. This kind of experience, I believe, is what Socrates had in mind when he said that the unexamined life is not worth living. It exemplifies an important *movement of consciousness* that is at the heart of the psychotherapeutic process, and, indeed, at the heart of any meaningful life.

The most straightforward way of describing this movement of consciousness, as I have experienced it, is that the painful experience of anxiety (often associated with shame and/or guilt) opens us to the possibility of change—the birth of new awareness—through the questions it forces us to ask ourselves. A less straightforward way of describing it, which captures more of what is "shocking" in the shock of recognition, is that the experience of painful discrepancy opens us to the possibility of anxiety, which opens us to the possibility of a deeper level of feeling, which ultimately opens us to the possibility of *joy* in discovering our True Self—the entire process being sustained by the spirit of questioning. This is what I experienced at the 1969 march on Washington. My attention was arrested by the mortifying discrepancy between the reaction I expected and the reaction I got from my companions. This discrepancy resisted all my efforts to rationalize it away, as I had been able to do with the similar discrepancy in the college bull session three years before. The discrepancy therefore made me anxious, and almost at the same time—because it reminded me of that earlier episode in college—gave rise to the exhilarating shock of self-recognition. My consciousness moved, in an instant, from discrepancy to anxiety to the stunning realization that the source of both the discrepancy and the anxiety was in me—in the urgent emotion of outrage that had impelled me twice now, contrary to my conscious intentions, to alienate my friends. That emotion represented the driving force of my repetition compulsion.

Had I been able to stay with my feeling of anxiety, it might have alerted me to the fact that, in my outrage, I was behaving just as hypocritically and oppressively as the Church and the political system I felt so driven to attack. The righteousness of purpose I had been professing (and feeling) was discordant with (and served to conceal) what I was actually doing (and unconsciously feeling), that is, showing a disdain for my friends' opinions, while arrogantly trying to force my own opinion down their throats. My anxiety then signaled the possibility, both joyful and fearful that, instead of foisting my outrage on my friends, I might consciously feel and accept responsibility for it, and for the wilfully self-aggrandizing motive it embodied. I would then have been able to say that I had met the self-righteous hypocritical enemy and he was me.

At the time I was unable to stay with the anxiety and went ahead immediately to one of those incomplete explanations that put the mind to rest, a compromise between self-awareness and rationalization. "It must be my parents I'm really angry at!" While this was a new idea to me, and there certainly was some truth to it, its primary effect (and purpose) at the time was to close off rather than open up the possibility of new feeling. Serious anger at my parents was far enough below the surface of my conscious awareness that I could easily think about it in the abstract, without feeling it, and so keep my attention comfortably distracted from the possibility of experiencing whatever unsettling feeling actually did lie just below the surface of my diatribe.

I was destined to repeat the same sort of experience again and again in different situations over the years. Each time it happened I became a bit more curious about what was driving me, and a bit more convinced that I needed to stay with the anxiety I was beginning to feel about that drivenness and explore its contours and layers. The early phases of this development occurred before I thought of getting into psychotherapy, but it was only through a psychotherapeutic process, in my personal psychoanalysis, that I gained a level of understanding deep enough to produce real change. It was only then that I did get in touch with the real anger I felt toward my parents, which eventually freed me to get in touch with the real love I have for them. In between I had to get in touch with real anger at my analyst, and come to appreciate that everything I hated in him, as in my parents, was a reflection of something I hated in myself.

In many ways my experience was similar to Mary's. Over time she became more aware of, and more curious about, the marked fluctuations in her attitude toward therapy. She, too, began to notice a glaring discrepancy, between her abiding regard for me as a nurturing, sustaining presence in her life that she could ill afford to lose, and her unaccountably blasé readiness to let me go in those impulsive moments when she suddenly felt like quitting. Recognizing that the key to this discrepancy must lie in her sense of urgency, she was eventually able to try out my suggestion and simply let herself be in the state of urgency without trying to do anything about it except to feel it.

10. Introspection and Putting It into Words

And as imagination bodies forth
The forms of things unknown, the poet's pen
Turns them to shapes, and gives to airy nothing
A local habitation and a name.
—William Shakespeare, *A Midsummer Night's Dream*

At another time she asked, "What is a soul?" "No one knows," I replied; "but we know it is not the body, and it is that part of us which thinks and loves and hopes."... [It] is invisible.... "But if I write what my soul thinks," she said, "then it will be visible, and the words will be its body."
—Annie Sullivan, epigraph to *The Miracle Worker*

Feelings, Tolerable and Intolerable

The turning point came approximately three years into Mary's psychoanalysis, the fourth time she had the urgent impulse to quit. At that time I told her that I thought the real point of her urgency must be to get out of the relationship with me before she felt something she couldn't tolerate feeling. This would mean, I added, that she must at that moment actually be on the edge of having feelings about me that she was afraid to let herself feel. She was struck by this formulation, and it helped her to notice more clearly that she did indeed feel an underlying uneasiness, an anxiety that fueled her sense of urgency to escape treatment. The uneasiness was in response to a subtle feeling tone that she had never noticed, or at least never taken seriously before. But once she paid attention to it, the feeling was clear. She was disappointed in me. That was the real reason she wanted to leave treatment. When she allowed herself to feel this disappointment, she noticed further that it had an angry edge to it, a bitter sense that I hadn't helped her very much, especially at times when she was in the most serious distress. It was very difficult for her to admit to herself or to me that she felt this way about me. If she admitted it to herself she would have to tell me, but if she told me she was sure it would hurt my feelings. Hence her uneasiness.

In fact I did find Mary's disappointment troubling, but not so much because I was offended or hurt by it as because I really wasn't sure what sort of "serious distress" she was referring to that I had failed to help her with! Although I had often had a sense of her feeling unsettled, tense, or confused, I couldn't recall ever seeing her in a state of acute emotional distress, pain, or panic. So I asked her to describe what she felt to be the most significant times that I had failed her in the way she was now alluding to.

She then reminded me of several occasions during the preceding year when she had called me from her job, feeling upset but not very articulate. She had said that she could hardly stand another minute of sitting at her desk, but was unable to explain clearly what kind of upset or agitation she was feeling or what had triggered it. Even when I had been able to reschedule her appointment to see her right away at those times, she got the sense that I never really understood how upset she was, and, more important, I had never done anything to make the painful feeling stop. That particular agitated unsettled feeling, she now told me, was sometimes so severe as to be simply unbearable. She recalled a number of instances when at a certain point in a session, after getting increasingly frustrated and frantic that I wasn't helping, she had flipped some sort of internal switch and had simply given up wanting help at all. In fact, now that she thought about it, that was pretty much the feeling—of having given up—that had most recently led her to want to end her treatment. She realized that she had probably never told me just how frantic she was getting at those times, because the upset feeling affected her in such a way, and was so difficult to describe, that it left her literally speechless. Of course she understood perfectly well—or so she reassured me—that I couldn't have known what the problem was as long as she couldn't put what she was feeling into words. Intellectually, she understood that this sort of difficulty is exactly the reason that psychotherapy usually takes such a long time, and that you can't rush it. Still, it was so difficult to tolerate this particular feeling that she had sometimes wished I would give her medication to relieve it. She had never asked for it, though, because she knew I was a psychoanalyst and assumed I had been taught not to use medication. She hadn't wanted to pressure me to do something I would be uncomfortable doing, and if she was honest with herself she had to admit also that she was sure I would say no and was too proud to put herself in a position (by asking for medication) where I could humiliate her by doing so.

Countertransference

My reaction to Mary's rich disclosure was complex; it evolved as she was talking, but it ended in my feeling insulted all over again. She probably didn't realize she was saying it, but she certainly seemed to be implying that I didn't care enough about her to offer comfort (in the form of medication) when she was in pain; that I cared more about some rules I had been taught about the proper way to do psychoanalysis than I cared about her. It took me several moments to absorb the impact of this criticism and get a full sense of my emotional reaction to it.

I began by registering an impression that Mary's depiction of me was reminiscent of a mother who ignores the painful crying of her baby because she is following her pediatrician's instructions to let the baby cry itself to sleep. I had always strongly disapproved of any pediatrician who would give this advice and of any mother or father who would follow it, so I felt an impulse to defend myself against Mary's accusation. I reassured myself that I was more than open to the idea of using medication. I was even considered something of a local expert on integrating the use of medication with psychotherapy. Still, that being so, I had all the more reason to ask myself: Why hadn't I ever thought of using medication with Mary? More than that, now that I was thinking about using it, why did I still feel some reluctance? Perhaps Mary was right in thinking that I was prejudiced by my training, or perhaps something more personal was going on, a hostile reaction that was making me want to withhold from her, but that I had not yet recognized as hostility.

One thing I did recognize was a feeling of guilt, a sense that Mary was right to feel disappointed in me. I felt that I actually had failed her on a number of occasions when I should have recognized more clearly than I had just how distraught she was. I remembered the phone calls and the emergency sessions, but somehow she had never seemed as upset during those sessions as she had sounded over the phone. I had never recognized her distress at those times as being nearly as severe as she was now describing it. Her complaint now forced me to reconsider my previous impression. I was surprised at how clearly I could remember the feeling I had had during those sessions: a pressured sense that Mary was counting on me, and a subtle, anxious feeling that I didn't know what I could do to help her. Now that I thought about it, this reminded me of feelings I had had as a parent, when my children were sick and in obvious distress but I couldn't figure out what was hurting them and they were too young to have the words to tell me. I vividly remembered the frantic feeling of helplessness that grew in me on a couple of such occasions when we couldn't reach the pediatrician for what seemed like a very long time. I now recognized that the subtle anxious feeling I had had with Mary was on the verge of being the same kind of frantic helplessness, but I had never allowed it to get to that point. In fact, I had never stayed with the feeling long enough even to identify it as anxiety, but instead had insulated myself from it by turning my mind away from Mary's distress. I could have recognized how frustrated and frantic she was feeling, even without her being able to tell me in words, but I would have had to be willing to feel my own anxiety first, in order to be able to recognize hers.

In effect, I had been turning a deaf ear to Mary's crying, detaching myself emotionally in a way that (unconsciously) mirrored her own inner process, as she had just described it—flipping an internal switch to shut down feelings. I had always been able to rationalize this sense of detachment toward Mary's distress because her episodes were, thankfully, self-limiting. Even if I didn't do anything about them, they went away on their own. And it wasn't as if I hadn't tried to do something about them. I regularly offered interpretations, tentative explanations of what might be going on psychologically, aimed at unblocking Mary's feelings.

For instance, I had suggested that, since the episodes seemed to begin most often at work, they were probably connected with unresolved tensions between Mary and her boss. As I described in Chapter 9, she seemed to get into situations with him where I thought she should have been angry but where she didn't feel any anger. There had also been a number of incidents in which she did feel angry over a decision he had made and had been able to tell him so. These had given her a great sense of accomplishment and left her believing that her problem with her boss was resolved. I was not so sure, suspecting a deeper layer in Mary's anger at arrogant, manipulative men than she had so far been able to tap. So I would typically try to find a way to relate her episodes of distress to some incident where she might have been angry at her boss without realizing it, where she might have felt forced to cover up her feelings—even from herself—because she had not felt entitled to them or had been afraid of provoking a confrontation. I had suggested to her that the kind of agitated unsettled feeling she was suffering from might result from just such a state of unconscious, stifled anger.

Still, I had had no real sense of conviction that such speculations were even on the right track. I knew that something had to be unconscious for Mary to be so inarticulate about what was upsetting her, yet how could it be anger when she was already conscious of being angry at her boss at least sometimes? Possibly she could feel anger only under certain conditions, or perhaps only a certain kind of anger. I suspected that this was the case. For instance, her anger at her boss might be more acceptable to her when she could relate it to some decision or policy she considered objectively unfair. In other situations where she was angry primarily at his arrogant attitude and bearing toward her, her anger would feel more personal, and might easily be complicated, in a way that made it less acceptable to her, by some combination of envy, resentment, dependency, or sexual attraction. But there was never anything in what she could tell me about her interactions with her boss that would have clearly supported or disproved these speculations. Indeed, I was able to get very little useful information at all from Mary to guide my speculations. When she was not in one of her states, it was as if they had never happened and she felt no motivation to talk about them. When she was in one of her states, she had considerable difficulty forcing herself to talk at all. She seemed completely unable to assess whether my interpretations "felt" right or not, or to tell me what if anything she had been aware of feeling toward her boss that afternoon.

In the end, I felt I was trying to guess at answers when I didn't even know the question. It wasn't that I didn't hear Mary crying, or that I didn't care about her. But I couldn't tolerate not understanding why she was crying and not knowing what to do about it. Feeling a responsibility to do something, and knowing that she was expecting me to be able to do something, I began to feel stupid and incompetent. I would certainly have gone on to feeling frantic and helpless had I not then turned a partly deaf ear to her crying. This mechanism of detachment did have a positive dimension, in that it enabled me to preserve my equanimity and go on trying to help. I could simply remind myself that sooner or later something always happens to clarify such murky situations, that sometimes the unconscious feelings have to come to a very painful head before they can pop into consciousness. I could even imagine that Mary would take some reassurance from my detached equanimity. Certainly she would have felt worse had she sensed that I was feeling helpless. So in that way I could think of my detachment as necessary, like a surgeon's, however disappointing it may have felt to Mary and now felt to me. On the other hand, I realized that Mary would have felt even more reassured by my equanimity had I not had to purchase it by distancing myself. Had I been better able to tolerate my own anxiety, I would have been able to stay in closer emotional contact with her, empathizing with her distress even if I didn't know how to relieve it. That in itself would have comforted her and perhaps made it easier for her to focus on and describe what she was experiencing. So by distancing myself, both from my own anxiety and from Mary, I had actually been perpetuating the problem, leaving Mary feeling worse than she needed to feel and leaving myself more helpless than I in fact needed to be.

A Brief Digression on the Science of Subjectivity, Inspired by My Insightful Editor

The inner response I have been describing—my initial countertransference reaction to, and then my reflections on, Mary's disappointment in me—is just the kind of unmeasurable subjective experience that I claim must be incorporated into a fully objective science of the mind. My editor inadvertently substantiated the validity of this approach with a question she posed to me in a marginal note toward the end of the last section (when the book was in manuscript form): "How much of this," she wrote, "given your own anger and polemics at 'unfair,' 'big business' type situations, might have been colored by your lens? Your anger shielding you from really trying to hammer out why Mary was crying? It would be interesting to look at this. Given a situation in one of your patient's lives that closely approximates the kind of situation that triggers off your own anger, are you not duplicating the same avoidance of feeling your patients are guilty of?"

Briefly put, my answer is yes! I hadn't realized that, in her states of mute distress, Mary might have been experiencing toward me the same sort of helpless outrage I had once experienced toward the Catholic church and the U.S. military-industrial complex. It didn't occur to me that I might have appeared to her at those times like a pig-headed oppressor who could not be influenced or moved to feel compassion. It was easier for me to think of her boss as being in that role. And why was this easier? Because I was not aware of my own anger at Mary and so didn't realize that I was, in a way, being pig-headed and oppressive, refusing to help her. But I hadn't wanted to know that I was capable of being a jerk, and so I hadn't been able to appreciate how Mary could experience me as such. The anxiety I had felt about not knowing how to help Mary was therefore at least partly a response to my own unconscious jerkiness—my unfair anger at her for "making" me feel helpless—threatening to become conscious. In this unconscious anger I had actually been experiencing Mary as the oppressor—impervious to my needs, opinions, and desires, forcing me into a position of helplessness by her impenetrable silence. I did gradually come to feel and understand all this consciously, but, as my editor suggested, I might have got there sooner, with less distress to Mary, had I not had the same problem she did.

Sounds bad, doesn't it? I had the same problem my patient did, and that interfered with my being able to help her. But as you will see in Chapters 11 and 12, this is pretty generally the way transference works in the psychotherapeutic process: Unconsciously, the patient actually needs to provoke the therapist to experience the same problem she has, so that he must then resolve that problem in himself *in order* to be able to help the patient with it. This means that sooner or later in every effective psychotherapy, I actually expect to develop the same inner conflict that my patient is struggling with, and to have to heal myself before I can properly treat the patient.

But my editor didn't know that! She simply recognized the parallel between the kind of anger I had experienced as an adolescent and the kind of anger I thought Mary should have been feeling toward her boss. From this, she correctly inferred that my own problem with anger had been interfering with my understanding Mary's problem with me. Thus, my seemingly gratuitous digression into the story of my own repetition compulsion actually helped meet Bohr's criteria for objective scientific description, as discussed in Chapter 8. It served to define my observational framework (which necessarily includes the emotional tendencies of my repetition compulsion) unambiguously enough that my editor (and presumably other educated readers) could understand even the *unconscious* details of my interaction with Mary. By helping readers identify with my personal *subjectivity,* my digression improved the *objectivity* of Mary's "case report," making my observations more objective in the sense that they are consensually validatable, independent of any *individual* subjectivity.

What About Medication?

I did now realize that I had been perpetuating Mary's problem by distancing myself emotionally, and that I had somehow been feeling more helpless than I needed to be. But there remained that nagging question of medication. Given that I *had* been feeling so helpless, why hadn't I ever thought of using medication when Mary was in one of her states? Well, for one thing, these states had been infrequent and brief, and I hadn't allowed myself to recognize how disturbing they were to her. For another, I wouldn't have known exactly what I was treating. Mary had repeatedly said that she was unable to identify her upset feeling as either depression or as anxiety, or for that matter as any other feeling that she knew the name of. She knew only that she felt paralyzed by it. Probably most of my psychiatric colleagues would have used medication anyway, on a trial-and-error basis. They would have decided what to name the symptom according to which medication relieved it. But that approach is based on a philosophy that is completely antithetical to my own. My medication-oriented colleagues think of a symptom as the direct result of an underlying disorder of brain functioning. I think of symptoms very differently, as the manifestation of an internal emotional conflict in which an emotion is stirred that has until then been kept unconscious because it is unacceptable to the conscious self. As the newly activated emotion begins to emerge into conscious awareness, it triggers the psyche's alarm system, producing anxiety; and because anxiety is such a uniquely uncomfortable state to be in, the psyche tries to turn off the alarm by creating a symptom that diverts or distracts attention from the unconscious emotion that is setting off the alarm (but at the same time expresses that emotion in a disguised way). Since my best guess had been that Mary's symptomatic state resulted from a repressed unconscious emotion of anger trying to come to the surface, and since I believed that Mary's symptom would disappear if she could feel that anger consciously, it simply didn't occur to me to use medication. Even if medication might have worked, it would have done so by suppressing or dampening the unconscious emotion, rendering it less accessible to consciousness. I would then have been relieving the symptom but perpetuating the underlying problem.

I might have felt differently had Mary's symptom been interfering significantly with her day-to-day functioning, or had she ever actually said to me, "I don't think I can go on feeling like this. I simply can't stand it." In that case I might have reasoned that the normally adaptive anxiety response was being overwhelmed by an unconscious emotion too intense and/or too frightening to be processed in the usual way. (In the same way, fever, normally an adaptive response that facilitates the natural healing process, can sometimes become maladaptive, raising the body temperature beyond the point where it helps to fight infection, so high that it begins to interfere with healing.) In such situations of overwhelming unconscious emotion, medication can often dampen the unbearable affective turbulence without completely suppressing it, thereby making the emotion less overwhelming and hence *more* accessible to consciousness. But of course Mary *was* now saying to me that her unnameable states were overwhelming and unbearable to her. Although they hadn't prevented her from performing well at work, they did seem to be interfering with her ability to participate fully in the psychotherapeutic process. After all, she could hardly talk to me when she was in one of those states. I could feel myself, in these reflections, almost trying to talk myself into offering her medication, as if I were feeling (uncharacteristically) pressured to do the politically correct thing. Yet still I hesitated. Why?

I decided to practice what I preached and, rather than try to talk myself out of the feeling, simply let myself feel my ongoing reluctance—even given the level of distress I now understood Mary to be suffering—to use medication. As soon as I focused in on the feeling, I became aware that my reluctance was a counterreaction to the strong temptation I felt to resort to medication not in order to calm Mary's agitation but to calm my own. It would be a great relief if I could simply forget about trying to figure out why Mary was crying and be content to settle her with a pacifier. I knew clearly that giving in to this temptation would be an evasion of my responsibility to her, but I would be the only one who knew it. To everyone else, including Mary, it would look as if I were doing just what a doctor is supposed to do. Of course I now recognized that offering Mary medication might actually be the right thing to do, but I was quite certain that offering it to her for the purpose of calming my own anxiety would be wrong. So until I found another way of dealing with my anxiety, I wouldn't be in a position to assess with any kind of objectivity whether Mary needed medication or not at this particular juncture.

Process Versus Content

Already in the few brief seconds in which I had been processing my reactions to Mary's criticism I had been gaining a much clearer awareness that my anxiety with her centered around my own feeling of utter helplessness—my inability to understand or relieve her distress. When I went back and felt again the similarity of this feeling to the frantic, helpless state of a parent whose infant is in distress, I also felt a whole new dimension of possibilities open up for helping Mary. My mode of attention shifted, from reasoning about what might be happening inside Mary, as I could only speculate about it from outside, to a feeling awareness of what was going on between us, as I could discern it within myself. I welcomed this familiar shift from content-thinking to process-awareness—from thinking of Mary (positivistically) as if she were a completely separate other and I a detached observer of her, to feeling the pushes and pulls of our evolving emotional interaction—a relationship in which I was participant as well as observer. While I wanted to reserve medication as an option, I saw no particular advantage and several obvious disadvantages to even considering it before I had exhausted the yet untested psychotherapeutic possibilities that now presented themselves with this new process-awareness.

So I returned from my reverie and said to Mary, "You know, until you told me just now, I hadn't realized just how unbearable your feeling was at those times. You certainly had good reason to feel disappointed in me. Thinking just now about what you were telling me, I was going back over those sessions in my mind, and I noticed an impression that had never quite registered before. The distress you felt then, that you seemed unable to talk about or even put a name to, reminds me of the kind of distress a sick or hungry baby must feel who is too young to have words and so can't say where it hurts. That could be a very frantic feeling for the baby if no one does anything to make it better, and I have the sense now that you felt something like that kind of franticness when I wasn't helpful in those sessions."

"Yes!" she said. "That's just what it felt like! I *was* frantic, and I couldn't do anything to make it stop, and there were no words I could find to tell you about it so that you could make it stop. . . . You know I probably never mentioned it before, but I did have colic for six months after I was born. I guess it must have been pretty severe because my mother still talks about it from time to time. I suppose this horrible feeling of mine might be like what a colicky baby feels."

"Hmm. Yeah, that makes a lot of sense. . . . So then if it is like colic, I would think it would have to feel almost more physical than psychological, like a generalized bodily agitation—a painful restlessness—rather than anything you would be able to recognize and name as a distressing feeling or emotion."

"Yes, that's right! It is definitely in my body, deep under my skin somewhere. It's like, when I'm that way, I can't be still. Nothing in my body is still."

Cellular Dysphoria

Mary had never described her distress so clearly as an experience of physical pain or dysphoria before. She had always seemed to accept my way of talking about it as more of a conscious emotional experience, a kind of "anger trying to happen." While I was not about to discard the assumption that her unnameable distress was psychological/emotional in origin, I was at this point forced to recognize that Mary was much more radically cut off from the psychological/emotional dimension of her distress than I had previously thought. She felt the turbulence in her body (an affect), but she was very far from feeling anything like an emotional quality in her unnameable states. What she felt was more like the dull agitation of a toothache, only spread through her entire body rather than localized in one tooth.

My instinctive response to this new appreciation of Mary's unnameable distress was that it needed a name. I began to refer to it as her "cellular dysphoria." In calling it *dysphoria,* a term derived from a Greek word meaning "hard to bear," I was thinking of its usage in neurology to denote a peculiar state of physical discomfort (often produced by nerve damage) that is not distinct enough to be called pain but can be even more excruciating. In calling it *cellular,* I was trying to capture the sense I had from Mary's description of it that her discomfort was deep in the cells of her body, deep enough that she couldn't soothe or comfort herself because she couldn't get at the place where it hurt.

Mary loved the name, not only because she felt it captured the uniquely unpleasant under-the-skin somatic quality of her experience but also because it made her feel special to be given a new term of her own, one that I had coined just for her and didn't use with anyone else. In addition, and what was particularly remarkable, Mary found that having a name for her distress made it much easier for her to recognize when she was feeling it. As we talked more about this over the next few weeks, it emerged that she felt some degree of cellular dysphoria much more often than either one of us had first imagined. In addition to the sort of occasional severe but brief episode that we had been discussing, she suffered a milder, more pervasive version of the same unsettling feeling. She began to notice that this milder dysphoria occurred during at least part of almost every session with me, and she reported that at work she would sometimes have it for what seemed like days at a time. She also realized that she had had the same kind of feeling off and on throughout her adult life, and that it was probably what had driven her to use drugs during a period of her adolescence.

A Brief Digression on Diagnosis

This discovery that Mary had been suffering from cellular dysphoria for years without realizing it had fascinating implications. For one thing, it took her out of the ill-defined category of the worried well and qualified her for an official *DSM* diagnosis. Previously she had shown no symptoms of any major psychiatric disorder—no psychosis, no panic anxiety, no obsessions or compulsions, no depression or mania, no dissociation, no anorexia or bulimia—nor was her social functioning disturbed enough to meet the criteria for a personality disorder. But now, taking her cellular dysphoria into account, it appeared that Mary had all along been suffering from a kind of depression. The acute episodes of severe distress that she had experienced during the last year were like what is called an *agitated depression,* except that they didn't last very long. The more chronic form of her symptom—the protracted periods of subtle, pervasive malaise that she now realized she had been suffering from since adolescence—were typical of a milder but still debilitating form of depression called *dysthymic disorder.*

Not that I had ever doubted Mary had a legitimate problem for which she needed treatment, with or without a *DSM* diagnosis. If, as Freud said, mental health consists of being able to love and to work, then Mary clearly had a mental illness. The impairment in her ability to love might not have counted as a problem in our official diagnostic manual, but in the book of life there is no problem more important. So the fact that her cellular dysphoria now qualified her as having a real mental illness where before she had seemed to have only a mild personality problem simply confirmed what I already knew—that there is a good deal more to the worries of the worried well than this trivializing label would suggest.

At the same time, the way Mary's cellular dysphoria had seemed to emerge in the context of her relationship difficulties—first with her boss, then with me—did shed some new light on an important diagnostic issue: the relationship between symptoms and personality. Mary's pattern with men of repeatedly breaking off relationships abruptly, though it was not severe enough to "count" as a personality disorder, certainly met the definition of a personality trait—a stable, stereotyped pattern of emotional and behavioral responses to particular interpersonal situations. But it seemed that the same pattern could now equally well be explained as a result of her symptom. Cellular dysphoria made it difficult for her to relax with a man and put her on edge in a way that could easily produce an impulsive need to flee a relationship. To me, this suggested that her personality difficulty and her symptom disorder were intimately related, and reflected the same underlying problem with intimacy.

Such an idea went against the prevailing psychiatric view at that time, which explained personality disorders psychologically and symptom disorders biologically. Personality disorders were thought of as habitual patterns of emotional and behavioral responses learned through repeated early experiences of dysfunctional family interactions. Symptom disorders were thought of as neurochemical imbalances that produce psychosomatic distress (anxiety, depression, etc.) irrespective of early experiences or personality type. But Mary's difficulty—a dysfunctional personality trait that had evolved into a state of psychosomatic distress—seemed to defy this simplistic dichotomy, and demanded a more integrated explanation.

Personality, Symptoms, and the Repetition Compulsion

Today, most Medical Model psychiatrists would favor an integration that explains both Mary's personality trait and her symptom disorder as manifestations of the same underlying problem of brain chemistry. This view, popularized in books like *Listening to Prozac* and *Shadow Syndromes*, rejects the traditional understanding of personality as an organization of learned responses. It considers personality problems like Mary's as having little or nothing to do with early experiences, but rather as being caused by a milder form (a so-called *forme fruste*) of the same sort of chemical imbalances that produce full-fledged symptom disorders.[1]

My own view, and that of the Psychotherapeutic Model, takes inner conflict rather than chemical imbalance as the unifying explanation for mental illness. I believe that all mental illnesses—personality disorders as well as symptom disorders—are caused by inner conflict, and that even a "normal" personality inevitably organizes itself around inner conflict. In fact, from an evolutionary perspective, I believe that the adaptive point of having a personality in the first place is to provide a solution to the problem of inner conflict!

Let me elaborate. If we define *personality* as an enduring organization of habitual interpersonal responses (behavioral, cognitive, and emotional), then it makes sense that having a personality would further the survival of the species because it provides emotional stability for the individual. Specifically, it allows us to engage in social interactions without being too disrupted by them (as we would be if we were never quite certain who we were or how we were going to react next).

But then, what is it that makes social interactions so disruptive that we need a stabilizing personality to protect us? It is that social interactions tend to evoke emotional responses in us, and often activate anxiety-provoking unconscious emotions. So it is not the social interaction per se that disrupts us, but the forces of inner conflict that the interaction stirs up in us—forces that are inherently destabilizing and push us toward change. At the same time, of course, the capacity for change that comes with inner conflict must itself be an evolutionary advantage. Anxiety, symptoms, and inner conflict are not only disruptive (swimming-pool perspective) but also adaptive (quest perspective). So, as a simple generalization, it makes sense to say that our personality maintains stability while our inner conflicts push us to grow.

In other words, the evolutionary function of a personality is to manage inner conflict and minimize anxiety through a pattern of habitual interpersonal responses. But recall that this is exactly the function of the repetition compulsion—to protect against anxiety through the repeated reenactment of an unconscious scenario. What gets repeated in this reenactment is exactly what gets repeated in a personality tendency: a habitual pattern of interpersonal responses. The point of repeating the unconscious scenario—like Mary's tendency to break off relationships with men abruptly, or my tendency to become outrageously polemical—is to divert the unconscious emotions into (interpersonal) action so that we can avoid the anxiety of having to feel the emotions directly. The repetition maintains our sense of stability by keeping us focused on the enemy (threat) outside us, so that we can put off having to meet the enemy within. So from a psychoanalytic/evolutionary perspective, *personality patterns are the outward conscious expression of the unconscious scenarios of the repetition compulsion.*

By this definition, the line between normal personality and personality disorder is ambiguous. It depends on the degree to which the acting out of the unconscious scenario—the habitual personality pattern—solves the primary problem of inner conflict versus the degree to which it produces a secondary problem of interpersonal conflict. Mary's personality pattern of cutting off relationships abruptly solved the internal problem of her unconscious anger (by getting her out of the situations that provoked it) but at the cost of creating the interpersonal problem of failed relationships. Now that she had decided she no longer wanted to depend on this familiar though dysfunctional reaction pattern in her relationship with me, she had been forced to fall back on the symptom of cellular dysphoria as an alternative way of managing her inner conflict.

Here was a convincing explanation of how Mary's personality pattern and her symptom could be products of the same underlying problem with intimacy: both were unconscious attempts to manage the inner conflict she repeatedly experienced in her relationships with men. I now believe that this sort of connection between personality and symptoms is a general feature of all mental illnesses. I think of a personality pattern, organized around an inner conflict, as being like a geological terrain that contains a fault line. Most of the time the terrain appears solid and stable, but too much pressure at the fault line can produce an earthquake. In the same way, a normally stable personality pattern can crack under pressure, giving rise to symptoms. In this sense, every personality could be said to have a trace of personality disorder—a fault line—that, given a particular kind of stress, can erupt into a full-fledged symptom disorder. That is why dynamic psychotherapy is so essential in the treatment of all mental illnesses, symptom disorders as well as personality disorders. The effect of making the unconscious conscious is to resolve inner conflict by integrating the anxiety-provoking emotions into a larger sense of self. This permanently releases the pressure at the fault line and thereby improves the balance and flexibility of the personality organization so that it is less vulnerable to stress and less likely to develop symptoms.

Recapitulation: Good News and Bad News

To sum up, Mary's achievement in being able to recognize and express her disappointment in me represented a psychotherapeutic turning point. Once she could feel the disappointment and, to some degree, the anger behind her impulse to quit her relationship with me, she no longer needed to resort to threats of quitting in order to express it. Now she could put the feeling into words, specifically into the complaint that I hadn't given her the help she so desperately needed with her cellular dysphoria. But in so doing, she had in effect created a new problem for herself. Her complaint, which served to focus our attention on her uniquely painful symptom, had thereby accentuated her awareness of that symptom as a prominent feature of her daily life. The good news was that her increased self-awareness, her relief in being able to tell me she was disappointed, and her delight in the special term I had coined for her had all helped to diminish the urgent impulsiveness that had made her repeatedly want to terminate treatment prematurely. The bad news was that her inner conflict around intimacy was far from resolved. In fact, by staying with me in analysis, she was actually aggravating that conflict—risking more intimacy than she ever had before! The result was, having given up the protection that her periodic brief impulses to quit had once provided her, she was now left with the much more pervasive—and at the same time much more obscure—symptom of cellular dysphoria.

11. Resistance and Transference

This thing of darkness I acknowledge mine.

—Shakespeare, *The Tempest*

Despite the illuminating insight it provided into the link between personality and symptoms, there was something disconcerting about finding the psychologically opaque experience of cellular dysphoria under the surface of Mary's more transparent impulse to quit analysis. After all, bringing the unconscious into consciousness was supposed to bring with it greater clarity, not greater obscurity. Peeling away layers from the onion of Mary's impulsiveness should have brought us closer to her underlying feelings—as indeed it did, initially, to her feeling of angry disappointment in me. But where this new feeling should have pointed us to other deeper feelings, it now seemed to be pointing instead to an experience far removed from anything that could be called a feeling at all. After being able to discern within herself a succession of deepening layers of emotional awareness—first impulse, then urgency, then anxiety, then disappointment and anger—Mary was now left only with the pure physical immediacy of her cellular dysphoria, in which she could discern no emotional quality whatsoever. She only knew that it hurt, that she needed me to make it stop, and that I wasn't making it stop.

But then, I reassured myself, wasn't this itself an emotional experience, and a new one at that, which had emerged only through the process of peeling the introspective onion? After existing for most of Mary's life as nothing more than uncontextualized, purely physical pain, cellular dysphoria had now been transformed by the psychotherapeutic process into an experience of physical pain within a painful relationship. In fact, once we had named it and began to pay more attention to it, Mary gradually (over a period of a month or two) began to experience cellular dysphoria much more regularly during her hours with me, and to be less troubled by it at work and elsewhere. She had, in effect, taken a problem that was originally outside of our psychotherapeutic relationship (one that she had always experienced in anguished isolation) and brought it into the center of that relationship, where it could now become a problem for both of us. In other words, cellular dysphoria had now become part of the transference.

Transference As a Remembering of the Past

It was typical of transference that Mary's cellular dysphoria should recapitulate something she had once experienced with her parents. Her mother had often told her that even as a baby she never liked to be held, and it was easy to imagine how a personality trait might have evolved: *Mary was colicky, wanting to be comforted. Her parents tried to hold her, but she was inconsolable and continued crying and squirming. Her parents felt helpless and hurt at her fending them off. Gradually they gave up trying to hold her. Mary felt abandoned by their apparent withdrawal, and her frantic sense of helplessness was so great that it triggered a self-protective switch inside her, so that she stopped wanting to be held or comforted at all. Eventually she began to push people away whenever they tried to hold her.* In terms of this hypothetical scenario, Mary's inability to talk during her episodes of cellular dysphoria was the "transference equivalent" of her inability to be comfortably held when colicky. My repeated attempts to engage her in the psychotherapeutic process—to talk with her about what she was experiencing in her mute distress—were the equivalent of her parents' attempts to comfort and hold her when she was colicky. My internal reaction of distancing myself from her in order to relieve my own anxiety was then the countertransference equivalent of her parents giving up trying to hold her (countertransference being the spontaneous inner reaction elicited in the therapist by the patient's transference).

This was an appealing explanation. It persuasively tied together Mary's transference experience with me, my countertransference experience with her, and the report from her parents about her never liking to be held. But of course it was an unconfirmable speculation that Mary's psychosomatic experience of cellular dysphoria in the present felt like her experience of colic as an infant. We can never know for sure what the experience of an infant is like; we can only make inferences, based on our sense of empathy for the infant's expressions of emotion, and based on the assumption that some of the inchoate emotional experiences of which we are capable as adults must be carry-overs from the experiences of infancy. On that basis, it does seem likely that fluctuating states of diffuse, intense bodily discomfort, like Mary's cellular dysphoria, are much more characteristic of an infant's experience than of an adult's. We assume that the infant's awareness is naturally more inchoate—like cellular dysphoria, inherently difficult to describe in words—simply because the infant cannot tell clearly that it is her experience, because she has not yet figured out where she ends and the world around her begins. In fact, there is a good deal of research to suggest that in the early months of life the infant has no differentiated sense of a self at all, separate from the mothering presence, or of a mother who has a life independent of the infant's awareness of her.[1] Therefore, if the infant's body is in pain, her whole world is painful and mother is part of that pain. If the infant could talk, she would not say "I am in pain" but rather "There is pain." As the infant grows, then, her growing capacity to distinguish inside from outside, and self from other, will roughly parallel her growing ability to use words to define individuated elements of her experience of the world.

Given that the most striking feature of Mary's cellular dysphoria was her utter inability to talk about it, it was easy to imagine that her experience actually lacked any of the differentiated quality that the use of words reflects—to think of it essentially as a "body memory" of her infantile colic. It was tempting to imagine that the transference and countertransference—Mary's inchoate, inconsolable distress and my internal emotional distancing—were a repetition of events from Mary's very early life, when her distress was unnameable because she couldn't yet talk and when her parents were unable to provide relief. Reliving this scenario in the present with me would then be the only sort of memory she could possibly regain of such an early traumatic experience—a remembering through repeating it.

At the same time, I knew that the function of repeating an early traumatic experience in the transference was not so much to remember the traumatic events as to feel the painful emotions. To Mary's immature infant psyche these emotions had been far too overwhelming to process consciously, but they had been registered unconsciously and remained embedded within the physiological affect state of cellular dysphoria. The inner conflict between these unconscious emotions pressing toward consciousness and Mary's resistance against feeling them was the ongoing source of her need to repeat that had now become focused in her transference relationship with me.

The Inward Face Is Resistance; the Outward Face Is Transference

To the extent that it was a body memory, Mary's cellular dysphoria reproduced a primitive mental state in which there could have been no inner conflict because there was not yet a differentiated conscious self who could feel her inchoate emotions as being clearly inside rather than outside. But now that she had become such a differentiated self, her cellular dysphoria had become the nexus of her inner conflict—a symptom that both disguised and expressed a disturbing unconscious emotion. On the one hand, she could use her capacity to re-create a primitive, undifferentiated state of pain as an internal resistance—a way of blotting out any awareness of any more differentiated and disturbing feelings toward me. On the other hand, in the very process of blotting them out, her cellular dysphoria also functioned as a disguised expression of those disturbing feelings. It stood as a mute reproach against me for not relieving her pain, for instance, and at the same time a silent rebellion, in which she refused to let herself open up and feel the painful emotions that I was encouraging her (or, as she probably experienced it, callously manipulating or pressuring her) to feel. In both these senses her cellular dysphoria was not just an internal resistance against self-awareness; it was also an external resistance against me—a negative transference.

So it seemed that Mary's symptom was both the reliving of a primitive undifferentiated mental state and, at the same time, as I had always thought, a kind of anger trying to happen. However much she may have wanted me to help her, by remaining mired in a purely somatic level of experience, Mary was unconsciously fighting my attempts to help her through talking. This symptomatic stonewalling suggested that she must at some level experience me as someone who could not be trusted with her feelings. It implied that there must be another layer to her negative feelings about me—deeper than the disappointment and anger she had so far been able to acknowledge—a layer of more disturbing mistrust, possibly even hatred, still buried within her cellular dysphoria. To the extent that it expressed these more disturbing feelings, however mutely and indirectly, her symptom represented not the resistance but the consciousness-expanding tendency of the transference.

Mistrust and Hatred

On a couple of occasions earlier in the analysis, Mary had described brief flashes of deep, almost paranoid mistrustfulness toward me; but each time she had been so unsettled by the feeling that she needed to block it out of her awareness, and so had forgotten it almost as soon as she felt it. Although she was not now aware of any difficulty in trusting me, she did think of herself generally as a mistrustful person. With other people outside the analysis, she often felt a sense of guardedness and wariness whenever she began to feel close enough to the other person to be vulnerable. She tended to become easily suspicious that she was being taken advantage of, yet at the same time she would feel pressured to please the other person. This left her torn between an impulse to break off the relationship on the one hand and what looked like an overdependent need for the relationship—really a need to please—on the other. I speculated that she was afraid, were she actually to let herself feel taken advantage of—for instance, by allowing herself to stay with her feeling of mistrustfulness toward me when she felt it—that her strong protest would incur the other person's dislike and disapproval or, even worse, that it would put her in touch with the disturbing force of her own hatred. Either way, the danger was that a relationship in which she had been able to feel some degree of closeness and comfort would be destroyed, and her reaction was to ward off this danger by needing to please—making herself more dependent on the other person for reassurance and approval.

Recently Mary had felt this fluctuation between mistrustful wariness and pressured dependency particularly strongly with her boss, but she had felt the same feelings many times before—with former husbands and boyfriends, with both parents and siblings, and with her closest friends. With me, the ambivalence was much more subtle. Consciously, her feelings toward me had been almost entirely positive, with frequent feelings of gratitude for all the help I had given her in the analysis. Nevertheless, her quickly forgotten flashes of mistrustfulness together with her periodic urgent (but also quickly forgotten) impulses to end treatment suggested that there was a certain tenuousness to these good feelings about me, as if she expected our relationship to become contaminated sooner or later by bad feelings and would have preferred to "get out while the gettin' was still good." At the same time, she had tried to hold on to my goodwill by not complaining too much about her cellular dysphoria, fearing that her complaint could disrupt or even destroy our relationship. Although her new awareness of disappointment and anger at me had now taken the edge off any impulse to end treatment, it had also brought her closer to the deeper layer of bad feelings from which that impulse had always distracted her—the disturbing feelings of mistrust and hate that were simultaneously expressed and concealed in her cellular dysphoria.

The Fault Is Not in Our Stars but in Our Moms?

Again it was easy to imagine that this whole complex of bad feelings embedded within her symptom was modeled after Mary's early experience of colic, when she had given up wanting to be held in reaction to her parents' giving up their efforts to comfort her. Her mistrustfulness as an adult could then be considered essentially a learned response according to which she expected people to be unavailable or uninterested in her the same way her parents had been.

The problem with this point of view was that it was one-dimensional. It presupposed that Mary's mistrustfulness was warranted—and could be explained—by the behavior of her parents. It presupposed that her parents had failed, however understandably, to be "good enough" parents to a child with severe colic. But there was an equally plausible alternative scenario according to which Mary could have reacted with anger and mistrust even if her parents had never given up or withdrawn from her. This scenario would start from the idea that we all instinctively experience pain as an affliction visited on us from outside ourselves, and therefore instinctively tend to blame someone else for any pain we might feel.

Every mother will certainly recognize this as a basic truth of human nature. Children do tend to blame Mom for everything that goes wrong in their lives. But this blaming tendency is not limited to children. If I leave a cabinet door open, for instance, and then inadvertently bang my head on it, my immediate reaction is not to blame myself for my own forgetfulness, but to curse the unidentified so-and-so (presumably a close family member) who (I automatically assume) carelessly left the door open and did this to me. Or if I misplace my keys, I instinctively want to blame whoever must have moved them from the spot where I normally leave them. In the same way, as Shakespeare has reminded us, people have always tended to find the fault in their stars (gods, devils, parents, spouses, children, and bosses) rather than in themselves. I believe, with Shakespeare, that a blaming mechanism of this sort is inherent in human nature, and that it appears in the universal tendency toward transference projection. Many developmental psychologists believe that projection and blaming constitute the infant's earliest mechanisms for establishing the distinction between inside (self) and outside (world). The crying infant shows the same sense of outrage at the way hunger, or intestinal gas, has painfully disrupted his previously comfortable condition as he does at a harsh noise or other disruption coming from outside. The reason, almost certainly, is that he experiences all pain as coming from outside. The roots of adult prejudice, nationalism, and paranoia lie in this instinctive equation of infancy: good = me = inside; bad = not-me = outside. The infant embraces good feelings as belonging to the self while projecting (transferring the locus of) all bad feelings into an alien (m)otherness. The subsequent development, in toddlerhood, of the capacity to say no is a later evolution of this same projective mechanism of individuation, the implication being that I am the one who has a right to want/feel this way and Mom is the one who wrongly wants/feels that way.

It was inevitable then that, as an infant, Mary would have needed to blame someone for her unrelieved colic, projecting all inner sense of pain and/or badness to the outside. Of course, her actual feeling at the time would have been a relatively inchoate precursor of blaming, but as she grew and gradually became able to have a more differentiated self-experience, she would have begun to blame her parents, experiencing them as persecutors who had betrayed her (the external causes of her pain) rather than as earnest but ineffectual helpers. She would have had no way of understanding that her parents were not godlike in their omnipotence, and would have assumed that if they were not providing the solution then they must be causing the problem. Her crying and squirming would then have taken on a tone of outrage and eventually hatred toward her parents, and she might easily have withdrawn from them, feeling hurt, bitter, and betrayed, even if they themselves had never flagged in their efforts to comfort her. According to this alternative scenario, Mary's eventual adult tendency to be mistrustful of people who tried to hold her (stay with her in a long-term relationship) would be the natural evolution of her very early "paranoid" reaction to her parents as perpetrators of her pain.

Nurture and Nature

I realized that these two hypothetical scenarios I had formulated for the origin of Mary's cellular dysphoria reflected the perennial polarities of the nature–nurture debate: Did Mary develop her symptom because of a failure of her parents or because of a flaw in her own nature? Theoretically, the correct answer is undoubtedly both; but in practice, a psychotherapist must choose which paradigm to emphasize at any given clinical moment. Psychoanalysts have traditionally emphasized nature rather than nurture, teaching their patients to look for the fault in themselves rather than in their parents. It is not that parents are never to blame, only that they are easy targets. It is much easier to see the qualities we hate in someone else than to see, much less accept, those same qualities in ourselves. The goal of the psychotherapeutic process—healing the soul—requires that we take the less traveled path, looking honestly at ourselves and taking responsibility for our own faults.

Nevertheless, it is healthy and sometimes necessary to be able to blame other people. Blaming one's parents, and one's therapist, for what they have really done wrong (and, given the universal flaws of human nature, they have always done something wrong) is an essential step toward growing up and becoming one's own person—as essential as the toddler's developing the capacity to say no. As part of the negative transference, it is also a necessary element in the psychotherapeutic process. By itself, however, blaming is only one step—necessary but not sufficient—in the processes of growing and healing. True maturity and healing come only after repeated bitter experiences have brought us to the place where there is nobody left to blame for our pain but ourselves. Luckily, we all seem to have an unconscious knack for acquiring such bitter learning experiences, through the operation of the repetition compulsion. Dynamic psychotherapy is simply a way of harnessing this knack—concentrating, focusing, and framing the tendencies of the repetition compulsion in a way that seldom happens in ordinary life, through the intensification of transference.

Transference As a Manifestation of Inner Conflict

Mary's cellular dysphoria was an example of just such an intensification. It was a symptom that had been with her to some degree, off and on, since adolescence, but until she got into psychotherapy she had never had to pay much conscious attention to it. Whenever things would get too uncomfortable, she had always been able to run away somehow, whether by doing drugs, breaking off relationships, quitting jobs, switching departments, or even, a couple of times, moving to a different city. Through repeated attempts to run in the same way from psychoanalysis, she had now come to recognize the inner urgency and anxiety that drove her, and to understand that she was really trying to run away from something in herself. Her conscious decision to stay with analysis and work on staying with her uncomfortable feelings was an acknowledgment that the problem was in her, not in her environment. But precisely because she chose not to run away from it, the pressure of Mary's disturbing emotions began to build up, and hence her cellular dysphoria gradually increased in frequency and intensity within the analytic setting. This was a manifestation of her unconscious feelings of mistrust and hatred—her disowned need to blame me—coming closer to consciousness, and stirring up correspondingly greater resistance. Her symptom was a compromise, as all symptoms are, between Mary's need to feel these conflicted feelings and her need to run away from them.

In this context it would have been a serious mistake for me to interpret her cellular dysphoria simply as a body memory and learned response to what had happened between her and her parents in her first six months of life. To do so would have provided her with an easy rationalization for running away—from the immediacy of her newly emerging negative feelings about me, and her inner conflict over them, into the remoteness of a theoretical fantasy about hypothetical events from her distant past. In fact, it occurred to me that by spending so much time on these speculations about Mary's infancy, I myself was running away from my feelings about her cellular dysphoria in the present. There was no need to speculate about what might or might not have happened in Mary's unrememberable past, after all, because we were reliving it in the here-and-now of the psychotherapeutic process. It was clear enough that I had failed to comfort her at times of her greatest distress, and that, in my emotional withdrawal at those times, I had been acting very much like a *not*-good-enough parent. Instead of empathizing with Mary's plight, I had been angry at her for her transference colic and had left her to cry herself to sleep! That was why I suspected Mary must be harboring much more anger at me—even hatred—than she knew, and must be in a state of unconscious conflict over it. In a very real sense I *deserved* more anger than she had yet consciously felt! How could she not feel abandoned, betrayed, and deeply mistrustful about my attitude toward her? How could she not feel at some level that I didn't care enough about her to even want to help her (as by giving her medication) when she was hurting?

I knew that Mary was not eager to dwell on such feelings. Up until now, she had always been able to dismiss the brief, disturbing flashes of mistrustfulness she had occasionally felt toward me. In fact, it had been a great source of comfort to her that she did not feel with me the kind of guardedness and pressure to please that she felt with so many other people. Rather she had always felt that I gave her the space to be herself. But this idealized picture of me was now threatened by her experience of cellular dysphoria. What she had always taken as my caring gesture of giving her space, she might now easily begin to experience as my cold, rigid, uncaring detachment. What she had previously felt as a relaxed absence of pressure, she could easily experience more mistrustfully as a silent pressure—my arrogant, selfish expectation that she do all the work of analysis herself while I sat back passively doing nothing. In fact, my ongoing experience of her cellular dysphoria was that it "embodied" just these complaints against me, in a kind of global, mute reproach that she was still unable, or afraid, to formulate in words.

Transference Cure Versus Existential Responsibility

So if I did interpret Mary's cellular dysphoria and her disappointment in me in terms of her early experience with her parents, I would only be encouraging her denial, deflecting her attention from these disturbing new feelings about me in the present. This could subtly suggest to her that I would rather have her idealize me than feel whatever she really felt. It would encourage her idealization, by suggesting that anything negative she might feel about me was really a feeling about her parents, and by giving her the reassuring impression that I (unlike her parents) was now finally doing something (giving her an ostensibly deep interpretation) to comfort her. This might actually help her to feel better, since strengthening the idealization would alleviate the anxiety of her underlying mistrustfulness. But the problem would be that she would then have to suppress the mistrustfulness without ever becoming aware of the negative emotions that fueled it. This would leave her with pretty much the same neurotic handicap that she had when she came into therapy—a need to limit the degree of intimacy she could permit herself in any relationship, in order to limit her vulnerability to feeling betrayed and thus limit the danger of an uncontrolled, potentially destructive outbreak of hostile emotions.

There would be an inherent instability in such a therapeutic result—sometimes called a transference cure—because it would depend on an idealizing positive transference in which Mary saw herself as the helpless victim of an external dragon (her parents) and me as the white knight who was rescuing her. The problem with such a cure is the same as the problem with a medication cure: it involves a disclaimer of existential responsibility for one's own dark side—for the guilt/shame/anxiety-provoking emotions that come out in the universal need for negative transference (projection and blaming). That's always the problem, I reflected, with understanding transference simply as a repetition of early childhood experiences. Past trauma cannot cause present pain unless there is a current, active inner conflict within the traumatized person that is, in effect, perpetuating the trauma. It is that current conflict, not the old trauma per se, that causes symptoms and generates transference.[2]

Transference As Projection

For Mary to understand her difficulties with me in terms of an inner conflict in the present, we would need to think of her transference as a *projection,* in which she would be seeing in me (and blaming me for) an emotion or attitude that she could not tolerate feeling in herself. Her transference, according to this view, would be a way to get rid of the (unconscious) "badness" within herself, and at the same time to make me into a mirror in which she could confront that badness face to face. In this sense, her disappointment in me would be a reflection of what she might find disappointing, were she aware of it, in herself; and her mistrust of me (to the extent that she felt it) was a reflection of what she could not trust in herself.

It used to be thought that transference projection involved only the patient's neurotically distorted image of the therapist, which the patient projected onto him as if he were a blank screen that has no responsibility for what appears on it. Psychoanalysts were taught to be objective observers, who should, in their neutrality, serve as blank screens for their patients' projections. Any kind of emotional engagement with or reaction to a patient was considered a countertransference "error"—an avoidable failure in the analyst's proper function. But we now know that this was a misguided view, based on the failure of analysts as a group to acknowledge the ubiquity and intensity of our own countertransference reactions. The myth of the blank screen was popular at a time (the 1950s and 1960s) when counter-transference was only beginning to be understood theoretically, and it has long since disappeared from psychoanalytic teaching.

The currently accepted view of transference projection is exemplified in my experience with Mary. What Mary was projecting was not only an image but the (unconscious) feelings and attitudes that went into that image. These she projected not only *onto* me, but *into* me, according to the law of like evokes like. Remember that my automatic reaction to her cellular dysphoria, and to her inability to talk about it, was to withdraw from her emotionally. Her symptom, which contained the implicit (unconscious) angry, mistrust-ful expectation that I would withdraw from her as she felt her parents had, ac-tually elicited my real tendency to do so. But her symptom itself represented a tendency to withdraw (by not talking) that replaced her earlier impulse to quit analysis. By expressing this withdrawal unconsciously in her symptom, she was able in effect to put (project) *into* me her own unacceptable emo-tion—the harsh, cold, rejection of intimacy—while getting rid of (disown-ing) it in herself.

According to this understanding of transference, the patient actively but unconsciously provokes behavior and attitudes in the therapist that conform to, and seem to justify, an image already present in the patient's unconscious—the image of what the patient can't tolerate in herself. Being unconscious, this image does not exist in the patient's mind in a form that she can recognize or describe. Rather, it is a projective tendency, a personality dis-position awaiting the opportunity to play itself out in a relationship. It can be seen and described as an image only when it appears in the behavior and at-titudes of the therapist, and the patient can then be in conscious conflict with the therapist instead of unconscious conflict with herself.

Thus transference projection functions to make an internal conflict into an external, interpersonal one. The mechanism is as follows: Internal conflict over an unacceptable (unconscious) emotion produces anxiety in the patient. The anxiety then prompts an (unconscious) projection of the unacceptable emotion into the therapist. The projection pushes an emotional button in the therapist, provoking a countertransference response, in which the therapist consciously experiences and/or unconsciously acts out the projected emotion that the patient can't tolerate. Now that the conflict has become externalized through transference projection, it serves to distract the patient from the disturbing emotion that is the source of anxiety within herself, but at the same time it brings that emotion closer to conscious awareness by putting it right in her face (metaphorically) whenever she looks at the therapist.

Looking in the Mirror

Such projective transactions are by no means confined to psychotherapeutic relationships. They are ubiquitous, and any patient will have projected the same transference feelings and experienced the same transference–countertransference conflict with many other partners before ever experiencing them with the therapist. The difference is that outside of psychotherapy, in the neurotic conflicts of everyday life, it is much more difficult to tell who is projecting what into whom.

Consider paranoia, the prototypical example of the projective process. Imagine a paranoid man walking into a small, quiet waiting room and finding it occupied. He enters with eyes sharp, suspicious, darting from person to person, looking for the danger he knows is lurking. Perhaps he frowns ominously or shows muted alarm on his face. Now imagine the reaction of the other people in the room. They sense something strange—a potential danger—in the intruder and are put immediately on guard. They don't want to stare, but they watch him carefully, self-protectively out of the corners of their eyes. The paranoid man, ever vigilant, notices these furtive glances and says to himself, "Hah, I knew it! There really is a conspiracy, and these people are in on it, too."

In this extreme example, what the paranoid man projects is his own unconscious hostile, predatory disposition. He projects *onto* the other people in the waiting room the predatory image, perceiving them as people who are out to get him. He projects *into* them the corresponding predatory emotions, provoking them to a condition of fight-or-flight activation. He himself is aware only of fear and suspiciousness, but his unconscious hostility shows in his eyes and triggers counterprojective suspiciousness and hostility in the other people. When he looks at their reaction to him, he is looking in the mirror, but he does not know it. What he sees appears alien and predatory to him, which is exactly what he expected, and exactly what he cannot tolerate seeing in himself.

In the same way, but usually more subtly and more gradually, we all create self-fulfilling prophecies in our interactions with others. We expect people to behave according to our projective expectations and without intending it we elicit in them reactions that confirm those expectations (sometimes our worst fears, sometimes our most fervent hopes). Like the paranoid person, we are often aware of our mistrustful (or idealizing) expectations, but are seldom aware that we elicit the expected reactions, still less that these mirror our own unconscious attitudes. To the extent that the other person's reaction conforms to our expectations, we don't recognize it as a reaction and therefore can't learn anything useful about ourselves from it. So we keep running the same movie, oblivious to the fact that we ourselves have produced and directed it. We see the projection but never notice the projector.

Consider another typical example: the evolution of a marital conflict. Imagine a husband who enters a marriage thinking that women generally are demanding and bitchy, but that his wife is different. Unconsciously he would love to be tough and intimidating, but consciously he looks down on macho men and thinks of himself as a nice guy who tries to please. Imagine that his wife enters the marriage thinking that men generally are selfish and ungiving, but that her husband is different. Unconsciously she would love to be more self-indulgent and even whimsically capricious, but consciously she looks down on vain childish women and thinks of herself as a responsible, nurturing caretaker. Now it isn't too difficult to imagine what will happen next. Sooner or later, the husband will do something—perhaps have one too many glasses of wine and fall asleep without doing the dishes—that conforms to the wife's negative expectations of men, and she will feel badly treated and react angrily. Or the wife will do something—perhaps comment on the mess her husband leaves when he does the dishes—that conforms to his expectations of women, and he will feel badly treated and react by indulging himself in a sulk and an extra glass of wine. A gradually escalating vicious cycle will then ensue in which the wife becomes more demanding and begins to openly blame her husband for being such a lazy slug, while the husband becomes more self-indulgent, spending more time at the gym or the bar while secretly blaming his wife for being such a bitch. The wife will feel unfairly neglected and rejected, and the husband will feel unfairly put upon and maligned. Both will feel victimized, and neither will recognize how their own behavior has provoked and perpetuated the problem.

In such a vicious cycle, each partner's overt reactions are a mirror image of the other's covert expectations *and unconscious wishes*—that is, the husband acts selfishly, as the wife has always thought most men act and as she would secretly like to act herself, while the wife acts aggressively, as the husband has always thought most women act and as he would secretly like to act himself—but neither notices the reflection. You can't recognize yourself (especially an unfamiliar, unwelcome aspect of yourself) in a mirror unless the mirror remains still long enough for you to see clearly. In a marital conflict, as in any dysfunctional relationship, neither partner is willing to sit still for being used as a mirror. Each responds to the transference projection, and blaming, of the other by throwing back a countertransference projection, and *counterblaming*, becoming in effect a mirror image with a vengeance.

In psychoanalysis and psychodynamic psychotherapy things are supposed to be different. It is precisely the therapist's job to sit still long enough to be used as a transference mirror. Not that the therapist doesn't experience countertransference. As some of my own reactions to Bill and to Mary illustrate, the psychotherapist will inevitably experience the same sorts of countertransference impulses and feelings that spouses and parents (and children, and friends, and people in waiting rooms) experience. The difference is, hopefully, that the therapist can accept and process these projections in a way that significant others in the patient's everyday life cannot be expected to do, experiencing the countertransference emotions fully as feelings, without having to blame or react impulsively to the patient.

Projection, Counterprojection, and Enactment

When both parties in a relationship are projecting—like the dysfunctional couple just described—the problematic interaction that results from the vicious cycle is what psychoanalysts call an *enactment*. This is defined generally as any interaction in which two people inadvertently incite each other to act out their respective unconscious expectations. In psychotherapy, enactment refers more specifically to an interaction following the pattern of the patient's repetition compulsion, in which the therapist unconsciously colludes with the patient's need to stage a particular unconscious scenario—as, for example, when I colluded with Mary's "colic scenario" by withdrawing from her emotionally. This is called enactment because emotions are expressed *in action* but do not become fully conscious as feelings. Enactment may take the form of overt and obvious behavior, as when the patient quits treatment or the therapist violates sexual boundaries. But usually it is more subtle, limited—by the built-in psychotherapeutic expectation that emotions should be put into words rather than into actions—to the kinds of emotional pushes and pulls that are communicated between the lines of verbal exchanges. In such exchanges words (and nonverbal behaviors like inflection, tone of voice, rhetorical suggestion, facial expression) are used *as* actions, to move the other person without physical contact—to hurt, seduce, endear, make guilty, and otherwise manipulate, rather than to communicate.

When this sort of thing goes on in politics, in academics, in business, or in marriage, it is considered par for the course. When it happens in psychotherapy, it indicates a countertransference problem. It means that the therapist is being made anxious by the patient's transference projection, and is treating it (unconsciously) as a hot potato that must be reflexively thrown back with an equal but opposite counterprojection. Every therapist will to some extent become caught up in such countertransference reactions, because we all have inner conflicts that make us vulnerable to anxiety. What makes the ensuing enactments in psychotherapy different from those in politics, academics, business, and marriage is that the therapist is (or should be) able to catch himself in the enactment, to notice his anxiety as he is being driven by it, and stop, to get in touch with the disturbing feelings that are producing the anxiety.

My task with Mary, then, was to stop enacting my countertransference and instead simply let myself feel it. I had to be able to contain Mary's projection by accepting in myself, without acting on them, the negative emotions that Mary was eliciting in (projecting into) me through the sense of betrayal, mistrust, and hatred that was implicit in her cellular dysphoria.

Negative Transference

Negative transference—the patient's need to project the worst (what she hates in herself) into the therapist and then blame the therapist for it—is an absolutely essential step in the process of making the unconscious conscious. The blaming is necessary because it puts the hated image or quality into words, making it fully conscious though in projected form. To become more conscious of the "bad" feelings and motives she harbored toward me, for instance, Mary would first need to acknowledge her mistrust—voicing her worst suspicions about my bad feeling and motives. Before she could recognize what was hateful and untrustworthy in herself, she would first have to experience it as being in me, and then experience herself hating me for it. If I could tolerate her thinking the worst of me, without needing to retaliate or discount her accusations—that is, if I could contain her projection without enacting it—then she could risk consciously thinking the worst of herself as well, and could ultimately allow herself to feel the feelings that she now had to disown. She would then be able to *reclaim* her projection, saying, as Prospero did about Caliban, "This thing of darkness I acknowledge mine." In achieving this goal of recognizing and taking responsibility for her negative emotions, she would be freed from the unconscious compulsion (the repetition compulsion) to enact them in her relationships.

Of course that's a very big proviso. "*If* I could tolerate her thinking the worst of me, without needing to retaliate or discount her accusations"; in other words, if I could tolerate my countertransference anxiety. The automatic temptation would be to try to get rid of my anxiety by putting the blame back on her like a hot potato. For instance, I could tell her that she was "only" projecting—that her feelings about me were based on a neurotic distortion, or that she was replaying an old tape that had to do with her parents and not with me. Even if I didn't say any of this in words, it would be all too easy to convey such a counterblaming message through a subtle intonation of protest, reproach, or surprise, as if to say, "How could you think such a thing of me?" or "Now don't you think that's just a little unfair?" or "How curious that you would think that of me!"—the common but covert theme being "If you have bad feelings toward me then they are your problem. Don't blame me for them. I don't want to be thought of that way." In other words, "Nothing human is foreign to me except *that*. It makes me too anxious to think that I might actually be—or that I even have it in me to be—as disappointing, untrustworthy, or bad as you feel that I am."

The skill of the therapist is to be aware of wanting to throw the blame back on the patient, but without needing to actually do it, whether by overt counterblaming or covert insinuation. I managed to contain Mary's projection in this way, as I described in Chapter 10, when she expressed her disappointment in me and implicitly blamed me for not offering her medication. But in that instance, my unusually felicitous awareness and processing of countertransference feeling had been possible only because of Mary's unusually rich articulation of transference feeling. Neither would have been possible without a lot of preliminary trial-and-error work. Transference is not something that springs fully formed from a patient's consciousness like Athena from the brow of Zeus. Because it is a manifestation of unconscious conflict, it always starts out unconsciously as an impulsive or compulsive action, an absence, an avoidance, or a disclaimer of certain thoughts and feelings, or a physical discomfort or anxiety that cannot be put into words. In these early stages, the countertransference is correspondingly likely to be ambiguous, most commonly an ill-defined pressure, push, or pull to respond in certain ways, which the therapist is unlikely to notice until it produces a more distinct discomfort or anxiety, or perhaps until he hears it in his own counterblaming tone of voice. Let me give you an example of how I fell into this kind of subtle counterblaming countertransference with Mary.

Blaming and Counterblaming

It was during the early months of her analysis, when Mary was experiencing what we now called her cellular dysphoria only as an occasional feeling of discomfort that made it more difficult for her to talk. At those times, she would tell me that she was feeling a bit pressured because she really didn't have anything to talk about that day. She would then complain, very hesitantly, that she wished I would talk more. "I know you want me to talk more," she said on one occasion, "to try to describe what I'm feeling. But the problem is that I'm not really feeling anything; at least nothing that's clear enough to put into words. I realize you're trying to follow the proper psychoanalytic method, but I'm worried that maybe it isn't working with me. Maybe I'm not cut out for it, because I only end up feeling as if you're too distant, too unemotional. It's pretty difficult to talk about my feelings when you're not giving me any input that I could have feelings *about*. But I do think it would be a lot easier for me to feel something if *you* talked more. That way, you know, I would have something to react to."

This complaint was very far from a blaming accusation, or from the more overt feelings of disappointment and mistrust it foreshadowed. In fact, Mary was not consciously blaming me at all. She assumed that detachment and unemotionality were perfectly acceptable parts of standard psychoanalytic technique, and the tone of her complaint was more one of apologizing for herself than of blaming me for not talking. Nevertheless, my unconscious guilt must have resonated with her unconscious reproach, because I responded with a subtle, unintended counterblaming reproach of my own.

"Well, there's a chicken-and-egg issue here," I said. "I think some of what you experience as my being too detached and unemotional is actually my response to *your* detachment. Since the idea of analysis is to follow the thread of your associations, I have to wait for you to talk. When you don't talk, then *I* don't have any input to react to, so I have to keep waiting. I think you then *interpret* my waiting as an emotional withdrawal. But in sessions like this one, when you're not talking, I get the sense that it is *you* who are emotionally withdrawn from *me*. I suspect that's because you're feeling some anxiety. Perhaps there's an uncomfortable feeling coming up in our relationship that you would rather not feel, so you withdraw instead and wait for me to talk."

Of course there was a good deal of truth in this interpretation, and Mary acknowledged that she could indeed feel herself withdrawing. Yet at the same time, as I heard the inflection I had put on certain of my words, I became uneasy about the counterblaming tone they seemed to carry. Officially, I had been trying to encourage Mary to talk about whatever uncomfortable feeling might be prompting her emotional withdrawal. But unofficially, and unconsciously, I was actually discounting her efforts to do just that! After all, she had just told me about an uncomfortable feeling—her feeling that I was too distant and unemotional. True, she hadn't come right out and said, "I think you're a manipulative jerk, the way you sit there so cold and detached and just leave me here squirming—but I hate to think so badly of you, so it's a lot easier to just withdraw instead." She hadn't said this because she wasn't fully conscious of feeling it, but what she had said was close enough. Had I been more comfortable at the time with her feeling that way about me, I could have recognized her reproach between the lines and then been able to help her recognize it in her own feelings. All I would have had to say was "So tell me more about this sense you have of me as detached and unemotional. What comes into your mind, what else do you feel, when you think about me in that vein?" Instead, I distanced myself from feeling her reproach and unemotionally threw a counterblaming reproach back at her, saying in effect (but without much *affect*), "Hey, don't blame me! I'm not the one who is withdrawn. You are!"

It was through catching myself in this kind of enactment—noticing and becoming anxious about my counterblaming tendency—in basically the same way on several different occasions that I gradually got to the point where I was able to hear Mary's reproach and accept it without having to throw it back at her. It was true: I really did become too detached and unemotional when she was in her cellular dysphoria. Even if I was reacting to her uncommunicativeness, it was nevertheless my reaction, based on my own inner conflicts. After all, she could easily say, and essentially had said, that her uncommunicativeness was a reaction to me. So if I ever expected Mary to recognize her feelings as her own, I first had to take responsibility for mine. Otherwise our transference and countertransference would remain a vicious cycle of covert blaming and counterblaming under the unconscious sway of our respective repetition compulsions.

Make Anxiety, Not War!

In such a vicious cycle, the feeling of anxiety is a two-edged sword. When both parties involved are running away from their anxiety, it keeps the cycle going. But if at least one of them can feel his or her own anxiety, it serves to break the cycle. It forces the person who feels it to stop and pay attention, thereby inhibiting the tendency to impulsive action. In this context a little inhibition can be a very good thing, affording not only a therapeutic but also a cultural and evolutionary advantage. To the extent that it prevents us from acting reflexively—not only in subtle enactments between therapist and patient, but in the ubiquitous power struggles, wars, and other vicious cycles of everyday life—anxiety makes room for the development of consciousness. At the center of all the distracting enactments of transference and countertransference, anxiety stands as a silent signal pointing inward, from action toward reflection, from projected enemies without to the undiscovered self within. Where the impulsive cycle of blaming and counterblaming stops, the inward journey begins.

At the same time, however, enactment does seem to be an inevitable, and even a useful, part of the psychotherapeutic process. As in the episode just described, when the patient cannot articulate transference feelings and attitudes in words, it is only by noticing a countertransference response within himself that a therapist can become aware of the transference at all. In the ideal case the therapist notices this response immediately and fully as a conscious feeling, one that he does not feel impelled to act on. But more often he becomes aware of countertransference only after the patient begins to complain about it (as Mary complained that I was too unemotional) or when he catches himself in the middle of an enactment (as when I became aware of anxiety over my counterblaming tone of voice). In such cases, the new awareness that ensues is never stable and never happens all at once. Any new awareness will be subject to the repetition compulsion and will tend to sink back into unconsciousness, only to emerge again in the next enactment, which will again trigger anxiety and a slightly fuller awareness, which again tends to sink back into unconsciousness. This is why the resolution of unconscious conflicts and the integration of disowned emotions into self-awareness generally takes such a long time. It can happen only gradually, through the dialectical opposition of the need for enactment and the need for consciousness.

How I Came to Realize I Had the Same Problem Mary Did

My counterblaming response to Mary's complaint that I didn't talk enough was part of such an evolving dialectic. Initially, my dawning self-awareness was limited to noticing some anger in the inflection of my voice, and recognizing that it was a reaction to Mary's veiled reproach. I did not then stop to ask what made me so reactive to her reproach—what the unsettling emotion was that I didn't want to be blamed for. As a result, I didn't really hear the reproach for what it was, taking it more as an unreasonable demand (that I should talk more) than as an expression of her hurt feelings. It would require repeated variations of the same enactment, centered around Mary's gradually intensifying (not yet named) cellular dysphoria, before I was ready to really hear her reproach and understand the difficulty I had with it. In each of these repetitions I would catch myself feeling angry at her, and from that infer that Mary herself must be angrier than she sounded, or that her painful silence was an angry one. I would interpret to her that her not being able to talk must be a symptomatic expression of unconscious anger—a rejection of me through mute withdrawal—that she could not otherwise allow herself to feel or express: "As if your unconscious believed that if you can't say something nice about me then you shouldn't say anything at all."

Eventually, when Mary was able to express her disappointment, and to some degree even her anger, over my not helping her in her times of distress, I became aware that I had indeed given her some real justification for feeling angry, by withdrawing emotionally from her distress (to avoid feeling helpless). I understood then that the reason I had had such trouble hearing her reproach for so long was that I didn't want to recognize this tendency in myself. I didn't want to think of myself as the sort of person who could be so uncaring—even coldly rejecting—of someone who needed me. Yet it was hardly surprising that my countertransference experience should take this form. It reflected one of the primary problems that Mary had come into treatment for—an aversion to needy crying infants! It made sense that if she couldn't tolerate such a feeling in herself, she would need to project it into me—unconsciously provoke my own tendency to feel just that way—so that she could see what she hated in me (and see how I handled being confronted with it) before she had to confront it in herself.

Yet I sensed that something was missing from this understanding. Even acknowledging that I did have it in me to be so uncaring and rejecting, I knew that this was far from the whole story of my relationship with Mary. I began to feel that I was painting much too negative a picture—both of Mary, whom I genuinely liked, and of my work with her, which I actually felt pretty good about. Even in her cellular dysphoria and my reaction to it, I realized that there was much more going on than our cold, angry, rejection of each other.

What's Wrong with This Picture?

As I reflected on the course of the analysis up to this point, I realized that I had been thinking of Mary's transference almost exclusively in terms of her projection of "bad" feelings—the kind that could inspire disappointment, anger, mistrust, or hatred when she saw them in me, and guilt if she were to feel them in herself. But I knew that transference typically includes the projection of good feelings as well—the kind that inspire affection and intimacy. Projection is simply a mechanism for dealing with intolerable feelings, and good feelings can sometimes be just as intolerable as bad ones. For one thing, they entail a degree of openness and vulnerability that can be terrifying. For another, they may be intensely embarrassing or may provoke guilt (over being too happy or successful), or feelings of unworthiness. Indeed, I suspected that Mary's aversion to infants and children stemmed from just such an intolerance of good feelings—specifically from an intolerance of her own maternal feelings.

Thinking of Mary's cellular dysphoria (before we had given it that name) in terms only of the negative transference, I had understood it as "anger (reproachful mistrust) trying to happen." Taking both negative and positive transferences into account, I could now think of it as a conjunction of conflicting projections, in which Mary was simultaneously crying for me to hold her and furiously fending me off. In the positive transference, she was crying for me to hold her because, having projected into me her good maternal feelings, she felt "bad"—painfully alienated from her own sense of inner goodness, which I was now holding for her and which she needed to get back from me. At the same time in the negative transference she was fending me off because she saw me as cold, angry, and rejecting—a projection of her bad feelings of disliking children. In that sense, the cellular dysphoria, and the conflicting transferences it contained, could be seen as Mary's unconscious attempt to integrate her loving and her hostile feelings, an anxiety-laden synthesis of her conflicting needs for engagement and for disengagement.

I knew that such a dialectic was active in Mary's transference symptom because I could feel the same dialectic in my own countertransference response to her symptom. When I allowed myself to stay with the anxiety that I still felt to some degree whenever Mary was in a state of cellular dysphoria, I could recognize two sides of an inner conflict that paralleled Mary's. To the extent that I felt her silently crying for help, I wanted urgently to reach out to her. To the extent that I felt her pushing me away—mistrustfully refusing to be held—I reacted with hurt and angry frustration. The combination of these conflicting feelings left me both with an impulse to withdraw from her—feeling rejected, helpless, and angry—and with a competing impulse to pursue her more aggressively, determined to find a way to reach her, but with a chip on my shoulder.

The compromise I had unconsciously arrived at was to withdraw from Mary emotionally while aggressively trying to reach her from an intellectual/theoretical distance. It was in the spirit of this compromise that I had been so determined not to let her quit the analysis, despite her repeated impulse to run away and my angry counterimpulse to just let her go. And it was in the same spirit that I had repeatedly pushed the one-sided interpretation that her cellular dysphoria, like her urge to quit, must be a disguised expression of anger. I now realized that this interpretation had reflected only a half-truth—one that served as a disguised expression of my own anger. If Mary's cellular dysphoria expressed a transference conflict between her need to be taken care of and her angry refusal to let me take care of her, then my interpretation that she was angry reflected a similarly conflicted countertransference. It expressed my need and desire to take care of her, but at the same time it pushed her away, by defining her as primarily angry and ignoring the needy wanting-to-be-held side of her feelings. In that sense, the interpretation had actually been a kind of countertransference insult to her—discounting her positive efforts to reach out to me, as I felt she had discounted (by refusing to be held) my positive efforts to help her. I would now need to correct the imbalance and help Mary recognize that her cellular dysphoria expressed not only her anger but her longing for closeness and need to be taken care of as well.

Interpreting the Cellular Dysphoria

With these considerations in mind, I began to talk to Mary about her cellular dysphoria in a way that would leave room for the positive feelings it embodied. Instead of interpreting it as anger trying to happen, I described it as an anxiety equivalent: a somatic expression of an anxiety now stirring in her relationship with me, that she did not yet experience as anxiety. I suggested that we should tentatively think of this as we would any other anxiety, as a signal of unconscious emotions threatening to become conscious. Given that the cellular dysphoria now seemed to be occurring mostly during her sessions with me, I said, it was a pretty safe bet that the emotions it signaled must be taking the form of disturbing feelings about me. Of course she had experienced cellular dysphoria long before she ever knew me, so the anxiety-provoking emotions were not originally about me, but it seemed they had now become focused on me through the natural workings of the transference.[3] Since she had experienced several memorable episodes of cellular dysphoria at work, it seemed likely that whatever unconscious emotions she was then having toward her boss she was now having more toward me.

Mary objected that this went strongly against her conscious feelings, which were almost entirely negative toward her boss and still (despite occasional blips of negativity) almost entirely positive toward me. I acknowledged this, but reminded her that if her cellular dysphoria was a manifestation of anxiety, then it signaled an inner conflict over emotions that had to be at least partly unconscious. I pointed out that there had been discrepancies in her conscious experience to indicate that she had such conflicted unconscious emotions about both her boss and me. For instance, she had initially greatly admired her boss, much as she now admired me, and had only gradually become intolerant of what she now felt to be his controlling sexist attitudes. Perhaps her turning against him was partly a reaction against letting herself feel too admiring, or too dependent on him. As far as her feelings about me, I thought she had a similar problem. Although she had very positive feelings toward me, she couldn't easily let herself feel dependent on me either. In fact, her positive feelings were the kind that put me at a distance, on a pedestal. "When it comes to more personal feelings like dependency," I reminded her, "you've said more than once that you don't see how you would ever be able to let yourself feel that way about me, because you get no indication that I have any such personal feelings about you."

"Yes. It would absolutely make me too vulnerable to feel dependent on you."

"And I think then you would tend to get angry, so as to counteract the vulnerability. Which could lead to your turning against me just as you turned against your boss. In fact, I think that's what was beginning to happen recently when you felt disappointed in me for not offering you medication. You took it as a sign that I didn't care about you, and that it wasn't safe to let yourself feel dependent and vulnerable. But you then had to stop yourself from dwelling on those feelings for fear that it might open up a Pandora's box of anger and you would risk losing me as someone on whom you really can and do depend."

Intellectually, Mary understood that these speculations made sense, but at a feeling level she was unimpressed. "I don't know," she said. "I'm not aware of feeling afraid to get angry. In fact, I think I would really like to feel some anger at you—not just disappointment, but real, red-hot anger. I feel so dull sometimes, and I imagine that a little anger would be exciting. I know you would like it—you've told me often enough how I must be angrier at you than I realize. But there's no way I'm going to be able to just walk in here one day and get angry, when you're sitting there being so calm and reasonable all the time. If you really want me to be angry, you're going to have to provoke me."

12. But Isn't Psychoanalysis Supposed to Be About Sex?

I used always to warn my pupils: "Our opponents have told us that we shall come upon cases in which the factor of sex plays no part. Let us be careful not to introduce it into our analyses and so spoil our chance of finding such a case." But so far none of us has had that good fortune.

—Sigmund Freud, "The Question of Lay Analysis"

When Mary said that if I wanted her to be angry, I would have to provoke her, I smiled somewhat ruefully, feeling stymied and at the same time playfully teased. For one thing, it wasn't really anger, but dependency feelings, that I had been trying to emphasize in the interpretation I had just given her. For another thing, Mary was encouraging me, almost daring me, to do something that, if she stopped to think about it, she knew was against my principles. It would be contrary to the purpose of psychoanalysis for me to provoke her—whether to anger or dependency or to any other feeling. If an emotion was present and trying to come to the surface in her, then I shouldn't need to provoke it but only to point out where I thought she might be resisting awareness of the emotion. It was then up to her to determine whether she could notice herself resisting, and whether, by directing her attention toward what she was resisting, she could actually feel the uncomfortable emotion in question. If she felt something only after I provoked her, as she was now inviting me to do, then she wouldn't be able to tell whether the feeling came from her or from me—whether it expressed primarily her need or mine. Such a confusion would be in the service of her resistance, interfering with the psychotherapeutic goal of getting in touch with, and owning, her own feelings.

There was a familiar story here. First, it was that if I wanted her to talk more then I had to talk more. Now it was that if I wanted her to be angry then I would have to provoke her. In either case, the message was the same. If I expected her to have personal feelings about me, I would first have to show that I had feelings about her. *She would show me hers, but I would have to show her mine first.* "Hmm," I thought, a bit startled by this idea. "So cellular dysphoria must really be about sexual feelings after all!"

This was an intriguing and unexpected turn of inner events. I had just been immersed in thinking about the infantile, nonsexual aspects of Mary's symptom—conceptualizing it as a mixture of her urgent need to be taken care of and her hurt and angry refusal to trust anyone who dared to try. Considering her early traumatic experience of colic as a kind of psychophysiological template for her current experience of cellular dysphoria, I had been imagining the latter as an intensely uncomfortable, diffuse bodily craving and need to be held, suffused with anxiety and frustration. Now suddenly it struck me that in her grown-up body, the frustrated needs most likely to produce such a state would have to be sexual ones. In other words, whatever it might reflect about her experience as an infant, cellular dysphoria was now, in the present, almost certainly an expression of Mary's conflicted, frustrated, sexual desire.

Peeling the Onion of Memory and Desire

Now it may strike the reader as odd or even disingenuous of me to say that I was surprised by the thought that Mary's symptom must be sexual in origin. After all, psychoanalysts are always looking for the sexual meaning in everything, aren't they? Well, yes and no. I do have the theoretical expectation that if we keep peeling, we will all eventually, like Adam and Eve, find a sexual conflict at the heart of the introspective onion. But in my daily work with patients I am by no means looking for that conflict, any more than I would be looking for the center of an actual onion as the primary object of my peeling. Rather I try to maintain a state of "evenly hovering attention" in which I am not looking for anything at all, but simply listening, both without and within, to the patient's unfolding communications and to my own unfolding emotional response to those communications.

The attitude I aspire to is perhaps best captured in British psychoanalyst Wilfred Bion's admonition that the analyst should be without memory or desire:

> If the psycho-analyst has not deliberately divested himself of memory and desire, the patient can "feel" this and is dominated by the "feeling" that he is possessed by and contained in the analyst's state of mind.[1]

Bion's precept should not be taken quite literally. Without any memory at all, I would be unable to recognize repeating patterns of emotion and behavior in my patients. Without any desire, I would have no motivation to devote myself to their growth. Yet memory and desire are the very form and substance of the repetition compulsion. To the extent that I am under the sway of memory and desire, I will tend to see my patients primarily in terms of my own unconscious scenario and so have trouble distinguishing *their* memory and desire—the proper object of analytic attention—from my own.

Bion's point is that the analyst must not be controlled or driven by his memory and desire in the sense that he would have a personal need for the analysis to proceed in a particular way or for the patient to achieve certain goals. Following this prescription in my work with patients, I try simply to take things as they come, without imposing preconceived theories and agendas on them. I try to let myself be in the present moment as it is, and allow my patients to be and become whoever they are, without trying to force their experience of today into the mold of what I thought was happening yesterday (memory) or of what I hope will happen tomorrow (desire). That is how I came to spend three years focusing on Mary's conflict over her anger, then shifted to thinking about her conflict over dependency feelings, and only now for the first time registered the thought that her primary conflict must be about sexuality. I was trying as much as possible to let Mary dictate the flow of our interaction—determining what we talked about according to whatever came into her mind—and then to follow that flow with my evenly hovering attention. I would listen to what she was saying and how she was saying it, noticing my inner reactions and using them to help locate the theme of her communication, and would then formulate comments that invited her to consider whether or not she could feel that theme in herself.

As I explained in Chapter 8, this method—in which I derive my understanding of what is going on in Mary's mind primarily from what I notice going on in my own inner response to her—is the only legitimate scientific method for observing inner experience, the only method that takes adequately into account the interaction between the observer and the observed.

Following this method, I have tried to tell Mary's story in a way that accurately depicts the process of observation, describing and explaining as fully as possible my feelings and thoughts as they arose in my interactions with her. In this context, to be without memory and desire is a scientific as well as a moral requirement. It means being objective and unprejudiced in my observational attitude, not only in the way I listen to Mary but in the way I listen to and report my own inner responses.

Not that I and all analysts (like all people) don't have preconceived ideas and wishful thinking—elements of memory and desire, patterned by our repetition compulsions—that prejudice us for or against particular elements in the patient's experience, and dispose us to see only certain things while blinding us to others in our own experience. That, after all, is how transference–countertransference enactments happen: as vicious cycles in which the patient's neurotic patterns of memory and desire trigger neurotic reactions in the analyst that inadvertently reinforce the patient's patterns. My goal as an analyst then is not to eliminate all my prejudices (which would be impossible), but to be able to take an unprejudiced attitude toward them, to be able to be without memory and desire about my own memory and desire so that I can observe my need for enactment just as I observe a patient's need, compassionately, from a place where I am not emotionally embroiled in it.

Achieving this unprejudiced observational position is not a one-time event but an ongoing dialectical process. In the day-to-day flow of analysis, I will repeatedly tend to slip into a mode of unconscious enactment and must repeatedly step back from it into a mode of more detached conscious awareness, divested of memory and desire. What typically alerts or reminds me that I need to take this step back is an experience of *discrepancy*—the sort of moment that occurs in almost every psychotherapy session when I am surprised by an experience that runs counter to what I would have expected or wanted.

In noticing such discrepancies, I am operating from a place in myself—and in human nature generally—that transcends the influences of memory and desire. It is a place of elemental, naive clarity, a state of quiet awareness that admits of wonder and surprise—and anxiety—just because it is open to the unexpected and the unwanted. Without this kind of awareness, no one would ever have a new idea. Scientific theories would never evolve because no one would ever be able to observe anything that they weren't already predisposed (by memory and desire) to look for. Since I aspire to being scientific in my observations, I consider it important to cultivate this natural condition of awareness that is open to the new and unexpected—so that I would notice, for instance, if I were ever to meet a person in whom there was no sexual conflict at the heart of the onion. This same openness would then have the additional benefit of allowing me to be pleasantly surprised when, without looking for it, I came upon the theoretically expected sexual conflict anyway.

It was just this sort of pleasant surprise that prompted me to smile when Mary's remark—"If you really want me to be angry, you're going to have to provoke me"—made me think of sexual teasing. But there was also something of an unpleasant anxiety in the surprise that gave my smile a rueful twist. My immediate impulse was to verbalize my thought and actually say, "So you'll show me yours, only I have to show you mine first." But I hesitated, arrested in my impulse by that twinge of anxiety I felt, which pointed to two simultaneous, interlinking but distinct trains of thought, one triggered by memory, the other by desire. I must warn you that it will now take quite a few written pages to describe these trains of thought, but the inner process itself occurred in a matter of seconds, so that Mary did not experience it as a break from our usual mode of communication. Even so, it may appear to you in what follows that I am overly absorbed in my own thoughts and out of touch with Mary. Quite the contrary, I will be attending precisely to the place where I was most in touch with her—the inner place where our emotional interaction was happening. I will be trying to map the contours of this place in all the detail necessary for an unambiguous scientific description, including a complete description of the process of observation—the way I became aware of successive layers of feeling in the anxiety that made me hesitate. In describing this process of getting in touch with feelings, I also hope to clarify why I call it listening to the soul. On the surface it may appear to be a commonplace experience that has nothing particularly spiritual or soul-like about it. Yet at its heart the process depends on that unprejudiced openness and clarity of awareness, without memory or desire, which is the very essence of the spiritual—the still center of the soul.

Memory: Déjà Vu All Over Again

One part of the anxiety that was making me hesitate was that I knew exactly how Mary would respond if I said, "So you'll show me yours, only I have to show you mine first." She would say, "So you think this is really about *sex?* I don't know. What makes you think *that?*"—with an intonation suggesting one part curiosity, one part skepticism, and one part frank mistrust. I would then feel stuck, wondering how I could possibly say anything at all that Mary wouldn't now construe as a subtle attempt to impose my own prurient interest and/or Freudian ideology on her. As I played out this anticipatory scenario, I immediately recognized it as a familiar one. The reason I knew how Mary would respond was that I had been here with her before. I remembered a whole series of exchanges that followed the same pattern, going back to the early months of the analysis. Where just a minute ago I had been thinking almost as if sex had never come up as an issue in the analysis, I now remembered that it had indeed come up repeatedly and dramatically, albeit very fleetingly, like lightning on the horizon.

The scenario had typically begun when, at some point in a session, Mary would mention a sexual situation with Henry, the man she was then involved with, that was making her anxious. She usually introduced the subject with a comment like "I wish I didn't have to talk about this, but I know I have to, if I ever want to figure out this problem I have with men." Mary had long been aware of a subtle anxiety that came up regularly in her sexual interactions with men—and that was reflected in many of her nonsexual interactions as well, with her boss for instance—related to a sense of struggle about who was on top or in control. Each time she talked with me about a sexual situation, she would get to the same point of identifying this anxiety yet would have trouble going any further with it. To get beyond the simple formulation that she was anxious because of a power struggle, she needed to feel what the power struggle was really about—specifically, what it was that made her uneasy about a man being in control. To do this she would have to talk about the details and emotional nuances of particular sexual encounters. But whenever she would begin to do this, or when I asked her a question that invited her to do it, she became increasingly anxious and unable to proceed. She said she felt embarrassed to talk openly to me about something so private. At a deeper level, she was aware of a more specific sense of shame about something in her sexual feelings that she experienced as bad or unacceptable.

"I know I shouldn't feel so guilty about sex," she would say, as if trying to dispel the guilt simply by labeling it as neurotic.

"But you also know that the best way to get rid of a feeling you don't want is to let yourself have it," I would reply, "and that would certainly include guilt. When you say 'I know I shouldn't feel so guilty about sex,' you're actually trying to put the guilt out of your mind without having to feel it. But the only way to know what the guilt is about—and whether you should or shouldn't have it—is to let yourself feel it and get the sense of exactly what it is pointing to in your sexual feelings or fantasies."

But Mary never seemed to get very far in identifying this specific guilt-provoking element. It seemed that the more she tried, the more anxious and uncomfortable she became. When that happened, I would hesitate, with the uneasy sense that by expecting her to talk about her sexual feelings I might be forcing her to do something that would be terribly humiliating for her. Eventually it occurred to me that this uneasiness I felt about forcing something on her was a countertransference clue to the nature of her anxiety about power struggles. It suggested that Mary was now beginning to experience with me the very feeling she was trying to talk about, a sexual anxiety about what might happen—having something forced on her against her will—if she gave up too much control to a man.

"Perhaps you are now experiencing with me the very anxiety you were just talking about in your relationship with Henry," I would say. "Perhaps there is something in the process of talking with me about sex that stirs up the same bad feelings as if this were a sexual relationship rather than a psychoanalytic one."

The Problem Is in the Process

This is the sort of situation that psychoanalysis is designed to capitalize on, when the problem being discussed by patient and therapist becomes activated by their discussion and is played out between them in the transference and countertransference—in this case, through Mary's difficulty in talking about sex and my reluctance to push her. I was now in the ideal position to understand Mary's conflict. Not only was I hearing how she experienced the conflict outside of treatment, but I was now experiencing the conflict first-hand, having myself become half of the conflict through the action of transference projection. Mary confirmed that, in trying to talk to me about sex, she did feel the same sense of struggle about who was on top as she did during sex itself. As the patient, she felt at a disadvantage. She worried a good deal about what I would think of her, that I might judge her harshly, looking down on her not only for the sexual feelings she was so reluctant to talk about but for the reluctance itself, which she assumed would make me think of her as a bad patient. On one occasion she mentioned another worry: that, as a Freudian and a man, I might not be able to appreciate her experience as a woman but would try to impose my sexist theory of penis envy on her. Both of these worries sprang from her uneasy sense that, as the analyst, I was automatically in a position of control, which gave me the power to hurt or humiliate her.

This was about as far as we would typically get in one session. We had identified an important theme in the transference—Mary's mistrustful anxiety that I would try to control her or force something on her—and were just beginning to explore it. I thought it likely that this power to hurt or humiliate that Mary feared in me was a projection of something she feared in herself—the real unconscious source of her anxiety. But this could only be confirmed through the further unfolding of the transference and countertransference, so I would always leave these sessions looking forward to continuing that process. I was always surprised, then, when in the very next session Mary would act as if there were no process—no unresolved or unsettling issues on the table. She would come into the session comfortable and relaxed, and would launch into a completely new topic, as if sexual anxiety were the last thing on her mind.

Free Association As Resistance

It is integral to the so-called fundamental rule of psychoanalytic free association that the patient determines what to talk about each day by tracking the flow of thoughts, images, and feelings as they emerge into awareness during the session, whether they seem to make rational, linear sense or not. It is understood that the analyst will give the patient enough space, in the form of relaxed silence, to settle into the session, make the necessary inward shift of attention, and begin to notice and talk about whatever is on his or her mind. This requires that the analyst himself be relaxed, in a condition of "evenly hovering attention" that is free enough from the pressures of memory and desire that he can refrain from insinuating his own agenda or otherwise controlling the flow of the session.

It is in the nature of this unusual state of consciousness required of both patient and analyst that often neither one will remember at the beginning of Tuesday's session what they talked about on Monday, but that in the course of Tuesday's free associations some thought or feeling will emerge that brings Monday's session back into conscious memory. Such spontaneous associative links between sessions generally provide more illuminating information about what is important, and what is related to what, than a more directed cognitive effort to follow up on yesterday's session could ever produce. Nevertheless, there are always some sessions that are more dramatic, more emotional, and generally more memorable than others, when it would be surprising if patient and analyst did not both begin Tuesday's session with some interest in following up on Monday's. The sessions in which Mary talked about her sexual anxiety certainly had that memorable quality of emotional intensity for me, and so, when she would begin the next day's session with no reference to the previous one, and would then proceed far into the session with neither a reference to sex nor a hint of anxiety, I found myself in an awkward but interesting position.

As the minutes ticked by, my initial surprise that Mary didn't seem to remember yesterday's session gradually turned into restlessness and then frustration, as I became more and more aware of the activity within me of Bion's analytic vices, memory and desire. I remembered yesterday's session even if Mary didn't, and it seemed a whole lot more interesting and important than what she was talking about today. I found myself wanting to interrupt her, to say something like "I notice you haven't mentioned anything about our last session. Are you aware at all today of the kind of anxiety you were feeling yesterday?" Such a question might have been completely reasonable in terms of its content, but I could feel something uncomfortable in the process—a certain pressure in my need to ask it. The question was coming from an unsettled, frustrated place in me, where what I really wanted to say was "Hey, I liked it better when you were talking about sex. Let's do that again!"

Resistance As Sexual Teasing

In feeling this way, I was responding to an unconscious transference projection. Mary had disowned both her own memory of the sexual theme we had been talking about and her desire to pursue it further, and had in effect put these into me—leaving me as the one who wanted to talk about sex. In my urge to forcibly remind her of yesterday's session I was wanting to throw the projection back to her, by reminding her that it was she who had wanted to talk about sex first. But I came to understand this only gradually, over the course of several repetitions of the same scenario. The first couple of times I simply went ahead and asked Mary about the previous session, not thinking about what my motives might be for doing so until her response put the question (and the hot potato) right back on me: "Gee, I can hardly remember yesterday's session. What was it we were talking about?"

No matter how I tried to answer such a question, I always had the uneasy sense that I would end up appearing more interested in talking about sex than Mary was, or even as if I were trying to force her to do something (talk about sex) that would be humiliating for her but fun for me. It seemed that, by not remembering yesterday's session, Mary had unconsciously set me up to enact her worst fear about me. So I tried to answer in a way that would put the focus on her fear of my exploiting her rather than on my interest in doing so.

"Perhaps the vagueness of your recollection is a way of protecting yourself from feeling again the anxiety you were beginning to feel with me in the last session," I suggested.

But Mary had an answer for that, too. "Do you think so? I don't know. Yesterday's session seems so distant right now that I can't remember what I was feeling. But you do have me curious now about why you think it's so important. What were you feeling about yesterday's session?" In other words, "So you want to see mine? I don't know about that, but if you're so interested then why don't you let me see yours first."

At that point I had to bail out with a comment like "Well, I think it's important that we stay focused on what you are feeling. If I told you what I remember or what I was feeling, then we would be talking about my psyche and not yours." Eventually, I was able to point out to Mary that there was a pattern in the way she talked about sex. She didn't do it very often and, when she did, it was only for one session—a productive but anxiety-provoking one—after which the subject seemed to vanish without a trace from her consciousness.

"When that happens," I said to her, "it puts me in a funny position. If I remember the last session and you don't, and I don't say anything about it, then I'm making it easy for you to avoid the uncomfortable feelings that we both agree you need to deal with. But if I do say something, then it looks like I'm the one interested in talking about sex. And then I think you begin to be suspicious about my motives, wondering whether I might be trying to foist some Freudian agenda on you, or even worse, whether I might have some voyeuristic interest in hearing you talk about sex."

"So it's kind of like I'm teasing you, and then blaming you for being turned on."

"Yes, and I think the point of that is to get out from under the situation where you feel I will blame you or think badly of you for what turns *you* on, which you are afraid might come out in a humiliating way if you talk more about sex."

In this last response, I was saying something important, but it was a good deal less than I was thinking—only the part that I thought Mary would be able to hear. What I didn't tell her was that I heard her response as itself a kind of tease, almost like an acknowledgment that she could feel the teasing/blaming impulse as her own. But it wasn't really an acknowledgment. She didn't say, "Yes, I must admit, now that I think about it, that I probably was getting a little charge out of teasing you." What she said was more noncommittal, implying that although she might have been teasing me, it might equally well be my own sexual need that led me to perceive her that way. She needed to maintain this ambiguity, I assumed, because she was afraid to ask herself whether she really was teasing me and, even worse, to risk discovering that it could turn her on to tease me. That was why I framed my response to include an implicit reassurance—that even if she was teasing and blaming me, I understood it was to protect herself from feeling blamed by me for her sexual feelings. But at the same time, I realized that her teasing impulse, however self-protective, had an autonomous sexual energy of its own, which served to provoke in me the very response from which she then needed to protect herself.

I was pretty sure that underneath Mary's fear that I would blame her for her sexual feelings was another fear: that if she talked about sex as she was tempted to do, it would turn me on. Indeed, that was probably what she most feared I would blame her for, and what had brought her up short each time she began to talk with me about sex. She feared my criticism because, unconsciously, she wanted to turn me on by teasing. This secret, forbidden desire was so unacceptable to her that she could experience it only in projected form—as an anxiety that I was trying to force my sexual desire on her from without by making her talk about sex, rather than as a perception of her own desire to talk about sex in a way that would turn me on against my will. So her mistrustful suspicion of what I might be trying to do to her was really an inverted image of what she unconsciously wanted to do to me.

In sum, I realized that the issue of who was responsible for wanting to talk about sex, and the question of whether talking about sex is good (a natural and productive part of the psychotherapeutic process) or bad (an act of sexual teasing on Mary's part or of sexual domination on mine) had been recurrent themes in the analysis long before I felt the impulse—and then hesitated—to say, "So you'll show me yours, only I have to show you mine first." These themes brought into Mary's transference relationship with me the same kind of power struggle and anxiety that she had experienced in previous sexual relationships, and in relationships with men generally. As I reviewed how difficult our interactions had been whenever the topic of sex came up, I began to realize how dangerous these power struggles really felt to her. Although it was subtle, her anxiety about men wanting to dominate and control her was actually quite intense, and she was always feeling a need to protect herself. No wonder I could never find a comfortable way to talk to her about her contribution to the power struggle—how she (unconsciously) used teasing provocations to elicit the male-dominance responses to which she then objected. And no wonder I was hesitating about what to say now. Anything I tried to say about her pattern of sexualized power struggles would only raise her anxiety level beyond the point where she could think productively about it. She would only feel all the more that I was like any other man, trying to force my sexual or Freudian agenda on her.

The Oedipus Complex

By inferring that Mary was unconsciously provoking the very response she feared, I *was* thinking in very Freudian terms. It is a commonplace of Freudian logic that what we fear most is what we secretly desire. If we think of anxiety as a warning signal that an unconscious emotion is trying to become conscious, then the most anxiety-provoking emotion is always a forbidden desire. More specifically, it is a unique combination of forbidden sexual and hostile desires, in the archetypal motivational pattern that Freud called the Oedipus complex.

Perhaps the most common manifestation of the Oedipal pattern in everyday experience is the fact that we tend to want people (and things) we can't have, or who are hard to get. Very often, the feeling that it is wrong, hopeless, off-limits, or dangerous to pursue an object of desire makes that object all the more desirable. There is excitement in violating a taboo or in overcoming resistance to make a conquest. In the original Greek myth of Oedipus, the hero does both. He wins the forbidden, dangerous object of desire through taking it by force: killing his father, and taking possession of his father's crown together with his father's wife (his own mother) as the spoils of his triumph over the dreaded Sphinx. In these actions (though he takes them unwittingly—not realizing *who* he has killed or who he has taken in conquest) Oedipus expresses the deepest unconscious meaning of our everyday conscious pattern of wanting what we can't have. Freud saw this pattern as an expression of a universal childhood wish to become the center of one parent's attention by displacing the other parent—to steal the love of one parent away from the other, or simply to claim one parent's love by getting the other out of the way.

There has always been a good deal of debate about how sexual, in the adult sense, the child's experience of Oedipal wishes may be, but there is no doubt that it becomes sexualized as soon as the child does—during puberty. When that happens, the wishes must be repressed, that is, disowned and banished from consciousness, just as Oedipus had to be banished from Thebes. The reason for the repression is twofold. On the one hand, we all have a childish fear of inadequacy (performance anxiety) and/or retaliation (punishment) if we were actually to win the forbidden object of desire. That is, we feel inadequate or fear retaliation with the same inner sense of smallness and weakness we had as children. On the other hand, we also have an adult shame and guilt that comes with the incipient knowledge of good and evil—a sense that however good it may feel, our sexual desire at the same time also feels disquietingly wrong.

The fact is, a good deal of the excitement of Oedipal desires revolves not around love for the other person, but around hostility: the urge to exploit, control, humiliate, or hurt the other person, treating him or her as a sex *object*—a possession to which we are entitled—rather than as a person we love. The very sense of unattainability that makes another person desirable makes us hate as well as love him or her. The sadomasochistic satisfactions of exploiting, controlling, and humiliating are guilty, shameful compensations for the underlying feeling that we can never truly have the other person.[2] This hostile motive in sexual desire is represented in the myth of Oedipus by the fact that Oedipus *wins* his mother, who has no say in the matter, as a kind of trophy—the spoils of his conquest. He has no guilt about thereby exploiting her, or about killing his father for that matter, *until* he discovers that they are his parents—in other words, until he feels the discrepancy between his lustful and murderous impulses on the one hand and his loving feelings (and need to be loved) on the other. So if the curse of Oedipus was that he was fated, as all of us are, to have murderous and exploitative impulses toward those he loved, then his feelings of shame and guilt were a counterbalancing blessing, signaling the birth of his moral consciousness.

Although most people aren't aware of the deeper unconscious layers of their Oedipal impulses, most people are aware from time to time of certain sexual fantasies or urges that secretly (e.g., in masturbation) turn them on, but that they would hesitate to enact with a partner they love. Or they may enact them and then, like Oedipus, become aware of uneasiness about what they have done only after orgasm. In either case, the hesitation or the uneasiness reflects a universal anxiety about being responsible for the evil elements of Oedipal desire. *The anxiety is that, in our most private experience of sexual excitement, it feels so good to do something that feels so bad.*

Mary's Oedipus Complex

No doubt my evolving thoughts about Mary's teasing pattern—talking about sex one day and dropping it like a hot potato the next—were influenced by my understanding of the Oedipus complex, and by my belief that there is always an uneasy fusion of love and hate in sexual desire. Given this background, I expect that a desire to seduce, excite, manipulate, or control (i.e., possess) the analyst is something that will come up eventually (meeting tremendous resistance along the way) in every analysis, an expression of the forbidden Oedipal desires that are reactivated by the evolving transference. In the transference, the analyst becomes the personification and avatar of everything the patient loves and wants, but also hates, because she feels she cannot have it.

Still, in my day-to-day listening and being with patients, I do try to leave such expectations in the closet of memory and desire. If my Freudian expectations are valid, I know that the expected feelings will emerge in their own time, without my having to push or provoke them. If the expectations and the theory are not valid, the only way to find that out is to leave room for something different and unexpected to emerge. That is why, even after I began to feel teased by Mary's pattern of talking about sex one day and completely forgetting about it the next, I did not talk to her about this until she had repeated it often enough that I was sure it was *her* pattern. Theoretically, I recognized that the interaction was probably generated by her Oedipus complex: She experienced me as unattainable, controlling, and judgmental (like a father) and unconsciously desired to turn the tables—to control and conquer me by turning me on and then judging me for it. But in what I said to her, I tried to limit myself to what Mary was, or could be, conscious of— the element of teasing in her pattern of talking about sex. I hoped to encourage her to focus inward on her own experience, simply to confirm or deny that she could feel the impulse to tease me, without feeling pressured to conform to my theoretical expectations. When I suggested that teasing me and then blaming me for being turned on would be a reaction to feeling blamed by me for what turned *her* on, the comment was certainly informed by my theoretical expectations but was based primarily on my sense of Mary's guardedness in that moment (reflecting her anxiety about being controlled/blamed by me) and on my repeated experience of her uneasiness in talking about sex, informed by the history of all she had said about her mistrustful power struggles with men.

Desire: What My Own Anxiety and Guardedness Were About

These then were the memory-thoughts stirred by my impulse—and my hesitation—to respond to Mary's teasing challenge to provoke her. Processing these associations during the few brief moments of my hesitation, I was left with a distinct overall impression that Mary's comment fit a long-standing pattern of unconscious sexual teasing, suggesting that her cellular dysphoria almost certainly did have something to do with conflicted sexual feelings about me. But I sensed that she was too far from being aware of those feelings to understand what I was talking about if I said, "So you'll show me yours, only I have to show you mine first."

To complicate matters, during the same few seconds of hesitation, I had been running through a separate but interlinking train of thought, one that left me with a very different impression—that Mary was *too close* to feeling her sexual feelings (and hence far too anxious) to be able to process such a comment from me in a useful way. In fact, it occurred to me that if I said, "So you'll show me yours, only I have to show you mine first," it might actually turn *her* on.

In this second train of thought, I was hesitating not because of anything

I remembered about Mary's pattern in talking about sex, but because I felt a more immediate anxiety about the impact the words I was tempted to say might have on her. Specifically, I was worried that my proposed comment might be a kind of countertransference countertease. My intended purpose was to highlight the teasing implications of Mary's comment ("If you really want me to be angry, you're going to have to provoke me"), hoping that she would then be able to feel and reflect on the impulse that prompted it. But maybe that was all a rationalization and what I was really up to was the same kind of sexualized power struggle that all the other men in her life seemed to get into with her. By implying that Mary was really talking about sex when she thought she was talking about anger, it might even appear that I *was* trying to provoke her—not to make her angry but to seduce her—or that I was trying to foist a Freudian agenda on her. Well then, I had to ask myself, was I?

When I stopped to think about it, I could easily imagine that the unexpected sexuality of what I was tempted to say to her might indeed take Mary by surprise and turn her on. As I had this thought, *I* was taken by surprise, by a brief rush of sexual feeling in myself. Apparently, the idea of teasing Mary was also a turn-on for me. No wonder I was hesitating.

So where was this sudden upsurge of sexuality coming from? My first defensive impulse was to blame it on Mary: If I was turned on at the idea of teasing her, then it must be an enactment of her scenario—my reaction to her unconsciously teasing me. But of course, I knew that even if Mary was provoking such an enactment—projecting her unconscious sexual impulses into me—it didn't mean I wasn't responsible for what I was feeling. She couldn't have activated a sexual feeling in me if it wasn't already in me waiting (and wanting) to be activated. So my first priority was to identify and understand the source of this feeling in myself. When I thought about it, I realized that when Mary had said, "There's no way I'm going to just walk in here one day and get angry. If you really want me to be angry, you're going to have to provoke me," I had initially, momentarily, taken it more as a rejection than an invitation. Recall that I had just offered her a new—and what felt to me important—interpretation of her cellular dysphoria as having to do with dependency feelings rather than anger. In her teasing response, she seemed to be dismissively rejecting my interpretation without even giving it a thought. This left me feeling both ineffectual—once again I had failed to reach her—and helpless. She was saying, in effect, "The only way you're going to get what you want from me (that I should feel any of my feelings) is to do something we both know you are forbidden, in your position as analyst, to do (provoke me)."

In my momentary feeling of rejection, then, *I* was suddenly the dependent child, needing Mary's validating response but feeling hopelessly unable to get it. In other words, I was experiencing her as a painfully unattainable object. This was not something I was eager to feel, and my counterteasing impulse—an activation of my own Oedipal desire—was a convenient way of not feeling it. I would in effect be saying, "I refuse to feel small and helpless the way you're trying to make me feel. I'll show you how big and strong I am by controlling your feelings, by being sexually provocative and making you want me." But this turning-the-tables motive was almost certainly a countertransference mirror image of Mary's transference. My interpretation that her cellular dysphoria had to do with her needy, dependent feelings threatened to put her in touch with feeling like a dependent child—something she was even less eager to feel than I was. So she had to push the interpretation, and the feelings, away. She did this by teasing me (projecting the feelings into me) with the unconscious subtext: "I refuse to feel weak and dependent the way you're trying to make me feel. I'll show you how powerful I am by manipulating your feelings, by being unreachable and making you want me!"

Recognizing this transference–countertransference power struggle over who was going to have the power to make the other feel something, I realized that, in part at least, Mary must have reacted to my new interpretation as a kind of male-domination power trip, in which I was keeping myself emotionally aloof toward her while expecting her to feel dependent on me. This would have felt terribly humiliating to her, and it was to avoid that danger of humiliation that she needed to turn the tables on me with her teasing, rejecting response.

So After All That Hesitation, What Did I Finally Say?

I hope this account of the unconscious subtexts of desire in the interaction between Mary and me will suggest to the reader the mixture of love (Mary wanting me to take care of her and me wanting to take care of her) and hostility (both of us feeling rejected and wanting to take control by making the other feel something) that typically infuse sexual feelings in the Oedipal pattern of desire. In the moment of my hesitation, of course, I was thinking not in such theoretical terms, but in very personal terms of the sexualized power struggle that I knew Mary was both drawn to and afraid of, and that I could now feel activated within myself. The overall impression I was left with was that sexual feelings were close to the surface of Mary's cellular dysphoria, but too volatile with humiliation and hostility for us to focus on them right now. She would need to feel a stronger sense of trust in me as someone she could count on to take care of her before she could risk being aware of and exploring the sexual dimension of our relationship. So in response to her comment, "If you really want me to be angry, you're going to have to provoke me," I said simply, "Well, you know, I didn't mean to be talking just about anger. I don't think anger is the only feeling you have trouble with, or the only feeling that's contained in your cellular dysphoria. As I said, I think there are also feelings of neediness and dependency, but I think perhaps you would *rather* feel angry than feel that kind of vulnerability."

A Controversial Footnote on the Oedipus Complex and the Nature–Nurture Debate

The fact that the sexual impulse I felt was clearly associated with, and experienced as a reaction to, feeling like a helpless, rejected child, I take as important presumptive evidence that the sexual impulses of the Oedipus complex do in fact originate earlier than puberty. But as I mentioned earlier, this is a controversial position. It has been claimed by Heinz Kohut, for instance, that the overt indications of Oedipal sexuality so often seen in the play of young children do not represent a basic instinct in the same sense that the sexual behavior of adolescents does but are rather a compensatory reaction to a certain kind of parental rejection. My own experience, as well as common sense, tells me otherwise. Sexual desire, whenever it occurs, is *both* a basic instinct and a response to an external stimulus. It is wishful thinking indeed to suppose that because an impulse occurs in reaction to something else that the impulse is therefore not an inherent disposition of human nature. This is the same sort of wishful thinking, by the way, that has produced the age-old nature–nurture debate, and the perennial question about whether human beings are innately destructive (have original sin) or are born innocent and become destructive only in response to the destructive influence of family or society. The answer, of course, is that both are true. Our destructive impulses always occur as a reaction to a perceived threat or attack from outside. But at the same time we would never be able to react that way unless we had an innate disposition toward destructiveness within us.

To see this more clearly, compare the reactions of a human being with those of a sunflower. No matter how badly you treat it, a sunflower cannot be provoked to fight back, nor will it ever develop a mean streak of hostile aggression (nor will it ever get turned on if you tease it), because it is simply not in its nature to react that way. People, in contrast, will predictably react that way with relish, and you don't even have to attack them to elicit the response. You can easily provoke another person's hostility (or sexual desire) simply by ignoring him or her, or putting your own needs first. Why? Because it is in our nature to be hostile (and sexual). Even more dramatically, we will become hostile without any external provocation whatsoever, in response to hunger, pain, or any other discomfort from within (as we will become sexual in response to boredom). However, because of the universal projective blaming impulse, we inevitably feel this willful hostility or sexuality (and invent rationalizing theories about it) as coming not from our own nature but from the willful provocations of others (the objects of our projection).

The conclusion is clear. Whether in the case of adult hate and destructiveness or the childhood sexuality of the Oedipus complex, if it weren't in our human nature to be that way, then we simply wouldn't ever be that way.

A Skeptical Question

But perhaps I have strained the credulity of some of my readers. It is clear enough that the Oedipal power struggle I have described was going on in my head, but how could I possibly be sure that Mary had all the feelings I was attributing to her? After all, it was I, not she, who was thinking all the thoughts about dependency and teasing/controlling sexuality. And these thoughts were based on what I was feeling, not on anything Mary had said directly. How could I know that the whole train of thought wasn't simply a product of my own neediness and/or sexual desire rather than Mary's unconscious projection of these emotions into me?

The answer is that I was being scientific. I was practicing the kind of participant observation outlined in Chapters 6 through 8, based on the principle that we can objectively observe another person's inner life only by observing its interaction with our own inner life as registered in the feelings it evokes in us. From this perspective, I understood that the feelings I felt were the product both of my own desire and of Mary's projection—a conscious response in me to emotions that remained unconscious in her. But then, how could I tell that I was observing this interaction objectively—that it was generated primarily by Mary and reflected her repetition compulsion and not the disruptive intrusion of my own sexual need and anxiety into our relationship?

I could tell based on two criteria. First, what I observed in myself didn't feel disruptive or compelling in the way that I would have expected had it been driven primarily by my own repetition compulsion. Instead, I registered it more as a signal—an anxiety-provoking temptation to make a counterteasing comment—that I was able to feel and reflect on without being unduly pressured by it. Second, what I observed in myself was consistent with everything Mary had told me over the years about her typical relationships with men. She did have a long-standing tendency, which she was both aware of and anxious about, to get caught up with men in a sexualized power struggle over who was on top. Though she had never felt more than hints of this struggle with me, she had repeatedly come to the edge of feeling it and then acted it out (instead of feeling it) in her here-today-gone-tomorrow approach to talking about sex.

Soon after the session I have been discussing, Mary had two dreams, on different nights, which provided further indirect evidence that what I had registered in my unspoken trains of thought and feeling did indeed reflect something that was pressing to come to the surface in her.

Messages from the Unconscious

In Mary's first dream, I was holding her in a way that felt unlike anything she had ever experienced in her waking life. "You were so incredibly loving!" she said. "You were sort of enfolding me, like a nurturing mother, except you were definitely male. I guess there was also something sensual, though it wasn't exactly sexual, in the way you were holding me. It was amazing, almost like a religious experience. You know what it reminds me of—that scene in the movie *Cocoon*, when the man and the alien woman are in the swimming pool and they are sort of blending energies."

In the second dream, Mary was by herself, visiting the birdhouse of a zoo. She was struck by the variety of small but wonderfully colorful tropical birds flying all around. Suddenly they swooped down on her, hundreds of birds all at once, attacking her, relentlessly pecking and pecking into her skin. It was awful and it seemed to take her a very long time to wake up.

About the first dream, two things were striking: first, that as the creator of the dream, Mary clearly had the capacity to experience—indeed, to generate from within herself—such a blissful feeling of love; and second, that she seemed so far from being able to feel anything like that in her waking life. "That's what I'm looking for from analysis," she said. "To be able to feel that way with another person when I'm awake." The second dream suggested what was stopping her from being able to feel that way when she was awake. Where the first dream associated sexuality with feelings of nurturing intimacy, the second dream associated it with anxiety and danger—not just the danger of anger, but of greedy/devouring lust, as represented by the attacking birds. It struck me quite forcefully that the intolerable pecking of these birds was a perfect dream symbol for Mary's "attacks" of cellular dysphoria, and a clear indication of the anxiety-laden sexual feelings that probably lay behind it. On the one hand, the birds were exotically foreign, outside her, representing the (projected) excitement and danger of intrusive male sexual desire. On the other hand, they were under her skin, like the cellular dysphoria, representing the dangers of her own sexual desire: first, the danger of feeling her adult sexual power to excite me—and thereby make me dangerous—provoking (teasing) me into a sexual power struggle; and second, the danger of feeling the needy/greedy/urgent/hostile/aggressively sexual feelings of a colicky baby in an adult body. Of course, I could not be certain that this interpretation was correct. Whereas in the first dream Mary was consciously aware of a sexual dimension in her ecstatic feeling, in the second dream there was nothing she recognized as sexual about her frightening experience. But this difference was consistent with my impression that Mary's sexual feelings were coming closer to the surface in the transference but that something in them was still too volatile and threatening for her to face.

Another Question: Why Now?

If, as I believed, Mary was not yet ready to talk comfortably about sexual feelings with me, then why would an unconscious sexual impulse be stirring in her at precisely this point in our interaction, when we were ostensibly discussing a conflict over anger and dependency, and when neither of us had said anything about sex for weeks previously? The answer, as I have already suggested, is that I provoked Mary's sexual impulse. I didn't do it through sexual teasing, however, but simply through my interpretation that her cellular dysphoria was an expression of uncomfortable dependency feelings. Her teasing impulse was a reaction to—and against—the feelings of closeness and wanting-to-be-taken-care-of to which my interpretation called her attention. To the extent that she could feel her wish to be taken care of, it was natural that she would experience some sexual stirrings along with it, associated with the hungry yearning for physical closeness and "blending energies" that would be the adult counterpart of her infantile colic. But to the extent that she could not tolerate this yearning, or trust the closeness and dependency feelings involved, she would tend to experience these as something I was manipulating her to feel, a painful sign of my being on top, trying to tease and humiliate her. Here, too, she could easily feel sexual stirrings—as a reaction *against* the dependency feelings: wanting to turn the tables by teasing me, making me feel the humiliating neediness. Her resultant sexual desire (if she were to feel it) would then be a combination of wanting to be taken care of and wanting to be on top.

It was just such a combination of loving and hostile feelings that I became aware of in my countertransference impulse to tease Mary with a sexually provocative comment. On the one hand, my impulse was a way of trying to connect with her emotionally—to blend energies—in a way that would help her connect with her own feelings. On the other hand, it was a way of trying to break through her resistance (her teasing me, playing therapeutically hard to get) with the sexual implication of taking her by surprise and making her respond to me sexually. But there had been no such sexual implication in my original interpretation about Mary's uncomfortable dependency feelings. The sexual desire had first emerged in Mary, as an unconscious teasing impulse, and then in me as a conscious counterteasing feeling. These transference and countertransference reactions were in one sense resistances against feelings of closeness and dependency, but in another sense they were therapeutic progress—bringing the unconscious two steps closer to becoming conscious in the gradual unfolding of the psychotherapeutic process.

Dialectic and Integration

It was now beginning to make sense to me how this unfolding process had come to include both here-today-gone-tomorrow impulses to quit treatment and here-today-gone-tomorrow bursts of interest in talking about sex. These were the two sides of Mary's ambivalence about engagement versus disengagement, wanting to feel close versus wanting to keep me at a distance, transference versus resistance. In the early stages of the analysis, when Mary had had less reason to trust me, she had kept herself as detached and unemotional with me as she felt I was with her. Whenever she then began to have more feeling toward me, whether positive or negative, it stirred up a burst of anxiety that threatened her detached equilibrium. The positive feelings came out in her attempts to talk about sex. The negative feelings came out in her impulses to quit the analysis. In one case there was an anxiety-laden impulse toward emotional engagement with me (the anxiety being generated by unconscious sexual feelings), and in the other an equally anxiety-laden impulse toward disengagement (the anxiety being generated by unconscious mistrust and hostile/destructive feelings).

As we weathered these brief but frightening storms of emotional intensity, a change had evolved in which Mary began to feel closer to me much more of the time, but now too close for comfort. Her response was the transference symptom of cellular dysphoria, incorporating in a single psychophysiological movement both the impulse toward engagement (transference) and the counterbalancing impulse toward disengagement (resistance). As distressing as it was, this symptom was also a positive achievement, the first stage of a psychological integration of her two opposing tendencies into a new way of being with me in which she could feel something without having to run away from it the next day.

Psychoanalysts Do Make Predictions

If this understanding was correct, I expected that Mary's cellular dysphoria would gradually evolve through the psychotherapeutic process into a more effective synthesis of emotional opposites. Her conflicting needs for love and hate, engagement and disengagement, would ultimately come together in a full conscious experiencing of her sexual desire. In fact, this was already beginning to happen. Mary was trusting me more and was able to feel a lot closer to me before she felt too close for comfort. As a result, she could now begin to feel the loving component of her sexual desire for me, at least in her *Cocoon* dream, though the hostile component remained unconscious (disguised in her other dream by the symbolism of attacking birds). In such an evolving context, it was to be expected that she would continue to experience intermittent bursts of sexual interest and anxiety, and that pretty soon one of these bursts would bring her forbidden sexual impulse directly into consciousness.

This expectation was so intrinsic to my understanding of the psychotherapeutic process that it had the strength of a scientific prediction: If Mary actually had the unconscious sexual impulse I was attributing to her, then the psychotherapeutic process would eventually bring that impulse fully into consciousness as a sexual feeling. She would become able to feel, and describe in words, the conscious temptation to tease me sexually—not in reaction to something provocative I might say, but in a spontaneous urge that she could recognize (and feel anxious about) as an expression of her own sexual desire. As a corollary prediction, if her cellular dysphoria was indeed an expression of this unconscious, conflicted sexual desire—as I had speculated—then as she became able to feel her desire consciously, the symptom would disappear, because she would no longer need it to disguise her sexual desire from herself.

Both these predictions proved correct. Within about two years from the time we first gave it the name cellular dysphoria, Mary's symptom was gone and she had become fully conscious of a sexual impulse to tease me. During those two years, our psychotherapeutic work had focused more and more on her sexual anxiety. As it turned out, the impetus for this development came not only from within the analysis but also from the intensification of a serious new relationship that Mary had entered into early in the third year of her analysis. In fact, the notable intensification of cellular dysphoria that began as soon as we had named it had coincided not only with her working through the impulse to quit analysis (which meant staying too close to me for comfort), but also with her decision to move in with Robert—an important step for her in this new relationship.

Mary reported that Robert was more open to his own feelings, and to hers, than other men she had been involved with. Being with him, she felt challenged to be more open herself, and so was forced for the first time to admit to herself just how inhibited sexually she had always felt. Previously she had told herself the story that her sexual experimentation during the "free-love" era of the sixties proved that she was a liberated woman. Now she recalled that she had never felt fully present emotionally during those early sexual relationships—never able to let down her guard, not even with the two men to whom she was briefly married. Some of this she had already reported to me in the context of her here-today-gone-tomorrow attempts to discuss sexual experiences. It was only after she moved in with Robert, however—and at the same time moved closer to me in the analysis—that she fully began to appreciate the importance of sexual anxiety and inhibition in her relationships with men.

This is the sort of thing that happens regularly during long-term psychotherapy. Something opens up in the therapy that facilitates a change in the patient's outside relationships (like Mary becoming involved with Robert), which in turn activates feelings that feed back into the psychotherapeutic process (as in her increased awareness of sexual anxiety). In that way, a synergistic combination of events in Mary's two ongoing intimate relationships, with Robert and with me, had now focused her sexual awareness and anxiety to the point that she could clearly notice herself feeling too close for comfort with one or the other of us, on an almost daily basis.

It is worth emphasizing that this increase in sexual anxiety was actually a sign of the great progress Mary was making in dealing with her difficulties with men. These difficulties—her mistrustfulness, her tendency to become caught up in power struggles, and her impulsive need to run away from any relationship that threatened to become too intimate—had all, in an important sense, been the result of her inability to tolerate anxiety. The fact that she now felt safe enough to *feel* her anxiety with me and with Robert, without needing to run away, was a major achievement—an indication of how well Mary had been able to use, and grow from, the psychotherapeutic process. It showed that Mary was much more capable of trust, and therefore able to feel comforted and sustained in her relationships. It also meant that she was better able to trust herself—to feel comforted and sustained from within—and therefore much more capable of loving in return. These two movements went together: becoming secure enough within herself to recognize her anxiety as her own problem rather than a reaction to dangerous men, and becoming able to trust, appreciate, and love Robert and me as comforters rather than having to run away from us as oppressors. Mary's growing capacity for love (the waking counterpart of her *Cocoon* dream) was a natural corollary of her growing capacity to experience and stay with her anxiety (the waking counterpart of her "attacking birds" dream).

Validating the Prediction

Mary's conscious awareness of a sexual desire to tease me emerged gradually (accompanied by a lessening of her cellular dysphoria) in a process that had three identifiable stages. In the first stage, she approached the subject of sexual desire from a considerable distance, by talking about the strong feelings of disapproval she felt toward a co-worker who dressed "too provocatively." As she introspectively unpacked these feelings, Mary realized that what troubled her was the idea that men would look at this co-worker and feel turned on by her. She felt jealous of the woman's sense of inner freedom to show herself openly in a way that would turn men on. Mary could never bring herself to do that, she said. It would make her too self-conscious.

The next stage came through analyzing her reasons for not attending a lecture of mine that she had very much wanted to hear. She had done this several times before—planning to come to one of my lectures, feeling a sense of eager curiosity about it, but then at the last minute finding a reason not to come. This time, however, she was particularly struck by the discrepancy between how eager she had felt to hear me speak and how gratuitous her reason was for missing the lecture—she had too much work to do around the house! When I asked her to review what she had felt on the day of the lecture, she recalled that as it came time to get herself ready to go, she had begun to feel a distinct sense of reluctance and ennui. This reluctance really had nothing to do with having too much work, she admitted, but stemmed rather from another, more troubling feeling—a worry that it might not be proper for her to go to one of my lectures, that I might not want her there. She found herself imagining that she would come into the lecture hall and I would suddenly notice her from the podium. She then became afraid that when I saw her, I would become flustered and unable to speak.

"What would I be feeling so flustered about?" I asked her.

"I don't know really," she answered initially. "It would just feel too personal somehow for a public arena, like I was intruding on your space."

Then, as she imaginatively projected herself into this fantasy, she recognized what the real intrusion would be: "I guess what I was fantasizing is that you would feel suddenly attracted to me, and that's what would throw you off balance, because you would know that you shouldn't be feeling that way about one of your patients." As she related this thought to me, Mary noticed that she felt turned on by it.

It is worth emphasizing how much change really took place between these two stages of Mary's awareness of her sexual feelings. Most important was a change from passive to active in which Mary began to feel more in charge both of her feelings and of her treatment. Initially, she had described her distress over her co-worker's sexual provocativeness much as she had described her cellular dysphoria, as an affliction visited on her from outside rather than as an emotion generated from within. It took considerable introspective work over a period of months before she could identify that the vague but compelling discomfort she felt in her co-worker's presence involved very specific feelings—disapproval of the way this woman teased men and self-consciousness at the thought that she herself could ever do such a thing. Even then, what she was aware of was not her own forbidden sexual desire but only feelings (disapproval and self-consciousness) that opposed her desire. In the second stage, analyzing why she had missed my lecture, her feelings were much better defined and she was able to recognize them as products of her own fantasy. Although her most prominent feelings continued to be those that opposed her desire—feelings of reluctance, guilt about intruding on my privacy, fear of my disapproval—she was able to analyze these feelings further (by asking herself what would be the intrusion, what would I disapprove of) to the point of becoming consciously aware of the forbidden sexual desire that was provoking this resistance.

In the next step of this progression from unconscious to conscious—the step that would fully confirm my prediction—Mary felt a direct upsurge of spontaneous, unguarded, sexual excitement, prompted by a fantasy of teasing me, which came up on two separate occasions, simply in the normal course of her associations. The fantasy was that she would describe a sexual situation or fantasy to me, ostensibly for the purpose of analyzing her sexual anxiety, but in a way that was covertly intended to turn me on.

Sex, Revenge, and Morality

Significantly, Mary was able to tell me about this fantasy, each time she had it, in a way that was not itself sexually provocative. In other words, she was able to *feel* the exciting temptation as a feeling, without having a need to act on it. She recognized as part of her awareness of this feeling that acting on it could only defeat her psychotherapeutic purpose. Indeed, the main charge of excitement in the temptation lay precisely in that forbidden possibility—of defeating not only her own purpose but mine, by rendering me powerless to maintain my position of therapeutic "neutrality," just as in her earlier fantasy she had rendered me speechless at the podium. This possibility felt exciting because it gave her a sense of unaccustomed power over me. For such a long time she had felt (in her negative, mistrustful transference) that I had all the power, and that my so-called neutrality was simply a way of lording it over her from my detached psychoanalytic throne. Now, in her fantasy, she could feel how delicious it would be to "get even," by turning the tables and using *her* power on me.

The fact that sex, power, and revenge were thus intertwined in Mary's fantasy—linked together in the idea of "making a conquest" of me—went a long way toward explaining why she had had trouble becoming aware of her desire in the first place. She was conflicted not so much about the sex as about the hostility of her revenge motive. But once she could feel it, and accept it as part of herself, this motive turned out to be very liberating for her. It inspired her to want to openly claim the equal power she had always denied herself, not only in the area of sexuality but in all areas of her relationships with men. With her boss, with Robert, and with me, she became better at recognizing when she was angry or disagreed with us, and much better able to put forward her own needs and perspective without worrying about incurring our disapproval. In her day-to-day interactions with me, she became noticeably less hesitant, needing less to depend on me to help her make sense of what she was feeling, and generally taking charge of her own analysis.

At the same time, with the awareness of her power came an awareness of her responsibility to use that power well, and a mature sense that it would be not only counterproductive for her therapy but morally wrong were she to try to put her fantasy of teasing me into action. What made it wrong was that the fantasy scenario was based primarily on a negative transference attitude toward me, informed much more by hostility than by love. The analyst of whom Mary was tempted to make a conquest was a one-sided caricature of myself—an object rather than a person. That caricature enjoyed keeping himself cold and aloof, manipulating and cynically exploiting her, and thus deserved to be put in his place. That's what made the fantasy so exciting, and also what would have made it wrong to act on it: it represented a longed-for vengeful triumph over a tantalizing figure (me) who stood for the unattainable, forbidden objects of desire (her parents) by whom she had felt rejected and humiliated in childhood. In consciously feeling the sexual excitement of this fantasy, then, Mary was confronting the moral crux of the Oedipus complex, the knowledge of good and evil in the awareness of her own sexual desire.

It is significant—and quite typical of what happens in psychoanalysis—that the result of Mary's getting in touch with her sexual feelings was not a greater tendency to hedonism but rather a more refined moral sense. Being able to feel that the excitement of her fantasy came from a hostile power motive made it easier for her to choose not to act from that motive. At the same time, being able to feel what was good in the fantasy—the sense of having a right to personal power in her relationships with men—made it easier for her to recognize and assert her power in more positive ways, toward equality and respect rather than revenge.

This was by no means the end of the treatment, or even the end of our analysis of Mary's sexual anxiety. It was enough, however, to complete the cure of her cellular dysphoria, by transforming it into a consciously experienced moral and emotional conflict. In situations where she had previously felt paralyzed by the inchoate physical distress of her symptom, she now experienced a differentiated and much more tolerable feeling of anxiety. This change culminated a gradual evolution of diminishing cellular dysphoria and increasing awareness of sexual anxiety and sexual desire over the period of two years or so that she was working through her sexualized power struggles with men in her transference relationship with me.

Considering that her cellular dysphoria was a crystallization of Mary's experience of herself as a passive, helpless victim—at the mercy of emotions and people she could not control—it was only natural that the symptom should disappear once she was able to experience herself as having power in her relationships. The overall shift was from feeling like a helpless child to feeling like a competent adult. She now felt freer and more relaxed than she had ever felt before, not only sexually but emotionally in general. Perhaps the most dramatic example of this change was that her aversion to infants disappeared. Now that she no longer felt trapped in the experience of a colicky infant, she could accept feelings of dependency and vulnerability in herself and in others, and so was able for the first time in her life to enjoy being around children, and to want children of her own. Meanwhile, her relationship with

Robert continued to flourish and she eventually married him. They are still together today, many years later—the first time Mary has ever been able to stay in any romantic relationship for more than two years.

Sexuality and Healing the Soul

Mary's experience exemplifies the way healing occurs in the simple process of getting in touch with feelings, and illustrates, I hope, why I describe this process as listening to the soul. It involves the movement of consciousness I referred to earlier, in which paying attention to an experience of anxiety opens us to a deeper level of feeling, and ultimately to the joyful discovery of our true self. In the process, as we become more open to our own anxiety-, guilt-, and shame-provoking emotions, the inward movement of self-discovery becomes at the same time a movement toward intimacy, opening us to others in a fuller experience of love. There is an inner sense of wholeness that comes with such an experience that has a distinctly spiritual quality—as Mary felt most vividly in her *Cocoon* dream but increasingly in her waking life as well—an awareness of the healing activity of love in the soul.[3]

From this perspective it is easy to see why sexuality plays such an important role in the psychotherapeutic process. As a source of anxiety, guilt, and shame, and at the same time an impetus toward intimacy, sexual desire combines and energizes the two movements—toward self-discovery and toward intimacy—that together constitute the process of healing the soul. The overall psychotherapeutic development is from a compelling experience of inner conflict to a joyful experience of love.

One Last Question

Through the story of Mary's treatment, I have presented elements of the psychotherapeutic process that stem from the universal inner conflict over forbidden sexual desire—something that I believe should (or could) be recognizable to all my readers from their own sexual feelings. Nevertheless, I expect that many readers of this chapter will be left with an uneasy question: "Isn't it wrong, and dangerous, for a patient and a therapist to be feeling sexual feelings toward each other?"

As you might imagine, the answer is complex, and must be given from both the side of the patient and the side of the therapist. The most important thing to keep in mind is that it is one thing to feel a sexual feeling, and to talk about it for the purpose of understanding what the feeling contains and points to, yet quite another to have a sexual impulse that triggers immediate action, whether a physical action or an emotional enactment like teasing. It is the latter that many people think of as "being in touch with" their sexuality, but in fact just the opposite is true. The impulsive need for immediate action and reaction is a way of trying to get rid of uncomfortable sexual feelings by discharging the inner tension they produce. It is a way of not feeling the power of, and responsibility for, one's own sexual desire, with all the guilt, shame, and anxiety that attend it. It is *acting instead of feeling.*

Still, as I have tried to illustrate in describing my interactions with Mary, a certain degree of impulsiveness and unconscious tendency to enactment are a natural and integral part of the psychotherapeutic process, a result of the patient's inevitable transference projection of disowned unconscious emotions into the therapist. When properly handled by a self-aware therapist, such enactment tendencies are simply grist for the mill. They reveal in interpersonal form, via the countertransference, the nature of the patient's unconscious conflict, and they serve to make the unconscious conscious by creating a mirror in which the patient can see his or her own forbidden emotions as a projected image. When that happens, the patient may very well fall in love with, feel desire for, or be tempted to seduce the therapist, but he or she will also become more aware of what makes such emotions forbidden (guilt/shame/anxiety-provoking) to begin with, and will have correspondingly less need to act on them.

The therapist's having sexual feelings toward the patient is also to some extent inevitable, but with an important difference. Whenever a patient has unconscious sexual emotions that are pressing toward consciousness but still barred from it, those emotions are likely to express themselves in some form of unconscious teasing or seductiveness. It is natural that the therapist will register a sexual response to this enactment pressure, as I did to Mary's unconscious teasing. But where the patient is enacting the sexual emotions without feeling them, the therapist must be able to feel the feelings without enacting them. It is always improper for a therapist to use a patient, however indirectly, to gratify his or her own sexual or romantic needs. Any sexual response in the therapist should be a distilled conscious feeling, modulated enough to be used exclusively as a signal—to alert the therapist to what is happening in the transference and countertransference without disrupting his state of receptive attention. It should never be an impulsive need that the therapist is driven to enact with the patient rather than feeling within himself.

In other words, it is not sexual feelings that are dangerous, but rather sexual needs and impulses that are not fully experienced as feelings. *Those who cannot feel their emotions are condemned to enact them.* This is one more reason why anyone practicing psychodynamic psychotherapy or psychoanalysis should undergo intensive psychotherapeutic treatment themselves. The treatment should be long enough and deep enough for the therapist-patient to become fully aware of, and no longer driven by, his or her own forbidden, conflicted, sexual desires.

But there are a couple of important qualifications that must be added. For one thing, there is a good deal of psychotherapeutic benefit that can be gained without ever getting to the level where sexual conflicts and anxieties come to the fore. I may have given the impression that the only productive events in Mary's therapy were our brief, intense transference–countertransference interactions around her impulse to quit and around unconscious sexual teasing, but in fact we accomplished a good deal during the long in-between periods when we focused on her life outside of analysis. As a result, by the time she said, "If you really want me to be angry, you're going to have to provoke me," she had already learned to be much more comfortable with her anger and more aware of it as it surfaced in her dealings with her boss, with members of her family, and with friends. She had become more confident and assertive, and was better able to stand up for herself in the world. At that point it was only in her most intimate relationships, with me and with Robert, that she remained significantly inhibited in terms of being able to feel her anger and stand up for herself. In these relationships, her unconscious sexual conflicts and anxiety were definitely getting in the way.

The second qualification is that, while it may be natural for a patient to feel or unconsciously enact sexual and/or romantic emotions toward the therapist, it is quite unusual—and a definite danger signal—for a patient overtly and intentionally to try to seduce the therapist or to turn the therapeutic relationship into a romantic one. When patients do this, there are two possible explanations. The more ominous possibility is that the therapist is being unconsciously seductive, so that the patient is the one experiencing countertransference. In other words, a patient who attempts to seduce the therapist may well be enacting the therapist's unconscious transference projection. What makes this ominous is that the therapist seldom knows how to recognize it—or what to do about it—when it happens. If he did, it wouldn't be happening in the first place, because the therapist would have been dealing with his transference needs in his own psychotherapeutic process, not projecting them into his patients. It is typically therapists who have had inadequate training—especially inadequate personal psychotherapy of their own—who unconsciously exploit their patients in this way.

The other possibility when a patient consciously tries to seduce the therapist is that the seduction is serving as a resistance against awareness of powerfully painful and/or humiliating feelings that are not primarily sexual. It may be an attempt to avoid therapy (and consciousness) altogether, whether by provoking the therapist to show that he cannot be trusted, or simply by defeating his or her therapeutic purpose. This extreme form of resistance indicates the patient's absolute underlying lack of trust that anyone could be sincerely interested in helping—as if to say (unconsciously), "I'm sure this person is going to end up using me just like everyone else has, so I might as well beat him to the punch and use him first." Here again, the question becomes one of whether the therapist has enough awareness of and comfort with his or her countertransference reactions to be able to recognize that the sex or the romance for these patients is essentially a red herring—designed to subvert a therapy that the patient never really believed in to begin with (whatever story they may have told themselves and the therapist about why they wanted therapy).

The Answer? It Depends

Returning then to the question of whether it is wrong or dangerous for a patient and therapist to be experiencing sexual feelings during treatment, perhaps the best way to answer is to say that it depends, both on the goals of the treatment and on the skill of the therapist. In the case of cognitive-behavioral psychotherapy, supportive psychotherapy, problem-focused counseling and other forms of short-term psychotherapy, the goals of treatment are generally limited to providing symptomatic relief and improving social or occupational functioning. The therapist is typically not paying attention to transference and countertransference, and is not practiced in dealing with them.

Having sexual feelings come up in these therapies, therefore, tends to interfere seriously with the treatment. It often indicates a problem—an unconscious enactment—in the therapist–patient relationship that neither therapist nor patient is aware of. It may also mean that the patient needs a more intense transference relationship than the therapy he or she has chosen is designed to deal with.

In psychoanalysis and psychodynamic psychotherapy, on the other hand, problems are addressed not only at the more superficial levels of relieving symptoms and improving functioning but also at the deeper level of improving the patient's acceptance of self and others and thereby his capacity for true intimacy. The goal of treatment is ultimately to expand the patient's consciousness through a healing transference relationship, in which the patient is able to re-create and more fully experience his or her problem with a person who knows how to recognize and handle countertransference. Through accepting, containing, and processing the patient's projections, both positive and negative, the therapist establishes a safe "facilitating environment" where the patient can project whatever he needs to, then catch himself in the enactment, and ultimately feel his own feelings, in a way that can seldom happen in "real life." In this context, it is to be expected that both patient and therapist will at times become aware of conflicted sexual feelings—but only to the extent that they are part of the patient's currently pressing problem—simply as part of the normal course of peeling the introspective onion.

V. History Lessons

Those who cannot remember the past are condemned to repeat it.

—George Santayana

13. Respect the Symptom

[A]s you ought not to attempt to cure the eyes without the head, or the head with-out the body, so neither ought you to attempt to cure the body without the soul. And this . . . is the reason why the cure of many diseases is unknown to the physicians of Hellas, because they disregard the whole, which ought to be studied also, for the part can never be well unless the whole is well.

—Plato, *Charmides*

Nature is the physician; we only her assistants.

—Galen

The Repetition Compulsion and the Adaptive Value of Symptoms

We have seen how Mary's story—both before and during her analysis— was largely the story of her repetition compulsion: a recurrent pattern of transference–countertransference interactions that shaped all her important relationships. In the same way, everyone's life—including yours and mine— is dictated to a significant degree by our repetition compulsion, and so is really a story being written by an unconscious author. We spend most of our time reacting automatically rather than acting self-reflectively, responding to situations and people according to stereotyped personality patterns that are essentially involuntary—like a neurologically programmed instinct or conditioned reflex. In that sense, Mary's goal in treatment reflects what many of us would call our goal in life: to free ourselves from these automatic emotional and behavioral patterns of the repetition compulsion and become the conscious authors of our own story.

In Mary's case, as often happens, developing a symptom was an important step toward becoming conscious. Mary's cellular dysphoria helped contain the conflicting needs and passions that for years had provoked so much anxiety in her that she needed to avoid or flee all intimate relationships—the pattern of her repetition compulsion. Developing the symptom forced her (and me) to pay attention to her anger, her feelings of dependency, and her sexual anxiety. Becoming able to feel these feelings was the beginning of a new freedom from her repetition compulsion and a new capacity for intimacy.

How Medical Is the Medical Model?

The general idea that symptoms are adaptive, you will recall, derives from the ancient Hippocratic teaching that symptoms are manifestations of a healing energy—the *vis medicatrix naturae*—that is inherent in all natural processes. In more modern, scientific terminology, we would say that symptoms are products of evolutionary adaptation—the organism's genetically programmed healing response to disease. In American psychiatry, this view was widely accepted as recently as the first half of the twentieth century, and was the central teaching of Adolf Meyer (1866–1950), generally recognized as the father of American psychiatry. Meyer classified the common psychiatric symptom clusters as *reaction types:* characteristic patterns of psychobiological response, elicited by psychosocial stress, that represent different styles of adapting to stress, and that presumably have a genetic basis.

Unfortunately Meyer's teaching has in recent years fallen out of fashion. Psychiatrists continue to view symptoms as genetically encoded responses, but now believe they are genetic defects rather than genetic adaptations. This belief reflects the Medical Model's swimming-pool assumption that symptoms are bad—painful and disruptive to functioning—and therefore *must* be diseases. It ignores the ways that symptoms promote healing and growth; it blurs the fundamental distinction between symptom and disease; and, ironically, it puts the Medical Model at odds with the deepest principles and traditions of medicine.

The Adaptive Function of Symptoms in Physical Illness

Most of us are familiar with the adaptive, healing function of symptoms from our everyday experience of physical symptoms like fainting, fever, and cough. Fainting solves the problem of insufficient blood flow to the brain, forcing the lightheaded person into a position where blood can get to the brain more easily. Fever has been genetically programmed over the course of evolution to facilitate the action of the immune system. Coughing aids recovery from upper respiratory infections by clearing the bronchial passages of noxious phlegm.

Pain itself is perhaps the most obvious example of the healing function of symptoms. Pain facilitates healing by signaling us that something is wrong, and making it less likely that we will continue to do certain things (like throw a baseball with a broken arm) that might aggravate the problem. If I come to the emergency room with a red, blistering hand and complain of physical pain, for instance, the doctor will assume that my pain is a natural, adaptive response to the burn I suffered. He may want to alleviate the pain, but he would never think that the pain was itself the primary problem. Yet amazingly, if I come to the same emergency room, now gaunt and sleepless, complaining of emotional pain, the doctor will not think for a minute that my pain might be an adaptive response to some psychic burn I have suffered, still less that it could be genetically programmed to alert me to a sickness or disharmony of my soul. Instead, he will assume that my pain is an abnormal neurophysiological event, a genetic mistake, not a symptom but a disease called depression.

Nature Is the Physician, Except in Psychiatry?

The theory of evolution tells us that genetic errors are maladaptive and so tend to die out gradually over time. By this logic it seems highly implausible that depression and anxiety could possibly be as widespread as they are currently (and who has not experienced them in one form or another?) unless they had survival value for the species. Even schizophrenia, whose sufferers are far less likely to produce offspring than the general population, nevertheless shows no indication of diminishing in frequency, as we would ultimately expect it to if it were a maladaptive genetic defect.[1] The truth is, we have no scientific evidence that any psychiatric symptom is a disease rather than—like fever, cough, fainting, and physical pain—part of a natural healing process. *Genetic researchers have absolutely no way of knowing that depression and anxiety have not been hardwired into the genes in exactly the same way fever and cough have been, through a slow evolutionary process that is ultimately beneficial for the survival of the species.*

The fact that doctors respect the symptom when it is fever but not when it is depression reflects a serious limitation in their materialistic philosophy. They can see the adaptive value of fever through the lens of that philosophy because the healing action of fever is purely biological: fever promotes the swimming-pool equilibrium, or chemical balance, of the body. But the adaptive value of depression cannot be seen through swimming-pool lenses because the healing action of depression is not on the body but on the soul, promoting a more effective integration of the conflicting needs of body, brain, mind, *and* spirit. As in the stories of Anne and Joe, depression forces the sufferer to pay attention to something important within himself that he would otherwise be inclined to ignore. To understand this adaptive, healing function of depression—or of any psychiatric symptom—requires a quest philosophy that allows us to look beyond the symptom as neurobiological event to the person within whom the neurobiological event occurs. If we think of psychiatric symptoms as produced by persons in their wholeness rather than by brains in their brokenness, then we can see that they are more than disruptions of biological equilibrium. They are adaptive attempts to master the trials of the life cycle, integrative self-healing responses to a disruption, not of chemical balance in the body, but of the inner harmony of the soul.

Yet the fact that I consider psychiatric symptoms adaptive doesn't mean that I am oblivious to the suffering they entail or that I am opposed to using medication to alleviate that suffering. What it does mean is that I would never use medication to treat the symptom without also using psychotherapy to treat the underlying disease—the inner conflict—that is generating the symptom and the suffering. What I am opposed to is a psychiatry that relies *exclusively* on medication because it equates getting rid of the symptom with curing the disease. Medical students learn very early in their training that they should never give painkillers to patients with abdominal pain, because in taking away the pain they might mask the warning signs of appendicitis. Understanding this, what patient would insist on taking a painkiller for a stomachache? Although the danger of treating the symptom as if it were the disease may not always be so obvious, it is safe to assume that there is always some risk involved when we try to eliminate a symptom without considering the vital, adaptive purpose it may be serving.

Symptoms Are Good for the Soul

I have treated a number of patients like Anne and Joe, for instance, whose disabling symptoms forced them to grow—who were freed from unrewarding careers or from destructive relationships only by their unremitting psychiatric illnesses. For patients like this, it is difficult to believe that their lives would have been better had they been "cured" with medication. Sometimes you have to fall down to realize you are on the wrong path. I have also treated several seriously depressed patients who dropped out of psychotherapy—ignoring significant marital or family problems—because they felt miraculously cured by an antidepressant, but whose depression later returned and was no longer responsive to the same dose of the same antidepressant. Biochemically, no one knows why antidepressants tend to lose their effectiveness like this, but it isn't so difficult to explain if depression is understood as the muffled voice of the soul, trying to call the patient's attention to something he or she is trying to ignore. If that is true, it makes sense that an adaptational need for a depression might supersede the biological action of an antidepressant that had once worked.

It is a well-known but poorly understood fact that the risk of suicide becomes greater when a depressed patient begins to recover. This doesn't fit well with the usual assumption that the symptom of depression itself is what makes the person suicidal. Rather it suggests that the biological shutdown of depression may actually protect against suicide—by making it more difficult for the patient to take *any* action—and that reactivating the patient with medication may then increase the risk of suicide unless adequate attention is paid to the patient's underlying reasons for hopelessness.[2]

Agnes

Agnes was a former high school cheerleader who became profoundly depressed in her third month of college. She responded very well to antidepressant medication but as her depression improved she developed uncontrollable urges to cut herself. Referred to me for hospitalization, Agnes explained that she felt *compelled* to cut herself, specifically to make a scar on herself *so that she would never forget her depression.* She could not explain why she was willing to go to such lengths to remember an experience she described as having been unimaginably painful. Indeed she begged me never to take her off the antidepressant because she was terrified of ever feeling that pain again. But if the pain was that awful, then why would she want to memorialize it by scarring herself?

What emerged over many months of psychotherapy was that the pain of Agnes's depression had, in an important way, been good for her. She recalled that in the weeks before she got depressed she had become painfully self-conscious, aware of what seemed an unbridgeable gap between the empty despair she felt on the inside and the compulsively cheery smile she showed on the outside. Feeling the pain of her symptom had been a solution to this underlying problem of emotional deadness. Her incapacitating depression was an open expression of what she had always put so much energy into hiding, and a significant improvement over a life of debilitating pretense. In that sense, the antidepressant had actually interfered with Agnes's healing, taking away her genuine feeling of despair, which the depression had forced her to acknowledge and to show openly for the first time. With the depression "cured," she had gone back into hiding, cutting herself in secret while trying to act on the surface as if all were well. But at the same time, cutting herself was also an attempt to bring her despair back out into the open, by producing a visible scar that would reveal it to the world and help her remember it herself. Wanting to remember her depression meant wanting to remember that she did indeed have the capacity to feel.

"Though This Be Madness, Yet There Is Method In't"

Like Agnes, most psychiatric patients tend to feel highly identified with what psychiatrists call their illnesses. Against all appearances, they sense that their symptoms somehow express what is best, most alive, in them. Anorexic patients, for instance, may feel free only when they are starving themselves. So-called borderline patients often feel alive only when they are cutting themselves. Many manic-depressive patients are reluctant to take lithium because they don't want to give up the productivity and creativity that come with their manic episodes. Likewise, schizophrenic patients often feel energized and healthy only when they are psychotic; apathetic and sickly when they are not. But whether patients experience their symptoms as valuable or not, it always becomes clear in the course of psychotherapy that there is a way in which the symptom is good for the soul.

There is a fascinating illustration of this principle in the movie *The Ruling Class*. In it, Peter O'Toole plays the overtly schizophrenic product of a covertly pathological family of British Lords, who are in turn the product of a secretly sick, hypocritical society. O'Toole's delusion that he is a loving Jesus Christ protects him from having to participate in the corruption of his family and his society. But his family expects him to rise to his station, so they arrange to have his delusion corrected through a frightening kind of shock treatment. The treatment is an apparent success, and O'Toole becomes to all outward appearances a paragon of sanity, assuming his destined role of leadership in the House of Lords. But inwardly, we soon discover, his humanity has been destroyed. No longer allowed to seal himself off from the sickness of his society and the hidden sickness within his family, he turns from open schizophrenia as Jesus Christ, to a surreptitious schizophrenia in which he acts as Jack the Lord by day but becomes Jack the Ripper by night. His Jesus Christ delusion, it turns out, had been a healthy adaptation, through which he had actually been saving mankind from his own potential to become Jack the Ripper.

The Ruling Class is a modern treatment of an old theme, most memorably treated by Shakespeare in *Hamlet*. Hamlet, too, is expected (by the armored ghost of his murdered father, who represents the cultural expectations that go with Hamlet's lineage) to assume leadership of a war-mongering society. Denmark is rotten not only because of Hamlet's dead uncle and voluptuous mother, but because of his murdered father, a warrior who had spent his life indiscriminately killing people in battle. As the play opens, Hamlet wants to escape this destiny—and his own warlike disposition—by leaving Denmark to become a student, but his family will not permit it.[3] He then resorts to madness, still trying to avoid the necessity of becoming like his violent and lecherous family. As in *The Ruling Class*, the tragedy is that his madness failed. It was an adaptive response to an impossible predicament, protecting him from evil as long as he was able to maintain it. But circumstances (most notably the direct threat to his life posed by Rosencrantz and

Guildenstern) in the end force Hamlet to become sane again, and in so doing he becomes a murderer.

Artistic portraits of mental illness like *Hamlet* and *The Ruling Class* present a stylized but psychologically valid picture of the deep unconscious method in their protagonists' madness. They help underscore the very real danger we court in treating the symptoms of mental illness as meaningless by-products of bad brain chemistry while ignoring their deeper purpose of healing the soul. We all have within us the makings of both philosopher and murderer, Jesus Christ and Jack the Ripper. When conflict between these antithetical tendencies begins to threaten our integrity, symptoms act to restore some measure of inner harmony. Even the most bizarre and terrifying symptoms of psychosis are adaptive—if only partly successful—acts of integration.

The Ecological Versus the "Foreign-Body" Conceptions of Disease

It is worth reemphasizing that this concept of symptoms as nature's attempts to heal a disharmony within the soul (including its relation to the environment)—known as the holistic or ecological conception of disease—has been the dominant paradigm throughout almost the entire history of medicine. Originally called "humoral pathology," it was developed between the sixth and fifth centuries B.C. by Pythagoras, Empedocles, and Hippocrates, who viewed health as a harmony and disease as a disharmony between four inherently conflicting physical elements (Air, Earth, Fire, and Water) and their corresponding physiological "humors" (blood, black bile, yellow bile, and phlegm).

The idea that disease was caused by discord among antithetical elements and humors and that health required the harmonizing of these physical opposites was the earliest precursor of the Psychotherapeutic Model's current idea that healing the soul requires a resolution of inner conflict. But it was only with Plato (c. 428–348 B.C.) that the centrality of the soul in the healing process was fully recognized, and that inner conflict was understood not simply as a physical opposition of elements and humors but also as a conflict between different levels of experiencing within the soul itself. Plato's basic model, as he spelled it out in the *Republic*, the *Phaedrus*, and the *Timaeus*, was that the soul has three levels of desire. The lowest level was appetite—the hedonistic desire for physical comfort and pleasure. The middle was ambition—

the desire for success, glory, and honor. The highest was philosophy—the desire for wisdom and virtue. True healing, Plato argued, operates not only at the level of physical health—the kind of humoral balance that Hippocrates emphasized—but at the levels of worldly success and moral virtue as well. It requires a complex harmonizing of all three levels of desire in the soul, with each other, with the humors of the body and with the elements of the environment.[4]

Plato's model of the tripartite soul contained all the necessary elements for a clinically useful psychiatric theory of inner conflict, but these would remain dormant seeds for many centuries, flowering briefly during the Renaissance (with Burton's *Anatomy of Melancholy* and other similar treatises on depression and the soul), but growing to full fruition only with Freud, whose model of the tripartite soul (the *It,* the *I,* and the *I that stands above*) resembled Plato's but, as we shall see in Chapters 14 and 15, was more specifically designed to explain the processes of inner conflict.

Humoral pathology remained the dominant paradigm in medicine until the early 1800s, when it was gradually superseded by the new paradigm of "cellular pathology" that still predominates in medicine today. Developed by pathologist Rudolf Virchow and bacteriologists Louis Pasteur and Robert Koch, cellular pathology advanced the radical notion that individual cells (like cancer cells or bacteria) could cause disease of the whole organism. Whereas humoral pathology viewed disease as a disharmony of the whole person, cellular pathology viewed disease as *external* to the person, resulting from a parasitic or invasive attack by a "foreign" disease-carrying microbe or cell against an otherwise healthy body. In more recent times this "foreign-body" conception of disease has been extended to its submicroscopic limit, where we see disease as centered not in the whole organism, or even in a whole cell (whether domestic or foreign), but simply in alien (defective, bad) molecules. As Harris Dienstfrey has put it,

> The medical community [now] generally presumes that the source of each definable illness is likely to be a single physical entity—if not a "germ," then a deficient gene or an improper amount of a chemical produced by the body.[5]

Harmony Versus Homeostasis

It is sometimes said that our modern concept of chemical imbalance is a return to the old paradigm of humoral pathology. Not so. When psychiatrists today refer to a chemical imbalance, they do not mean an imbalance that involves all the physiological processes of a person in interaction with his environment, still less a disharmony between different levels of desire in the soul. What they mean is a very localized imbalance between "transmitter" molecules and "receptor" molecules in the microscopic spaces ("synapses") between nerve cells in particular areas of the brain. They see this imbalance as a neurological glitch, like a foreign body, that is disrupting the "homeostasis" of an otherwise healthy person.

Homeostasis, first described by nineteenth-century French physiologist Claude Bernard, is defined by the *Encyclopaedia Britannica* as the inherent tendency of biological systems "to reach a steady state, a balance that resists outside forces of change." Where Pythagorean–Platonic harmony referred to a dynamic, evolving state of interactive balance between inherently conflicting elements, the very term homeo*stasis* implies a much more static, noninteractive, condition. It assumes that the only inherent tendency in a person is toward biological equilibrium, and that any disruption of that equilibrium would therefore have to come from outside (i.e., a foreign-body model of disease).

This homeostatic conception of health and disease defines a distilled swimming-pool philosophy of life. It pictures a human being as a purely biological system, designed to avoid or minimize change while expending no more energy than is necessary to survive and maintain stability against outside forces of disruption. The goal is to keep swimming laps (maintain a homoeostatic equilibrium) and avoid collisions with "foreign bodies"—bad genes, damaged or defective cells, and unbalanced neurotransmitters that can upset your equilibrium by causing symptoms. In contrast, the harmonic conception of health and disease define a quest philosophy. It pictures a human being as an evolving soul or self—unsettled and spurred toward growth by a disharmony of body, brain, mind, and spirit. The goal is to pursue an ever-elusive state of integration by harmonizing these conflicting elements as we grow and develop through interaction with others. The anxiety and symptoms that emerge during this process are a falling down that is good. They may be painful, but they are the seeds of healing the soul.

The Medical Model May Be Hazardous to Your Health: Symptom Chasing

There have recently been widespread signs of a countercultural revitalization of the holistic, harmonic conception of health and disease. In response to the dehumanizing, technologizing trend in mainstream medicine (and its even more dehumanizing economic by-product, managed care) there has been a good deal of interest in "alternative" approaches to healing. Central to all these approaches is an emphasis on the mind or soul as the active, harmonizing agent in the healing process. Even within mainstream medicine there has been a growing appreciation that our state of mind has a profound influence both on the disease process and on the healing process. Yet oddly enough it is psychiatry, the discipline that specializes in phenomena of the mind, that has been most resistant to this new awareness. The resistance takes the form of the Medical Model's materialistic swimming-pool philosophy, which defines symptoms as bad and health as homeostasis. Though called the Medical Model, this approach is no longer medical in the truest sense of the term. It no longer respects the soul's need for harmony and no longer respects the symptom as part of the healing process.

I have seen the harm this approach can do when I have been called on as a consultant for "problem patients" who are taking four or more different psychiatric drugs and remain in significant distress. I tell all such patients that I have a rule of thumb: *Any psychiatrist who prescribes more than three psychiatric drugs at one time for one patient is trying to fix something with medication that isn't really a medication problem.* What has typically happened in these situations is something called symptom chasing, where the patient keeps experiencing new symptoms (or a recurrence of old ones) and the psychiatrist treats each new symptom with a different medication. He thinks of each new symptom as a chemical imbalance in a different neurotransmitter system that calls for another drug designed to act on that particular neurotransmitter system.

Here is a hypothetical but by no means far-fetched example of symptom chasing. A patient presents with paranoia and is given an antipsychotic (dopamine system), which can have sedating side effects. At the next visit, four weeks later, the patient seems strikingly slow and apathetic—symptoms of depression—and so is given an antidepressant (norepinephrine system), which in a small percentage of patients can increase paranoid anxiety. At the third visit, the patient complains of new obsessive-compulsive symptoms and is given a selective serotonin reuptake inhibitor like Prozac (also an anti-depressant, but working on the serotonin rather than the norepinephrine system), which is known to be useful for obsessive-compulsive disorder but can also increase paranoia and cause agitation. At the fourth visit, the patient seems restless and agitated and is given an anti-anxiety agent like Valium (gamma-aminobutyric acid system). At the fifth visit, the psychiatrist notices that the patient's paranoia and agitation still haven't entirely disappeared and he wonders whether they might be symptoms of manic-depression, so he prescribes a mood stabilizer like lithium (norepinephrine, gamma-aminobutyric acid, and/or possibly the glutamate system). The psychiatrist may realize that each new symptom the patient has developed is a possible side effect of the last medication added to the mix. He may even realize, if he has a sense of humor, that some of the patient's paranoia and agitation now reflects a valid feeling that his brain is being controlled by irrational outside forces. What the psychiatrist will not realize is that all the patient's symptoms and neurotransmitter imbalances, even those that are side effects, are also and most importantly mechanisms for coping with the anxiety of one basic inner conflict—in this case probably a conflict over unconscious rage. The patient's paranoia, his oversedation and apathy, his obsessive-compulsive symptoms, and his agitation, all reflect changes in the balance of unconscious rage versus unconscious inhibitions and defenses. Each change in medication changes the biological pressure of either the emotion trying to become conscious or the resistance against it, and thereby changes the symptoms and the level of anxiety. The psychiatrist will not realize this because he is limited by an incoherent theory of symptoms as foreign-body glitches that in the end leaves him with nothing else to do for a persistently symptomatic patient than to prescribe yet another medication. He lacks an integrative theory of the soul in conflict that would allow him to understand the effects (and side effects) of medications *not* in terms of what they do to neurotransmitters but in terms of how they relieve or exacerbate the disharmony of emotional forces within the soul.

The Skeptic Responds

"That's all well and good," a skeptic might say, "but the fact is that patients suffer tremendously from their symptoms and often experience great relief with medication. Aren't you being irresponsible in minimizing how important that is?" My answer is that I am not opposed to using medication to relieve suffering. I do it frequently. What I'm opposed to is the misguided attempt to *eliminate* suffering without respect for what is causing it. It is a matter of philosophy. Suffering is an inevitable aspect of falling down, and whether we are justified in trying to eliminate it or not depends at least in part on whether we think falling down is bad or good.

I have suggested a number of the ways in which eliminating a symptom that is actually a healthy adaptational response can lead to other serious problems. Most of the time it doesn't seem to, as far as we know, but then how *would* we ever know? We literally have no idea why the mind-altering medications we use have even their intended therapeutic effects,[6] let alone any unintended ill effects that we probably wouldn't recognize as medication effects if they did occur. Even for those patients who seem to respond to medication as if they are totally cured, we don't know that their lives won't in the long run be emptier, that they won't develop high blood pressure or a bad back or begin to mistreat their children because of the way medication has readjusted their personal ecology.

On the Other Hand . . .

Still, none of these considerations has ever stopped me from taking aspirin for a headache. Falling down may be good, but there are many times when I'd rather be comfortable. I should admit, too, that despite the lesson I learned from Gregory about falling down, I still found myself instinctively using the father-knows-best method to help my daughter, Nicole, learn to ride a two-wheeler. With her, it worked like a charm. Even as a psychotherapist, much of what I say to patients could be taken as expressing a swimming-pool philosophy. The impulse to say anything at all reflects some degree of discomfort with allowing them to fall down in their own way without trying to control or influence it. Whether I offer medication or interpretation, a hand on the back of the bicycle seat, or an admonition to watch out for cars, all my interventions are at least partly swimming-pool interventions, designed to foster equilibrium at the moment.

But at the same time all interventions, including medication, can also be viewed as attempts to rock the boat, to change the current equilibrium (or disequilibrium) to a new one. In that sense, all interventions are to some degree quest interventions, designed to provide new experiences that can foster further growth. An intervention designed at one level to protect the patient from a particular kind of falling down may be used at another level to open up new possibilities for falling down more productively. I may want to medicate a symptom like severe anorexia, for instance, not only because I want to protect the patient from being killed by the symptom but because I want her to be able to feel the anxiety and self-hatred she has been acting out through the symptomatic behavior. Even the father-knows-best method of teaching bicycle riding is not exclusively a swimming-pool technique. Part of why it worked better for Nicole than it had for Gregory (besides the difference in their personalities) was that I was much calmer about the fact that at some point in the process Nicole, too, would have to fall down. Therefore, my use of the technique with her was less anxiety-driven and philosophically more open-minded than it had been with Gregory.

My conclusion is that we are all swimming laps even as we are simultaneously engaged in a quest. The soul needs the growth of the quest while the body and brain need the stability of the swimming pool. Mental illness—indeed any illness—reflects a disharmony in both realms of experience. In the Age of the Brain the key question is whether we will choose a model of healing that understands our swimming-pool needs within the larger context of the quest, or remain content with a model whose therapeutic horizon extends no farther than the edge of the pool.

But Doc, I Really Need Something Right Now!

"That's all very inspirational," protests the skeptic, "but with your head so much in the philosophical clouds, how do you ever make a practical decision about when to write a prescription?" A good question, but remember that all of us—even psychiatrists who do nothing but write prescriptions—have our heads in one philosophical cloud or other, and every practical decision we make crystallizes out of that cloud. As for myself, I make decisions about medication based on my sense of the transference. I think of transference as the vehicle of the quest. So whenever I find myself reacting to a patient's pain, distress, or complaint by wanting to prescribe medication (whether or not the patient is asking for it), I think of my reaction not only as an indication that the patient might actually need medication but also as a countertransference response to the patient's unconscious transference projection. Am I wanting simply to quiet the patient's sense of urgency, and the disturbing unconscious emotion that is provoking the urgency, because that emotion is too disturbing to me? Or am I accurately perceiving that the disturbing emotion is too overwhelming for the patient to handle consciously right now? At issue is whether the patient and I, at that point in our evolving relationship, are ready to experience the transference and countertransference consciously and to make productive use of the experience.

In those frequent situations when the patient's pain and urgency are great, when he feels the need for immediate relief and I don't have a very good sense what is going on in the transference, I try to enlist the patient in the decision on medication. I explain that the urgency he is feeling is actually the pressure of unconscious feelings trying to become conscious; that this is good if he can stay with the process but bad if he can't tolerate it. I may explain that medication can relieve the pain and urgency, making it easier to tolerate the unconscious feelings, but that it can also potentially suppress them, making them more difficult to feel. I may add that the unconscious feelings won't go away, and that even if we do quiet them with medication now, we will get another chance at them later, when we both may be in a better position to deal with them. When this sort of situation comes up—as it often does—in the first session, a patient may say he is only interested in medication to help him feel better. When I do prescribe medication in such cases, I will also recommend that the patient try four or five psychotherapy sessions to get an idea of what the process is like. I will explain that although medication can certainly relieve symptoms and may even temporarily quiet the underlying emotional conflict, it can do nothing to resolve that conflict or tap the growth potential embedded in it. If the patient still isn't interested, or if he tries a few sessions but doesn't find the process helpful, I will refer him to a colleague who has a philosophy more in line with what he is looking for. Just because a person doesn't want to listen to the soul and its quest right now doesn't mean he won't change his mind five years from now, and when that happens I want him to remember that there are psychiatrists who specialize in that, too.

14. Freud's Theory of the Soul: From the Swimming Pool to the Quest

But the direction taken by this enquiry was not to the liking of the contemporary generation of physicians. They had been brought up to respect only anatomical, physical and chemical factors. . . . They obviously had doubts whether psychical events allowed of any exact scientific treatment whatever. . . . [T]hey regarded such abstractions as those with which psychology is obliged to work as nebulous, fantastic and mystical; while they simply refused to believe in remarkable phenomena which might have been the starting-point of research. . . . Even the psychiatrists, upon whose attention the most unusual and astonishing mental phenomena were constantly being forced, showed no inclination to examine their details or enquire into their connections. They were content to classify the variegated array of symptoms and trace them back, so far as they could manage, to somatic, anatomical or chemical aetiological disturbances. During this materialistic or, rather, mechanistic period, medicine made tremendous advances, but it also showed a short-sighted misunderstanding of the most important and most difficult among the problems of life.

—Sigmund Freud, "The Resistances to Psychoanalysis"

History Repeats Itself

The epigraph to this chapter is Freud's account of the situation he encountered when he first proposed his psychoanalytic theory of inner conflict in the early 1890s.[1] Had he been talking instead about the end of the 1990s, he would not have needed to change a word! If you stop to think about it, this is really quite astonishing. Freud's theory, after a rocky start, was ultimately so convincing to so many people that it overcame the materialist prejudices of his day and grew to become one of the most important and influential ideas of the twentieth century. Meanwhile, quantum physics proved the inadequacy of any purely mechanistic science and validated the need for a non-mechanistic science of the mind—like Freud's—that took into account the crucial element of subjectivity in the interaction between observer and observed. Yet, after all that impressive progress, psychoanalysis at the beginning of a new century is confronted by exactly the same materialist prejudices—and is attacked with the same dismissive contempt by purveyors of the same mechanistic worldview—as it was at the beginning of the twentieth century. How in the world could this have happened?

Looked at in broad historical perspective—in terms of the conflict between humoral pathology and cellular pathology—it appears that Freud's theory of inner conflict was an attempt to reinstate the ancient harmonic/ecological model of health and illness, and was bucking an irresistible historical tide that has been drawing medicine toward the homeostatic/foreign-body model. In other words, Freud was trying to reestablish the perennial philosophy of the quest in a swimming-pool world dominated increasingly by a mechanistic conception of human nature and a hedonistic—"creature comfort"—conception of the good.

But though it is true as far as it goes, this is not a very psychoanalytic way to look at things, because it locates the problem outside rather than inside. It paints psychoanalysis as the good guy, the virtuous champion of humanism, and blames the recurrent antipsychoanalytic prejudices of the 1890s and 1990s on dehumanizing historical and cultural forces—external enemies—that have been too powerful to overcome. A more psychoanalytic explanation would look for the enemy within and would suspect a repetition compulsion at work, driven by an inner conflict within Freud and within the psychoanalytic community after Freud.

Freud's Inner Conflict and Psychiatry's Repetition Compulsion

As I discussed in Chapter 5, Freud's theorizing did suffer from an inner conflict—both emotional and philosophical—between the swimming pool and the quest. He spent his entire career torn between a need to fit in with the mechanistic scientific thinking of his day—explaining mental life in the purely biological terms of his libido theory—and an opposing need to create a new science of subjectivity that would explore the inner conflicts of the

Flesh and the Spirit in light of the more metaphysical principle of Eros. So the fact that psychoanalysis is met with the same kind of scientific prejudice now that it was more than a century ago reflects, at least in part, Freud's inability to make up his mind. He spent his entire career struggling to integrate his two ways of thinking, to the point that, between 1893 and 1926, he made at least eight major changes in the direction and organization of his theory.

In the end, Freud never fully resolved his inner conflict. Although his mature theory did have all the makings of a potential integration—one that could include the biological dimension of his libido theory *within* a more comprehensive model of the soul in conflict—Freud was never entirely comfortable with the spiritual implications of this new theory, nor did he ever give up his attachment to the materialistic standards of positivist science. The result was that neither Freud's final theory nor his followers quite hung together. By 1959, twenty years after Freud's death—when psychoanalysis was at the height of its popularity and was dominating psychiatry in the United States—psychoanalysts found themselves split into two opposing camps. In one camp were people like Erik Erikson, who minimized the biological dimension and emphasized the psychosocial and spiritual aspects of the quest. In the other were people like Heinz Hartmann and David Rapaport, who were still trying to explain everything in the swimming-pool terms of Freud's original libido theory.

What happened then was especially interesting. The next generation of psychoanalysts, led by the students of David Rapaport (notably George Klein, Robert Holt, Merton Gill, and Roy Schafer), successfully challenged and refuted the libido theory, which soon disappeared altogether from psychoanalytic thinking. At the same time, those psychiatrists who preferred biological explanations gradually abandoned psychoanalysis and joined the psychopharmacological revolution. Since the 1970s, then, psychoanalysis has improved considerably both as a theory and as a treatment, but it has been steadily losing prestige and influence to biological psychiatry. Today psychiatry is right back where Freud started from. The current split between the Medical Model and the Psychotherapeutic Model is a repetition of the psychoanalytic split in the 1950s, which in turn was an externalized repetition of Freud's unresolved inner split between the materialistic values of the swimming pool and the humanizing purpose of the quest.

The Soul and Its Brain: A Freudian Model

According to Freud's theory in its final form—completed in 1926, summarized in a series of lectures in 1933—there are two distinct agencies or processes that reveal themselves in states of inner conflict. One is the *It (das Es)*, comprising the neurobiological dimension of experience. The other is the *I that stands above (das Über-Ich)*, comprising the spiritual dimension of moral and self-reflective awareness. Chemical imbalances and the needs of the swimming pool belong to the *It*. Anxiety, shame, and guilt—the knowledge of good and evil and the aspirations of the quest—belong to the *I that stands above*. There is then a third, integrating agency, the *I (das Ich)*, whose function is to harmonize the conflicting operation of the other two agencies (in light of the *I*'s own perceptual/cognitive assessment of reality) in a unified expression of the soul—a symptom, a dream, a work of art, or even a scientific theory. In this integrative activity—resolving disharmonies between body/brain, mind, and spirit—the *I* encompasses but transcends any chemical imbalance in the brain, knitting the brain's functioning as well as its malfunctioning into the seamless cloth of experience.

Although Freud never explicitly acknowledged Plato's model of the tripartite soul as the prototype for his own tripartite model, the close parallels between the two are strikingly apparent. Freud was probably uneasy about the growing similarity of his thinking to Plato's (beginning with his introduction of the principle of Eros in 1920), because its implicit spirituality represented a radical departure from the neuroscientific emphasis of his original theory of the mind. But the seeds of his later theory had been present even in Freud's earliest thinking, and his theorizing had always been in a sense torn between the Flesh and the Spirit—between unconscious brain processes and self-reflective inner experience. His very first psychoanalytic writings (from 1893 to 1895) reflected this deep philosophical ambivalence in the form of two opposing theories of mental illness. On the one hand was a theory of *psychoneurosis* that emphasized inner conflict. On the other was a theory of *actual neurosis* that emphasized chemical imbalance. These conflicting models of neurosis were, in fact, the original patterns for the Psychotherapeutic Model and the Medical Model of psychiatry as we have them today.

Psychoneurosis Versus Actual Neurosis

Initially, in the early 1890s, Freud believed that psychoneurosis (including hysteria, phobias, obsessional neurosis, and some forms of psychosis) was caused by the delayed impact of a childhood sexual trauma, memory of which had been repressed. He believed that cure required a cathartic recovery of the repressed traumatic memory with all its associated emotion. This theory, which came to be known as the *seduction theory*, is still widely used as a model for treating certain dissociative disorders in adults who were once victims of childhood sexual abuse. Most of the therapists who treat such illnesses nowadays, however, focus exclusively on the element of abuse—the physical violence, the violation of the child's psychological integrity, the immoral exploitiveness of the perpetrator. They think of the illnesses that result, typically years after such abuse occurred, as caused by the external trauma rather than by internal conflict. Freud's view was more complex. He emphasized that what was intolerably traumatic to the patient was not only the painful, loathsome, or terrifying violation by the perpetrator but also the fact that this violation typically involved a "seduction," in which the perpetrator forced on the child a premature and terribly unsettling experience of sexual feelings. Freud's point was not that the children were in any way to blame for these feelings or for what was done to them, but simply that the deepest cause of their illnesses later in life was inner conflict over the sexual feelings that had once been aroused so disturbingly against their will. Freud theorized that, with the onset of puberty or with the initiation of sexual relationships in adulthood, the newly emerging sexual desire that for most people would be experienced simply as a normal part of life becomes for these traumatized individuals an unbearable source of shame, guilt, and anxiety, and hence of symptoms.

Freud soon modified this theory of psychoneurosis, after a few years of clinical experience led him to conclude that most (though by no means all) of the childhood sexual traumas being reported to him by his patients were in fact not accurate memories of actual events but rather anxiety-laden fantasies reflecting the unconscious emotions of the Oedipus complex. Instead of believing that psychoneurosis was caused by the delayed impact of relatively uncommon childhood traumas, he now believed it was caused by the delayed impact of universally occurring childhood wishes and fears. His model of cure changed correspondingly, from recovery of a repressed memory to recovery of a repressed fantasy (again with a full experience of all the emotions embedded in the fantasy). Of course, Freud still recognized (contrary to the claims of some modern critics) that real sexual abuse of children did occur and that it predisposed those children to the later development of psychoneurosis. But he now recognized that there were other predisposing factors—nonsexual childhood traumas, current emotional stresses, and constitutional factors— that could easily aggravate the Oedipus complex to the point of psychoneurosis even when no direct sexual trauma had ever occurred.

Alongside this evolving theory of inner conflict in the psychoneuroses, Freud proposed an utterly different, purely physiological, explanation for the symptoms of anxiety neurosis and neurasthenia, the so-called actual neuroses. Based on a superficial similarity between the symptoms of these disorders and the physical manifestations of sexual arousal and discharge, Freud speculated that the symptoms of anxiety neurosis (dizziness, tremor, sweating, restlessness, rapid breathing, and palpitations) were toxic physiological by-products of sexual frustration (incomplete discharge) due to forced abstinence or coitus interruptus; while the symptoms of neurasthenia (fatigue, weakness, and intestinal disturbances) were toxic by-products of sexual enervation (repeated inadequate discharge) from excessive masturbation. He believed that cure depended either on achieving adequate discharge through normal sexual intercourse or on avoiding arousal in the first place when adequate discharge was unavailable.

The official glossary of the American Psychoanalytic Association, *Psychoanalytic Terms and Concepts*, summarizes the difference between Freud's two models of mental illness as follows:

> (1) the cause for actual neuroses was to be found in individuals' contemporary sexual life (the German *aktual* means "present-day") while that for psychoneuroses was related to events in early childhood; (2) the etiology of the actual neuroses was somatic while that of the psychoneuroses was psychical; the symptoms of actual neuroses were physiological reactions to current faulty sexual practices and did not require the psychodynamic mechanisms underlying the symptom formation of the psychoneuroses; and (3) actual neuroses were not amenable to psychoanalytic treatment. (p. 5)

To modern readers, and even to other psychoanalysts during Freud's own lifetime, the idea of actual neurosis has always seemed implausible at best. Yet when we step back from the idea of sexual frustration as the specific cause (not an uncommon idea in nineteenth-century medical thinking by the way), it is pretty difficult to tell the difference between the biological thinking behind Freud's theory of actual neurosis and that of our own Medical Model. Both rest on the fundamental premise that mental illnesses are chemical imbalances devoid of psychological meaning, and both reflect a swimming-pool philosophy in which symptoms are seen as *harmful* disruptions of equilibrium, and cure is equated with restoring the old equilibrium.

In contrast, Freud's theory of psychoneurosis, reflected the quest philosophy as we still know it today in the Psychotherapeutic Model, where symptoms are seen as *beneficial* disruptions of equilibrium (expressions of repressed memory or desire trying, against resistance, to become conscious); and where cure involves a new harmonizing of inner conflict through an expansion of consciousness (a fuller emotional awareness of the repressed memory or fantasy).

Creativity, Conflict, and Anxiety

For Freud, as for any great thinker, there was a creative tension between two poles in his thinking. His biological theory of actual neurosis represented the *regressive* pole, in which he was loyal to, and constrained by, the ideas of his teachers and the dominating cultural assumptions of his era—specifically, by the mechanistic, positivistic paradigm of nineteenth-century science. But at the same time there was a dialectically opposed, *progressive* pole in Freud's thought—his psychological theory of inner conflict in the psychoneuroses— representing his authentically original, "countercultural" contribution. True creativity in general depends on a thinker's progressive, antithetical mode of thought being strong enough to transcend the limitations of his old paradigm, but this process is never a clean one. In the end, all great thinkers are subject to what literary critic Harold Bloom has called the *anxiety of influence*, and remain to some degree, like Michelangelo's prisoners, entangled in the worldview of their predecessors. Freud's theoretical and philosophical ambivalence reflected just such an entanglement—an anxiety-provoking inner conflict between his deference to the mechanistic worldview of his medical/ scientific fathers and his true calling to explore the mysteries of the human soul. In a sense, Freud's whole career became a quest to resolve this central conflict—and in the process his own anxiety of influence[2]—by finding a way to bring together the either–or antitheses of actual neurosis and psychoneurosis into one synthetic science of the soul.

The Libido Theory

Freud's first attempt at integration was based on his observation that anxiety was the common element in both forms of neurosis. Whatever the specific symptoms were, and whatever he thought might be causing them, Freud noted that a low-grade anxiety often accompanied the symptoms, and that every symptom seemed to serve a defensive function, aimed at preventing or minimizing this anxiety. Under stress, however, this defensive function of symptoms had a tendency to break down and give way to a more severe outbreak of anxiety, in the same way that a patch on a heating pipe might break down and give vent to a burst of steam.

The good news was that the libido theory provided a single explanation that applied both to psychoneurosis and to actual neurosis. The anxiety and/or symptoms of both illnesses could be attributed to the same toxic physiological process of arousal and interrupted discharge. Recall (from Chapter 5) that libido was the neural energy of the sexual drive, and that too much libido accumulating in the neurons of the brain produced a chemical imbalance that needed to be discharged. If discharge was blocked—either by the inner conflict of psychoneurosis or the sexual frustration of actual neurosis—the quantity of undischarged libido would either spill over in a toxic discharge process that was experienced as anxiety or divert itself into neurotic symptoms that served to "bind" the anxiety (prevent the discharge, like the patch on the steam pipe) and keep it unconscious.

The bad news was that there was a serious and fundamental inconsistency in this apparently unitary theory. If a buildup of libidinal pressure was supposed to create a need for discharge—either as sexual release or as anxiety—then why and how could such a buildup divert itself into a symptom designed to *prevent* discharge? This would be as if leaking steam from a pipe could somehow form itself into a patch designed to stop the leaking!

Clearly there was something missing from the libido theory, but at first Freud didn't seem to notice. He was so taken with the idea that one theory of anxiety could explain both kinds of neurosis that he then tried to expand this theory into a complete "scientific psychology" that proposed to explain all human motivation in terms of libido. This theory—first formulated in Chapter 7 of *The Interpretation of Dreams* (1900)—equated the soul with the brain, describing it as an elaborate neurological stimulus-response reflex apparatus *(Seelischen Apparat)*. The stimulus-response mechanisms of this "soul–brain apparatus" were assumed to be a product of evolution, whose function was to discharge libido as efficiently as possible (consonant with the swimming-pool need of the constancy–pleasure principle).

In this expanded version of the libido theory, Freud pictured all motivation as a kind of "wishful thinking," aimed at fulfilling the primary biological need of avoiding unpleasure and seeking pleasure by discharging excess libido.[3] Inner conflict he explained as a result of an inhibitory neuronal process that blocked the free discharge of libido, causing it to accumulate in the brain and thereby produce a wish. Although libido started out as the energy of the sexual drive, Freud argued that when sexual discharge was blocked or delayed, libidinal energy could be diverted into other, nonsexual paths of wishful thinking and discharge—*sublimations*—and in that way ultimately provided the energy for all motivated activity. Only when both paths to wish-fulfilling discharge—directly sexual and sublimated nonsexual—were blocked would libido accumulate to the point of producing anxiety and/or symptoms. *In this expanded version of the libido theory, Freud had taken the concept of homeostasis—the constancy principle—and elevated it to serve not only as a model of physical health but as the purpose of life itself.*

How Can You Get an Inner Conflict from One Motivation?

Ironically, the problem with the libido theory was exactly the same problem Freud had complained about when he encountered it in medical colleagues who rejected psychoanalysis. In trying to reduce all human experience to the mechanistic terms of nineteenth-century physics, the libido theory itself showed "a short-sighted misunderstanding of the most important and most difficult among the problems of life." Probably the most obvious misunderstanding was in the theory's implicit assumption that the purpose of life (as hard-wired in the evolutionary structure and function of the brain) was hedonism: an essentially amoral pursuit of the quickest possible tension-relieving discharge-pleasure. In fact, this was not at all what Freud believed. Although he did think that human cultures tended to impose unnecessary and unhealthy restrictions on sexual expression (the underlying cause of actual neurosis), he also thought that some degree of cultural restriction was necessary and inevitable, a by-product of the universal inner conflict and self-imposed morality of the Oedipus complex (the underlying cause of psychoneurosis). The problem was that at this early stage of his career, Freud's theory was itself neurotically restricted by his allegiance to scientific materialism, so it did not fit what he really believed—and what he was observing every day—about human nature. It accounted very well for the drive toward hedonistic discharge and for the unconscious drivenness of human motivation generally. But it could not account for the neurological forces that *opposed* discharge in states of inner conflict, or for anything like conscious intentionality or moral choice. Although the theory did try to explain inner conflict—as an inhibitory neuronal process that opposed or delayed hedonistic discharge—it could not explain the motive for this kind of inhibition. The constancy principle was essentially *monistic,* allowing for only one source (libido) and one purpose (discharge) in human motivation. It left no room for any motive that opposed hedonism (as would be necessary to produce an inner conflict) because such a motive would cause a buildup rather than a discharge of libido—a direct violation of the constancy principle.

For example, the constancy principle could not explain why a man would ever refrain from having sex with a beautiful woman who excited him and wanted to have sex with him. To explain such a decision in terms of a neuronal inhibition of discharge couldn't work, because there would have to be a second motivational principle (that violated the constancy principle) to produce such a neuronal inhibition. Moreover, it was difficult to get around the fact that when people actually feel both sides of an inner conflict consciously, they always seem to experience their conflicting motives as flowing from two fundamentally different inner sources, and serving two inherently different purposes. The man who refrains from having sex with a beautiful and willing woman, for instance, may very much want the sexual gratification but feel that he doesn't deserve such a woman, or that he doesn't want to exploit her or feel obligated to her. Observations of conflicts like this in his patients gradually made it more and more apparent to Freud that he needed a *dualistic* theory of motivation, one that included some nonmaterialistic principle of morality or values. Yet his loyalty to scientific materialism held him back, so his progress toward that dualistic theory had to go through gradual stages.

Initially, given that the constancy principle allowed for only one source and purpose of motivation within the soul, and since the other source and purpose simply wouldn't disappear from the lived experience of inner conflict, Freud realized that he had to put it somewhere else—if not within the soul, then outside it. He therefore tried to describe the force opposing hedonism as arising externally, in the behavioral restrictions imposed by family and society, to which the growing child must learn to accommodate. Inner conflict he then conceptualized as a conflict between an *Unconscious*—the biological–neurological force of the sexual drives that he would eventually call the *It*—and a *Conscious,* a self that interfaced with the external world and made the necessary accommodations to ensure maximal discharge pleasure. This *Conscious*—an early version of the *I*—was aware of what parents and society would and would not allow, and made its accommodations accordingly—either delaying gratification or substituting indirect (more socially acceptable) sublimation for direct sexual gratification—following what Freud called the *reality principle.*

On the surface this seemed to solve the problem of how internal conflict could actually be generated out of a single motivating impulse. The opposing motive was seen as externally imposed by parental and societal restrictions that essentially forced an internal conflict on an inherently "singleminded" psyche. The *I* was not considered an autonomous intentional agent but rather a motivationally passive function of the unconscious drive for libidinal discharge, whose purpose was to facilitate that discharge within the constraints of the reality principle. But there was a fudge factor in this solution: a covert dualism, concealed in the very notion of a reality principle that required an accommodation to parental or societal restrictions. After all, if motivational energy came only from the drive toward libidinal discharge, and if there was nothing in that drive that was inclined toward delay or substitution (i.e., that violated the constancy principle), then where would we ever get the impulse, or even the capacity, to delay and sublimate? If the *I* were simply a function of the unconscious drives, then how could it ever learn the value of accommodation? Why would it suffer the slings and arrows of parental and societal restrictions for even a minute, when it could simply defy them? Why didn't every little Oedipus simply kill his father and take his mother to bed as soon as he became physically able to do so? There had to be something in the individual that agreed with—even valued—the restrictions imposed by parents and society, and was motivated to oppose the drives rather than to serve them. Once again, it seemed necessary to posit a second, nonhedonistic inner source of motivation.

The I That Stands Above

Freud came to this realization in 1914, midway through his psychoanalytic career, as he was trying to formalize his libido theory in a series of metapsychological papers. This project, which he ultimately abandoned, made him increasingly aware of exactly what there was about inner conflict that the libido theory couldn't explain. Specifically, he recognized three psychological functions—idealism (the setting of ideal goals for the self), self-observation, and conscience—that all seemed to require a second *inner* motivation, opposing the push of the drives for uninhibited sexual discharge. At first, Freud tried to modify the libido theory to allow for a new agency—what he eventually called the *I that stands above*—that could perform these functions while still "driven" by the energy of libido. He was still hoping to be able to explain everything in neurological terms, so he preferred to minimize the disembodied, spiritlike quality of consciousness—the self-observing and evaluating function—that belonged to his new agency. Even after he had officially abandoned the libido theory and introduced the concept of Eros, Freud tended to limit his discussions of the *I that stands above* to its function as conscience, the internalized voice of parental and cultural authority that we know as the "superego," because that was the sort of thing he could imagine as being located somewhere in the brain's memory banks. Still, the very term *I that stands above* seemed to imply something beyond the brain—an inner observer/evaluator who is both intrinsic (an "I") and transcendent ("standing above")—more consistent with Freud's initial ideas about an agency of idealism and self-observation as well as conscience.

Despite Freud's ambivalence, the spiritual implications of this original, more complete concept of the *I that stands above* remained important influences in the evolution of psychoanalytic thought. In 1930, Robert Waelder summarized these implications in a seminal paper that defined the *I that stands above* as the particular element of the soul that "distinguishes the nature of man from that of animals":

> It is the element by which man . . . goes beyond himself, taking himself as an
> object, whether acting in a punishing, aggressive way [as in the voice of a

harsh conscience], or lovingly caring [as in self-respect], or, finally, being disinterestedly objective, as in self-observation and the ability to depart from his own point of view.[4]

Waelder highlighted the dualism that is implicit in the very concept of an *I that stands above:* an inner self that is autonomous and *transcendent* (i.e., nonbiological), opposed to the discharge-drives of the *It* both in purpose and in kind.[5] But Freud himself continued to vacillate in his discussions of the *I that stands above,* picturing it sometimes as the neurologically recorded voice of external authority and other times as the authentic inner compass of the soul.

The Soul and Its Discontents

It is a common misconception that Freud's theory of inner conflict was about nothing more than the opposition of instinct and culture. Instead of an inner moral conflict between an *It* and an *I that stands above,* this view sees neurosis as a political conflict between a hedonistic individual and a repressive society—with the Freudian "superego" representing the values of society. What is missing from this picture is what Waelder clearly understood: that the Freudian superego is a spiritual agency, the center of human consciousness, an intrinsic I that stands above both instinct and culture and is in fact responsible for creating culture in the first place.

Freud himself finally came to just this conclusion in *Civilization and Its Discontents* (1930), where he proposed a theory about how the *I that stands above*—and with it, inner conflict—first developed in primitive man. Freud proposed that prior to the development of civilization, prehistoric man must have lived as an animal, in social groups controlled through power and fear by a dominant "alpha male," the *primal father.* In this prehuman "primal horde," Freud argued, there was no inner conflict because we had not yet developed beyond animal consciousness.[6] There was no sense of morality, no cultural values, no social taboos to internalize, and no individual superego–conscience to internalize them. At some point then, a group of primal sons must have risen up in rebellion to kill the alpha-male primal father, driven by both lust for the women he controlled and envy of his power to control them. At that moment, Freud speculated, individual conscience and cultural taboo (i.e., the superego) must have come into being simultaneously. How? Through the great remorse the brothers would have felt immediately after their murderous deed. Presumably, such primal murders could have occurred many times previously without provoking any remorse—as they do among lions, for instance—but conscience, inner conflict, and civilization could not have begun until human nature had evolved to the point that it was capable of remorse.

In this theory Freud clearly did not view inner conflict in terms of instinct versus culture, because he thought that the experience of remorse had to occur *first,* in order for culture to develop. This remorse, coming before the establishment of any cultural values or taboos, could not have been produced by an internalized superego–conscience. Rather it was produced by the innate, unconditioned love the sons felt for their father, just as the primal murder was produced by their innate lust for sexual domination—two halves of an archaic ambivalence.

From such speculations Freud concluded that the opposition of instinct and culture is derived from a more fundamental internal opposition between lust and love, the Flesh and the Spirit. This origin of both the superego–conscience and cultural taboo from an intrinsic tendency to love, independent of any cultural conditioning, implies an innate and universal moral sense—a more feeling-based version of Kant's categorical imperative. In that sense, Freud's myth of the primal sons killing and eating the primal father is a more viscerally compelling version of the biblical myth of the Fall. Just as Adam and Eve acquire the knowledge of good and evil through the shame they feel after their willfully defiant act of self-assertion, Freud's primal sons acquire it through their remorse, and the awareness it brings of their conflicting purposes of love and lust.

Eros: The Principle of Love and Life

Freud had now clearly identified the second fundamental motivation he needed to explain inner conflict but that had been missing from the libido theory. It was *love*—not as a "sublimated" form of libidinal discharge, but as an independent force, operating through the moral consciousness of the *I that stands above* to produce emotions, like remorse, that opposed the need for discharge. Although a conflict between love and lust had always been basic to the Oedipus complex—the lustful desire for one parent being opposed by filial love for both parents—the libido theory had prevented Freud from recognizing love as a motivation fundamentally different from lust. The constancy principle had reduced all motivations, including love, to the pursuit of discharge-pleasure. But now, by associating love with the independent agency of the *I that stands above,* Freud was clearly pointing to something "beyond the pleasure principle," to an autonomous moral/spiritual purpose in love that could no longer be explained away as a discharge of "sublimated" libido.

To go with this new motivational purpose Freud needed a new motivational source or principle—something to oppose the swimming-pool hedonism of the constancy principle with the loving, consciousness-expanding purpose of the quest. He called his new principle *Eros,* borrowing the name from Plato's *Symposium,* in which Eros is described as the desire to reunite with one's lost "other half," rejoining two sides of a primal human nature that was originally torn asunder by Zeus. Generalizing on this model—and incorporating further meanings of Eros from the *Symposium*—Freud saw Eros not only as the motivating principle of human love that brought people together in couples, families, communities, societies, and civilizations but also as a basic life force, comparable to Henri Bergson's *élan vital,* or Hippocrates' *vis medicatrix naturae*—a universal force of integration, a tendency within physical matter, within living organisms, and within the human soul to bring separate, opposing elements together into states of higher energy and more complex organization.

Initially, Freud conceptualized Eros merely as an extension of libido—a more generalized way of describing the physical energy of the sexual drive. But in fact Eros represented a radically new understanding of the sexual drive—as seeking communion—diametrically opposed to libido seeking discharge. Unlike the sexual drive of the libido theory, Eros was stimulus-seeking rather than stimulus-avoiding, tending toward higher rather than lower levels of energy, promoting growth and conflict-resolving harmony rather than stability and tension-reducing homeostasis. Where the constancy principle had reduced all movements of the Spirit to sublimated impulses of the Flesh, the principle of Eros now redefined impulses of the Flesh as localized manifestations of the Spirit. This was very much in keeping with Socrates' view, as presented in the *Symposium,* that Eros is the motivating energy of the quest, a tendency toward higher consciousness of which the sexual drive is only the lowest expression. Seen in the terms of Freud's new tripartite model of the soul, Eros was the synthetic energy of the *I,* integrating the swimming-pool passions of the *It* with the loving intentions of the *I that stands above,* harmonizing both these opposing motives within the dialectical self-actualizing purposes of the quest.

The Death Instinct (Thanatos)

Opposed to Eros, Freud then posited a second universal tendency, which he called the death instinct or *Nirvana principle,* also frequently called *Thanatos.* He described it as a tendency within physical matter, within living organisms, and within the human soul to fall apart or break down into simpler elements, disintegrating, gravitating to a state of zero energy (i.e., nirvana or death) or as close to it as possible.[7] Perhaps the most disturbing and controversial element in all of Freud's thought, this concept of the death instinct has been almost universally rejected, even by otherwise doctrinaire Freudian analysts, even in Freud's own day. And no wonder. Thanatos represented a paradox that threatened to turn the first twenty-five years of Freud's theorizing completely upside down. As a principle of swimming-pool homeostasis, it was actually a reformulation in only slightly different terms of Freud's old constancy principle. But by redefining that constancy principle now as Thanatos—a tendency to disintegrate toward the ultimate constancy of the inorganic state—Freud seemed to be suggesting that what he had all along been calling the sexual drive under the libido theory was really a drive toward death!

Freud might have resolved this paradox by admitting that his original concept of sexual libido had always included two incompatible elements— the I–Thou element of love and the I–It element of lust, the desire to come together in intimate union versus the self-centered need to use another person, or allow oneself to be used, for purposes of tension-reducing discharge. He could have rectified this old inconsistency by recognizing Eros and Thanatos as inherently conflicting tendencies of love and lust within the unitary experience of sexual desire. Had he done so, the concept of a death instinct would have made a good deal more sense. It would have helped explain why inner conflicts over sexuality are universal, for instance, and shed new light on the biblical link between sexual desire, shame, and the knowledge of good and evil. The problem was that, in so doing, it would also have shifted the meaning of Eros and Thanatos from that of value-free motivational principles to that of moral categories. The very distinction between love and lust, after all, is primarily a moral distinction—between I–Thou and I–It attitudes toward another person. So it would have been difficult for Freud to draw the parallel between Eros/Thanatos and love/lust without moving psychoanalysis openly into the realm of moral philosophy. This Freud was not prepared to do, for fear it would destroy the scientific status of psychoanalysis. He clung to the idea of Eros as a simple extension of libido, ignoring or glossing over the disturbing connection between libido and Thanatos. He explained the Eros/Thanatos duality not as love versus lust, but in the more value-free terms in which analysts still think of it today, as love versus destructiveness:

> According to our hypothesis human instincts [drives] are of only two kinds: those which seek to preserve and unite—which we call "erotic," exactly in the sense in which Plato uses the word "Eros" in his Symposium, or "sexual," with a deliberate extension of the popular conception of "sexuality"—and those which seek to destroy and kill and which we group together as the aggressive or destructive instinct. As you see, this is in fact no more than a theoretical clarification of the universally familiar opposition between Love and Hate. . . . But we must not be too hasty in introducing ethical judgements of good and evil. Neither of these instincts is any less essential than the other; the phenomena of life arise from the concurrent or mutually opposing action of both.[8]

War, Death, and the Repetition Compulsion

In terms of the Oedipus complex, Freud's emphasis on love versus hate rather than on love versus lust did have some justification. It certainly made sense to say that the primal sons, and Oedipus himself, were motivated as much by murderous ambition—blood-lust against the primal father/king—as they were by sexual lust for his women. Previously Freud had always focused on forbidden sexual desire as the core of the Oedipal problem, ignoring the problem of human destructiveness. Now, by introducing the concept of the death instinct, he was correcting that imbalance. But Freud's emphasis on destructiveness made even more sense when considered in the historical context of 1920. The world had just been through an unimaginably violent and degrading "war to end all wars" and there was no more pressing need in psychiatry at the time than to understand the roots of human destructiveness.

Psychiatrists like Freud had been uniquely privy to the private horrors of World War I through their work with patients suffering from "war neurosis," who were forced in their symptoms to relive the most terrifying battle experiences again and again in recurrent flashbacks and nightmares. In fact, it was this repeated reexperiencing of traumatically painful events—familiar to us today in the posttraumatic stress disorders of Vietnam veterans—that first led Freud to conceptualize a death instinct. It convinced him that there must be a need or force in human nature beyond what could be explained by the libido theory. He called this force the *repetition compulsion,* because it reminded him of the way patients in analysis tended to repeat what they could not remember—reliving even very painful past experiences through the transference—and also of the need he had so often observed in children to repeat over and over again their intense experiences both of pain and pleasure. In all these phenomena, Freud hypothesized that the need to repeat was a conservative, stabilizing tendency, a way of avoiding disruptive changes, or, in the case of traumatic experiences, a way of undoing the disruptive changes that have occurred—trying in effect to stop or reverse time—by repeating previous experiences. It was then only a short leap from this compulsive going back over past experiences to a full-blown death instinct— *"an urge inherent in organic life to restore an earlier state of things,"* ultimately "to return to the inanimate state."9

Thanatos and Eros As Emotional Dispositions

To modern readers, Freud's leap may seem a strange one. For one thing it seems to ignore the impulse toward mastery—the need to keep doing it until you get it right—that is clearly involved in the repetition compulsion. For another, the idea of an urge to return to the inanimate state seems a far cry from the drive "to destroy and kill" that Freud described in the passage quoted above and that seems the much more obvious fact about war that needs explaining. The first objection Freud would have answered simply by saying that all the phenomena of life reflect the combined operation of Eros and Thanatos, so that the impulse toward mastery can be thought of as the contribution of Eros toward the repetition compulsion and the urge toward death as the contribution of Thanatos. The second objection can be answered by saying that the urge to die and the drive to kill, when considered at an emotional level, are really two sides of one coin. Perhaps the best way to appreciate this would be to imagine Thanatos as one of the characters from an old joke:

> A psychologist was doing research on the difference between optimism and pessimism. He took a pessimistic child and left him alone in a room full of

new toys. At the same time he took an optimistic child and left him alone in a room full of manure. When he came back to check on the two children after a half hour, he found the pessimistic child sitting in the middle of the room crying, surrounded by broken toys. "Why are you crying?" he asked the child. "Your toys suck! I can't make them work right!" the child wailed, as he threw a toy against the wall, barely missing the psychologist's head. "I hate you for making me play with these stupid toys. I want my own toys!" Meanwhile, the optimistic child was up to his elbows in manure, whistling and smiling, happily digging away. The psychologist was amazed. "Why are you so happy?" he asked. "Well," replied the child, "I figure with all this horseshit, there's bound to be a pony in here somewhere!"

The pessimistic child in the joke is like Thanatos. He operates on the swimming-pool premise that falling down (trial and error) is bad, and so is intolerant of any frustration or tension, and hates anything new. He experiences new things and new people as threats to his self-esteem (emotional equilibrium). He reacts to such threats by wanting to retreat to the familiar patterns of compulsive repetition (playing with his own toys) or, when that isn't possible, by destructively attacking whatever threatens him (breaking the new toys, throwing them at the psychologist), and/or by self-destructively falling apart. In that sense, the need to repeat, the urge to destroy, and the tendency to fall apart and die all reflect the same basic emotional impulse. They are all homeostatic, swimming-pool mechanisms—reactive, tension-reducing processes of stabilization and/or discharge.

The optimistic child in the joke, on the other hand, is like Eros. He operates on the premise of the quest, that falling down (getting your hands dirty) is good, so he is curious and interested in trying new things, even when they seem unpleasant on the surface. He is happy to endure the frustration of compulsive repetition, endlessly digging through all the horseshit, because he expects that in doing so he will eventually uncover something new and wonderful—bring the unconscious pony into consciousness. He is the energy of healing and growth—the *vis medicatrix naturae*—personified.

Thanatos, Eros, and the Repetition Compulsion

At this point it would be fair to ask why I have gone to so much trouble to explain the logic of Freud's death instinct. Why try to rehabilitate a theory that was so disturbing and confusing that hardly anyone has ever used it? My answer is simple: because the theory flat out works! If you leave out the inconsistencies stemming from Freud's neurotic attachment to his old libido theory, Thanatos and Eros become a coherent and useful way of describing the two basic motivational systems in human nature: the swimming pool and the quest. They also correspond very nicely to the dualistic perspectives of Bohr's principle of complementarity: analysis and synthesis—breaking things down into parts and integrating parts into a whole. In that sense, they provide a useful framework for understanding that all psychological experience is the product of inner conflict and requires two mutually exclusive scientific perspectives to be adequately explained.

We might think of Thanatos as combining all our swimming-pool impulses toward discharge–enactment in the service of constancy–homeostasis. This includes both lustful impulses toward sexual discharge (as in the original constancy principle) and "aggressive" impulses toward destructive and self-destructive discharge, as in the pessimistic child's temper tantrum. As reactive tendencies, these "discharge-drive" impulses can be explained in neurobiological terms, as automatic, instinctive stimulus-response patterns— the stimulus being the pressure of a disturbing unconscious emotion and the response being a mechanism for discharging–enacting the emotion so as to minimize disruption and reestablish homeostasis. Considered purely from the perspective of Thanatos, however, there is no pattern or coherence to these reflexive tendencies. Any emotional stimulus will trigger whatever discharge–enactment response works quickest to get rid of the stimulus. The problem is, we couldn't survive for very long if we were operating entirely in this mode of Thanatos—which is why it's called the death instinct—because we would have no mechanism for delaying discharge in the interests of food, shelter, and safety. That's where Eros comes in, to integrate our inchoate Thanatos-tendencies into the unifying pattern of the repetition compulsion: a more complex mechanism of discharge–enactment that minimizes disruption but also promotes survival and growth, by organizing our otherwise unintegrated instinctive discharge-responses into an adaptive personality-defining scenario.

We could say, then, that the repetition compulsion embodies the discharge–enactment tendencies of Thanatos as integrated by the central organizing tendency of Eros, so that our biological need for homeostasis becomes part of our larger personal needs for identity and growth. In terms of identity, we might think of the repetition compulsion as the soul's mechanism of homeostasis—a way of establishing and reestablishing our "sameness" over time, as encoded in neurological patterns of memory and desire that define our familiar sense of self or (looking at it from the outside) our personality. The idea is that when we are confronted with something or someone new, we experience an influx of neural stimulation (excitement and/or anxiety) that threatens to disrupt our sense of identity (cohesiveness of our personality). We then have a reflexive tendency—as dictated by the repetition compulsion—to preserve identity by discharging the excess tension through characteristic (repetitive-compulsive) patterns of emotional and behavioral response. To the extent that we perceive the threatening stimulus as coming from outside, we will tend to preserve identity through the enactment of characteristic sexual and hostile-competitive fantasies—outerdirected expressions of the repetition compulsion as lustful or destructive patterns of discharge–enactment. To the extent that we perceive the threatening stimulus as coming from inside, from an anxiety-provoking unconscious emotion, we will tend to preserve identity by "breaking down" into a characteristic pattern of inner conflict, using defense mechanisms of repression and/or symptom formation that reflect our own particular personality style. For instance, the pessimistic child's temper tantrum represents both sides of this reaction—the outer-directed breaking and throwing of toys and the inner-directed anxious frustration that produces the emotional breakdown.

Seen in this way, the repetition compulsion is a disposition toward conflict in the service of constancy: a fundamental impulse that says, "I'd rather fight than change," where the fight can be directed either externally or internally or both, and where the goal of the fighting is to get rid of the enemy (anxiety). But if we look at the same pattern differently—from the perspective of the quest, in terms of mastery and growth—it then becomes a disposition toward conflict in the service of integration: an impulse that says, "The only way to change *is* to fight," where our external battles change the balance of our internal conflicts, which then feed back on our external battles, and so on, in a dialectic of conflict and reintegration that evolves, over the course of many repetitions, toward the goal of meeting the enemy—experiencing our disruptive anxiety instead of discharging it—and thereby becoming more fully ourselves.

For a real-life example, recall Mary's personality pattern, and the symptom of cellular dysphoria that emerged out of it. As a tendency to withdraw abruptly from uncomfortable relationships, Mary's personality pattern allowed her to discharge (enact) anger without feeling it, while at the same time avoiding any disturbing dependency feelings. Her symptom of cellular dysphoria served much the same function within the relationship, except that it was less of a discharge–enactment and closer to an inner experience of her disturbing emotions. As a kind of psychic shutdown that left her unable to communicate, her cellular dysphoria was directed externally—as both an emotional withdrawal from the disruptive relationship and an unconscious mute reproach, a rejection of my inadequate and untrustworthy efforts to help her. At the same time it expressed an inner-directed self-reproach, a rejection of her own unconscious anger and dependency emotions that were expressed physiologically in her symptom. Both the outer-directed and the inner-directed reactions were expressions of Thanatos—an attempt to preserve her psychic equilibrium by warding off the external and internal stimuli that were threatening to change her. But her symptom was not only a defense against this threatened change. At the same time it also was the change—a development from discharge–enactment toward conscious feeling—trying to happen. As such, it was a manifestation of Eros, expressing the stirring of Mary's repressed unconscious emotions, and her need to feel and communicate these emotions, however unsettling they might be to her or to me. Here the repetition compulsion—manifest first in her personality pattern of withdrawal from relationships and then in her persistently recurring symptom of cellular dysphoria within relationships—was operating in the service of Eros, as a principle of mastery and growth, a drive to "keep experiencing the conflict until it becomes conscious."

The Repetition Compulsion and the Psychotherapeutic Process

Applying these ideas to the psychotherapeutic process, we can think of the repetition compulsion as the force that drives the psychotherapeutic process. It enlists the energies of both Eros and Thanatos, the transference and the resistance, the movement toward change and the tendency toward stabilization. The process begins with the Thanatos-activating stress of an unconscious emotion pressing toward consciousness (the movement of Eros). Under this stress the soul tends to "fall apart" into the inner conflict between the *It* and the *I that stands above*. Such a tendency is built into the structure of the personality—and the sense of ego-identity—so that each person tends to fall apart in his or her own characteristic way. Freud first recognized this "disposition to fall apart" as a manifestation of the repetition compulsion when he began to encounter it in his patients as a tenacious resistance to treatment—a tendency to react to any positive change, even to the possibility of positive change (the inner prompting of Eros), in a negative way, by suffering a worsening of their illnesses. This worsening, which Freud called the "negative therapeutic reaction," involved a stereotyped pattern of psychological "regression," a return to an earlier state of functioning which, though painful, is also familiar and therefore experienced as safer—better insulated from the threat of change.

Freud attributed the negative therapeutic reaction to a deep unconscious sense of guilt manifesting itself as a need to be punished whenever something good threatens to happen. This need to be punished, and the tendency to regression that went with it, was what first put Freud on the train of thought that led both to the death instinct and to the tripartite model of the soul. He recognized that the need to be punished for "getting better" (for the impulse to change and to grow) was a general manifestation of the death instinct, not limited to the negative therapeutic reaction but an aspect of all inner conflict. He thought of it as a self-destructive attack on the "instinctive" self that is trying to become conscious by an overly sadistic superego/conscience that is afraid to grow. In these terms, the pessimistic child's temper tantrum was a self-punitive attack by his mean-spirited superego against the joyous part of himself that was tempted to have the same unguarded spontaneity in playing with the new toys as the optimistic child had in digging through horseshit. By the same token, the optimistic child's happy quest for the pony was itself a kind of victory over the pessimistic part of himself that was tempted to feel deprived and put upon by his shitty predicament. In either case there is a dialectic between pessimism and optimism, between Thanatos and Eros, falling apart and getting it together.

But the point of the joke, and of the psychotherapeutic process itself, is that Eros ultimately prevails. To understand how this happens, consider what makes us laugh at the joke—the unexpected joy we feel at the sudden expansion of consciousness that comes with the punch line. The point of the joke, as of the psychotherapeutic process, is precisely to produce this expansion of consciousness. The joke does it by provoking in us a tension between Thanatos (our unhappy identification with the pessimistic child and our cynical reaction to the optimistic child) and Eros (our expectation of a happy punch line)—a tension that is then resolved as we get the meaning of the joke and discover the pony within ourselves. This is also pretty much the way it happens in the psychotherapeutic process, through resolving a dialectic of Thanatos and Eros, the difference being that the punch line is in our own unconscious and the only clue we have that it is coming is the anxiety we feel—to which we tend to react negatively, like the pessimistic child—so it takes a lot longer to get the joke.

The point of the joke, then, is that there is no such thing as a purely pessimistic or a purely optimistic child. We all have elements of both inside us, so that even in our most desperate moments there is a life force, an agency of hope, at work within us. The dialectic between the two—the interaction of Thanatos as a principle of disintegration and Eros as the complementary principle of integration—defines an ongoing process of growth, evolving through a sequence of discord and harmonization, conflict and resolution between the inner agencies of the soul and the outer world that impinges on them. The overall process is the work of Eros, the healing power of nature, incorporating swimming-pool processes of homeostasis in the brain within the larger dialectical quest of the soul, through the self-reflective moral agency of the *I that stands above.* The result of this process—the unconscious becoming conscious—is a shift from being driven by the neurobiological forces of the *It* and automatic reflexes of the repetition compulsion to having a fuller human experience of autonomy and self-actualization: a condition of free will in which I am able to choose, to direct my life according to my own authentically personal ideals and values, acting from the spiritual center of my self-reflective moral consciousness. Freud summed up this humanizing action of the psychotherapeutic process in a famous aphorism: "Where *It* was, there shall *I* become" *(Wo Es war, da soll Ich werden).*

15. Integrating the Swimming Pool Within the Quest: "Where *It* Was, There Shall *I* Become"

[T]he freedom of the will is . . . a feature of conscious life which corresponds to functions of the organism that not only evade a causal mechanical description but resist even a physical analysis carried to the extent required for an unambiguous application of the statistical laws of atomic mechanics.

—Niels Bohr, "Light and Life"

An Ambivalent Integration: Freud's New Theory of Anxiety

Anxiety was always central to Freud's theory of inner conflict, but in 1926 he radically changed the way he thought about it. Whereas he had originally pictured anxiety as an automatic neurological reflex generated by the *It*—a toxic discharge of excess (repressed) libido—he now saw it as a purposeful signal generated by the *I* to warn itself of the pressure of forbidden (repressed) emotion.

This new theory of anxiety became the cornerstone of Freud's mature theory. The change from automatic anxiety generated by the *It* to signal anxiety generated by the *I* culminated the series of important theoretical advances Freud had been making since 1914. It seemed to complete his transition from the swimming pool to the quest: from a mechanistic theory that pictured the soul as a "mental apparatus" under pressure, seeking discharge and stability, to a dualistic theory that pictured the soul as an intentional self in a state of inner conflict, seeking integration and growth. But there was a problem in Freud's presentation of his new theory. He left it ambiguous—and clearly himself felt confused about—whether the new theory of signal anxiety should (1) replace the old theory of automatic anxiety because the old one was simply wrong, (2) be applied to most cases of anxiety but not to cases of actual neurosis where the old theory applied, or (3) somehow incorporate the old theory within it.

Two Kinds of Anxiety, Two Kinds of Love: Passion Versus Action

Not surprisingly, this confusion about his two theories of anxiety was the same confusion that had made it so difficult for Freud to integrate his two theories of love: libido and Eros. In both cases, the earlier theory defined an experience (anxiety or love) as a *passion,* generated by the neurophysiological energies of the *It* seeking discharge, whereas the later theory defined the experience as an *action,* generated by the *I* seeking to integrate the conflict between the Flesh and the Spirit.

To fully appreciate this distinction, it is important to understand the root meaning of the word *passion.* According to the *Oxford English Dictionary*, the word originally meant simply "the fact of being passive, acted upon by an external agency or force." In other words, passion is etymologically the opposite of action: passive—active, passion—action. In the same vein, the word *passion* was also used synonymously with the word *affection*, meaning the state of being affected by a strong emotion. In a state of passion, then, I am not the active agent of my life but rather experience myself as passively swept up in emotions that happen to me as if produced by an outside force. In a state of action, on the other hand, I am motivated by conscious intention— free will—and experience myself as having the power to choose my own direction from within.

In terms of Freudian theory, we might say that passion is generated by the unconscious biological drives of the *It*-repetition compulsion, while action expresses the conscious intentions, goals, and values of the *I–I that stands above.* More simply, passion reflects the influence of *It* over the *I,* action the influence of the *I* over the *It.*

Integration in Process

Freud's confusion about the proper relationship between his two anxiety theories, then, reflected a more fundamental confusion about the relationship between passion and action in human motivation generally. From the beginning, Freud had emphasized that most of our mental, emotional, and behavioral life is driven by the unconscious forces of the *It* (and repetition compulsion) to which the *I* must accommodate as best it can. But Freud's new anxiety theory implied an entirely different perspective, in which all of our mental life is motivated (not driven) by the purposes and intentions of the *I*. Freud's ambivalent vacillation between these two perspectives is evident in the following account taken from a 1933 lecture:

> We are warned by a proverb against serving two masters at the same time. The poor ego [the *I*] has things even worse: it serves three severe masters and does what it can to bring their claims and demands into harmony with one another. These claims are always divergent and often seem incompatible. No wonder that the ego so often fails in its task. Its three tyrannical masters are the external world, the super-ego [the *I that stands above*] and the id [the *It*]. . . . [The ego] feels hemmed in on three sides, threatened by three kinds of danger, to which, if it is hard pressed, it reacts by generating anxiety.[1]

Notice that Freud pictures the *I* here first as a passive accommodator of the forces impinging on it (following a swimming-pool philosophy) and then as the active harmonizer of those forces (following a quest philosophy). Although he never fully resolved this ambivalence, the trend of his thinking was clearly toward a solution that integrated the drives of the *It* within the larger motivational purposes of the *I* (passion within action, the swimming pool within the quest).

Such a solution is implicit in his important aphorism "Where *It* was, there shall *I* become." Intended as a summary of how the unconscious becomes conscious in the psychotherapeutic process, this aphorism is probably the closest Freud ever came to a fully integrated theory of the soul in its quest: the unconscious activity of the brain (the reflexive *It*) becomes part of the conscious activity of the soul (the intentional *I*) through an evolving process of inner conflict with the *I that stands above*. This is exactly the same process, by the way, that Freud had described in his myth of the primal sons' transformation from animal instinct to human moral responsibility: *It* becomes *I* through the dawning consciousness (the feeling of remorse) of the *I that stands above*. It is also the same process that is artistically represented in the Disney film *Pinocchio*: a wooden puppet, an *It*—passively pulled by the strings of neurological reflex toward the hedonism of Pleasure Island, pulled back by his Jiminy Cricket superego–conscience—is transformed into a real boy, a fully human *I*, through a joyful experience of active, unconditioned love for his father, inspired by his fairy/angel *I that stands above.*

So What Was Wrong with This Picture?

This quasi-integration of Freud's was easy enough to understand intuitively—as expressed in an aphorism, a myth, or a children's movie, or as experienced in the psychotherapeutic process. The trouble was, Freud could never work out the theoretical details of this intuitive integration in a way that could account for the interrelationships between the motivating forces or drives on the one hand—Eros, Thanatos, and the repetition compulsion—and the three agencies of the soul on the other. He remained ambivalent, holding out hope for a simple biological explanation based on the drives of the *It,* even as he was increasingly emphasizing the irreducible motives and autonomous intentions of the *I* and the *I that stands above.* As a result, not only could Freud never quite make up his mind what anxiety was, he could never quite make up his mind what the *It,* the *I,* and the *I that stands above* were, either. Were they neurological functions of the brain (obeying the homeostatic principle of Thanatos), or were they spiritual agencies of the soul (animated by Eros)?

What Would the Resolution of Freud's Ambivalence Have Looked Like?

In hindsight, it is clear enough that Freud had all the elements he needed for a fully integrated theory, and that the proper solution would have been to recognize both dimensions—neurological and spiritual, passive function and active intention—as complementary and equally necessary aspects of the soul and its three agencies. Such a solution might have gone something like this: There are two basic motivating forces in human nature, Thanatos and Eros, or, more simply, *passions of the flesh* and *actions of the spirit.* Passions of the flesh include all motives—both sexual and hostile—that are driven by unconscious neurobiological forces impelling toward discharge in physical action. Actions of the spirit include all motives that are determined by free will: intentional choices based on acts of emotional and moral discernment that transcend the influence of neurobiological forces and cannot be explained in physical terms. Passions of the flesh are produced by the unconscious biological drives of the *It*–repetition compulsion while actions of the spirit are produced by the conscious intentions of the *I–I that stands above*. Passions of the flesh reflect the influence of matter over mind; actions of the spirit reflect the influence of mind over matter.

Unfortunately, this is not a solution that Freud could ever have endorsed. Given his lifelong ambition to establish psychoanalysis as a legitimate science—and given the materialistic prejudices of his age—he believed he had to ground his theory exclusively in the physical. So his official science of the mind—his metapsychology—was always about how neurophysiological events determine conscious experiences, never the other way around. That's why he tried to define Eros and Thanatos as physical tendencies of chemical and biological systems (e.g., the tendency of atoms, cells, and organisms to come together into states of higher energy and complexity—molecules, organs and colonies—versus their tendency to die and fall apart into lower-energy states). Even though Freud typically spoke of Eros as love and Thanatos as hate, it was with the underlying assumption that both these motives were generated by the forces of matter over mind. To admit that the theory of psychoanalysis included anything spiritual—especially anything so mystical as the action of spirit over matter—would, in Freud's mind, have been to destroy its scientific credibility.

However, it is difficult to imagine that a man like Freud, who was such a master of language, would have been so careless in his choice of words that he wouldn't have recognized the spiritual implications of the names he chose for his two motivational principles. By taking the name Eros from Plato's *Symposium*, Freud was implicitly equating it with the highest spiritual value in Western philosophy. By describing the death instinct as the Nirvana principle, he was implicitly equating it with the highest spiritual value in Eastern philosophy. Perhaps this was Freud's way of implicitly acknowledging the importance of the spiritual dimension while at the same time maintaining his official loyalty to scientific materialism by defining Eros and Thanatos in strictly physical terms.

Clinically, in fact, psychoanalysis and dynamic psychotherapy have always included the spiritual dimension. Not only do they revolve around the conflict between the Flesh and the Spirit, but their effectiveness ultimately depends upon the action of Spirit over matter. When we talk about the goal of making the unconscious conscious, after all, we are really talking about the spiritual concept of free will—the idea that as we become more conscious we are less controlled by our drives and have more possibility of autonomous conscious choice that is not biologically determined. Simply put, the goal of the psychotherapeutic process is to foster the action of the Spirit by enlarging the range of free will. This is exactly what Freud meant when he wrote, "Where *It* was, there shall *I* become": where once I was controlled by the unconscious neurobiological forces of the drives, I will become free to direct my life from the spiritual center of my self-reflective moral consciousness.

Again, Freud may well have realized that his aphorism implied some kind of spiritual agency in human nature that transcends the physical—that can transform an *It* into an *I*—but he could not discuss this openly (or perhaps even acknowledge it to himself) because he thought it wouldn't be scientific. As we have seen, of course, the lesson of complementarity was that every scientific theory has a spiritual or transcendent dimension. The very act of scientific observation introduces an irreducible element of wholeness—an observing consciousness—into the natural world that is forever beyond the reach of natural science to explain it. Unfortunately, Freud had to develop his theory of the soul without the benefit of ever knowing about Bohr's principle of complementarity, which was not published until 1928, two years after Freud completed his last major theoretical revision. As fate would have it, however, this was just about the time when Robert Waelder first entered upon the psychoanalytic scene.

Psychoanalysis Meets Quantum Physics: Waelder's Principle of Multiple Function

Waelder was himself originally a physicist, having earned his Ph.D. in 1920 at the ripe age of twenty. He then changed course to became a psychoanalyst, and by 1926 had been accepted as part of Freud's inner circle. It is a fascinating piece of intellectual history that Waelder made this particular career switch at this particular time. The period between 1913 and 1927 was probably the most exciting time in the history of physics—beginning with Bohr's quantum theory of the atom and culminating in quantum mechanics. Coincidentally and quite independently, the period between 1914 and 1926 was the most exciting time in the brief history of psychoanalysis—beginning with Freud's first discussion of the *I that stands above* and culminating in his new anxiety theory. Waelder's background in physics made him uniquely able to appreciate the scientific and philosophical implications of Freud's latest theories better than Freud himself could. He was not hampered, as Freud still was, by any residual attachment to the old libido theory or to the nineteenth-century positivism it embodied. He came to psychoanalysis with a sophisticated twentieth-century understanding of science, kept up with developments in physics, and probably knew about the principle of complementarity almost as soon as Bohr first presented it in 1927.[2] By 1930, in fact, Waelder had already published a paper using Bohr's principle to solve Freud's problem integrating his two theories of anxiety:

> In his earlier concept, Freud assumed that anxiety erupted from the [It] as the immediate result of the tensions of excessive, unsatisfied needs, and that the [I] was, as it were, a defenseless victim. The new concept modifies this; Freud states that in a situation of danger . . . the [I's] anticipation of this state may result in the experience of anxiety. This anxiety is at the same time a signal which causes a readjustment of the organism for the purpose of avoiding the danger . . . This new concept naturally was not intended to set aside or replace the earlier concept, nor did Freud mean that anxiety might come about at one time in this way and at the next time in the other way. Undoubtedly it meant that in each concrete case both theories—anxiety sweeping over the [I], and anxiety formed as a danger signal by the [I]— represent two sides of one actual phenomenon, described one time from the side of the [It] and the other time from the side of the [I].[3]

Here, in less than one paragraph, Waelder resolved Freud's lifelong philosophical ambivalence by settling the question of how his two theories of anxiety were related. Although he gave Freud credit for the resolution, the key idea that anxiety generated by the It and anxiety generated by the I represented "two sides of one actual phenomenon" was definitely not Freud's idea. Rather, it was Waelder's application of Bohr's principle of complementarity to Freud's two theories. In the light of complementarity, Waelder realized, anxiety should properly be viewed as both a passion and an action. Viewed as a passion, it was a neurological discharge generated by the It and sweeping over the I. Viewed as an action, it was a warning signal generated by the I to help control the It and to respond more adaptively to a danger situation. The two points of view were mutually exclusive but both were true and both were necessary to understand any individual experience of anxiety.

Waelder then expanded this dualistic view of anxiety into a larger dualism of passion and action in human experience generally. "In its division between a person's *I* and *It*," he wrote, "psychoanalysis recognizes the two aspects of his being driven and his being directed." In this deceptively simple reframing of Freud's familiar concepts, Waelder was really proposing a psychoanalytic version of the principle of complementarity—*the principle of multiple function.* Waelder's new principle held that the dualism of the *It* and the *I* was a necessary and intrinsic characteristic of all mental phenomena:

> a twofold . . . approach to each psychic act would be not only admissible but even required by psychoanalysis.
>
> In the [*It*] . . . there is gathered together everything by which a person is driven . . . In the [*I*] . . . reside all man's purposeful actions, his direction.[4]

In other words, to be properly understood, every human experience must be viewed from two complementary perspectives: both as driven by the *It* and as directed by the *I*, both as a passion and as an action.

To What Does the "Multiple" Refer in the Principle of Multiple Function?

As clarifying as this understanding was, Waelder recognized that much more goes into any moment of human experience than could be explained by a simple complementarity of the *It* and the *I*. He expanded this complementarity into a full eightfold principle, seeing the *I* as both passive and active not only toward the *It* but toward the external world, the repetition compulsion and the *I that stands above* as well.

For example, consider what *I* am doing when I punch someone in anger. In relation to the external world *I* am passively reacting by fight-or-flight to how threatening and how big the other guy is and at the same time I am actively dealing with the challenge he presents me. In relation to my *It*, *I* am passively discharging my anger and actively mastering my fear. In relation to my repetition compulsion *I* am passively enacting my knee-jerk anger scenario (being my favorite kind of hero or victim toward my favorite sort of bad

guy) and actively preserving my sense of identity. In relation to my superego—
I that stands above, I am passively feeling obligated to live up to familial/
cultural standards of behavior and actively choosing to stand up for what I
believe.

The Principle of Multiple Function in Historical Context

Waelder's principle redefined Freud's tripartite soul in a subtle but profoundly important way. Where Freud saw the *I* as one of three agencies—and
a relatively weak one—that together constitute the soul, Waelder was saying
that the *I is* the soul, the integrative center of all the passions and the actions
of our inner life. In other words, he was correcting the imbalance in Freud's
theory, by putting the biological forces of the *It* into the larger context of the
harmonizing activity of the *I.* This was a modern version of the ancient
Pythagorean/Platonic theory of the soul as a harmony of conflicting humors
and desires, or, as Waelder put it, "a kind of polyphonic theory of psychic life,
in which every act is a chord, either consonant or dissonant" (p. 16).

Freud had never been able to explain exactly how the conflicting forces of
Thanatos and Eros operated within the three agencies of the soul. This
Waelder was able to do with his principle of multiple function. The passive
drivenness of the *I*—being pushed and pulled by four competing influences,
trying to accommodate them all, and, in the process, tending to "fall apart"
into a state of inner conflict—reflected the operation of Thanatos. The active
directedness of the *I*—integrating and harmonizing these four competing
influences—reflected the operation of Eros. The complementarity between
these two sides of the *I*—as seen from the analytic perspective of the swimming pool and the synthetic perspective of the quest—completed Freud's unfinished theoretical symphony. It defined the soul as an evolving process of
the "*I* in its becoming," a dialectic of inner conflict and reintegration, driven
by lust *and* inspired by love, in which passions of the flesh (under the principle of Thanatos–constancy) become part of a larger action of the spirit (under the principle of Eros–growth). In other words, "Where *It* was, there shall
I become."

There Was Only One Problem

There was only one problem. Waelder never actually said any of that! In fact, he never even mentioned Eros or Thanatos or the principle of complementarity. Those concepts fit Waelder's principle so perfectly that it is impossible to imagine he didn't realize what he was implying, but he never stated it explicitly. We can only speculate about Waelder's motives, but I suspect that he didn't want to compete openly with his teacher. Waelder was a young man of thirty when he wrote "The Principle of Multiple Function." Freud was seventy-four, and suffering from cancer. Waelder was probably reluctant to say openly that he had now completed the solution of some of Freud's most serious theoretical problems and had done so using a revolutionary idea just proposed by a man who perhaps represented Freud's strongest competition for the title of greatest genius of the twentieth century! So instead, Waelder took the low-key approach, going out of his way to give the impression that he wasn't introducing anything new to psychoanalytic theory but was merely elaborating and clarifying what Freud had already written.

The unfortunate result of Waelder's reticence is that psychiatry today is still caught between the poles of Freud's philosophical ambivalence, in our ongoing conflict between the Medical Model and the Psychotherapeutic Model. But stay tuned. In Chapter 16, I will try to resolve this modern version of Freud's mind–body problem by using Waelder's principle of multiple function as the framework for an integrated theory that incorporates the Medical Model's homeostatic chemically imbalanced brain within the Psychotherapeutic Model's harmonizing dialectically conflicted soul.

VI. The Mind–Body Problem and the Crisis in Our Culture

We know two kinds of things about what we call our psyche (or mental life): firstly, its bodily organ and scene of action, the brain . . . and, on the other hand, our acts of consciousness, which are immediate data and cannot be further explained by any sort of description. Everything that lies between is unknown to us, and the data do not include any direct relation between these two terminal points of our knowledge. If it existed, it would at the most afford an exact localization of the processes of consciousness and would give us no help towards understanding them.

—Sigmund Freud, "Outline of Psychoanalysis"

The way we as a society conceive of mental illness matters. . . . It affects our moral instincts about what it is to be human. . . . The real dilemma is faced by our society. It is whether we will allow the seductions of the vulgarized biomedical model to overcome our own responsible commitment to a complex view of human life. . . . whether to understand [the mentally ill] only as the detritus of a broken brain or also as people whose suffering implicates us, whose struggles are resonant with our struggles, . . . whose complexity and depth demand that we see their suffering as engaged in the struggle to be decent, responsible people.

We are so tempted to see ourselves as fixable, perfectible brains. But the loss of our souls is a high price to pay.

—T. M. Luhrmann, *Of Two Minds: The Growing Disorder in American Psychiatry*

16. What Is the Soul?

[A]n analysis of the very concept of explanation would, naturally, begin and end
with a renunciation as to explaining our own conscious activity.

—Niels Bohr, "Light and Life"

When both hands are clapped a sound is produced.
Listen to the sound of one hand clapping.

—Zen koan

Laura

I still remember Laura's eyes, the impossible combination of vacancy, terror, cold rage, teasing seductiveness, and a compassionate wisdom so deep it
threatened to make me believe in reincarnation. I remember how she seemed
to be looking right through me—or rather through the flimsy therapeutic
identity I was then trying to inhabit—in a way that made me uncomfortably
aware of the discrepancy between how I wanted to appear and who I really
was. Every day in the classroom I would sit down with Laura and she would
look through me with those unfocused eyes, slowly intoning, as if chanting a
mantra, "Would ya like ta kno-o-o-o-w? Would ya like to know what's on her
mi-i-i-i-nnd? Would ya like to kno-o-o-o-w? Would ya like ta know what
Laura's thinki-i-ng?" This daily ritual never failed to leave me with the uncanny feeling that there was somebody else present—a third person in our
dialogue—speaking through Laura, the eight-year-old autistic girl, to me, the
novice teacher-therapist. It felt as if this mysterious third person was indeed
looking through me, intent on protecting Laura from my budding *furor
sanandi* and at the same time trying to mock me, gently, into self-awareness.

Sadly, I never did find out what Laura was thinking, but her daily incantation forced me to pay a good deal more attention to what I was thinking. It forced me to look at myself, especially at the overzealousness of my wish to help her. Indeed I very much did want to know what was on Laura's mind, to an extent that she must have experienced as frighteningly intrusive. Her traumatic history had given her ample reason to be suspicious of hidden pressures in the minds of her adult caretakers. Now, in my eagerness to know what was on her mind, I had been imposing my own subtle pressure on her—a pressure to prove myself by curing her, or at least figuring her out. Laura was more attuned to this motive in me than I was, and her questions were like a Greek chorus, commenting on the unconscious hubris of my therapeutic urgency, and warning me of the threat it posed to her and to me.

Now a Medical Model psychiatrist might well dismiss this account of my experience with Laura as a romanticized story I am telling myself about her, a story created out of neuronal surcharges in my own presumably undamaged brain. Current theories about the neurological basis for autism suggest that I should consider Laura's eyes and her words as a kind of brain-damaged blank screen on which I was simply projecting my own private movie. The third person I sensed in the interaction would then have been my own incipient self-awareness, which I incorrectly attributed to her. Maybe so. Certainly I had no scientific evidence to support my intuition that there was someone important, intact, intuitive, even wise, hiding behind Laura's autistic eyes. It was only an uncanny feeling I had as I listened to her words. Yet the more I have practiced psychotherapy, the more I have come to trust that such moments of unusual or unexpected feeling are important guideposts to the soul, signals not only of something in the therapist but also of something in the patient that needs to be recognized though it cannot yet be put into words. Such signals can only be received by someone attuned to the nonverbal channel of communication, in the mode of awareness that I have been calling "listening to the soul."

Although in describing my experience of Laura I have used standard visual metaphors like she "looked through me" or "made me look at myself," I don't think those metaphors quite do justice to the inner processes they describe. At the time, Laura seemed to be looking through me because her eyes were unfocused, but I think that's because what she was doing was more like listening than looking. In order to look at something one must be able to focus, and, since eyes are designed to focus on objects at a distance, "looking" is the appropriate metaphor for scientific observation of the "objective" physical world. "Listening" is a better metaphor to describe observation of the inner subjective world of oneself and another—the sort of listening Theodor Reik described in *Listening with the Third Ear.* Whether Laura—or the observer I imagined hiding behind her eyes—knew that she was doing it or not, I believe she was using her third ear to listen to the soul. And in her mantralike repetition of the question "Would you like to know?" I believe she was inviting me, and at the same time teaching me, to do the same.

Roy

Twelve years later, as a psychiatry resident, I was sitting in a hospital seclusion room with Roy, a sometimes violent schizophrenic young man who hardly ever talked and was generally incomprehensible when he did. After about twenty-five minutes of withdrawn silence, punctuated by occasional incoherent phrases spoken strangely to the walls or ceiling, Roy looked straight at me and said, completely deadpan, "My neocortex is asleep." He seemed to be expecting a reply, but I was speechless, struck dumb with an uncanny but familiar feeling. Roy's comment seemed to come from someone I hadn't realized was in the room—not from the Roy I knew, but from someone else who was apparently inhabiting the same body. Not only had he put the comment in the form of a coherent and comprehensible sentence, unlike his typical psychotic communications, but I recognized immediately and without question that what he had said was profound, like a message from the Delphic oracle, with layers of meaning that demanded serious attention.

My first thought was that Roy was proposing a neurobiological theory of schizophrenia, the idea being that his illness reflected some uncontrolled activity of his allocortex (the so-called visceral brain—the deepest, oldest part of the brain that includes the emotional centers of the limbic system), resulting from a chemical imbalance that had deactivated (put to sleep) the rational, organizing functions of his neocortex (the outer, most recently evolved layer of the brain, which is much more highly developed in humans than in "lower" species). A remarkably rational theory coming from a crazy person who had never finished high school and had recently been smearing feces on the walls of his seclusion room. But even more remarkable was the fact that Roy's words seemed to mock the very theory they espoused. Knowing his circumstances at that moment, it was difficult not to hear his statement as an ironic complaint about the treatment philosophy which dictated that he be heavily medicated and locked in a room with padded walls and a barred window. It was as if he was saying, "I know you've drugged me because *you* think my neocortex is asleep and I am reduced to the state of an irrational animal. But here's a news flash: My neocortex is alive and well and very much present in my illness, and it's your therapeutic methods that are putting it to sleep. Maybe my illness is threatening to tell you something that you don't want to hear, and your treatment is really an unconscious attempt to shut me up." In other words, "My neocortex is asleep. Is that what you were trying to accomplish all along?" The irony in all this, of course, was that this poorly educated man, who had acted and been treated for years as if he had no neocortex to speak of, apparently understood the word *neocortex* and the theory of evolution to which it alludes. A person whose neocortex was asleep (from whatever cause) could never say, "My neocortex is asleep."

There is an old idea in psychiatry nowadays dismissed as "the myth of the noble schizophrenic": that the sufferings of schizophrenic patients often put them in touch with a deep existential wisdom. In that vein, I found myself imagining that Roy had been speaking not only as a patient but as Everyman, commenting on the collective neocortical somnolence of our culture. I recalled that Erich Fromm once wrote about a "low-grade schizophrenic process" in the patterns of modern society.[1] Could it be that schizophrenics like Roy were actually more awake and sensitive to such subtle processes than the rest of us? I thought of the cold war—the United States versus the Soviet Union, the Eagle versus the Bear, each with an allocortical finger on the trigger and a neocortex asleep at the wheel. It occurred to me that to survive in a world like that *without* going crazy, it probably helps if your neocortex isn't too alert.

Mark

If I were to have the same encounter with Roy today I would probably not be, as I was then, at a loss for words but would say something like "Well, Roy, your neocortex may be asleep but somebody's certainly awake in there!" Now, I am no longer surprised when I encounter an intact and healthy core self in even the sickest patients. Nor are such encounters always so subtle and elusive as those I've just described with Laura and Roy. I worked for several years with another chronic schizophrenic patient named Mark, who had long stretches of time when he was not psychotic and whose healthy core was evident even in the worst stages of his illness. Mark once tried to describe to me the anguish of this illness, and his sense of helplessness about it, by saying, "It's in me and it gets out of me and it comes back at me." At one level, he was simply reporting the terms of his paranoid delusions. He was secretly horrified at his own murderous thoughts (It's in me). When he heard about a murder on the evening news he felt that his thoughts had caused it through "bad vibrations" that were broadcast like radio waves (it gets out of me). He therefore fully expected to be murdered himself—or lobotomized—as a retaliation and punishment (it comes back at me). Yet the statement itself was not paranoid. It was more like a theoretical explanation of paranoia. In fact, it was a pretty accurate summary of the process of transference projection and enactment, as I described it in Chapter 11. Like Roy's comment, it was also a statement about the human condition—a theory of the origins of evil in original sin.

In addition, I felt that Mark too, like Roy, was making an ironic commentary on his treatment. He saw me as the delegate and enforcer of the retaliation that was "coming back at him," and was telling me that what I thought of as psychotherapy seemed to him like sadistic punishment. Every time I entered his room, he assumed I had come to lobotomize him, either physically or psychically. He therefore responded to my therapeutic efforts to "understand" him by taking to his bed, where for session after session he would lie mute and motionless with an overcoat covering his head. It took weeks of futile attempts on my part to interpret this behavior before it finally dawned on me that the strained psychological theories I was spinning (which I'm much too embarrassed to report here) were as delusional as the psychosis I was trying to explain, and equally unhelpful in making contact. The more I tried to talk to him, the more his silence forced me to recognize that my words and my theories were getting in the way of communication. I needed to think less and listen more.

The I That Stands Above Versus the Superego

At first blush, it would seem that patients like Laura, Roy, and Mark should pose the greatest challenge to proper listening because of their idiosyncratic way of using, and not using, words. Indeed, if one is listening only to the words, it is exceptionally difficult to understand what autistic and schizophrenic patients are trying to communicate. What Laura, Roy, and Mark taught me, however, was that proper listening means listening not only, or even primarily, to the words but to something between and behind the words as well. Doing that, I became aware of an inner presence in each of them— an observer standing apart from their illnesses and wisely, compassionately, with an ironic sense of humor, commenting on those illnesses and on my fumbling attempts to treat them. Certainly they evoked such a presence within me—a self-conscious I that "stood above" our interaction—a compassionate, ironic, moral observer who was listening in on us, aware of the deeper implications and subtle overtones, both sinister and joyful, of what we were doing together.

It is by no means a coincidence that this kind of awareness was evoked in me by patients suffering from schizophrenia and autism.[2] Freud's first speculations about the *I that stands above* were based on his impressions about just this group of patients:

> It would not surprise us if we were to find a special psychical agency which performs the task of seeing that . . . satisfaction from the ego ideal is ensured and which, with this end in view, constantly watches the actual ego and measures it by that ideal. If such an agency does exist, we cannot possibly come upon it as a *discovery*—we can only *recognize* it; for we may reflect that what we call our "conscience" has the required characteristics. Recognition of this agency enables us to understand the so-called "delusions of being noticed" or more correctly, of being *watched,* which are such striking symptoms in the paranoid diseases and which may also occur as an isolated form of illness. . . . Patients of this sort complain that all their thoughts are known and their actions watched and supervised; they are informed of the functioning of this agency by voices which characteristically speak to them in the third person ("Now she's thinking of that again," "now he's going out"). This complaint is justified; it describes the truth. A power of this kind, watching, discovering and criticizing all our intentions, does really exist. Indeed, it exists in every one of us in normal life.[3]

Freud's account of this self-observing power raises the important question of how one person's conscience becomes another person's hallucination or delusion. Putting it in terms of my own experience, the question would be: How is it that the inner observer I sensed in Laura, Roy, and Mark, if it was so compassionate and wise, could have left them so horribly tormented by their illnesses?

The answer has to do with the distinction I introduced in Chapter 14 between the *I that stands above* and the superego. The *I that stands above* is a self-observing agency that in a sense really does "stand above" or outside the personality as an autonomous, dispassionate awareness. It can observe—without being controlled by—the more reflexively passionate, self-interested (and symptomatic) tendencies of the personality. But these embedded tendencies of the personality (functions of the *It* and the *I* as organized by the repetition compulsion) can at times co-opt the autonomy of the *I that stands above,* appropriating its neutral self-observing function to the purposes of a harsher, internalized self-criticism. It then becomes not an autonomous and accepting "I" that "stands above" the personality but rather an automated and punitive superego-agency within the personality, with reflexively passionate, self-interested needs of its own. When this happens, the capacity for dispassionate self-observation that in moments of reflective calm is the source of our most enlightened consciousness, can become temporarily inactivated—taken over by the self-attacking needs to whose use it is being put. This is very dramatically the case in schizophrenia, where the self-observing third-person voices Freud described can turn suddenly and unpredictably vicious, and begin to make frightening, degrading, and insulting second-person comments, like "Slut! Whore! Pig! Murderer!" "You should just kill yourself right now!" or "They all hate you because you're so incredibly stupid!"[4]

Schizophrenia and the Mind–Body Problem

On the surface, the relationship between schizophrenia and the mind–body problem may seem obvious enough. The very term *schizophrenia* refers to an extreme "split" in the personality between the mental and the physical, described classically as a split between ideation and affect. A more down-to-earth way to put it would be that schizophrenics attempt to live exclusively in their heads because they are alienated from, indeed often horrified by, their bodies. It is as if they are trying to keep their thoughts pure—free from contamination by their dirty, violent passions. But to do that, they must turn those passions against themselves in the most extreme form of repression—a sadistic, self-destructive attack on the natural linkage between their thoughts and feelings. The unfortunate result is that the schizophrenic literally loses "touch" with the physical reality of his emotions. His mind, cut loose from its proper mooring in the body, tends to run wild, getting lost in elaborate, un-realistic paranoid or grandiose delusions or in the disconnected irrational logic known as "thought disorder."

This kind of schizophrenic mind–body splitting is very different from the mind–body division of experience Descartes described. The "mind" in schizophrenic splitting is not the autonomous self-reflective consciousness of Descartes's *cogito,* but a compulsively self-attacking "conscience" (the in-sulting, humiliating voices and paranoid delusions). The passionate self-punitiveness of this superego/conscience is not a clear moral awareness but rather an automatic reflexive drive, much like the passionate drives of the *It* that it is defending against. As an internalization (and exaggeration) of parental and cultural authority, this superego/conscience is at least as much physical as it is mental, being embedded and structuralized in the brain through neurological processes of perception, memory, and learning.

In that sense, both sides of the body–mind split in schizophrenia—the physical passions and the punitive superego—belong to the body side of the mind–body problem. Yet, as I discovered in my encounters with Laura, Roy, and Mark, there is not only a superego in schizophrenia but an *I that stands above* as well, a self-observing consciousness that can feel the anguish of the schizophrenic split without being controlled by it. This would mean that the real Cartesian dualism in schizophrenia is not the pathological split between the superego and the *It,* but rather the same split we all experience between the clear consciousness of the *I that stands above* and the reflexive biological impulses of the superego–*It*–repetition compulsion.

And If You Doubt That, Therefore You Are

What I am getting at here is a distinction between an element within the soul that is clearly distinct from the brain, and another element that is embedded in the brain, both elements participating in what we ordinarily think of as the "mind." I believe that this distinction reflects a universal dualism in human nature that cannot be dismissed simply by calling it Descartes's error. In fact, all the standard arguments against Cartesian dualism themselves depend upon exactly the same kind of dualistic distinction. There is an idea in Eastern mysticism, for example, that dualism is a delusion that distracts us from awareness of the essential oneness of being. But this idea invokes a mind–body split of its own, between a higher self that is able to experience the oneness, and a lower self, the "ego," that is compulsively attached to the thoughts, emotions, and impulses of the everyday personality. James Carse describes this kind of dualism as a central feature of all mystical traditions. "Mystics often distinguish between the ego and the soul, or the ego and the self," he writes:

> The terms are not so important, but the distinction is. The ego is the dualist in us. It is the habit we have of seeing ourselves over and against someone else. As ego, my inwardness remains inward because it is completely closed off to you by my outwardness. As ego, my wealth, intelligence, moral goodness, social class are what they are only in contrast to the person next to me. . . . All such oppositions are creations of the ego.
>
> From the perspective of soul, however, we see each opposing either/or as a conjoined both/and. . . . "When there is no more separation between *this* and *that,* it is called the still-point of Tao. At the still-point in the center of the circle one can see the infinite in all things." I can be separate from you only because at a deeper level we are joined in something inseparable. . . .
>
> The still center, the soul, does not oppose anything. Not opposing anything, it does nothing. As soul, we do not act; we are. As ego, we cope with the world, change it, arrange it, try to improve it. We cope with our-selves, too, becoming our own projects, struggling to be who and where we are not. When we become aware of the still-point in a person, of a deed that has no doer, we are aware of soul; we are in the presence of presence.[5]

What Carse describes here as "the still-point in a person" is very close to the experience I believe Descartes was trying to capture in the words *Cogito, ergo sum.* It is also very much what I experienced with Laura, Roy, and Mark. With each of them there came a moment when I felt that I was *in the presence of presence.* This presence, which Carse calls the soul, is the self-reflective consciousness of the *I that stands above,* the compassionately dispassionate observer I could hear between the words of Laura's mantra, "Would you like to know?" Carse's distinction then between the undivided "presence" of the soul and the divisive "attachments" of the ego (my attachment to my therapeutic zeal, for instance, and Laura's attachment to her autistic defenses) is the same fundamentally Cartesian distinction I have just described in schizophrenia between the *I that stands above* and the "split" (superego–*It*–repetition-compulsion) personality.

At the opposite extreme from mysticism, the other major argument against Cartesian dualism is that of materialism. Where the mystic objects to dualism because it denies the essential oneness of the soul, the materialist objects to the fact that it has any concept of a soul at all. He dismisses the autonomous Cartesian consciousness as a myth—"the ghost in the machine" as philosopher Gilbert Ryle mockingly referred to it.[6] The materialist claims that all the functions traditionally ascribed to the mind or soul can be better explained as functions of the brain. Most often nowadays, he will invoke a computer model of the mind that views the brain as neurological hardware and of the mind as the (equally neurological) software program running on it.

If the Mind Is a Computer, Then Who Is That Guy Sitting at the Keyboard?

Ironically, this attempt to replace the immaterial ghost in the machine with the materialistic software in the machine ends up in the same place as mysticism—reaffirming rather than refuting Cartesian dualism. It simply brings in the ghost covertly, through the back door (or disk drive) so to speak, not as an immaterial consciousness residing in the machine but as a virtual consciousness residing in the software that runs the machine. To understand this, it helps to recognize first that there are some functions of the mind that a computer model does account pretty well for—the superego, for instance. As an internalized agent of self-criticism, the superego is very much like a software program, written by parents and culture and loaded into the memory banks of the growing child's brain. Such a software model is a useful way to describe the large component of learning and memory that is clearly involved in the development of a conscience and that must somehow be structurally encoded in the brain. The same model can then be extended to apply not only to the superego but also to certain elements of the *It* and the *I,* which can be thought of, respectively, as an instinct program written by the genes and as an adaptation–learning–socialization program written jointly by genes, parents, and society. In various combinations and interactions, these software programs of the superego, the *It*, and the *I*, can account for all the habitual, structuralized tendencies of the repetition compulsion—the repeating patterns of thought, attitude, emotion, and behavior that constitute what we call personality. These would be the same thoughts, attitudes, emotions, and behaviors that the Eastern religions refer to as karmic attachments of the ego—patterns of memory and desire to which we are attached quite literally because they are physically encoded (as software) in our brains.

Of course, this model by itself doesn't explain why the schizophrenic personality would be so different from the "normal" personality—why the schizophrenic superego is experienced as hallucinated voices, for instance, or why it is so much more cruel than in most people. These might be direct effects of harsher life experiences, or of more radically inconsistent parental attitudes that the growing child has had to internalize (in an inherently self-alienating way). Alternatively, they might be indirect neurobiological effects of a glitch or incompatibility in the genetic program for processing trauma or for imitating and internalizing parental attitudes. But in any case, an overall computer model of the mind that conceptualizes personality as software and the brain as hardware does seem to work, up to a point. It allows us to explain, for instance, how medications like Prozac can shift the balance of personality (though, as I will explain in Chapter 17, they do not transform it) through their neurobiological effect on the brain. The Prozac acts like another software program, a disk-repair utility that optimizes the performance of whatever personality programs are already running—or at least some of them—and changes the way background colors (overall moods) appear on the screen of consciousness. But it is also at just this point—when we begin to focus on the screen of consciousness—that the real problem with the computer model appears.

It is a remarkable fact that those who advocate a computer model of the mind never seem to include the computer's screen in their model, or to think carefully about what a phrase like "screen of consciousness" suggests. The screen itself belongs to a computer's hardware, and the contents that appear on the screen belong to its software, but the consciousness that reads the screen and finds meaning in its contents is neither hardware nor software, but belongs to a human observer sitting outside the computer.

Information and Consciousness

The computer model tries to get around both the screen and the observer by equating consciousness with the so-called information-processing activity of the computer and of the brain's neural network But the appeal of this idea depends entirely on a misuse of the term *information*. Computers do not process information. *Conscious minds* process information and they use computers to help them do so. What computers process is meaningless on/off electrical currents that in themselves contain no information. Only when organized and interpreted as a computer language *by a human consciousness* do these electrical currents become bits and bytes of digital information. In the same way a brain's electrical impulses become information only when experienced as meaningful by a human consciousness.

Consider a simple analogy: When I look at a grandfather clock or listen to its chimes, I get information about the time. I could say that the clockwork mechanism "informs" the operation of the chimes, or that it "tells" the hands how to move. But this would not justify my saying that the clock/chimes system "processes information," because that system is just a bunch of moving pieces of metal. There is no information about time being processed until an outside observer is included in the system who can interpret the movements of hands and chimes in his or her private nonmechanical consciousness.

In terms of complementarity, information implies meaning, and the meaning of any physical system—like the meaning of the Mona Lisa—can exist only in the synthetic perspective of a conscious observer. To equate information processing with events occurring in a network of electrical circuits is to spuriously conflate the observer with the observed—"collapsing the wave function" of information-as-meaning into an incoherent concept of information-as-electricity. To say that there is information in a neural network, then, is just another way of saying that there is a "ghost" in the machine.

Consciousness Rationalized: It Thinks, Therefore It's Me?

The computer model of consciousness violates the principle of complementarity by relying exclusively on what philosopher Daniel Dennett calls "the third-person materialistic perspective"[7] (i.e., positivism). It considers consciousness as a neurological process while ignoring the most essential feature of conscious experience: the element of wholeness, the experiencing first-person *I*. Without this first-person observer, the computer model of the mind can never be more than the model of a robot, an unconscious automaton. It can account for the contents of consciousness—thoughts, impulses, emotions, memories, fantasies, personality patterns—but not for the consciousness that experiences and finds meaning in these contents and can discern the difference between thought, impulse, emotion, memory, fantasy, and personality. Ultimately, it leaves out the very element of a computer it is supposed to be explaining, the consciousness of the guy sitting at the terminal.

In that sense, the computer model is not a scientific theory of consciousness, but only a bad analogy—a *scientific rationalization* designed to make it appear to be a scientific fact (rather than a philosophical assumption) that brain processes cause consciousness. Another such rationalization that is popular nowadays tries to explain consciousness as a biological product of natural selection that "emerged" during the evolution of the cerebral cortex. As Gerald Edelman puts it in *Bright Air, Brilliant Fire*, when the neural networks of the evolving brain reached a certain level of complexity, they simply "gave rise" to consciousness.[8] Philosopher John Searle tries to explain the logic of this process in *The Mystery of Consciousness*:

> [T]he brain is an organ like any other; it is an organic machine. Consciousness *is caused by* lower-level neuronal processes in the brain and is itself a feature of the brain. Because it is a feature that *emerges from* certain neuronal activities, we can think of it as an "emergent property" of the brain. An emergent property of a system is one that *is causally explained* by the behavior of the elements of the system; but it is not a property of any individual elements and it *cannot be explained* simply as a summation of the properties of those elements.[9] (Italics mine.)

The Hidden Duplicity of Materialist Explanations of Consciousness

Like the information-processing explanation, this "evolutionary emergence" explanation of consciousness relies on a misuse of words to compensate for the missing synthetic perspective. It replaces the precise scientific concept of "causality" with the nebulous nonscientific concept of "emergence" and then treats the two concepts as if they were synonymous. As the italicized phrases in the Searle quotation illustrate, this strategy is a blatant semantic evasion—a way of claiming that consciousness is causally explainable even while admitting that it cannot be so explained. In fact, there are no known laws of physical causality that can explain how brain processes could ever produce consciousness.

As for the idea that consciousness must be biological because it "emerged" through the biological process of natural selection, the truth is that consciousness is entirely different from any biological function that has ever emerged through natural selection. It cannot be explained the way biological functions can—as a result of genetic mutations producing new proteins producing new biological processes producing a new function. No doubt the brain processes that are necessary to support consciousness did emerge in this way through natural selection. But they are only the necessary biological conditions for consciousness, not its sufficient causes. Without a direct causal link between brain processes and consciousness, there is no persuasive reason to believe that consciousness emerged from the brain, or through natural selection, at all. Since it is a phenomenon of a fundamentally different order from any brain process, it would be much more logical to assume—if we are going to assume anything—that consciousness emerged from a source outside the brain.

Certainly it is no less mysterious, metaphysical, or mystical to say that consciousness suddenly arose out of the evolving brain without any identifiable cause than it is to say that consciousness suddenly "descended into" the brain without any identifiable cause. In fact, biologist Rupert Sheldrake (following Niels Bohr) argues that both points of view are necessary. He criticizes modern science for trying to explain phenomena only "from the bottom up," in terms of the lowest level particles and processes of physical science. Many biological phenomena—e.g., the development of an egg into an embryo, the regeneration of cells and tissues after injury, the homing of homing pigeons and various other animals, and mind-over-matter phenomena like the placebo effect—make sense only when viewed "from the top down," in terms of how a higher-level process or organization impacts on lower ones. Based on his study of such phenomena, Sheldrake has proposed that there must be a kind of force, cause, or guiding principle operating in the physical world—what he calls a "morphogenetic field," what Hippocrates called the *vis medi-*

catrix naturae, what Bohr called the "element of wholeness," what Freud called Eros—that is entirely different from the mechanistic forces of physics and chemistry. Applying this idea to the question of how consciousness appeared during evolution, Sheldrake comments:

> There could be an overall organizing principle immanent within the cosmos, maybe transcending the cosmos . . . that draws evolution toward the evolution of human consciousness or consciousness in general. . . . Materialists will always say it's chance, you see [i.e., natural selection], and it's a philosophical position. I'd like to have an open mind on that one. . . . I don't think we can rule out the possibility that consciousness could descend from a higher source, as one theory of it, in favor of the idea it ascends from a lower form of organization. They seem two different ways of looking at it.[10]

Materialism Refuted: A Thought Experiment

Consider for a moment what would it would take to *prove* scientifically that consciousness is caused by brain processes. Imagine that you are a scientist of the future who has absolute control of the machinery of the brain. You can hook a person up to your experimental equipment, measure and record all brain events as they occur during his conscious experiencing, and can then reproduce each brain event at will. You want to show that every time the subject has a particular experience it goes with a particular brain event, and that every time you reproduce that brain event in him it goes with (i.e., causes) the same conscious experience. Of course, the only way you could do this would be to ask the person to describe what he is experiencing as you manipulate his brain events, and track how his description changes with your manipulations. Otherwise—unless he told you—you couldn't know for sure, certainly not with any kind of scientific reliability, that he was having a conscious experience at all.

But then the whole procedure would depend on the subject's being able to report his neurologically induced experiences reliably and objectively, which means that his observing consciousness would have to be completely unaffected by those experiences and the brain events that caused them. In other words, you couldn't do the experiment unless there was an element of consciousness in the subject that was *outside* your experimental control, and—since you control everything in the brain—that consciousness would have to be outside the brain! If it weren't—if the subject's observing consciousness could itself be influenced by his brain events—then the subject might keep talking as you manipulated those brain events, but you would have no way of knowing whether the words coming out of his mouth reflected genuinely conscious experiences or were merely the kind of unconsciously reflexive "sleep-talking" that occurs in certain epileptic seizures.

Although this thought experiment does not prove that our observing consciousness is an autonomous agent or process outside the brain, it proves that it will always be outside the box of what science can explain. In the end, whether we call it a soul, a mind, a spirit, a ghost, a property that emerges mysteriously from the brain, a property that descends mysteriously into the brain, a *res cogitans,* or an *I that stands above,* we are forced to admit there is *something* that we all experience that simply cannot be explained in physical, chemical, or biological terms.

Wilder Penfield and the Mystery of the Mind

As it turns out, we don't really need a thought experiment to disprove the biological theory of consciousness because, in a primitive but compelling form, the real experiment has already been done by neurosurgeon Wilder Penfield. Penfield did the experiment during the course of more than twelve hundred operations he performed on patients with intractable epilepsy—seizures that could not be controlled with medication. He applied electrical stimulation to different areas of the surgically exposed brains of these patients (who were conscious during the operations) and asked them to describe what they experienced as he did so. The primary purpose of this procedure was to locate and surgically remove the disruptive focus in the brain that was generating the seizures. But in the process of doing so, Penfield took the opportunity (with his patients' permission, of course) to extend the procedure for the scientific purpose of mapping out the functions of the cerebral cortex—delineating just which area of the cortex produced just which type of experience.

What he discovered was that electrical stimulation to different areas of the cortex would predictably induce different conscious experiences, but only of certain types: sensory experiences, physical movements (that the patient was aware of but experienced as involuntary), and memories of all sorts, including vivid flashbacks of an entire stream of consciousness associated with a previous life event. At the same time, Penfield was struck by the fact that no electrical stimulation ever seemed to cause what he called "mind-action"— intentional conscious acts of faith, hope, choice, reasoning, introspection, empathy, and the like. The only sort of conscious experience he was able to evoke electrically was the passive experience of something happening to the patient or impinging on his awareness—what Penfield called "brain-action." This was not at all what he had expected. He had started out with the materialist assumption that all conscious functions and experiences must be controlled by the brain and would therefore be affected by the brain events he evoked with his stimulating electrode. But what he discovered instead was a presiding awareness in the patient that was utterly separate and unmoved by any of these brain events—that could recognize, remember, compare, and report on the various conscious experiences evoked by Penfield's electrode but was itself unaffected by them. Penfield wrote:

> The patient's mind, which is considering the situation in such an aloof and critical manner, can only be something quite apart from neuronal reflex action. It is noteworthy that two streams of consciousness are flowing, the one driven by input from environment, the other by an electrode. . . . The fact that there should be no confusion in the conscious state suggests that, although the content of consciousness depends in large measure on neuronal activity, awareness itself does not. . . .
>
> When I have caused a conscious patient to move his hand by applying an electrode to the motor cortex of one hemisphere, I have often asked him about it. Invariably his response was: "I didn't do that. You did." When I caused him to vocalize, he said: "I didn't make that sound. You pulled it out of me." When I caused the record of the stream of consciousness to run again and so presented to him the record of his past experience, he marvelled that he should be conscious of the past as well as of the present. He was astonished that it should come back to him so completely, with more detail than he could possibly recall voluntarily. He assumed at once that, somehow, the surgeon was responsible for the phenomenon, but he recognized the details as those of his own past experience.[11]

Over the course of more than thirty years of doing these experiments, Penfield came to recognize that the division of labor involved—he supplying the brain-action, the patient supplying the mind-action, the awareness that actually experiences this brain-action as a conscious experience—was the same division of labor that occurs naturally between brain and mind in everyday life, and that in fact no conscious experience is possible unless both functions are operating.[12] The experiments he had begun as a materialist, then, he completed as a confirmed Cartesian dualist, convinced that he had actually met the ghost in the machine.

From Neurosurgery to Psychoanalysis

Penfield's experiments provide a useful model for understanding the psychotherapeutic process. We can think of Penfield's stimulating electrode as a metaphor for all the stimuli to which we react automatically, reflexively, unconsciously—with a sequence of neurological events that triggers a bodily affect and/or action. The repetition compulsion would then be a counterpart to the electrode-induced reliving of past experiences by Penfield's patients. In the psychotherapeutic process this reliving takes place via transference projection—an emotional impulse (generated from an unconscious place we cannot control) that feels like something happening to us from outside rather than something we ourselves produce from inside. Under the influence of transference projection, the psychoanalytic patient will often say to the analyst exactly what Penfield's patients said to him: "I didn't do that [provoke that emotion]. You did!"

The anxiety stirred up by such transference experiences might be compared to Penfield's question to his patient—"What are you experiencing right now?"—as he stirred up the patient's brain with his electrode. The anxiety is an invitation to pay attention, to listen to the soul. The part of the patient that can do that—become aware of anxiety and then step back from the immediacy of transference affect and enactment enough to notice and report on what he or she is experiencing—is the same presiding consciousness that Penfield discovered hovering ghostlike over the machinelike circuits of his patients' brains. It is the higher self, reflecting on the karmic attachments of the ego, or the autonomous awareness of the *I that stands above,* observing the automatic patterns and reflexive passions of the repetition compulsion. In psychoanalysis this awareness is sometimes referred to as an "observing ego"—the part of the patient that is allied with the psychoanalyst's attitude of acceptance and reflective listening, even while the other, less conscious parts of the patient are driven (electrically stimulated) into the repetitive enactments that constitute the transference.

The psychotherapeutic process, then, is an evolving dialectic between these two elements of the soul—the brain-action of the repetition compulsion–transference tendency on the one hand, and the mind-action of the *I that stands above*–observing ego on the other. One element is encoded in the brain like software, whereas the other is as distinct from the brain as the human data processor is from the computer. The overall process involves a mysterious two-way interaction in which competing but complementary levels of experiencing come together in the act of listening to the soul. On one level there is a matter-over-mind experience of being passively caught up in the affects and enactments ("particles") of the moment. On another level there is a mind-over-matter experience of active self-reflection—listening to the feelings ("waves") of the soul. Both levels of experience are represented in the psychoanalytic method of free association, which involves passively allowing the stream of thoughts, emotions, and impulses to flow spontaneously as it will, and at the same time actively attending to those thoughts, emotions, and impulses in a way that inevitably changes the flow, guiding it toward the quiet, centered pool of conscious feeling. It is the dialectic between these two levels of experience that brings the unconscious into consciousness in the integrative moment of listening to the soul.

Feelings, Doubts, Logs, and Particles

I should reemphasize here that when I talk about "listening to the soul," I am trying to describe something much more profound than what people usually mean by terms like introspection, empathy, or getting in touch with feelings. My sense is that in using these familiar terms, we fail to capture, and probably don't even notice, the truly amazing nature of the inward act of consciousness we are referring to. Most of us have little idea of how incredibly powerful this apparently simple act of attention can be *in actually changing us.* By bringing the disowned unconscious into the accepting light of consciousness, listening to the soul becomes the vehicle not only of self-discovery, as in Prospero's "This thing of darkness I acknowledge mine," but of self-actualization, as in Freud's "Where *It* was, there shall *I* become." As I have experienced it, this is exactly what happens—*It* becomes *I*—just in that inward moment of noticing what you're feeling. The simple act of paying attention to your inner world, to the finely differentiated layers and qualities of private experiencing, becomes a dawning recognition that each moment of that experiencing crystallizes the core meanings of your life as an individual. This recognition involves a mysterious shift from content to process, from the perspective of distance—"What is that feeling impinging on my awareness?"—to that of immediacy: "I am who now feels this, and in so feeling recognize and become myself." The result is a unique experience of "consciousness in the act of expanding itself" that is not only the heart and soul of the psychotherapeutic process, but an experience of the soul itself.

It is interesting in this light to compare the psychotherapeutic process with the traditional practice of meditation. Both methods seek to expand consciousness but they go about it in ways that, on the surface at least, seem directly opposed to each other. In free association attention is expressly directed to the thoughts, emotions, and impulses that flow through consciousness. In meditation these associations are considered distractions—undesirable attachments of the ego. They are sometimes compared to logs (contents of the egoistic self) floating on a river (the higher self, consciousness in process). The meditator is directed to focus attention not on the logs but on the river, not on thoughts and emotions but on the inner presence that lies between and beyond them. But there is more than one path to this awareness of inner presence. Even if you start out by focusing on the logs, you can easily end up in the river. That's what I believe happened to Descartes in his epiphany, for instance, when the focus of his attention shifted suddenly from an endless stream of doubts to the indubitable *I* that was producing those doubts. The same sort of thing happened to me when Laura's repeated mantralike question "Would you like to know?" prompted a shift in my attention from what I wanted to know about her to the I who was wanting to know it. It happened again at the Phillies–Braves playoff game, when the unexpected experience of not being able to hear the familiar sound of my own shouting pulled the logs out from under my ordinary sequential awareness ("Only twenty-two more!") and I fell into the silent, inner presence—the river—beneath the shouting. In fact, I have on several occasions experienced exactly the same kind of meditative shift during psychoanalytic free association, when, in the midst of tracking a particularly vivid sequence of thoughts and feelings, I became aware of a larger, mysteriously beautiful order out of which all the individual thoughts and feelings seemed to be emerging into consciousness, and from which they took their sequence and meaning.

On the basis of such experiences, I conclude that whether you focus on the logs or meditate on the river, you can get to Rome either way. To appreciate this, imagine psychoanalytic free association as a method for peeling logs rather than onions—uncovering successively deeper and deeper layers until you finally get to the subatomic level at which the distinction between the logs and the river completely disappears. In fact, that's not just a metaphor. Peeling logs until you get to the river is actually a pretty accurate description of how Niels Bohr and a whole generation of atomic physicists became mystics: by pursuing their ordinary positivistic scientific method to its extreme limit, focusing in closer and closer on the objects and particles they could see "out there," until they realized that what they had really been observing all along was themselves—the subject "in here," who creates the object in the very act of observing it.

The Passions and the Actions of the Soul

The point of these reflections is that all roads do lead to Rome. Whether the path we take to understanding human experience is psychoanalysis, meditation, quantum physics, evolutionary biology, or artificial intelligence, when we follow that path all the way to the place where experiencing happens, we will always come to the same inner observer. Whether we call this observer an *I that stands above,* an observing ego, a higher self, an awareness that can discern and choose between analytic and synthetic perspectives, an "emergent" consciousness, or ghost of information in the machine, it is the same self-reflective consciousness Descartes discovered at the still center of his own restless doubting. So Descartes was right. The presence of this inner observer does define an irreducible dualism in human experiencing. Whether we describe this dualism in terms of the superego–*It*–repetition compulsion and the *I that stands above,* the ego and the higher self, logs and the river, observed and observer, brain-action and mind-action, or experiencing consciousness and observing consciousness, we are talking about the same old Cartesian theme of body and soul, and the mystery of what we are really experiencing when we experience ourselves.

In light of this, the fact that Descartes is nowadays best remembered—

and almost universally criticized—for describing body and soul as if they were things (*res extensa* and *res cogitans*) appears to be just another materialist strategy for evading the real Cartesian mystery of consciousness, a strategy that says more about our materialist worldview than it does about Descartes. It is we who can only think of the world in terms of material (visible, measurable) things, and who then need to dismiss the disturbing private experience of our completely un-thing-like consciousness by scoffing at Descartes's awkward way of describing it. But if you actually read Descartes's account of the process by which he arrived at his dualistic conclusion, it is pretty clear that he was thinking of body and soul not as fundamentally different kinds of thing, but as fundamentally different kinds of experience.[13] This is especially apparent in his last work, *The Passions of the Soul* (1649), where he describes the relationship between body and soul as one between movements (e*motions*) that originate in the body–brain and the more dispassionate feelings and desires that originate in the soul itself. The former he calls *passions* of the soul (the soul being passive with respect to the body–brain), and the latter he calls *actions* or "interior emotions" of the soul.[14] He notes that these actions of the soul "are frequently united to the passions which are similar to them" but are more likely to become noticeable when discrepant with the passions. As an example he cited the common experience of attending the theater, where the soul may passively experience pain from the unhappy emotions stirred up by a tragedy, for instance, but at the same time actively take "intellectual joy" in apprehending the meaning and value of those painful emotions within a larger artistic context.[15]

Passion and Action in Descartes and Freud

Unfortunately, Descartes died before he had a chance to develop the implications of this important division of emotional experience. In retrospect, it appears that his account of the passions and actions of the soul was far ahead of its time. It anticipated by about two hundred years Penfield's experimental discovery of the distinction between "brain-action" and "mind-action." More important, it foreshadowed Freud's account of the conflicting but complementary influences of the superego–*It*–repetition compulsion and the *I that stands above* (observing ego) in the psychotherapeutic process. In fact, Descartes's example of actively apprehending the meaning of a passively experienced emotion in the theater provides a useful model for thinking about free association—as an experience of attending the theater of the mind—involving both the passions and the actions of the soul. On the one hand, we can feel ourselves, in the course of our associations, being swept up passively in the unconscious drivenness of an emotion. On the other hand, we can step back and notice that our experiencing of that emotion includes a conscious feeling, that goes with the emotion but is more of an active choice, value judgment, or intention than a passive compulsion. This "feeling" would be an apprehending of the meaning and value that we assign to whatever evoked the emotion, so that we can say not only "*It* makes me angry" but "*I feel* it as something worth getting angry about" and, perhaps, "In acknowledging my anger, I recognize and stand up for the personal sense of values that my anger embodies."[16]

Descartes and Freud would have agreed that the far more interesting and illuminating circumstance is that of a discrepancy between the passions and the actions of the soul—when we are moved to say "It makes me angry but I can recognize that it *isn't* worth getting angry about" or "It makes me angry but I am ashamed of the revenge motive and selfish values that are implicit in my anger." In this circumstance of inner conflict, the close fit between Descartes's categories and Freud's becomes more apparent. If we think of Freud's *I* as the experiencing self, then Descartes's passions of the soul would represent the reflexive influence of the superego–*It*–repetition compulsion over the *I* while actions of the soul would reflect the complementary autonomous influence of the *I that stands above,* acting through the *I*. It might even be said that the primary advantage of Freud's tripartite model over his original model of the soul (as a drive-discharge neurological reflex apparatus) was precisely that it enabled him to conceptualize in this way not only the passive but also the active dimension of emotional experience—not only unconscious affect but self-reflective feeling as well.

The Principle of Multiple Function Revisited

At this point I hope that my readers are beginning to get a feel for the way in which all the important themes in this book converge in the fundamental Cartesian dualism of passions versus actions of the soul. It subsumes the dualism of brain-action versus mind-action (matter-over-mind versus mind-over-matter), Thanatos versus Eros, the Flesh versus the Spirit (lust versus love), the swimming pool versus the quest, homeostasis versus harmony, particles versus waves, and analytic versus synthetic perspectives. It is the same dualism I described in Chapter 15 as *passions of the flesh* versus *actions of the spirit*. This is a dualism not of substances but of processes. It is what Robert Waelder was referring to when he described the *I* as both "driven" and "directed."

I come back again here to Waelder because I believe that his principle of multiple function not only captured what was best in Freud's theory, but did so in a way that is immediately relevant to psychiatry today. In highlighting the opposing processes of being driven and being directed, Waelder redefined Freud's concept of inner conflict as a complementarity of opposing passions and actions of the soul. He thereby provided a framework to resolve Freud's lifelong philosophical conflict between the swimming pool and the quest. I propose that we can use this same framework today, to resolve our current version of Freud's conflict—the competing values and visions of human nature espoused by the Medical Model and the Psychotherapeutic Model. The Medical Model is a legacy of Freud's original swimming-pool philosophy of the *It*. In Waelder's terms, it focuses exclusively on the dimension of being driven by impersonal neurophysiological processes that determine not only our symptoms, but our thoughts, emotions, and behavior generally. The Psychotherapeutic Model is an outgrowth of Freud's mature quest philosophy of the *I that stands above* in conflict with the *It*. In Waelder's terms it includes the dimension of being driven within the larger dimension of being directed. It views the human condition as that of living consciously, with a sense of personal meaning and purpose, while subject to the potentially disruptive— at times compelling—influence of neurophysiological forces (unconscious affects) over which we have little if any conscious control.

If we now consider the Medical Model and the Psychotherapeutic Model together under Waelder's principle of multiple function, the result is an integrated "psychotherapeutic model" of the soul viewed as *a harmonizing of conflicting processes:* the neurophysiological affect-forces of the *It* incorporated within the personal intentions and purposes of the *I.* This model not only integrates the Medical Model's materialistic swimming-pool philosophy within the Psychotherapeutic Model's dualistic quest philosophy (the need for stability within the need for growth) but also reaffirms the ancient Pythagorean/ Platonic ideal of healing the soul—a harmonizing of conflicting elements and humors—in light of the most modern concepts of quantum physics.

The I *and the Repetition Compulsion*

The key to understanding Waelder's harmonizing "soul of multiple function" is in the particular emphasis he placed on the repetition compulsion. Whereas Freud had always defined the repetition compulsion as part of the *It*—a manifestation of the drives—Waelder made a great point of distinguishing between the two, giving the repetition compulsion equal standing with the *It* and with the *I that stands above* as one of the three agencies or "subsouls" that are integrated (along with the external world) in the polyphonic harmony of the *I*. Where Freud had talked about the *It*, the *I*, and the *I that stands above* as three agencies of the soul, Waelder was talking about the *It*, the *repetition compulsion*, and the *I that stands above* as three agencies of the *I*. In effect, he was putting the repetition compulsion in the place of Freud's *I* as the middle element in the tripartite soul.

The point of Waelder's revision was to correct an imbalance in Freud's view of the *I* as only one part of the soul, and a relatively weak and passive one at that when compared to the *It*. Freud's *I* was primarily an agency of passive accommodation—an organization of defense-and-adaptation mechanisms reflecting characterological (neurologically encoded) patterns of "compromise formation." Its purpose was to minimize and stabilize the opposing influences of the *It*, the superego–conscience, and the external world. In short, Freud defined the *I* pretty much the way I have defined the repetition compulsion–personality: as a homeostatic neurological mechanism for maintaining ego-identity (the sameness and stability of the personality) by reacting to the threat of change with reflexive characterological (i.e., automatic stereotyped) patterns of outer and inner conflict.

In fact, this definition comes much closer to defining a *Me* than an *I*, not unlike what Eastern philosophy would call the "ego": the reactive mind that contains the neurologically programmed tendencies of instinct and culture (karmic attachments of memory and desire). Waelder's autonomous, problem-solving *I* of multiple function is very different. It includes the reactive ego but also includes something like the higher self of Eastern philosophy. Waelder's *I* is more of an active harmonizer than a passive accommodator, integrating Freud's neurological body–brain–mind *Me* within a larger body–brain–mind–spirit *I* that *incorporates* (literally) the higher consciousness of the *I that stands above*.

In effect then, Waelder was proposing a new way of conceptualizing the Cartesian dualism of the Spirit and the Flesh as a complementarity of "the soul and its brain"—the *I* and the *Me*. The soul was an autonomous, intentional *I* that included a passively reactive *Me* (the neurologically encoded repetition compulsion–personality)—the directedness of the self under Eros integrating the conflicting but complementary drivenness of the ego under Thanatos.

Complementarity and Conflict

There may be some confusion about this idea that the forces of inner conflict are both opposing and complementary. When Bohr talked about complementarity, he stressed that the analytic and synthetic perspectives are mutually exclusive, so that we can observe only one aspect of a phenomenon at any given time. This would imply that, if inner conflict involves such mutually exclusive experiences, then we could never become aware of the conflict, because we could experience only one side of the conflict at a time. We could experience it exclusively from the side of the *Me* (feeling driven, compelled, or impulsively reactive) or exclusively from the side of the *I* (feeling a sense of our own personal direction and purpose), but we would be unable to notice any discrepancy between the two sides.

The key to understanding this apparent paradox is to recognize that inner conflict can be experienced at two different levels of consciousness: the experiencing consciousness of the *I* and the observing, self-reflective consciousness of the *I that stands above*. At the first level of consciousness (the level at which we live most of the time) we are somewhat like an atomic physicist who can see only particles or waves, depending on his observational framework. In the same way, when operating at the level of our experiencing consciousness, we can experience ourselves only as victims (analytic perspective) or as authors–heroes (synthetic perspective) of our fate, depending on our own observational framework. This framework is defined by the unconscious emotional scenario of our repetition compulsion and the attitude with which we habitually enact it. In our ordinary state of experiencing consciousness we have no direct awareness of inner conflict because we are enacting the conflict instead of feeling it. Although it is true that our repetitive scenario does unconsciously embody both sides of an inner conflict, while we are engaged in enacting the scenario we are experiencing only one side of the conflict and projecting the other side into whomever we are enacting with (transference).

One of the central purposes of psychotherapy is to free ourselves from the grip of this compulsive reenactment (i.e., enhance the flexibility of our personality) by enabling us to experience both sides of our inner conflict and to shift from one mode of experiencing it to the other. Those of us who generally feel like victims become aware of how much we are actually directing our repetitive scenarios of victimization, while those of us who generally feel like captains of our ship become aware of how much we are actually driven by emotional tides and currents that seem to have a mind and a direction of their own. This expanded awareness generally dawns during the course of reenacting our unconscious scenario in the transference, through an experience of discrepancy that evokes a feeling of anxiety, shame, or guilt, and thereby engages the attention of our self-reflective, observing consciousness. It is only then, while we are operating at this higher level of consciousness, that we can simultaneously experience both sides of an inner conflict. Like an atomic physicist who steps back from his experimenting and notices an incompatibility between different sets of observations—an experience he calls the wave–particle paradox—so we can step back from our enacting and become aware of an incompatibility in our inner sense of ourselves, in an experience we call anxiety, shame, or guilt.

In brief, then: Unconscious inner conflict is organized in the habitually enacted scenario of the repetition compulsion. At the level of our ordinary experiencing consciousness, we experience one side of the conflict as coming from ourselves and the other as coming from an external (projected) enemy. At the level of our observing consciousness, we can feel both sides of the conflict within ourselves, meeting the enemy and discovering that he is us.

The Flesh, the Repetition Compulsion, and the Spirit

Perhaps the most important implication of this revised model of the soul in conflict is that the *I* can operate at three different levels of consciousness—the level of the *It*, the level of the ego (the repetition compulsion–personality), and the level of the *I that stands above*—corresponding to the three levels of desire in Plato's original tripartite model of the soul. The level of the *It* is the level of pure biological instinct—an unconscious species-consciousness in which I have no individual identity and my desire is an automatic event (an affect) not experienced as desire, but recognizable only after the (f)act as a drive to satisfy an impulse. At this level there is no inner conflict, only animal instinct.

The level of the ego is an evolutionary step up from this species-specific *It*-consciousness to a more individualized I–It consciousness—the level of normal, waking, unreflective awareness that most of us live in most of the time. This consciousness belongs to a relatively mechanical state of self in which my individual identity (i.e., personality) is determined by the neurological reflexes of the repetition compulsion. Desire at this level is a conscious but compulsive emotion—a passionate need to enact a repetitive personality-defining scenario that is itself largely unconscious. At this level there is inner conflict, but it is unconscious, embedded in the repetitive, neurologically encoded scenario and experienced only in the enactment of that scenario (via transference projection) as interpersonal conflict.

Finally, the level of the *I that stands above* is the level of self-reflective, moral consciousness that defines a fully integrated, nonmechanical human being. At this level, my identity is defined *and can be changed* by conscious intention rather than by neurological compulsion. My desire is not only a passion but an action—an I–Thou feeling of love that includes a yearning for intimacy, an inner calling to self-actualization and an aspiration to do the right thing. At this level, inner conflict is a conscious experience (a knowledge of good and evil) felt either as a disturbing signal of anxiety, shame, or guilt, or as a more articulated awareness of incompatibility between simultaneous impulses of love on the one hand and lust, power, or revenge on the other.

To illustrate, consider the classically "co-dependent" wife of an alcoholic, abusive husband. To the extent that she allows her husband to exploit and abuse her, while repeatedly complaining and belittling him (thereby provoking another round of abuse), she is operating at the level of the repetition compulsion, confirming and reconfirming her familiar identity as a victim. There may be moments of sexual passion, however, in which she can lose herself temporarily—operating at the level of the *It*—and which bring a kind of solace to her otherwise bleak existence. If, however, she can look at her situation dispassionately, recognizing that it is self-destructive and feeling the clear sense that she deserves better, then she is, for the moment at least, operating at the level of the *I that stands above.* She now has a choice. If she acts from the consciousness of the *I that stands above,* she may decide to leave her husband or perhaps speak to him with a different attitude—more reflective, less blaming—about their situation. If she acts from the consciousness of the *It,* she may give in to an impulse of tension-relieving rage or lust. If she operates from the consciousness of the ego–repetition compulsion (incorporating the superego–conscience), she will engage him in one of their typical knee-jerk blaming–counterblaming arguments that tends to provoke her husband's drinking and abusiveness but leaves her feeling sorry and responsible for him, guilty about blaming him, and in the end resigning herself to her fate.

This perspective casts new light on Freud's always controversial emphasis on sexuality, both as a condition of mental health and as a cause of inner conflict. Many other motivations that have been considered crucial to psychological functioning—for instance procreation, territoriality, attachment, safety, mastery, pleasure, power, social adjustment, cohesiveness of the self, intimacy, love, even spiritual growth—are limited by the fact that they operate on only one or two levels of consciousness. Sexual desire, on the other hand, has the virtue (and the vice) of operating at all three levels simultaneously. It serves needs for procreation, territoriality, tension relief, and attachment at the level of the *It;* for pleasure, power, mastery, and self-definition at the level of the ego–repetition compulsion; and for intimacy, love, and spiritual growth at the level of the *I that stands above.* In its harmonizing of these three levels, the soul could be said to have roots in the Flesh and leaves in the Spirit, with the indivisible whole—the living tree of the soul—formed in the full experiencing of sexual desire. As Waelder put it, "the incomparable significance of the act of love in the household of the psyche is . . . that it comes closest to being a complete and equable solution of the *I*'s contradictory tasks."[17]

At the same time, of course, sexuality does not always bring harmony between the three levels of consciousness. In fact, it seems to create contradictory tasks for the *I* at least as fast as it solves them. There are inherent contradictions—or, more properly, disharmonies—between the three levels of sexual desire, that produce in every person some version of the universal conflict between the Flesh and the Spirit. At the level of the *It,* sexual desire is an instinctive phylogenetic impulse of hunger in which there is no sense of self or other. At the level of the ego, it is a passion of lust, mastery, and even revenge—a compulsion to enact a repetitive fantasy scenario in which the other person is experienced and treated as an object in an I–It relationship. At the level of the *I that stands above,* sexual desire is an act of love in which I experience the other person as a unique individual, a Thou in an I–Thou relation where the self is actualized in the experience of intimate communion. When things are going really, really well, all three of these levels of desire—instinctive hunger, self-serving lust, and self-actualizing love—are harmonized in a full experience of sexual intimacy, culminating in a concentrated moment of orgasm that is simultaneously an experience of oblivion or dissolution of self (nirvana in both the Freudian and the Eastern sense) *and* triumph *and* love. But, as we all know, things rarely seem to go quite *that* well! Between any two levels of desire-moving-toward-orgasm there are significant incompatibilities, each of which can provoke the disharmony—the anxiety, shame, and guilt—of inner conflict.

The fear of the knowledge of good and evil that is symbolized by Adam and Eve covering their genitals is, from this point of view, a fear of the experience of inner conflict that is inherent in sexual desire. To put it bluntly, it is a fear of knowing exactly what it is that gets us off and makes us come. In more academically refined terms (hiding it under the fig leaf of theory) it is a fear of knowing—through fully feeling—the incompatible good-and-evil impulses that, in paradoxical combination, produce the compelling excitement of our most private fantasy of desire-culminating-in-orgasm.

The importance of sexuality can be summed up by saying that the Flesh and the Spirit converge in the experience of orgasm, and in their convergence produce both a joyful harmony and an alarming dissonance—the emotional core of the knowledge of good and evil. Torn between the two, we would scarcely know what to do with ourselves were it not for the blind push we can always count on getting from the repetition compulsion. This push—the emotional charge that drives us to reenact our personality-defining interpersonal scenario—is generated, at the deepest level, by the excitement of a core sexual fantasy that drives us relentlessly and repeatedly toward orgasm. In so pushing us, the repetition compulsion moves us from dissonance toward harmony, provoking the anxiety of inner conflict and in the process awakening our higher consciousness. Again and again it drives us to reenact the same identity-defining, orgasm-producing fantasy scenario, in our non-sexual as well as our sexual relationships, pursuing the same joyful harmony in the face of the same alarming dissonance, until we can hear the dissonance clearly enough—in the form of anxiety, shame, or guilt—that we begin to actually pay attention to what we are feeling, and so initiate a psychotherapeutic process.

In this process the animal impulses of our *It*-consciousness and the repetitive compulsions of our ego-consciousness become identifiable, through the loving attention of the *I that stands above* as conscious desires and intentions that then become integrated into a fuller sense of "I." Greater awareness and acceptance of sexual desire then leads not to hedonism (as Freud's critics have too often protested) but to an enlarged sense of self and other, a fuller capacity to love, and ultimately, as in Plato's *Symposium*, to a higher spiritual awareness. "Where *It* was, there shall *I* become" in that sense means "Motives of the Flesh become one with motives of the Spirit as I become aware of and accept the disowned emotions and incompatible desires that culminate in orgasm." In other words, "This thing of darkness I acknowledge mine." In this process of becoming, the intention and attention of the *I that stands above* bring the energy of Eros to bear in the central psychotherapeutic act of listening to the soul. But at the same time it is the repetition compulsion—the thing of darkness itself—that drives the whole *It-becoming-I* process, first by pushing us toward experiencing the paradoxical harmony and dissonance of orgasm (thereby getting the attention of the *I that stands above*), and then by making us keep doing it until we get it right.

17. What Are We Really Hearing When We Listen to Prozac?

> *. . . for miracles are ceas'd;*
> *And therefore we must needs admit the means*
> *How things are perfected.*
>
> —William Shakespeare, *Henry V*

A Rescue Fantasy

Considering the importance of dualism in my thinking, I suppose I should not be surprised to discover, on reviewing these pages, that my book has a bit of a split personality. Writing as a psychiatrist and psychotherapist, my purpose is to reclaim healing the soul as the proper goal of psychiatry. I want to foster an appreciation of dynamic psychotherapy both as an effective, scientifically sound treatment for mental illness and as a personally rewarding path of self-discovery. I want to reconceptualize the use of psychiatric medications as part of the larger task of resolving inner conflict in a psychotherapeutic process. In this connection, I want to emphasize two philosophical points: first, that the mind-body problem is something real—an inner conflict that we can actually experience during self-reflection; second, that the way psychiatrists treat symptoms reflects their underlying philosophy of life. But I must admit that in pursuing these high-minded professional and philosophical purposes I have also had a frankly political purpose: to rescue the practice of dynamic psychotherapy from the evils of managed care and from the oppressive, shortsighted, materialistic prejudices that currently threaten to destroy it in the United States.

That "rescue" part is where I become aware of my split personality. I am writing not only as a dispassionate professional but also as a passionate person who sometimes gets a little bit carried away with himself. Speaking from this more personal level, I would describe my purpose in the book very differently. It is to convey the great enthusiasm I feel about the inward journey, about the awakening of consciousness that can occur in the experiencing of anxiety, and the subsequent unfolding of the hidden possibilities inherent in our human condition. It is to impart a vivid sense of how this unfolding happens through a simple but powerful act of inward attention—listening to the soul—within the context of a healing psychotherapeutic relationship. At the same time, it is to sound a warning about the dehumanizing effects of a quick-fix philosophy—not only in psychiatry but in our society as a whole—that encourages us to medicate away our anxiety, suppress our inner calling to the quest and ignore the deepest needs of the soul, in pursuit of superficial swimming-pool goals that we all know in our heart of hearts to be meaningless. But this is where I begin to get carried away, as my sentences grow longer and the balance of my personally charged purposes shifts from reflective action to reflexive passion. What started as a wish to convey my enthusiasm for the inward journey begins to slide into a melodramatic rescue fantasy in which I am a white knight trying to rescue psychotherapy—and even society itself—from the tyranny of a dehumanizing, scientistic Medical Model, the evil dragon in the melodrama.

I find this rather embarrassing. My need to be a white knight rescuing a helpless victim from an evil dragon I recognize as an aspect of my own repetition compulsion that can be more than a little irritating both to the designated victim (who may not feel so helpless) and to the designated dragon (who certainly does not consider itself so evil). Moreover, as I have emphasized throughout this book, the whole point of the inward journey is to reclaim both the helpless victim (Miranda) and the evil dragon (Caliban) as parts of oneself. This means that in the interest of practicing what I preach, I really need to consider what I am tempted to demonize in the Medical Model as a reflection of something I don't want to recognize in myself.

A Brief Exercise in Listening to the Soul

This is where I become not only embarrassed but somewhat anxious, because I realize that most of what I object to about the Medical Model is crystallized in one book, Peter Kramer's *Listening to Prozac*. The reason this makes me anxious is that it makes me vividly aware that my white-knight fantasy is fueled by a personal feeling of anger—an urge to attack Peter Kramer as an enemy, not to discuss or debate the Medical Model philosophy he advocates—and this puts me into a state of inner conflict. What I would like is to be able to discuss the underlying theory of "listening to Prozac" as the paradigmatic example of how psychiatry and society have lost their bearings in the Age of the Brain. Three passages from Kramer's book stand out in this regard:

> When one pill at breakfast makes you a new person, or makes your patient, or relative, or neighbor a new person, it is difficult to resist the suggestion, the visceral certainty, that who people are is largely biologically determined. I don't mean that it is impossible to escape simplistic biological materialism, but the drama, the rapidity, the thoroughness of drug-induced transformation make simplicity tempting. (p. 18)

> The capacity of modern medication to allow a person to experience, on a stable and continuous basis, the feelings of someone with a different temperament and history is among the most extraordinary accomplishments of modern science. (p. 195)

> In doing just what psychotherapy aims to do, Prozac performs chemically what has heretofore been an intimate interpersonal function. (p. 259)

Intellectually, I can say that these passages exemplify the danger of Medical Model thinking: how the temptation to "simplistic biological materialism" can destroy our appreciation for what is uniquely valuable in the psychotherapeutic process and uniquely human in ourselves. But emotionally, I cannot ignore the untidy fact that it was a real person whom I have actually met—*not* an abstract Medical Model—who wrote these passages, nor can I deny that I find them not only philosophically and scientifically misleading but personally offensive.

Of course I realize that Peter Kramer was not consciously intending to undermine the legitimacy of dynamic psychotherapy as a treatment for mental illness, nor was he trying to legitimize the practices of a managed care industry that defines any psychotherapy lasting more than a few sessions as "not medically necessary." Nevertheless his words certainly do have that effect. Why would people want to endure the hardship or the expense of long-term psychotherapy if they believed Kramer's promise that they can get to the same place—even be transformed—simply by swallowing a pill? It has always angered me that Kramer could claim that the intimate interpersonal function of psychotherapy is replaceable with the anonymous chemical normalization of Prozac. Yet now that I have come to writing about it, this anger of mine is beginning to make me feel anxious.

Let me be a bit clearer about this. The anxiety I am currently feeling has emerged as a conscious experience only gradually during the course of writing, revising, and discarding numerous earlier drafts of this chapter. In working on these drafts I was aware of feeling angry at times, and of a tendency toward a certain harshness of tone, but at first I was not particularly anxious about this. In fact, I felt rather self-righteous. I only began to feel anxious as I began to recognize that I was having more trouble than usual finishing this particular chapter. I found myself doing more rewrites—without feeling satisfied with the results—than I had for any other chapter. It was at this point that I began to notice my anxiety, and to recognize it as a sign that there was something in my angry reaction to *Listening to Prozac* that I needed to pay more attention to, as I now propose to do in the next few paragraphs.

If I let myself feel it, my anger seems at one level appropriate to the very real danger that I perceive in the widespread acceptance of misleading ideas about human nature. At another level, however, the same anger also feels like shallow narcissistic pride, a readiness to take offense that anyone else's ideas should have priority over mine—the same kind of arrogant attitude that led Oedipus and his father to their fatal standoff on the road to Thebes. At this level, if I try to be more specific about what I find offensive in Kramer's book, I find it is not the shallow swimming-pool philosophy it represents or even the threat it poses to psychotherapy. Rather, it is the fact that it promotes a compelling rescue fantasy that competes directly with mine—the promise that Big Science will save us from the evil dragon—only in Kramer's rescue fantasy *I* am the evil dragon, an advocate of an outmoded, unscientific method and theory of treatment who promises to do in seven years what can easily be done in three weeks, all the while happily taking your money and allowing you to go on suffering unnecessarily. Suddenly things have begun to feel very personal indeed.

But on further reflection, I blush to admit that I recognize a deeper layer in my angry reaction to Kramer's rescue fantasy. What offends me most is not being painted as the bad guy, but the fact that deep down I, too, feel captivated by his fantasy! When I read passages like the ones I have quoted above, the Miranda in me cannot help but be moved (Oh brave new world that has such scientific miracles in it!) and the Caliban in me cannot help but be envious of Kramer's Prospero-like powers of enchantment. More to the point, the reason this bothers me is that it forces me to be aware of the uncomfortable fact that I have in me such a Miranda and a Caliban—embarrassing and anxiety-provoking parts of myself that it has been the point of my own rescue fantasy to disown and project onto others so that I can feel more like Prospero.

Kramer Versus Kramer

Please don't misunderstand me. I am not saying that deep down I really agree with Peter Kramer. I most emphatically do not. But being more in touch with the Miranda in myself, I do begin to understand better what Kramer and his readers and the president and the Congress and the National Institute of Mental Health have all been getting so excited about—the powerfully appealing idea that, if we find the right pill, we can not only relieve the sufferings of mental illness but also transform ourselves overnight into new and better people. At the same time, being wary of the envious Caliban in myself, I am more skeptical of my self-righteous impulse to demonize Kramer, and more appreciative of the fact that Kramer himself was quite ambivalent in his enthusiasm for the apparent miracle cures wrought by Prozac. In fact, as he describes it in his first chapter, entitled "Makeover," Kramer felt not only excitement but a good deal of anxiety when he first began to observe that Prozac seemed able to "transform" personality:

> It is all very well for drugs to do small things, to induce sleep, to allay anxiety, to ameliorate a well-recognized syndrome. But for a drug's effect to be so global—to extend to social popularity, business acumen, self-image, energy, flexibility, sexual appeal—touches too closely on fantasies . . . that medication will take over in a way that cannot be reversed, that drugs will obliterate the self. . . . When faced with a medication that does transform, even in this friendly way, I became aware of my own irrational discomfort, my sense that for a drug to have such a pronounced effect is inherently unnatural, unsafe, uncanny. (p. 13)

I have only one problem with what Kramer is saying here: his assumption that his discomfort was irrational. I believe he was absolutely right to be uncomfortable, though I think he came to the wrong conclusion about the source of his discomfort. I suspect it was not so much Prozac's "uncanny" power to "transform" as it was his own temptation to believe in such a power—his inclination to "listen to Prozac" rather than to his own deeper instinct about Prozac—that made Kramer uneasy. Certainly I think that is what he should have been anxious about. After all, he himself describes the effect of Prozac as "cosmetic"—a kind of "makeover"—implying that what Prozac produces is not a real transformation but merely the superficial appearance of transformation. The only question is why he didn't take his own choice of words more seriously and recognize that what made him so anxious was the very real danger of believing there is no difference between a cosmetic transformation and a real one.

Listening to the Soul Versus Listening to Prozac

Again and again, in various ways throughout his book, Kramer comes back to this anxiety about whether the compellingly attractive cosmetic transformations he endorses may after all be "inherently unnatural, unsafe, uncanny"—so much so that the whole book becomes a kind of point–counterpoint debate between his need to listen to his own anxiety and his need to listen to Prozac. In fact, I suspect that much of the book's popularity stems from the fact that we can all recognize our own inner struggle in Kramer's. We are all torn in the same way, caught like Homer's Odysseus between the deep inner voice that calls us to the quest and the alluring siren song of the swimming pool.

I believe that the anxiety we can all feel in this struggle constitutes the central dilemma of the Age of the Brain—our choice between the long, difficult task of self-actualization and the alluring promise of a quick, cosmetic fix. As Kramer himself seems to recognize, this is a fateful choice, and how we make it will depend ultimately on whether we understand our own anxiety as a meaningful signal of inner conflict or as a meaningless neurological glitch:

> Anxiety is at the heart of the psychological understanding of man. The "dynamic" in psychodynamic psychotherapy is anxiety; anxiety is the motor force behind psychoanalysis. . . . Beyond the profession, in the work of existential philosophers like Kierkegaard and Heidegger, the individual's

struggle with anxiety is the preferred route to self-discovery. As a psychiatrist, I have spent most of my professional energy attending to psychological issues—to the significance of anxiety. Now ... I appeared changed in my perspective: I had caught myself assuming that a patient's anxiety was meaningless. (p. xii)

As Kramer suggests here, the stakes are high. What we stand to lose in "listening to Prozac" is nothing less than the psychological understanding of man. If we dismiss our anxiety as meaningless—merely an "irrational discomfort"—not only do we lose the opportunity for the inward journey of self-discovery, but we may lose our inner lives altogether.

Healing the Soul Versus the Quick Fix

For those who have benefited, or whose relatives and friends have benefited, from Prozac and other psychiatric medications, I want to stress that I am not questioning the therapeutic value of these medications. Used properly, I believe they can be extremely helpful, even life-saving. However, I also want to emphasize that most of the psychiatric medications being prescribed nowadays are not being used properly. They are not being used in the service of healing the soul in the context of a psychotherapeutic process, but rather as a quick, cosmetic fix to produce temporary symptomatic relief. Indeed, most of the psychiatrists who prescribe medications today—especially those trained in the last ten years—know very little about the psychotherapeutic process and so have nothing to offer except a quick fix. Even worse, most of our psychiatric medications are not even being prescribed by psychiatrists. They are being prescribed by general practitioners who have no expertise or interest in treating mental illness but do it because they are required by managed care guidelines and financial arrangements to avoid referrals to specialists.[1] This situation is highly destructive, both to the lives of individual patients and to the humanistic values of our society as a whole. But it could not be happening without widespread and powerful support—not only from psychiatrists and their patients but also from big business, from our political leaders, and from the media. *And such widespread support could not be happening without a very popular philosophy to justify and sustain it.* Ultimately, this philosophy—the materialistic swimming-pool philosophy of Medical Model psychiatry—is what we are really hearing when we listen to Prozac.

I certainly do not mean to suggest that Peter Kramer is responsible for our cultural predicament. He did not invent the Medical Model or its philosophy. The popularity of *Listening to Prozac* in 1993 was clearly a result rather than the cause of our societal craze for the quick fix. Yet no other book before or since has explained so well the scientific rationale (and rationalization) for the Medical Model's quick-fix philosophy. More important, the exciting promise that Kramer holds out (however ambivalently) in *Listening to Prozac*—the promise of painless overnight transformation—does capture the essence of what makes the quick fix so powerfully appealing. How can we help but stand, Miranda-like, in awe and admiration of the dramatic, almost instantaneous, relief from suffering that Prozac and other psychiatric medications often bring? But there is a hidden cost to this chemical relief that has not been generally recognized. The idea that we can avoid the inherent pain and struggle of human existence, and be transformed, simply by taking a pill is a subtle but powerful dehumanizing force that undermines the life of the spirit and subverts the fundamental human quest for a more genuine transformation of the soul.

The fact is, a drug-induced cosmetic alteration of personality is not a real transformation. It is merely a shift from an unhappy condition of the brain to a happy one—essentially a shift in mood, triggered by a shift in swimming-pool equilibrium (chemical balance).[2] In and of itself, this is not a bad thing, of course. Such shifts in mood can greatly improve our overall sense of well-being and self-esteem. But when produced by medication, these shifts tend to bypass or suppress the experience of anxiety, and in so doing block the path to a deeper transformation of the soul—the real transformation we all yearn for in our heart of hearts. This deeper transformation is not a shift between two alternative states of the brain but rather the unfolding of an unconscious condition of the brain into a conscious experience of the self—what Freud had in mind when he wrote, "Where *It* was, there shall *I* become." Such an experience of self-actualization can never be achieved by taking a pill, but only by listening to the soul: paying active attention to the experience of anxiety as the path to resolving inner conflict in a psychotherapeutic process.

In that sense, the same thing that makes Prozac and other medications so effective in relieving suffering also makes them dangerous. They achieve their wondrous effects by interfering, in one way or another, with the experience of anxiety. They blunt the painful consciousness of inner conflict but, by themselves, do nothing to resolve that conflict. Unlike psychotherapy, which achieves its effects through an expansion of consciousness—a fuller awareness of the unconscious dark side of the personality—medication fosters a contraction (or distraction) of awareness, making it easier to ignore or deny the dark side, reinforcing the suppression of disruptive unconscious forces but at the potential cost of an impoverishment of experience and of the creative possibilities that come with inner conflict. It is worth emphasizing that this directly contradicts what Peter Kramer claims about Prozac—that it does "just what psychotherapy aims to do." The cosmetic use of Prozac as Kramer describes it aims to promote the swimming-pool stability of chemical balance and social adjustment, quite the opposite of psychotherapy's aim of promoting growth in the quest. Of course it is true that stability is a necessary condition for growth, and the aims of the swimming pool are in that sense complementary with the aims of the quest. Prozac and other medications therefore can be used in the service of the quest—to modulate the experience of anxiety without completely suppressing it, thereby facilitating awareness of inner conflict. But unless the swimming-pool aim of medication is consciously subordinated to the larger purposes of the quest, it is likely to interfere with the psychotherapeutic process—promoting calm at the expense of consciousness and stability at the expense of growth.

To get a better sense of what this all means practically—how the difference between the aims of medication and the aims of psychotherapy actually makes a difference to patients, and how it can be dangerous to listen to Prozac at the expense of listening to the soul—consider the stories of Elise and Phyllis.

Elise

Elise had survived a traumatic childhood with a mother who was alternately doting and rejecting. She told me that she had grown up believing she was the apple of her mother's eye, and that her mother would have done anything for her. But as she talked more about the details of her childhood experiences, the mother that emerged from her account seemed almost entirely self-involved—able to love and admire Elise as an idealized extension of herself, perhaps, but oblivious to her as a person. Elise recalled vividly, for instance, how at a neighborhood party once when she was six years old, her mother had sat by a pool sipping a martini and never noticed as Elise—who could not swim—fell into the pool and almost drowned. Mom couldn't have been prouder, though, when her daughter then grew up to become a championship swimmer, as well as a virtuoso musician and brilliant student, first in her class at one of the nation's top law schools. For Elise, the problem was that she had to be a superstar—the very best at everything she did—simply in order to stay in her mother's good graces. As Elise gradually came to understand, she had actually grown up in a state of almost constant anxiety. She was the apple of her mother's eye, but only as long as she continued to fulfill her mother's dream of having a perfect daughter. Otherwise she lived in fear that her mother would turn on her—that she would become the object of contempt and vicious criticism, just like her father and almost everyone else in Mom's world *except* Elise.

With this background, it wasn't surprising that perfectionistic tendencies and fear of failure began to haunt Elise's promising career as a brilliant young trial lawyer. She loved the performance aspect of captivating and winning over a jury, and she took great pride in her many early successes, yet she lived in perpetual terror of ever losing a case. Gradually the weight of this anxiety dragged her down into a chronic depression that made it excruciatingly difficult for her to prepare her cases and, over time, made it harder and harder for her to relate comfortably to people generally. By the time she was twenty-nine, she had already had five years of psychiatric treatment. She had tried multiple antidepressants along with three different courses of psychotherapy, all without much benefit. But then she found a psychiatrist, Dr. Q, who prescribed an MAO inhibitor antidepressant, Marplan, that changed her life dramatically. For the next eight years, Elise felt happier and calmer than ever before. Her career blossomed, her relationships improved, and she looked up to Dr. Q as the man who had saved her life.

Eventually, however, the Marplan simply stopped working—a very common occurrence with antidepressants[3]—and Elise went into a tailspin, falling gradually but inexorably into the worst depression of her life. For the next two years, she was suicidal enough to require two lengthy hospitalizations during which Dr. Q—whom she continued to trust and depend on—tried one new antidepressant after another, including Prozac, but without benefit. This lack of response to medication put a great stress on Elise's therapeutic relationship with Dr. Q. She felt that by not getting better she was failing him, which only aggravated her depression, because it was like her worst fear come true: disappointing her mother. Dr. Q, for his part, began to think of Elise as "treatment resistant." He suspected there was a psychological factor interfering with her response to medication. He told Elise that he thought she had a personality problem that was aggravating her depression. She was hypersensitive, he said, too quick to take offense and get "inappropriately" angry at people. She would then immediately feel horribly guilty about this inappropriate anger and that guilt would make her more depressed, and in turn more hypersensitive.

Although there was a good deal of truth to this interpretation, Elise took great offense at it and became angry at Dr. Q. She told him he had no right to judge the "appropriateness" of her feelings and was being horribly unfair to blame her for her worsening depression. Had Dr. Q reacted to this criticism with equanimity, Elise might very well have then gone on to feel guilty and more depressed, which really was her pattern whenever she got angry (whether appropriately or not). But instead, Dr. Q reacted defensively, took Elise's angry criticism quite personally, and quickly became openly angry back at her. Elise in turn felt betrayed by this reaction but also justified in her anger, to the point that she decided to discontinue treatment with him.

When Elise entered treatment with me, I listened carefully to this story with an ear to learning from Dr. Q's mistakes. I knew that whenever a therapeutic relationship as important as Elise's with Dr. Q ends so abruptly and painfully, it is generally the result of a transference–countertransference enactment, energized by the patient's repetition compulsion. I had further confirmation of this hypothesis from Dr. Q, who told me that he endorsed Elise's seeking treatment with me because he felt defeated with her, hopeless about being able to work out their conflict. So if this conflict was a transference–countertransference enactment, I reasoned, then what had just transpired between Elise and Dr. Q would have to be a familiar story in her life, enacting emotions of which she was largely unconscious but which must be contributing significantly to her chronic depression. Elise confirmed that the sequence of idealization, disillusionment, anger, and betrayal she had just gone through with Dr. Q was a very familiar pattern in her adult relationships. In fact, it was the very pattern that Dr. Q had been pointing out to her, but he had pointed it out in a way that felt disapproving and blaming—that simply reenacted the pattern without promoting awareness of the emotions generating it.

As it turned out—not surprisingly—this idealization–betrayal pattern of Elise's repetition compulsion was based on her relationship with her mother.

For years Elise had idealized her mom, just as her mom idealized her. She took comfort from the ways in which her mom doted on her and suppressed any awareness of the repeated little betrayals she felt whenever her mom ignored or rejected her for failing to live up to some idealized image of perfection. Eventually, however, there was a betrayal too big to block out. When Elise was twenty-three, she made an independent decision that went openly against her mother's wishes. She decided to get psychiatric treatment for her depression and asked her mom to help her pay for it. Mom was outraged. She could never accept that *her* daughter needed to see a psychiatrist. She took Elise's request as a personal insult and responded by turning on Elise viciously. Not only did she refuse to help her but she had never since forgiven her for having asked for help at all.

As typically happens, despite being able to describe this prototypical pattern of idealization and betrayal as she had experienced it with her mother, Elise could not fully feel its impact on her until she had reexperienced and worked through the same pattern in her transference relationship with me. Fortunately, I had warned Elise early on—at the first sign that she was beginning to idealize me, and based on her recent experience with Dr. Q—that sooner or later I would inevitably say or do something that she would feel betrayed by, much as she had with Dr. Q. So when this did happen (quite a bit sooner than I expected) there were some stormy moments, but neither Elise nor I took them quite as personally as we might have had we not recognized the repetition involved. I was more prepared to accept Elise's disillusionment and anger—in fact, rage—at me with nonjudgmental curiosity and understanding rather than with frustration and defensiveness. She in turn was able to allow herself to fully experience these emotions (without unbearable guilt and also without having to end the relationship) for the first time in her life. Only then could she recognize that the rage and sense of betrayal she was experiencing with me were reactions she should have felt toward her mother.

Here is how it happened: After an initial honeymoon period during which her depression lifted and she was able to leave the hospital—feeling thrilled with me as a therapist, and able to return to her law firm with renewed enthusiasm—the bottom quickly fell out again when Elise was put in charge of a big case. Within two weeks her depression had returned full force. She felt as if her worth as a lawyer and as a person depended on her winning this new case, and she was afflicted with a growing sense of dread each time she tried to work on it. Even worse, her psychotherapy sessions no longer seemed to be helping her, and she would leave each session feeling more hopeless than when she had arrived. Finally, after several weeks of this, Elise woke up one morning feeling so desperate that she called me to say she was afraid she was going to kill herself if I didn't hospitalize her again.

Hearing the urgency and despair in Elise's voice, I had a sinking feeling, which I attributed to my worry about her condition and to the stress of having to rearrange my schedule on very short notice in order to admit her once again to the hospital. While this explanation was partly true, it was also a rationalization, and it kept me from recognizing the most important meaning of my sinking feeling, as *an anxiety signal*—a warning to myself that I had already fallen into a transference–countertransference reenactment with Elise of her idealization–betrayal scenario. I had, without realizing it, become narcissistically caught up in Elise's early success with me, feeling inordinately good about myself as a therapist and more excited and proud of *my* patient than I should have been when she so quickly recovered from her depression, was able to return to work, and within a few weeks landed a prestigious case. So when she then so suddenly became depressed again, I was selfishly disappointed on two counts: first, that I wasn't such a wonderful therapist after all; and second, that I wouldn't have the pleasure of vicariously enjoying Elise's courtroom victory. In retrospect it is clear that in being disappointed I was already beginning to betray Elise, relating to her emotionally just as her mother had—needing her to succeed so that I could feel good about myself. At the time, however, I didn't recognize this because I wasn't consciously registering my feeling of disappointment. Everything was happening so quickly and so intensely—as if we were on an emotional roller coaster—that it never occurred to me to stop and get my inner bearings until, in the middle of actually admitting Elise to the hospital, I found myself suddenly snapping at her in anger (in response to an innocent request), with a tone of impatient irritation in my voice that was completely uncalled for by the situation.

At that point, under calmer circumstances I would have stopped to ask myself where my irritation had come from and would have remembered the sinking feeling from earlier that morning, which would in turn have pointed me to the selfish disappointment I had recently been experiencing. I would then (hopefully) have put this all together and realized that in my irritation I was reacting to Elise just as Dr. Q and her mother had. But these were not calm circumstances. I was unable to do any of this inner processing because, the moment that Elise heard the sudden irritation in my voice, she just as suddenly became furious at me. She felt utterly devastated by my reaction, she later told me, as if she were drowning and I had suddenly pulled away her last lifeline. She was outraged. She accused me of having betrayed her in the most callous and unforgivable manner—of never having cared about her but only about myself—and she continued to berate me in this way each day I came to see her during her week-long hospitalization.

To an outside observer this protracted outrage of Elise's might have looked like a considerable overreaction—and at first it seemed that way to me—but in fact it turned out to be a very centering experience for both of us. It gave Elise the opportunity to feel and to articulate, more fully than she ever had before, her deep-seated sense of betrayal—in particular, how my irritation signified to her that I didn't really care about her but only about myself. For my part, I knew it wouldn't help to try to defend myself, or to apologize unless I meant it, so initially I had little choice but to shut up and listen to Elise's angry criticism. This was good for me because it finally forced me to stop and reflect not only on what Elise was saying but also on what I had been feeling. In the process I finally did recognize that my unexpected burst of irritation at her had been an outgrowth of the disappointment I was feeling— without realizing it—about having to hospitalize her again. It was only then that I realized how, in my disappointment and irritation, I had been reacting to Elise just as her mother had. This meant of course that Elise was right to feel betrayed by me and that, in an important sense, I did deserve her criticism. With this new awareness, I was then able to apologize sincerely to Elise for getting irritated at her. I explained that my reaction had come from my own unacknowledged feeling of disappointment, which was, as she had accurately sensed, an expression of my needs rather than hers. I explained further that I thought this whole crisis between us had been a repetition of her idealization–betrayal scenario, in which I had done to her exactly the sort of thing Dr. Q had done and, more important, the sort of thing her mother had been doing to her all her life.

What made this repetition different—and therapeutically useful—was that I was able to acknowledge my own culpability in the scenario (partly because Elise was able to be so clear about what she was blaming me for) and at the same time see it as part of a larger pattern in Elise's life. This allowed Elise to feel validated in her angry feeling of betrayal and at the same time begin to see that there was an element of overreaction in it. The great intensity and urgency of her disillusionment and rage, both at Dr. Q and at me, had been out of proportion to what we had actually done to hurt her, but it was absolutely appropriate to what her mother had done to her. Elise was able to recognize this simply through being angry at me and then experiencing that I was accepting of her anger, without needing to counterattack or reject her. This was so different from the way her mother would have reacted that it brought home to her, and helped her feel for the first time, how badly her mother had really treated her over the years and how angry Elise had always been at her without knowing it. She realized that she had never actually allowed herself to feel her disillusionment and rage toward her mother—even though she could describe many experiences of frank abuse and neglect by her—because, since the incident at age twenty-three, she knew that whenever she crossed her mother, even unintentionally (never being quite sure what *would* cross her), Mom would once again attack her viciously.

Once Elise was in touch with how angry she really felt at her mother, and how betrayed by her—through being able to feel these emotions in relation to me—she soon realized that she had chosen to become a lawyer primarily to fulfill her mother's needs. However talented and successful Elise was in her career, she had felt increasingly weighted down by it over the years. Not only was she afraid of losing a case but she had become less and less able to tolerate all the attacking and counterattacking that went with being a trial lawyer. At the same time, she found herself becoming more and more emotionally involved with the predicaments of her clients. She now came to feel that this emotional involvement expressed what was best in her—her ability to care for people. Interestingly, this awareness crystallized during her mother's terminal illness, while Elise was tending her in the hospital over the last six weeks of her life. During that time, Elise was able to feel moments of loving connection with her mother that helped her let go of some of the deep bitterness she had been harboring over a past that she could never change. She then made a dramatic midlife decision to change careers, and returned to school to become a physician.

When I say that Elise's story illustrates the danger of listening to Prozac, I most emphatically do not mean that she needed a psychotherapeutic process *rather* than medication. There is no doubt that she needed *both*. The whole time I was seeing her in psychotherapy (initially five times a week, then three times a week for several years, eventually once a week) I continued working with her, calling in consultants as needed, to find an effective medication regimen. But I consider it significant that it was only after Elise and I had worked through and survived together her disillusionment and anger at me, and after she was beginning to understand her tendency to relive her difficulties with her mother in all her important relationships, that we finally did find an antidepressant that worked again. And she definitely needed that antidepressant. Her psychotherapeutic insight was immensely helpful but was still not enough at that point to protect her from the disturbing sense that, at any moment, she might rapidly slide back into the depths of despair. The antidepressant gave her a crucial sense of confidence that there was now "a floor under her depression," so that even if something happened that would trigger a depressive reaction in her, the floor would stop her fall and she could stand up again and regain her emotional equilibrium.

My point is that this never could have happened if Elise was being treated by a psychiatrist who was only listening to Prozac, that is, who took his concept of what caused Elise's depression simply from what relieved it and thought that the goal of treatment was to make her symptoms go away and get her functioning again. The fact that medication had produced an eight-year remission in Elise's lifelong depression did not mean that her depression was merely (or even mainly) a chemical imbalance or that the only psychotherapy she needed was five or ten or even fifty sessions per year of cognitive or behavioral or supportive therapy. What she needed was a psychotherapeutic process with a therapist who understood how to work with transference and countertransference. Without that, three vitally important things probably never would have happened. She never would have discovered that her career choice had been fostering a painful repetition of her unhappy relationship with her mother. She might never have discovered, or given herself credit for, her great capacity to love. And she might very well never have found another antidepressant that worked again. Although I can easily believe that the eight-year remission in her chemical imbalance (and the eight years of caring therapeutic relationship with Dr. Q that fostered it) might have been just what Elise needed at that time in her life, I have no doubt whatsoever that it was a great blessing to her when the antidepressant stopped working. However hellish the experience was, Elise needed to become severely depressed again in order to have the opportunity to confront her real emotional problem and resolve the inner conflict of her soul. For Elise, as for Anne and Joe in Chapter 5, falling down was a way of growing up. Her need for a growth-producing depressive crisis was so deep that it was embedded in her neurophysiology—the neurophysiology that stopped responding to antidepressants until she started to get in touch with what she really felt. By the way, I am happy to report that Elise breezed through medical school and now loves her new career as a physician. She does not feel the work as a burden even when she has to be up half the night on call.

Phyllis

Phyllis's story is similar to Elise's in that she got something crucial from psychotherapy that she did not and could not get from medication, even though medication worked extremely well for her. Like Elise, Phyllis was a successful woman who needed to become depressed in order to recognize that there was something wrong in her life that she needed to change. But unlike Elise, Phyllis didn't need intensive psychotherapy or an understanding and working through of the transference to make this change. In fact, it took only two to four sessions per month for less than a year.

Phyllis had worked as a nurse for twenty years. Whether in hospitals or private offices, she had always been a dynamo, doing the work of two ordinary nurses, loved by patients and doctors alike. The problem was that once those doctors learned they could always count on Phyllis, they soon began to take advantage of her willingness to work above and beyond the call of any reasonable duty. When I first met her, Phyllis had been working in a doctor's office, earning a substandard salary with minimal raises for doing a staggering quantity of work—including many exhausting hours of overtime—that most practices would require two nurses to perform. In five years of working in that office, she had never once complained about her work or her salary. She had simply told herself that she should feel grateful to have a job she liked, working for a doctor she thought of as a good man. She finally broke down only after struggling for close to a year with an increasingly severe depression. She had tried valiantly to write off her symptoms—her inability to sleep, her loss of appetite and energy, and the tormenting feeling of agitation in the pit of her stomach—as simply stress. Week after week, she forced herself to keep working until finally she realized that she couldn't go on even one day more. She then called in sick and came to see me.

By that time, Phyllis's distress and agitation were so urgent that it was obvious she needed both an antidepressant and anti-anxiety medication immediately. At the same time, however, it was also fairly obvious that her depression was a healthy response to an unhealthy situation. Given her personality makeup, it was clear that becoming too sick to work was the only way she could allow herself to say "No! I refuse to be taken advantage of anymore!" I commented about this in our very first meeting, even while I was writing out her prescriptions. I asked her whether all the job-related stresses she had just described to me had ever left her feeling mistreated or taken advantage of.

"Not really," she said. "Oh, I may have gotten a little irritated at times, but I never complained. I was raised to believe that I should always put the needs of others before my own, so I guess I've always tended to do more than my share of the work."

"I believe that tendency of yours is the root of your problem," I said. "I suspect that for a long time you have been much more irritated than you realize, even furious, about the demands placed on you at work—about how much you've been expected to do and how little you've gotten in return. But instead of ever saying no or getting angry, I believe you turned all your resentment inward, perhaps without even recognizing it."

I explained that depression usually does involve turning anger against yourself rather than against those you are really angry at but don't feel you have a right to be. "Of course, there is a definite biological aspect to your depression," I added. "You do have a chemical imbalance that needs medication. But even when the medication works and you begin to feel well again, your real problem won't be solved, because medication can't change the psychological causes for your depression. As long as you have this tendency to let yourself be taken advantage of—as long as you feel you don't have the right to stand up for yourself and say no—you will continue to be vulnerable to depression, even with medication. And for that reason, I think it would be a big mistake for you to even think about going back to your current job until we begin to deal with this personality pattern of yours in psychotherapy."

At first Phyllis had strong reservations about my recommendation. She agreed that she needed psychotherapy to work on her inability to say no, and she knew that her husband's income was ample to support their family, but she wasn't sure she *could* say no to going back to work once she began to feel better. For one thing, she would miss the patients, many of whom felt quite dependent on her. For another, she worried about the huge burden of work her absence would be putting on everyone else in the office. (Indeed, she later learned that they did need to hire two nurses to replace her!) But then she began to think about her son's bar mitzvah that was coming up in six months and she realized that it would be too much stress for her to handle all the necessary preparations for that major event and try to go back to work at the same time, even if she did get some relief from medication.

Fortunately, she got great relief from medication. Within three weeks on Zoloft (a serotonin booster similar to Prozac), Phyllis was able to sleep and to smile again and after six weeks felt fully energized and was hard at work preparing for the bar mitzvah. She was also able to use her psychotherapy sessions to get in touch with her deep, never-before-acknowledged resentment about the tremendous burden of obligation she felt—ingrained in her by her upbringing—that she should always think of others before herself. Phyllis discovered that she was genuinely angry, not only about being taken advantage of at work but more generally about the way friends and family had always expected her to be the caretaker as well. She began to say no in a number of personal situations where she would always before have felt obligated to help out. For instance, although she was in charge of the bar mitzvah preparations, she felt proud of herself for being able to delegate some of the responsibilities to other family members. For the five months leading up to the event—which turned out to be a huge success—Phyllis was actually feeling better about herself than she had ever felt before in her life.

It was quite a surprise to me, then, when Phyllis came in for her appointment two weeks after the bar mitzvah and almost immediately burst into tears. She had started to feel depressed again, she reported, with recurring symptoms of insomnia, tearfulness, and an almost constant state of formless anxiety. "I don't know what's happening to me!" she cried. "I was feeling so good and everything was going so well, but now all of a sudden I can't stop crying again."

I told Phyllis there were two possible explanations. Either the antidepressant had stopped working (though we hadn't changed the dosage) or she had become depressed again for emotional reasons that had overridden the antidepressant effect of the Zoloft. Perhaps the need to prepare for the bar mitzvah had been protecting her more than we realized from the pressure to return to work and she was now feeling that old pressure again. Phyllis raised her eyebrows at that comment. She confirmed that the office had called and left two messages on her answering machine recently, asking how she was doing with her medical problems (she had never told them she was depressed) and when she would be ready to come back to work. She admitted that her first reaction had been that if they still wanted her back after all this time, then she really should go back because, after all, she was feeling better and the bar mitzvah was over.

"And it sounds like your very next reaction was to get depressed again!" I put in. Then, hoping to relieve the urgent pressure of her sense of obligation, I added, "To sort out whether this is a medication problem or a psychological issue, I think you should wait at least another two months before considering going back to work. In the meantime, we'll try increasing the dose of Zoloft, and if that doesn't work, we can switch to another antidepressant."

At her next appointment Phyllis said she had felt so relieved when I told her she couldn't go back to work yet that she had begun to feel better almost immediately and had never even bothered to increase her medication. For the next five weeks she felt "better than well" again. But then she suffered a third recurrence of depressive symptoms, this time triggered by a comment from her sister-in-law that it would be a shame to give up such a good job (this in response to Phyllis telling her sister-in-law that she might change jobs, or perhaps switch to part-time private-duty nursing). It took Phyllis almost a week to realize—to feel—how angry she was at her sister-in-law for making this comment. Once she could feel it, however, that anger became crucial to her healing. It reminded her just how much she really did hate her old job and convinced her, once and for all, that she didn't ever want to put up with being treated that way again. She was then able to call the office manager and tell her personally that she definitely wasn't going to be coming back. Immediately her depressive symptoms disappeared once more—again without any change in her medication.

Respect the Symptom: Reprise

Phyllis's story vividly illustrates the value of symptoms as part of the healing process. Her depression was a healthy adaptation of the soul, a solution to the self-destructive tendency (repetition compulsion) of her personality—her need to allow herself to be taken advantage of. Phyllis's depression forced her to find a healthier way of reacting to her unhealthy job situation. It forced her to pay attention to what she really felt, to recognize how much she hated her job and that she had good reasons for hating it. In this context, the dramatic symptom relief she got from Zoloft actually interfered with the healing process. It made Phyllis feel so good that she quickly forgot her anger and fell back into her familiar personality pattern, feeling obligated to ignore any misgivings or selfish needs of her own and go back to work. Fortunately, the healing power of her symptom then reasserted itself and she became depressed again, despite the Zoloft, whenever she began to feel obligated to return to work at her old job. This experience confirms my theory that the adaptive need for a depression can override the biological action of an antidepressant. More generally, it suggests an explanation for the common but poorly understood phenomenon of "Prozac poop-out." When an antidepressant works well for a period of months or years and then inexplicably stops working, perhaps this always means—as it did for Elise and Phyllis—that the swimming-pool effectiveness of the antidepressant is interfering with the soul's need for growth. At the very least, there are many situations where adjusting the chemical balance of the brain may interfere with the proper harmony of body, brain, mind, and spirit. When this happens, the best way to reactivate the process of healing the soul is often to become depressed again.

Am I suggesting that perhaps I shouldn't have used an antidepressant with Phyllis in the first place? Absolutely not. For one thing, Phyllis felt desperate and needed immediate relief. For another, I have no doubt that the Zoloft actually helped her get more out of her psychotherapy. By freeing her from overwhelming pain, it allowed her to pay more attention to what else she was feeling. But this happened only because Phyllis was being treated by someone who believed it was absolutely essential for her to pay attention to what she was feeling! Had Phyllis instead been treated by a psychiatrist who "listened to Zoloft," then the medication could easily have done her far more harm than good. Such a psychiatrist might never have recognized Phyllis's self-destructive personality tendency. Even if he did recognize it, he would have considered it either unrelated to her depression or else the sort of personality pattern (a *forme fruste* of depression) that Zoloft would also take care of. He could easily have taken it for granted that Phyllis should go back to work once she felt better and so, when she became depressed again, would have gone on a wild-goose chase looking for a more effective medication. In his eagerness to relieve the pain of Phyllis's depression, he would not have recognized the adaptive value of that pain, as a warning from her unconscious that to go back to working as she had before would destroy her.

First, Do No Harm

Every medical student learns on his first day in class that the first task of a physician is *to do no harm.* The Hippocratic oath says simply "I will follow that system of regimen which, according to my ability and judgment, I consider for the benefit of my patients, and abstain from whatever is deleterious and mischievous." There's nothing in the oath about relieving suffering, because Hippocrates understood that suffering may be a necessary part of the healing process. Just as it would be harmful to use morphine to relieve a stomach pain without paying attention to its deeper cause in the abdomen, so too it can be harmful to use Prozac or Zoloft or Marplan to relieve the suffering of depression without paying attention to its deeper causes in the soul.

Of course, the individual patient certainly has the right to choose medication and may feel that the benefits far outweigh any such risk of potential harm. This was the argument put forward in a 1993 *Washington Post* article, "The Wizard of Prozac," by writer Tracy Thompson, based on her experience with Prozac:

> I simply feel . . . *normal.* As if I had been driving a car all these years with the parking brake on, and now it is off. I feel as if the real me has returned—perhaps all the way from childhood, where she lived before The Beast arrived. Sometimes I sense that I have lost something. An intensity of feeling, maybe—a way of noticing the world with wonder. It is a perspective I now find hard to summon. Those instants are Kodachromed in my mind, like one moment from that mockingbird year when I saw a poplar tree in the rain, its yellow leaves falling on the wet pavement, and glimpsed an indescribable sad beauty. I don't have those moments much anymore; they have mostly all gone, along with most of those moments of lacerating despair. I have greedily swapped them for ordinary life. That may sound dull, but I tell you it is sweet. It is not caviar I crave, but clean sheets and hot soup.

Certainly for patients like Thompson, who have been racked by the torments of severe depression for years, the relief that comes with antidepressant medicine can be a great blessing. But as we saw with Elise and Phyllis, there may be a hidden cost to this kind of relief. If the depression, painful as it may be, has a vital adaptive purpose in the patient's life, then there is a considerable risk involved in simply trying to eliminate it. Even for patients like Thompson, who feel so dramatically better on medication that they can't imagine how it could be a problem, it is worth considering that depression, or any other symptom, may be like the canary in the coal mine that warns the miners of dangerous fumes. Imagine what would happen if, when the canary became sick, we gave it a pill that could keep it alive and singing (and keep the minds of the miners at ease) even in the presence of toxic gas.

Of course there are many patients who would disagree with Thompson's conclusion that relief from suffering is worth the loss of feeling that often comes with Prozac and other medications. I was made vividly aware of this by a woman I saw in consultation who wanted to begin treatment because she could feel an episode of depression coming on. She had suffered a fairly severe depression one year previously, she said, and had been treated at that time with Prozac.

"So were you thinking you wanted to go back on the Prozac then?" I asked her. "Did it work well for you?"

"Oh yeah!" she replied, with a slight edge to her voice. "Prozac was great. While I was taking it I couldn't feel a thing. No pain, no grief, not even sadness. No emotions at all. . . . That's why I stopped taking it. I was afraid I could get addicted to that. So no, I guess I'll pass on the Prozac this time."

A few months later, I had a similar experience with a psychoanalytic patient, Denise, who suffered from upsetting, sometimes protracted, bouts of negativistic moodiness. Denise told me about a friend of hers who had just recently started taking Prozac and now seemed dramatically happier and much easier to be with. She complained to me that three weeks of Prozac had done for her friend what four years of analysis had failed to do for her. Although I felt this personally and took it as an important transference reproach that I had failed her, Denise denied that she felt any anger toward me or intended any reproach. She had gotten a lot out of analysis in terms of improved relationships, she insisted, but the one thing it had never seemed to help her with was these bouts of negativistic moodiness. She was extremely skeptical of my view that her negativism represented an unconscious anger at me or at any other person. She suspected rather that it was something physiological and impersonal—the result of a hormonal or chemical imbalance—that would be impervious to anything except medication. She wanted to try Prozac.

I explained briefly that I think of all depression as having both a physiological and a psychological dimension, and that for purposes of the psychotherapeutic process the main question was, supposing that we could take the edge off her moodiness with an antidepressant, whether this would help or hinder her in getting in touch with whatever feelings might underlie the moodiness. I told her that in my experience medication seemed to have different effects on different patients. For one patient it seemed to make it easier to get in touch with feelings; for another, it seemed to interfere. Although I hadn't thought that Denise needed medication, I had no objection to trying it, with the proviso that we both needed to pay attention to whether it was helping or hindering her in her effort to become more aware of her feelings. Denise agreed, and so I prescribed Prozac for her. The result was interesting. Her negativism quickly faded and for the next four months she was in a consistently good mood. She did not feel transformed, however, nor did she experience anything different about this good mood compared with other good moods. It was just that this one seemed to be lasting much longer than usual. Neither she nor I detected any clear signs that the medication was interfering with her ability to identify and describe what she was feeling. However, she wasn't feeling anything that would ordinarily make a person want to be in psychoanalysis. Then one day she came in and announced that she was going to stop taking Prozac.

"I went to see a movie last night," she said. "*The Joy Luck Club*. I brought a box of Kleenex along because several friends told me what a tearjerker it was, and you know I always cry a lot when I go to the movies. Actually, I guess you wouldn't know that, since I never cry when I'm in here with you. But anyway, I didn't cry a single tear last night. I couldn't feel even a hint of an impulse to cry. Oh, I knew very well exactly where I would have cried ordinarily, but I couldn't seem to access that place where the tears come from. I think it must be the Prozac."

I trust that most readers will understand intuitively why Denise chose to stop taking Prozac. After two weeks without it, she noticed herself feeling irritable and felt a great sense of relief at being herself once again. Interestingly, though, it had never occurred to her that she wasn't feeling herself during the previous four months. Consider the implications. Prozac had effectively eliminated Denise's painful symptom of negativistic moodiness. Indeed, it had apparently done everything for her that Peter Kramer had said it would—transforming her personality and making her feel better than well.

But there was a price to pay for this transformation. Prozac had also impaired Denise's capacity to feel emotion.

So Is It Transformation or Suppression?

Prozac had been on the market for at least five years before psychiatrists began to recognize just how frequently—it has been estimated for as many as 90 percent of patients—it interferes with sexual feeling and/or functioning. Recognizing this, it may be instructive to ask whether Prozac is really an antidepressant with sexual side effects or should more properly be considered a sexual suppressant with antidepressant side effects. Either way, a simple psychological explanation for the efficacy of Prozac clearly presents itself: by suppressing the sexual drive, Prozac diminishes the urgency of inner conflict (lessening pressure from the sexual fantasy that energizes the repetition compulsion), hence diminishing anxiety, hence alleviating the wide variety of symptoms to which anxiety gives rise. (Remember that symptom formation is an unconscious mechanism for relieving anxiety.) Further, the kind of experience Denise had with Prozac suggests that it may produce a much more general suppression of affect and emotion, one not limited to sexuality. This is not a widely reported phenomenon. It is barely hinted at in *Listening to Prozac* (which says very little about the sexual side effects, either). Kramer does refer briefly to a loss of sensitivity that he has observed with Prozac—a "slight blandness apparent in some cheerful, formerly sensitive patients" (p. 104)—but he concludes that this loss is more apparent than real because these patients had been much too sensitive to begin with. It may be that the more extreme instances of emotional anesthesia like those I just described are relatively rare, but I suspect that if we started to look for it, we would discover that Prozac and many other psychiatric medications always produce some generalized suppression of affect. This would then suggest a more general psychological explanation for how Prozac works. Acting on the primarily biological level of the *It*–repetition compulsion to diminish the pressure of any disturbing unconscious emotion, Prozac changes the balance of inner conflict within the soul. It makes it easier for the *I* to maintain its defenses to keep the disturbing emotions from becoming conscious, thus reducing anxiety and promoting a sense of autonomy and self-esteem.

Psychiatry Is Losing Its Mind

But if this suppression of emotion is so common, we might ask, why hasn't it ever been noticed, reported, and discussed in the scientific literature? For the Medical Model, the answer is simple. Emotional suppression due to medication hasn't been noticed or discussed because Medical Model psychiatrists (like everyone else) pay attention only to what has meaning for them. They notice symptoms and side effects because these have meaning in terms of their biological model of the mind. But they do not notice the qualities of a patient's emotional experience because the Medical Model has no theory of the mind or soul according to which these qualities could be considered meaningful. This is what Peter Kramer was alluding when he wrote, "I had caught myself assuming that a patient's anxiety was meaningless." If you can think of emotions only as secondary by-products of brain events that are themselves meaningless, then the emotions must be meaningless, too. It is typical of this materialist mind-set that the reason psychiatrists finally got around to noticing the sexual side effects of Prozac was not that they considered their patients' sexual feelings relevant to their illnesses and therefore worth asking about. Rather, it was that the patients started refusing to take their medicine and the psychiatrists recognized *that* as meaningful.

But what about the Psychotherapeutic Model, which understands symptoms as disguised expressions of repressed emotions? Through this lens, emotions are clearly viewed as meaningful, so why haven't we Psychotherapeutic Model psychiatrists noticed and reported the kind of affective suppression I have been describing in our patients taking Prozac? The answer here is more complicated. First of all, we may not have reported it but we have noticed it.[4] I have talked about the phenomenon, as I became aware of it, to many colleagues who, once hearing it labeled, could easily relate many similar observations from their own practices. But these observations are not so easy to make as one might think. Even knowing about the possibility of affective suppression, for instance, I still managed not to recognize it when it occurred in Denise, and that was over four months of meeting with her four times a week. I only became aware of it when she told me about it. And that's not particularly surprising. As a therapist, I become aware of what my patients are feeling either because they are showing (and/or describing) it in a way that I can understand empathically, or because they are unconsciously evoking a countertransference emotion in me, or because they are manifesting anxiety—which then alerts me to the fact that there is an emotion threatening to become conscious in them. If the level of emotion is muted by medication, it will be much less likely to show, to evoke countertransference, or to produce anxiety.

But there is another, more disturbing reason why Psychotherapeutic Model psychiatrists have failed to report the phenomenon of affective suppression, even when we have noticed it. The unhappy truth is that there are very few of us left who are wholeheartedly committed to the Psychotherapeutic Model. Most dynamic psychotherapists, and even most psychoanalysts, have been so mesmerized by the claims of Big Science that we have in bits and pieces abandoned our model of the mind, especially in those situations where the mind has been put on medication. We, too, have begun to listen to Prozac instead of listening to the soul. So we have not thought very clearly about what medication actually does to the mind, or what it means that it can do such things. In fact, most of us have simply borrowed the Medical Model's unproven assumption that psychiatric medications correct a chemical imbalance, without ever questioning or trying to integrate this idea within our own theory of inner conflict. I realize that some of my friends and colleagues may be offended by this criticism, so let me explain more specifically what I mean. Here's what we should, but typically don't, say to ourselves about the effects of medication:

> *I have a trusty psychological model of the mind in conflict, which I have excellent reason to believe is valid for all people in all circumstances. I am now confronted with this interesting phenomenon of psychoactive medications producing dramatic changes in mental and emotional experience. Clearly I need to work out how these changes can happen, and I need to work it out in terms of the trusty psychological model which I know to be valid.*

Instead, here's what we typically do say to ourselves:

> *Omigod! The psychopharmacological revolution is upon us. Medication produces dramatic changes in the mind—the mind that I have always thought of in terms of my once trusty model of psychological conflict. All the scientists seem to agree that the power of medication to alleviate psychiatric symptoms and alter mental events generally means that mental illness and the mind itself must really be bio-*

logical in nature. They say that my psychological model of inner conflict no longer applies. They must be correct, because they do real laboratory and statistical placebo-controlled, scientific research! I guess I'll have to change my model to accommodate this new knowledge, and will henceforth have to say that inner conflict exists only in psychiatric conditions that don't respond to medication (the number of which seems to be shrinking like an endangered species).

In these circumstances, with a Medical Model that denies the very existence of the mind, and a Psychotherapeutic Model that accommodates that denial by abandoning or qualifying its hard-won understanding of the mind in conflict, it is no exaggeration to say that psychiatry is in danger of losing its mind altogether.

A Prescription for Psychiatry

Let me state clearly what I believe should be the proper perspective for psychiatry: *Psychiatric illnesses are part of the human condition, and inner conflict is central to every one of them, whether they respond to medication or not, whether they involve a chemical imbalance or not.* I do not know whether affective suppression is the only, or even the primary, mechanism by which Prozac improves self-esteem, or by which Thorazine relieves anxiety. But whatever the neurophysiological mechanism involved, I am quite sure that the only way any medication can affect mental illness is by changing the brain's biology in a way that shifts the balance of inner conflict. In other words, it is inner conflict, not chemical imbalance, that causes symptoms and anxiety and that disrupts self-esteem, so that any effect medication may have on symptoms, anxiety, and self-esteem can operate only through its effect on inner conflict.

If this is so, then it follows that an understanding of inner conflict is an absolute practical necessity not just for psychotherapists but for any psychiatrist who prescribes medication! Without an understanding of their particular inner conflicts, for instance, no psychiatrist could prescribe rationally for patients like Elise and Phyllis. Without an understanding of inner conflict generally, all psychiatrists will become merely "symptom chasers," treating every symptom and painful emotion as a glitch in a different neurotransmitter system and medicating it accordingly, with no overarching theory to explain how all symptoms and emotions are related within the organization of an individual personality. Even worse, they will view individual personality itself—at least the sort of quirky, not-quite-ready-for-prime-time personality that most of us have—as being just like a symptom, a *forme fruste* of a full-blown psychiatric disorder that can easily be made better than well simply by taking a pill.

Personality, Inner Conflict, and Human Nature

This brings us to the most important, and potentially most disturbing, question raised by Peter Kramer in *Listening to Prozac*. What does it tell us about human nature that personality can (apparently) be transformed overnight by Prozac? Kramer's answer, and the answer of the Medical Model generally, is a simplistic biological theory that equates "the self"—*who I am*—with my personality: a collection of neurological dispositions and glitches *(formes frustes)* that is entirely a product of neurotransmitter processes in my brain and so can be transformed with medication (making me a "new person") as easily as a symptom can be relieved.

To summarize Kramer's theory briefly: Personality is a collection of habitual behavioral tendencies. Those tendencies that belong to *temperament* are biologically determined, either genetically or through the neurochemical impact of trauma. Those tendencies that belong to *character* can be thought of—or at least used to be—in terms of inner conflict, as psychological "defense mechanisms." Under the influence of Freudian theory, says Kramer, we used to think of personality as about 80 percent character and 20 percent temperament. But now, the power of Prozac to transform personality suggests that most of what we once thought was character (i.e., psychological) must really be temperament (i.e., biological). In fact, Kramer cites a rapidly growing mass of scientific evidence (concerning behavioral responses of laboratory animals to "psychosocial stressors," and concerning the effectiveness of drugs in treating human personality disorders) that, to him, suggests there is probably no such thing as character in the Freudian sense at all. Everything we used to think of as character, he says, will probably turn out to be either a genetically hardwired trait or a secondary reaction of the brain to traumatic experience. Either way, Kramer predicts, the Freudian concept of inner conflict will no longer be necessary because personality (as well as symptoms) will be completely explainable (and adjustable) in neurochemical terms.

The problem with Kramer's theory, of course, is that it is based entirely on a false dichotomy between temperament and character. In fact, the categories of temperament and character refer to different levels of experience. Temperament is personality as observed through biological lenses. Character is personality as observed through psychological lenses. Character and temperament are not either–or personality contents that "add up" to a whole personality. Rather, they are complementary levels of personality organization—two mutually exclusive but equally valid ways of explaining any personality trait.

Kramer's view of personality can thus actually be subsumed within Freud's. Temperament would consist of the biological (affective) dispositions of the *It*. Character would consist of the psychological (emotional) dispositions of the *I*, reflecting (and attempting to resolve) inner conflict between the Flesh and the Spirit, that is, between the brain-encoded impulses of the *It*–repetition compulsion–superego–personality and the moral direction (feelings, ideals, values) of the *I that stands above*. The fact that this dualistic perspective is required by Bohr's principle of complementarity is enough by itself to disprove Kramer's theory. Personality can never be explained completely in neurochemical terms, because a complete explanation must include both the analytic (neurochemical) and the synthetic (psychological) perspectives. In other words, from the perspective of complementarity human nature is an irreducible dualism of character *and* temperament. As a human being, I am a self who is more than the sum of my personality traits, a soul who is more than my brain, a psychological *I* who includes a biological *It* but also includes the irreducibly spiritual consciousness of an *I that stands above*—the element of wholeness that defines what is uniquely human in human nature.

Is That a Personality Transformation or Are You Just Glad to See Me?

Kramer's reductionistic biological theory typifies the alarming consequences that have ensued from the Medical Model's abandoning its understanding of inner conflict. Kramer's vision of the future for psychiatry—a future of biologically engineered "designer personalities"—could easily have been taken out of *Brave New World.* He writes, for instance, about Prozac "changing . . . the infrastructure of personality" to that of "someone born with a different genome and exposed to a more benign world in childhood" (p. 177). He foresees new drugs aimed at "recasting the foundations of normal variants in personality . . . to modify inborn predisposition" (p. 184), and he predicts that "as we have access to yet more specific drugs our accuracy in targeting individual traits will improve" (p. 249).

Although, as I discussed above, Kramer does express misgivings about the "unnaturalness" of this sort of personality manipulation, in the end he concludes that all such misgivings are outweighed by the potential therapeutic benefits. He is particularly swayed by the incredible transformations of personality he has seen in certain chronically unhappy, dysfunctional patients who, on Prozac, felt suddenly and dramatically better about themselves, and seemed able to function in ways they had never before been capable of:

> We think of self-image as something accreted over time, acquired through living, subject mostly to incremental change. But in my practice I have seen case after case in which self-image changes overnight. . . . The new valuation of self seems to come from nowhere. . . . [M]edication works like a switch. When the patient is taking medication self-esteem is high; when medication is interrupted, self-esteem is absent. There is nothing incremental about this change. The switch flips, and the whole package of self-valuation changes; beliefs about the self, assessment of personal history, sense of place in the world. (pp. 208–9)

As the tone of this and other similar passages in *Listening to Prozac* suggests, it was the great enthusiasm engendered (in doctor as well as patient) by these dramatic, seemingly miraculous shifts in mood and self-esteem that moved Kramer to believe his patients had undergone a transformation—the same sort of transformation, he tells us, that happens in a religious conversion experience:

> Prozac seemed to give social confidence to the habitually timid, to make the sensitive brash, to lend the introvert the social skills of a salesman. Prozac was transformative for patients in the way an inspirational minister or high-pressure group therapy can be—it made them want to talk about their experience. (p. xv)

The problem with Kramer's account here—and with his understanding of his patients' experience generally—is that he never looks below the surface. He simply takes for granted that the appearance is the reality: that because a patient's personality—including basic mood, self-image, self-esteem and habitual reactions to people—*seems* so dramatically different on Prozac, it must mean that the Prozac has actually transformed their personality.

To illustrate just how misleading a picture this is of what Prozac does to personality, recall the story of Phyllis. When Zoloft made Phyllis feel better than well, not only did it fail to transform her personality, it actually reactivated the oldest, most ingrained self-destructive element of her personality—her need to take care of others at her own expense.[5] As for the many cases Kramer reports where personality does seem to change overnight, it may be instructive to follow Kramer's own logic and compare these cases with the kind of overnight personality transformations produced by religious conversion experiences or by intense weekend-retreat/encounter-group experiences like est and Lifespring. There is no doubt that such "transformations" do occur, that they work just as much "like a switch" as those produced by Prozac, and that they produce personality changes that are equally dramatic. But if you have ever had such an experience yourself or know someone who has, then you probably also know that such transformations are generally unstable. They must be maintained by ongoing support from the group and can only last as long as the convert continues to believe in the group. In the same way, a Prozac-induced transformation must be maintained by ongoing medication and only lasts as long as the medication continues to work.

Yet I also know people who I would say have had genuine, lasting personality transformations that began suddenly and dramatically with a mystical experience (which was self-perpetuating because it inspired them to pursue an ongoing inward journey–psychotherapeutic process). However permanent or impermanent such conversion experiences may be, the fact that any such spiritually induced transformations occur at all is enough by itself to refute Kramer's argument that who we are must be biologically determined because our personalities can be transformed overnight by Prozac. After all, the same logic leads just as convincingly to the opposite conclusion: Who we are must be spiritual because it can be instantaneously transformed by a mystical experience! In fact, both conclusions make sense and both are equally true. We are biological and at the same time spiritual beings, in a perpetual condition of inner conflict. Both sides of the conflict contribute to the formation of personality, and both sides must be involved in a genuine transformation of personality as well.

There Are Two Sides to Every Personality

I should hasten to add that I am not trying to endorse religious conversion as an alternative to Prozac. I am as skeptical of the misuses of the one as of the other. Rather, what I am saying is that if we are going to be drawing conclusions about human nature based on what causes personality change, then we need to take seriously whatever causes personality change, whether it happens to fit with our philosophy or not. With this in mind, I would like to suggest that dramatic changes in personality can actually be produced in three different ways: through the action of body–brain over mind, as typified by Prozac; through the action of spirit over mind, as typified by a religious conversion experience; and through the dialectical integration of body–brain, mind, and spirit as it occurs in the psychotherapeutic process. Of these three, I believe the only one that reliably produces genuine, deep, and lasting personality change is the psychotherapeutic process.

I certainly agree with Peter Kramer that Prozac can produce a dramatic switch in mood, self-esteem, and overall sense of well-being and that this switch involves a change from negative to positive in some basic "visceral sense of self-worth." But I don't find this kind of change nearly as remarkable as Kramer does. On the contrary, I consider it quite commonplace. What I find much more significant is Kramer's observation that the switch is *reversible*. In fact, I believe people experience such reversible switches in self-esteem all the time, whether they are taking medication or not. I know for myself that there are many things besides Prozac that can produce overnight reversible changes in my "visceral sense of self-worth." Just hearing my daughter sing, for instance, can lift my spirits for a week, while hearing myself sing can easily have the opposite effect. At the office, there are days when all my patients seem to be making significant progress and I begin to feel like a miracle worker, but then there are other days (sometimes the very next day!) when all my patients seem stuck and I begin to feel stupid, uncreative, and somewhere south of competent. In my writing, I can predict that if I finish this chapter today I will feel much better about myself tomorrow, but if I don't finish it, I will probably wake up with a slightly depressive or discouraged sense of myself and the world.

I believe that such everyday, psychologically induced switches in mood and self-esteem are universal, that they happen at the same unconscious reflexive level of temperament as a Prozac-induced switch and have pretty much the same degree of reversibility once the stimulus that caused the switch is removed or changes. They are comparable to the sudden feeling of euphoria that sports fans experience when their team wins a come-from-behind victory in an important game. This reaction is a prototypical example of a quick fix; it is a reversible switch in mood and self-esteem—a switch from feeling like a loser to feeling like a winner—that can be maintained only through the continued operation of external forces. The patient has to keep taking the medication. The religious convert has to maintain his connection with church or guru. The sports fan has to hope that his team keeps winning.

My point, again, is that the kind of personality change produced by Prozac is not a genuine transformation. It is not a "stable and continuous" change from one personality type (temperament) into another, but rather an unstable and discontinuous shift between two brain-encoded "states of mind" (and mood) within an untransformed but inherently dualistic personality.

There is a general truth about human nature here that is very much worth emphasizing: *every person has two basic but opposing patterns of self-experience.* Clinically, I have never met a single patient, whether on medication or not, who didn't over time show some pattern of alternating between two distinct personality modes, one positive and self-assertive, the other negativistic with low self-esteem. Interestingly enough, however, the patients themselves often don't recognize this pattern. People who live predominantly in a mode of depressiveness, insecurity, irritability, anxiety, pessimism, or negativity tend to think of themselves as always feeling bad. They forget that occasionally they feel just fine, even happy, for brief periods of time. For instance, it's not at all uncommon for me to have to say to a patient, "Wait a minute, you're talking as if you've been depressed for weeks without interruption. But I was with you just Tuesday, and you were in a really good mood. What happened? When did your mood switch?" Sometimes the patient simply can't remember that he felt better on Tuesday. Or he might say something like "Oh yeah, I had forgotten. Tuesday wasn't too bad. But, so what? I may seem to be having a good day once in a while, but it's not the real me." When such patients do have good days—when they feel positive, confident, calm, assertive, loving—they can't fully enjoy the experience because they know it won't last, and when they then shift back into their more familiar state of negativity they quickly forget that they ever felt good. What this means is that if they happen to be seeing a psychiatrist who doesn't take the time to know them very well—who sees them infrequently and only briefly or who simply isn't paying attention to the nuances of their inner experience—then neither the patient nor the psychiatrist is likely ever to notice this fundamental dualism within their personality. If the patient then takes Prozac and suddenly begins to feel positive most of the time and negative only transiently, he will almost certainly experience the change not as a reversal from mostly bad to mostly good, but as a transformation from all bad to all good.

Psychoanalysts call this black-and-white alternation between incompatible, mutually exclusive mood states *splitting*. It is a particularly dramatic feature of certain kinds of mental illness, but in a milder form it is a universal pattern of fluctuating self-esteem that should be noticeable to anyone who takes the time to reflect on his or her own experience. The pattern begins in earliest infancy, when every baby has two basic emotional modes—*ego states* as psychoanalysts like to call them—crying and smiling.[6] The infant's globally happy, smiling state is the precursor to the adult's more organized state of positive mood and self-esteem. We might think of this as a "good self–good world" state, in which it feels as if "I'm OK. You're OK," and "God's in His heaven, all's right with the world." The infant's globally painful, crying state, in contrast, is the precursor to the adult's more organized state of low self-esteem—a "bad self–bad world" (or "pained self–painful world") state in which it feels, as my aunt Rosie used to put it, as if, "Nobody loves me, everybody hates me. I'm gonna go out and eat worms!" Just as every infant has a "split personality" that allows it to be desperately crying one minute and happily cooing the next, so every adult experiences the same kind of blackor-white alternations of ego state, only in a less dramatic form. Depending on the balance of inner conflict within the soul, we all fluctuate between a "Thanatos-dominated personality" and an "Eros-dominated personality"—a bad self–bad world ego state and a good self–good world ego state.

It is particularly striking that Kramer doesn't recognize this universal dualism of mood and self-esteem in his patients. Instead, he believes that Prozac transforms people from a monolithic condition of low or absent self-esteem to a monolithic condition of positive self-esteem. When his patients are in a state of low self-esteem, he attributes this to their biologically "disordered" personalities. When they have high self-esteem, he attributes this to their transformed Prozac-personalities. Either way he assumes that people have only one basic self-esteem state, and that they are in that state—either good or bad—"on a stable and continuous basis."[7] Not so. In fact, there are two basic states of self-esteem in every personality and we inevitably switch back and forth between them, depending on our degree of inner conflict, whether we are taking medication or not. The fact that Kramer doesn't recognize this suggests that he never really got to know the inner lives of the patients whose so-called personality transformations he chronicles. In fact, he saw many of them only briefly, or only for medication management.[8] And even for the ones he saw regularly in long-term psychotherapy, his account of their treatment suggests that he was focused much more on diagnosing and relieving their symptoms and modifying their dysfunctional behavior patterns than he was on getting to know the subtle nuances of their private experience of themselves in an open-ended psychotherapeutic process.

Had he been more receptive to his patients instead of listening to Prozac, Kramer might have noticed that there are two sides to every personality. We all have a bad self–bad world mode of experiencing in which we are dominated by inner conflict and all our new toys seem broken, but we also have a good self–good world mode of experiencing in which we can sense the healing power of nature within us and we know that there really is a pony under all that horseshit.

The Quick Switch Versus the Psychotherapeutic Process

From this perspective, it appears that Prozac does not "transform" us. It simply makes it easier for us to access our basic positive feeling about ourselves and the world for more of the time. The dramatic overnight improvement in self-image and self-esteem produced by Prozac is merely a switch between alternative dispositions that are neurologically encoded in every personality. Not only Prozac but anything that diminishes inner conflict can trigger such a switch. The trigger can be a disinhibiting process like alcohol intoxication, romantic infatuation, the varieties of sudden inspiration, or the emotional activation of transference. Or it can be an inhibiting process, like the neurochemical suppression of affect produced by medication or like the superego prohibition (repression) of affect reinforced by some forms of religious conversion experience.

In either case, the quick switch from bad self–bad world to good self–good world is inherently unstable. In fact, when it is produced by disinhibition, the switch is self-reversing. It liberates the emotional impulses of the repetition compulsion, permitting us to enact our unconscious scenario without a sense of inner conflict, but only until this puts us into conflict with other people, which then throws us back into the same bad self–bad world state of mind we started from. When the switch is produced by inhibition/suppression of emotional impulses, then the good self–good world state of mind cannot sustain itself but must be continually reinforced, whether through pharmacological maintenance or through superego support from an outside group. Any stimulus that arouses unconscious emotion can then reaggravate inner conflict, disrupting the unstable balance and triggering a switch back, temporarily at least, into the bad self–bad world state of mind.

As for the long term, the repetition compulsion cannot be suppressed indefinitely. In using medications with patients like Elise and Phyllis over many years, I have observed that any drug-dependent "makeover" of basic mood and self-esteem will sooner or later tend to reverse itself, and the underlying conflict encoded in the repetition compulsion will tend to reassert itself—either in a recurrence of old symptoms or the emergence of new ones—*even while the patient is still taking the medication.* (Similarly, as any Catholic schoolboy knows, the good self–good world feeling that comes with confession (superego support) inevitably gives way sooner or later to the repetitive (sinful) compulsions of the Flesh and the need for further confession.) This sort of reversible switch that happens in a pharmacologic (or confessional) makeover is very different indeed from the kind of change produced by the psychotherapeutic process, which is irreversible—not a switch between one reflexive disposition of the brain and another but a true transformation of the unconscious reflexes of the repetition compulsion into the conscious motives and intentions of the *I.*

The importance of this difference cannot be overestimated. In one case there is a dramatic but reversible black-to-white change, produced by a temporary suppression of inner conflict which *happens to us* at the unconscious level of neurological reflex. In the other there is a more gradual, incremental and irreversible change, achieved by a resolution of inner conflict that *we bring about* in ourselves through the conscious activity of inward attention. In both cases, we gain greater access to the good self–good world side of our personalities, but in one case the good feeling we experience from this change is superficial and unstable while in the other it is deep and lasting.

The difference is in what happens to the bad self–bad world side of our personalities. The problem with the makeover–conversion–confessional experience is that the good self–good world state is produced by suppression of the bad self–bad world energy (the anxiety-provoking part) of the repetition compulsion. *But this energy is absolutely essential to a fulfilling life.* The drivenness of the repetition compulsion, as unsettling and anxiety-provoking as it may be, is also central to who we are and to what makes us tick. A good self–good world state of mind that is purchased at the cost of suppressing the repetition compulsion therefore will be superficial at best—lacking the vitality that comes from being connected to the deepest energies of the body. Furthermore, the good feeling so produced will be inherently unstable, like Miranda's happiness at the beginning of the *Tempest*: a euphoric but shallow swimming-pool contentment, dependent on a protective but rigid and controlling Prospero (the inhibiting effect of Prozac, or of the superego) always working overtime to keep Caliban at bay.

The advantage of the psychotherapeutic process is that we achieve the good self–good world state not through an unconscious switch but through conscious self-reflective attention to the experience of anxiety; not by disowning and projecting our bad self–bad world emotions but by recognizing and claiming responsibility for them as part of ourselves. The result is that, instead of suppressing and cutting ourselves off from the vital unconscious energy of the repetition compulsion we integrate and use this energy in the service of becoming who we really are. Instead of restricting consciousness and with it the boundaries of the world in which the self can feel its goodness, we expand consciousness and with it the boundaries of the good self *and* the good world. This is not to say that the bad self–bad world reflexes of the repetition compulsion no longer exist, of course. As illustrated by the way I had to reanalyze and reintegrate my own repetition compulsion in order to complete this chapter, the energy of the repetition compulsion continues to fuel our motivation and provoke new editions of old conflicts as we meet fresh challenges in the course of life. An integration that has been achieved at one level will need to be worked through again and deepened at each succeeding level, through a renewed activity of inward attention, prompted by new experiences of anxiety. But the net result is that the happiness achieved through a psychotherapeutic process will be like Prospero's happiness at the end of *The Tempest*—the joyful acceptance of both Miranda and Caliban as essential elements of a fully human nature.

18. Repetition, Reflection, and the Search for Meaning

More and more, we are all becoming aware that our lives are being lived for us by influences that, however numerous they appear, are in fact only so many reflections of one kind of movement in the life of man, a movement toward externals, toward needs and gratifications that, however justified in their own right, become destructive when they pretend to represent the whole meaning of human life.

—Jacob Needleman, *The Way of the Physician*

The world is too much with us; late and soon,
Getting and spending, we lay waste our powers.

—William Wordsworth

Author's Message

Throughout this book, I have tried to convey a sense of the process of healing the soul—the inward journey of self-discovery and self-actualization—as I have experienced it in the psychotherapeutic process. My hope in doing so was to help individual readers to gain a greater appreciation of their own personal quest, especially of the ways in which their symptoms and other kinds of falling down are an integral part of the healing process. That is what I do for a living: as a psychotherapist, I work with individuals, helping them "in their becoming." But I probably would never have thought to write a book about this if my work with individuals was not being threatened by larger cultural forces: the popular craze for psychiatric drugs, the greed of the managed care industry, and a deeper problem of which these are merely symptoms—the dehumanizing materialism that pervades our culture at every level.

We are so consumed by the pursuit of physical appearances, material possessions, creature comforts, and addictive pleasures that we have lost touch with the deeper needs and values of the soul. We then rationalize the emptiness of our materialistic values by invoking another kind of materialism—that of positivistic science, which gives credence only to what can be seen and measured and which believes that only the physical is real. Any anxiety we might feel about the lack of meaning in our lives we can then dismiss as a chemical imbalance, transformable into a state of contented normalcy simply by taking a pill.

The dehumanizing influence of this shallow scientific worldview reinforces a dehumanizing impulse that is already present in human nature. We find it easy to ignore the inner voice of the soul in our pursuit of external tokens of happiness—not only because we are seduced by our culture's materialistic values but also because we are driven from within by our own materialistic passions and by our addictive need for quick, painless fixes for anything disturbing in our lives.

I have written this book in the strong belief that all of us—not just psychiatric patients—have a deep spiritual need for healing the soul, *a need that cannot be satisfied with a quick pharmacologic fix.* But unless we make a special point of listening to the soul, it becomes all too easy to ignore this vital need, and with it any sense of a larger meaning and purpose in our lives. The problem is, we are all tempted to do exactly that! We all fear consciousness—the knowledge of good and evil within ourselves—and so we would prefer to deny or dismiss the inner voice that calls us to the quest and content ourselves with the swimming-pool comforts of the quick fix.

The Cultural Problem

As a result, the tendency to short-circuit our higher consciousness and awareness of our deepest values in the shortsighted pursuit of the quick fix has become the dominating trend of modern life in the Age of the Brain. The quick fix *is* our prevailing cultural value, and we can see it operating at every level of society: from politicians who don't look beyond winning the next election, to CEOs who can't see beyond the next quarterly report, to news media clambering after sound bites and Nielsen ratings, to scientists doing only short-term, high-profile research (because that's what the businesspeople and politicians will fund and the media will publicize), to doctors who defer to the values of politicians, businesspeople, media, and scientists, and lose track of their inner calling.

In such a world, it is hardly surprising that addiction—the compulsive pursuit of quick fixes—has rapidly become our most pervasive societal problem. We are addicted to substances—drugs (both legal and illegal), alcohol, cigarettes, food. We are addicted to people—rock musicians, sports heroes, movie stars, TV evangelists, pop gurus, psychics, New Age healers, talk-show hosts. And we are addicted to activities—gambling, collecting, pornography, investing, shopping, dieting, exercising, spectator sports, video games, chat rooms, the World Wide Web. Some of us are even addicted to reading self-help books with inspirational titles. In every area of our lives, it seems, we are looking for external fixes and saviors to rescue (i.e., distract) us from the painful awareness of inner conflict—to give us a rush, a quick switch from feeling like a loser to feeling like a winner.

Unfortunately, the fact that our society and cultural values support and reinforce our addictions encourages us to rationalize the quick fix as "the American way" rather than to recognize it as an uneasy attempt to hide from our own higher values and deeper desires. One of the central lessons of dynamic psychotherapy is that people are always embarrassed and uneasy about their own deepest desires, and develop powerful mechanisms for remaining unaware of, and evading responsibility for, those desires. The pursuit of a quick fix, often manifesting itself as addictive behavior, is one of the most popular of these mechanisms, aptly captured in the well-known bumper-sticker slogan "The one who dies with the most toys wins!" The addictive pleasure never actually satisfies the deeper desire, but the endless pursuit of the next "toy" or "fix" serves to keep that deeper, more unsettling desire out of awareness. In this sense, the problem of addiction is a symptom of an underlying sickness in our society: a sickness of the soul, in which we are living on the surface, telling ourselves stories that somebody else has written about what we should be living for because we are afraid to listen to the sound of our own inner voice.

Does That Sound Too Preachy?

To those who may feel that I am being moralistic and judgmental here, I admit to making a moral judgment: that our current quick-fix culture is dehumanizing, destructive, and delusional. (We all know, after all, that the one who dies with the most toys *doesn't* win.) But I do not believe that making moral judgments is something we either can or should avoid. Having moral values and ideals—and making judgments based on them—is as intrinsic to human nature as breathing. Consciously or unconsciously, we are always making choices between the values of the swimming pool and the values of the quest, and every time we do that we are making an implicit moral judgment: falling down is bad or falling down is good.

I believe that our choice between two models of psychiatry is really a choice between two competing sets of moral values that will ultimately determine the kind of society we live in. One is the Psychotherapeutic Model's ideal of healing the soul with its values of self-awareness, autonomy, personal growth, an I–Thou spirit of love, respect, and compassion for others, and an acceptance of moral responsibility for our own egoistic impulses and emotions. The other is the Medical Model's ideal of the quick fix, with its swimming-pool values of stability and conformity, and an I–It orientation toward material success and other superficial addictive pleasures.

Psychiatry at the Center of Our Cultural Crisis: The Case of Tony Soprano

This choice is the underlying theme of the recent television smash hit *The Sopranos*, which—judging from its immense popularity and the extravagant critical acclaim it has inspired—seems to have struck a deeply resonant chord in our cultural consciousness. The hero, Mafia boss Tony Soprano, is a modern American Everyman, suffering from a modern American problem. He needs Prozac! The plot revolves around Tony's symptoms of anxiety and depression, and the fact that he has to see a psychiatrist. Every episode poses implicit questions about Tony's predicament that are at the same time larger questions to us about our cultural predicament: What do Tony's anxiety and depression mean? What does he want from the psychiatrist? What should the psychiatrist be doing for him? Does he suffer from a chemical imbalance for which the psychiatrist should give him Prozac so that he can function more effectively as a mafioso? Or are anxiety and depression exactly what he should be feeling as symptoms of his inability to be at peace with being a mafioso. Tony's psychiatrist can't seem to decide. On the one hand, she treats his symptoms with Prozac. On the other hand, she tells him that his symptoms reflect his feeling trapped by a sense of loyalty to parents (and the "Family"), whom he has always secretly feared and viewed as destructive.

Ultimately, the point of the series—and the reason for its popularity—is that Tony's dilemma is our dilemma. He is torn between his deeper spiritual values—his desire to be a good person—and the values of power, wealth, sex, fine living, and family loyalty that define modern American society as much as they do Tony's Mafia. Significantly, religion doesn't help Tony resolve this conflict. The Catholic priest who claims he wants to help is a self-described "schnorrer" who eats Tony's food and lusts after his wife but never actually talks to Tony at all. The only person who even comes close to speaking for moral or spiritual values in the story—and helping Tony recognize his own values—is the psychiatrist.

The Cultural Crisis As Reflected in the Practice of Medicine

Historically, physicians have often spoken for spiritual values. In the traditions of both Western and Eastern medicine, as in the shamanic traditions of indigenous cultures, physicians have served a dual role as healers and priests. In his book *The Way of the Physician*, Jacob Needleman reminds us of this age-old relationship between medicine and religion, and warns of the danger inherent in our modern tendency to dissociate the two. He points out that the familiar symbol of the medical doctor, the caduceus, originated as an ancient religious symbol of transformation. The two serpents represent two intertwined but opposing movements of the soul—the movement outward of the ego (its emotional attachments to power and success, winning and losing) and the movement inward toward the authentic self. Needleman argues that the true physician is one who integrates within himself these opposing movements of the soul through the healing power of conscious attention—represented in the caduceus by the wings hovering above the opposed serpent heads—and in so doing provides a model for leading a fully human life:

> Only through the appearance in ourselves of an attention that can care for both sides of our nature can we develop into the transformed being that is the real meaning of the symbol of the . . . "priest-physician."[1]

I agree with Needleman that our society suffers greatly from the loss of this vital role model that our physicians once gave us. The practice of medicine has now become an industry in which doctors are, in effect, employees of insurance companies, paid to put the needs of big business before the needs of their patients. The physician–patient relationship has been reduced from a sacred personal trust, as described in the Hippocratic oath, to a commodity— the delivery of a "product" by a "provider" to a "consumer" via a corporately managed "network of health care options."[2] *This rampant commercialization of the practice of medicine—degrading it from a calling to a commodity— epitomizes everything that is wrong with our addictive, quick-fix society. It has left us with a gaping hole in the fabric of our culture that used to be filled by its physicians.*

Speechifying

My intention here is not simply to add another voice to the chorus bemoaning the crisis of modern culture. Rather, it is to say that the Psychotherapeutic Model of psychiatry offers a uniquely valuable approach to understanding and healing this crisis. But perhaps I *am* being a bit preachy. What I have attempted to do above is to summarize the larger message of the book as implied by the title, *Healing the Soul in the Age of the Brain: Becoming Conscious in an Unconscious World*. Reading over my words, however, I recognize that it is an unbalanced summary. In my polemical enthusiasm, I have put too much energy into proclaiming what's wrong with our unconscious, materialistic world and not enough into explaining how we can heal our individual souls (and hopefully improve the world) by becoming conscious. That's really the point of the book, after all. That's why Part One was about "the importance of being conscious." That's why, throughout the book, I have gone into so much detail describing how people actually do become conscious through the psychotherapeutic process. But I realize that you may still be left with questions. You may be wondering how all those stories about my experiences with patients apply to you personally. How can you become more conscious in your own life, you might ask, whether or not the future of our culture depends on it?

You could begin by reviewing the steps of the psychotherapeutic process as I described them in Chapter 3. Recall that the process starts with the awareness of anxiety. If you are currently at a loss for something to be anxious about, try thinking about your relation to our addictive, quick-fix society. What is your own favorite addictive pursuit and what are you using it to distract yourself from? What kind of choices are you making each day between the swimming pool and the quest? Your choice could be watching TV instead of writing a letter to the editor. It could be writing a letter to the editor instead of playing a game with your children. It could be playing games with your children instead of working on your novel. It could be working on your novel instead of watching TV with your children. It could be having a beer with the guys instead of a conversation. It could be working late, or playing solitaire on the computer, instead of having a beer with the guys. It differs for different people, but we all spend more time than we like to admit following our own path of least resistance while avoiding or procrastinating doing what we consider more valuable. If you reflect on it carefully, I believe you will recognize that most of the time you aren't really choosing at all but are simply *reacting* to situations, unconsciously and automatically, according to the habitual tendencies of your personality—your repetition compulsion. In doing so you are instinctively following the swimming-pool values of the quick fix.

This is a crucial point. What I am really saying is that the addictive tendency in human nature—the inner pressure that impels us toward the quick fix and has become the major problem in society today—is none other than our old friend and nemesis the repetition compulsion. The addictive sequence of discomfort→quick fix→relief is unconsciously organized by an emotionally charged personal scenario whose plot is something like victimization→revenge→triumph, or accusation→justification→ vindication, or oppression→rescue→liberation. If your quick fix is TV, for instance, you may unconsciously experience it as a liberation from oppression by your job or your family. If your quick fix is playing games, you may unconsciously experience winning as a revenge for painful losses or humiliations in your life. If your quick fix is some form of living through your children, you may be unconsciously needing them to succeed as a way of vindicating yourself to a world that undervalues you. We all have such a scenario and we all have a powerful need to produce, direct, and star in it again and again, day after day, throughout the course of our lives.

The way I began this chapter is a good example. Although I am confident that what I said is important, I said it in a way that was more polemical than it perhaps needed to be. There was a touch of the same self-righteous outrage that fueled my adolescent diatribes against Catholicism and American imperialism (as I described in Chapter 9). Instead of communicating with you at a personal emotional level—as I try to do when I am writing at my best—I was distracted by the addictive drama of my repetition compulsion into doing what Martin Buber calls speechifying:

> By far the greater part of what is today called conversation among men would be more properly and precisely described as speechifying. In general, people do not really speak to one another, but each, although turned to the other, really speaks to a fictitious court of appeal whose life consists of nothing but listening to him.

Once More with Feeling

To restore the balance, let me give you the more personal side of what I have just been speechifying about. Perhaps the most important lesson about healing the soul that I hope you will take from this book is that the symptoms and painful emotions we instinctively want to get rid of are in fact integral to the process of becoming who we truly are. Symptoms are part of the healing process. Anxiety is consciousness trying to happen. Falling down is a way of growing up. In the Age of the Brain these are surprising, even radical, ideas. And yet they belong to a teaching that is as old as Western civilization. I learned them as people have always learned them—as you can, too—not from books or scientific experiments but from a disciplined practice of listening to the soul.

This book is the product of that practice. It reflects my ongoing personal quest to become conscious, to experience my anxiety, to feel and accept responsibility for the good-and-evil emotions of my own dark side. That's what I was referring to in Chapter 17 when I described how the passions of my repetition compulsion had put me into a state of inner conflict that produced writer's block. I was tempted—in fact, driven—to present myself as a white knight rescuing society from the evils of a dehumanizing Medical Model. But this made me anxious, because it involved an impulse to attack Peter Kramer as the villain in the story, which would have been unfair to him and would have made me guilty of the very evil I was objecting to: dehumanizing (demonizing) Peter Kramer, using him as a straw man to beat up on.

But that discussion in Chapter 17 was only the happy ending of the story, in which I became fully conscious of the problematic passion of my repetition compulsion and could then integrate it into what I hope is a responsible, balanced critique of *Listening to Prozac*. I didn't tell you the whole story of what my repetition compulsion and I had to go through—including a full-blown chemically imbalanced mental illness—to get to that point of integration. I'd like to fill in the rest of this story now, because I think it captures what healing the soul is all about. It illustrates how the impassioned need of my repetition compulsion to fight the evil dragons of materialism impelled me on an inward journey where I had to confront and accept the good-and-evil dragon within myself. The path of that journey was long and difficult, and it led directly through the writing of this book.

Ego Trip

My first attempt to challenge the cultural forces of materialism was an article I submitted in 1985 to a national essay contest run by the *Psychiatric Times* on the topic "The Most Important Problem Facing American Psychiatry."[3] My essay was a polemic against "the philosophical myopia of [psychiatry's] materialistic bias." I argued that an exaggerated emphasis on the brain at the expense of the mind and soul served to "vitiate ideals . . . of moral [and] legal responsibility" and "encourage the unrealistic popular drug-culture expectation of quick, painless solutions to problems." I took exception to the misuse of scientific research to justify a theory of mental illness—as a chemical imbalance—that was both dehumanizing and irrational. I cited the systematic misinterpretation of treatment-outcome research (as discussed in Chapter 4) that denied the obvious significance of the placebo effect:

> The essence of the current psychiatric world view is captured by a description I heard recently of a psychotic episode as a "hurricane in the brain." This perspective is limited by its inability to account for a brain hurricane being stopped by a placebo, a phenomenon equivalent to a real hurricane being stopped by a fervently believed weather prediction.

I then went on a more personal rant against researchers Robert McCarley and Allan Hobson, whose neurological theory of dreams had gained considerable notoriety in those days because it claimed to discredit the classic Freudian theory of dreams. From experiments performed on the brains of sleeping cats, McCarley and Hobson had drawn a rather momentous conclusion about human dreams: that they consist of a series of random neurologically generated images inherently devoid of meaning. The reasoning they had used to reach this conclusion was specious, I thought, and I was less than polite in saying so.[4] After taking them to task for their self-refuting neurological nihilism, I concluded that their theory was "far inferior to Freud's because it is, in the literal sense, Mind-less."

When Allan Hobson quickly responded to the essay by challenging me to a formal debate at a national meeting of the American Psychiatric Association, I was thrilled. Hobson's debate partner was philosopher of science Adolf Grünbaum, another well-known critic of Freudian theory, whose argument against Freud was different from Hobson's but seemed to me just as irrational.[5] When the debate was over, I felt great, confident that, with the help of my partner, dream researcher Ernest Hartmann, I had thoroughly demolished the pretenses of those arrogant Freud-bashers. From what I could tell, the audience thought so, too.

But had I really accomplished anything other than indulging my own arrogant pretenses and gratifying my own ego? That's the question I should have asked myself, but I didn't. I was on a roll. The arrogant combativeness of my repetition compulsion was like bananas in my ears. I felt entitled to be outraged because I was fighting the good fight. My friends were applauding me. The only people who complained were the designated bad guys in my scenario and I couldn't hear what they were trying to tell me from outside the box of that scenario. For example, when psychiatrist Ronald Pies published an editorial accusing me of "splitting the discipline of psychiatry" with my "self-congratulatory polemic against the medical model," I felt insulted and immediately fired off a caustic counterattack.[6] In retrospect, however, I can see the truth in Pies's accusation. The colleagues who appreciated my self-righteous speechifying were those who already agreed with me anyway. The people I really needed to convince—people like Pies himself, who I thought overemphasized drugs but was also interested in psychotherapy—were the ones I was demonizing, arrogantly dismissing their strongly held beliefs and then expecting them to listen respectfully to what I had to say.

Meanwhile, I continued to devote most of my professional energy to treating individual patients with an attitude of empathic understanding, knowing that in order to help them, I had to be able to respect and accept them—including their illnesses—which often meant having to confront my own prejudices and expand my awareness so that I could see and feel things from their point of view. So where was this enlightened empathic awareness in my writing and lecturing? Again, that's a question I *should* have been asking myself. I might have been more concerned about the danger of splitting the discipline of psychiatry had I been more conscious of the dramatic split within myself. On the one hand, I was aspiring to treat my patients, family, and friends with an I–Thou attitude of love and respect. On the other, I was thoughtlessly railing against my Medical Model colleagues with a disrespectful I–It attitude of contempt.

Consciousness or Bust

And then one day I found myself standing at a podium, calm and confident as I began to speak, when I was suddenly blindsided by a certified *DSM-IV* panic attack. My voice began to shake, my heart began to palpitate, my eyesight went dim, my hands went numb, and my face burned with shame as I heard my normally lively, authoritative delivery collapse into a humiliating stammer. I felt sorry for the audience, squirming in their seats as they watched me struggling to maintain a semblance of dignity, trying desperately to continue reading from my prepared text.

Somehow I managed to get through that speech, but I felt physically ill for a week afterward. For several nights I was jolted awake by a furious pounding in my chest, with no recollection of having been dreaming. Fortunately, my work with patients wasn't adversely affected. In fact, I felt a deeper empathy with people who were disabled by their illnesses because I felt suddenly disabled myself. I couldn't imagine ever being able to speak to an audience again. I wasn't even sure I could continue writing, because if people read my articles and then invited me to speak, what was I going to tell them?

When I tried to listen to my anxiety—to recall how the panic began and feel more clearly what I had been panicked about—I didn't get very far. I remembered vividly the physiological affect state, but had no recollection of any preliminary anxiety feeling, a sense of something I was afraid of that might have triggered that visceral upheaval. This was surprising. Before every talk I had ever given I had felt some anticipatory anxiety—which disappeared the moment I began speaking—but this time I hadn't been nervous at all! In fact, I remembered remarking to myself, as I sat waiting my turn to speak, how unusually relaxed and self-assured I felt.

So if symptoms are adaptive, I mused, then perhaps my unconscious had produced this humiliating symptom to warn me that I had grown a little too self-assured, like Icarus flying too close to the sun. This seemed plausible. I knew that I had a penchant for challenging the conventional ideas of received authority, and a talent for finding dramatic, creative ways to do so. I hadn't yet realized that this style was a product of my repetition compulsion but I certainly knew it involved a tendency toward arrogance in my writing and public speaking. Was I too complacent about this tendency, I asked myself? Was the self-assurance I had felt before my talk really arrogance, and the panic attack a way of punishing myself for an overweening desire to show off?

I reviewed the circumstances of the talk. I had been assigned to prepare a formal discussion of a paper presented by a distinguished, nationally respected colleague, Dr. Glen Gabbard. Ordinarily, this would have been a wonderful opportunity to exercise my penchant for challenging authority, but Glen also happened to be a good personal friend of mine. His paper was an excellent discussion of transference projection. This put me in an awkward position. I could find nothing to challenge in Glen's ideas and, as his friend, I didn't even want to challenge him. Yet the impulse to challenge authority was still there, and I had always relied on it to energize my thinking and spur my creativity. So maybe I *had* been trying to show off, I mused, because I remembered how worried I was about not having any creative ideas, and how excited I felt when I finally came up with one: I would show *mock* hostility toward Glen, evoking an *imaginary* competition which I could then use to illustrate what Glen had just said about projection. Well, judging from the panic attack, my unconscious must have taken this imaginary competition as real. In fact, my unconscious did to me exactly what I warned the audience that Glen might want to do (influenced by my projection) in retaliation for my mock hostility. It publicly humiliated me.

Falling Down Is Good

My humiliation turned out in the end to be a blessing. If it hadn't happened, I'm sure that I never could have written this book. In fact, it was only through writing the book that I was eventually able to understand and deal with my symptom. Here's how it happened. Although I never had another full-blown panic attack, I felt seriously hampered by the fear of having another one. Over the next few months, I managed to give a couple of talks to small, friendly audiences who probably couldn't tell how terrified I felt, but the weeks of worrying about those talks beforehand were exhausting. I felt deeply that I had an important contribution to make to psychiatry, but my symptom was stopping me and I needed to learn why. I knew I could treat the symptom with medication, but if my unconscious was trying to send me a message, it would be foolhardy to try to suppress or ignore it. So I decided to go back into analysis.

I explained to my analyst that I was pretty sure my symptom represented a conflict over envy and competitiveness toward Glen, which, in retrospect, I had been somewhat aware of and had tried to defuse (unsuccessfully) by inventing a mock competition. But I couldn't imagine (or feel) how these subtle negative feelings toward a man I respected and admired could have been so powerfully disruptive as to produce a panic attack. It seemed only natural that I would feel a bit of envy and competitiveness over Glen's success. After all, he was the one invited to present a major paper and I was only the discussant. Still, I really didn't begrudge him his preeminence. I knew he had earned it. And he carried it extremely well. I remembered being impressed by his relaxed but commanding presence on stage.

What I didn't know or remember—and what took me six years of analysis and four major rewrites of this book to learn—was that, unconsciously, I didn't care whether Glen had earned his preeminence or not. He was alpha male and I wanted to be alpha male and so, like the sons in Freud's primal horde, I had to kill him. Or, more to the point (given the constraints of civilization), I was driven to vanquish and humiliate him with my powerful words. Though it was largely unconscious toward Glen, this was exactly the same arrogantly contemptuous attitude I had been displaying consciously for years in my attacks against Medical Model colleagues. The difference was that I had been thinking of those colleagues as pill-pushing bad guys who (according to the script of my repetition compulsion) deserved to be vanquished, so I had no compunctions about attacking them. Glen, on the other hand, was my friend, my brother. He had even been a kind of father to me, encouraging me in my early efforts at writing, giving me much-needed validation. My envious need to vanquish him put me in a serious Oedipal dilemma. Consciously, I wanted to (and thought I did) have an I–Thou attitude of respect for him as my friend/brother/father who had supported me and whom I admired. But unconsciously I considered this friend an enemy, an alpha-male rival who was in my way, just another I–It straw man for my Oedipal ego trip.

That's when the healing power of nature intervened with the powerful message of my panic attack. "Wait a minute," it was trying to say. "Remember that you aspire to having an I–Thou attitude of respect for *all* people. That aspiration is central to what you do as a psychotherapist. And yet for years you have been disrespectfully treating your Medical Model colleagues as enemies, I–It straw objects of your alpha-male road rage. If you really believe that your values are better than theirs, then stop being such a hypocrite and start putting your values where your mouth is. Treat your colleagues with the same respect you give to your patients and they might even want to listen to what you have to say."

Discovering My Moral Consciousness: *Where I–It Was, There Shall I–Thou Become*

Of course, that's the way I understand the message now, in 2001, almost ten years after the panic attack. At the time of the attack, I wouldn't have understood such a message if it came in a telegram. I had no suspicion at all that there was a problem with my attitude toward the Medical Model, still less that it was a major reason for my symptom. This first began to dawn on me only several months into my re-analysis, when I remembered something new about that surprising sense of calm I had felt before the storm of my panic attack. I remembered that when I noticed how unusually relaxed and self-assured I was feeling, the thought struck me that finally (at age forty-five!) I had grown up. In all my earlier public-speaking engagements, I had seen myself as the young upstart, an adolescent trying to show how much smarter he was than the elders, never really expecting to be taken seriously. But now, I had established a reputation. I had published papers and lectured at national meetings. I was being invited to speak at conferences all over the place and some people were coming to those conferences specifically to hear me speak. There was no getting around it. I was one of the elders now and people were definitely taking me seriously. They thought of me as an expert.

In this context, I could see my panic attack as a way of telling myself that I wasn't ready to handle so much authority and responsibility. I had too much of a need to show off, which interfered with the clear expression of my ideas. Even worse, my arrogant polemics tended to alienate people and encouraged them *not* to take me seriously. Maybe I was one of the elders now, but I certainly hadn't learned how to act like one. As I was thinking about this, I remembered something my father had said to me when I was about to go off to college.

"Well, it's a pretty big thing that you're going to Harvard," he said, "but I do have one piece of advice. Try not to be such an ass as you were in high school."

I hadn't much appreciated this advice at the time, but now I was finally beginning to understand what my father meant. Being an ass meant indulging the arrogant polemical impulse of my adolescent rebelliousness. Being an adult meant being an authority, responsible both to my audience and to the important ideas I was trying to communicate. There was a significant discrepancy between these two motivations and I could now recognize that it was something about this discrepancy that was making me anxious.

The first time I recognized it, I was preparing a talk for a conference and the tone of my writing began to lapse into an all-too-familiar polemical stridency. As I imagined myself saying what I had been writing out loud to an audience, I began to feel anxiety. On the surface, this was simply the fear of having another episode of panic on stage. But the fact that this fear had surfaced just as I was going into polemical attack mode made me stop and think about who I was attacking and why. It struck me that my target was not an impervious straw man but a real person, a colleague who would be presenting at the conference and listening to my words. I began to worry then about his feelings. I had an image of the difference between speechifying at him and speaking *to* him—and to the audience generally—in a way that invited real conversation.

In other words, I was becoming more conscious. After years of writing and public speaking in which I had been mindlessly reenacting the scenario of my repetition compulsion, my panic attack had forced me to recognize that there were serious moral implications to what I was doing. I felt a new sense of responsibility for the tone and the emotional impact of my words, and I realized that I needed to be more mindful of what I was tryng to accomplish in my writing and lecturing.

When I reflected on it, I recognized that my most cherished goal was just what it had always been: I wanted to be a teacher, to carry on the work of those who had taught me, "helping others in their becoming." This had always been my calling as a psychotherapist and I knew now that it was also my calling as a writer. From there it was only a short step to realizing that, if I was to take my calling seriously, I needed to get off my adolescent ego trip and do something more substantive with all those important but half-developed ideas I had been playing with since the early 1980s. In other words, if I was going to be an elder then I needed to take on the responsibility of an elder. It was time to write a book.

Re-analysis, Rewriting, and Working Through

So that's why I say that this book is the product of my mental illness. My panic attack and the subsequent anxiety about it that impelled me back into analysis turned out to be labor pains. My difficulty in giving birth to the book—and the quest of my psychotherapeutic process—was how to integrate the conflicting forces that had produced my symptom and fueled my repetition compulsion: Thanatos and Eros—the self-assured, self-dramatizing, arrogant alpha-male outrage that made me such an ass, and the love, compassion, and self-reflective consciousness that were at the heart of my work with patients.

I discovered as I tried to write the book that my repetition compulsion remained my constant companion. Time and time again when I would finish a chapter and read over what I had written, or when I would get comments back from my editor, I found that I had produced a frustrating mixture of the good, the bad, and the ugly: engaging personal reflections, in which I was really speaking to the reader, interspersed with my typical polemical rants and an assortment of polysyllabic theoretical pronouncements that I could see in retrospect were merely a more subtle form of speechifying. As I struggled to integrate these ambivalent tendencies in my writing, and worked toward a more consistently personal style, I found myself repeatedly slipping back into self-indulgent diatribes against a large cast of unfairly demonized straw men (most notably Peter Kramer). But I could now recognize these outbursts as products of the same morally objectionable egoistic impulse that had triggered the panic attack in the first place, and they became increasingly unacceptable to me as I got better and better at writing from the heart. At the same time, I also became increasingly impressed by the relentless persistence of my egoistic impulse and how deeply attached to it I was. It really was a repetition *compulsion*.

There is a time-honored principle in psychoanalysis that a new insight by itself does not lead to change without a lengthy process of *working through* the resistance of the repetition compulsion. As the official glossary of the American Psychoanalytic Association explains it, "an instinctual process ongoing for decades is unlikely to immediately take a new path simply because one has just been opened for it."[7] What this means in practice is that any new awareness will tend to slip back into unconsciousness and the repetition compulsion will tend to reassert itself; this will happen again and again—regaining the awareness, from different angles and in different contexts, each time losing it again to the repetition compulsion—many, many times over the long course of an analysis, until finally the awareness becomes fully integrated into the personality.

My experience writing this book is a good example. The first draft came very easily and took only a year to complete. As I wrote it, I felt inspired and excited by the influx of new ideas. But much of my excitement came from the still unintegrated passion of my repetition compulsion. My editor, Pam, reacted accordingly. She said the book was far too polemical and too academic as well. Pam appreciated that the principle of complementarity was important to me, but, she said, I needed to be a whole lot clearer about it—and briefer, too. She loved my writing when I was reflecting on my own inner experience but found it overbearing and tedious when I was philosophizing about science, psychoanalysis, and the mind–body problem.

It took me two months to absorb the impact of Pam's blunt but necessary criticism and recover enough self-esteem to begin writing a second draft. That second draft was painful and labored and took two full years to write, but it did force me to do some serious working through of my repetition compulsion. Each time I was faced with a difficult section to rewrite, I would tend to regress into speechifying, either polemical or pedagogical. Each time, too, I would be dissatisfied with the result, which forced me to become more aware of the tendency.

Meanwhile, I was working through the same tendency in my analysis, where I was spending a lot of time talking about the book—trying to work out more effective rewrites and articulate my evolving ideas—and in the process was doing a lot of speechifying at my analyst. This would have happened anyway—speechifying being a universal I–It tendency of the repetition compulsion that invariably comes out in the transference—but needing to talk so much about the book accentuated the tendency in a useful way.

Talking to my analyst and writing to my readers had parallel meanings in terms of my unconscious scenario, and I became more conscious of that scenario as I cast my analyst in different roles in relation to the book on different days. Sometimes he was the admiring audience of my adolescent display, other times the disapproving critic (reminding me not to be such an ass). Sometimes he was one of the bad guys, a cardboard caricature Freudian trying to dehumanize me with a benighted libido theory. Other times he was an innocent victim, brainwashed by the nineteenth-century materialism of the libido theory and needing me to rescue him with my more enlightened understanding of Freud. Sometimes he was the wise teacher—my muse—who was patiently guiding me to that more enlightened understanding. Other times he was a receptive student who was open to learning something new from me.

And sometimes he seemed a lot like Glen, a more accomplished alpha-male rival in a battle for power and prestige that only one of us could win, and at the same time a good friend who was happy to share the podium and the rewards of success with me. Ultimately, I realized that when I had the panic attack, I had been using Glen as a stand-in for my analyst because I had never completed the essential work of my analysis—experiencing and reclaiming my transference projections—the first time around.

In this way, the work of my analysis and the work of my writing were interwoven and merged into one inward journey. In both endeavors I aspired to the intimacy of I–Thou communication. In both I struggled with a tendency to I–It speechifying. As I worked toward integrating these conflicting needs and values within myself, I was at the same time gradually refining my integration of conflicting theories and philosophies in psychiatry. One of the most interesting and useful things I learned in this process is that I tend to speechify (fall into the pattern of my repetition compulsion) when I am insecure (as a defense against anxiety). In analysis my speechifying was an expression of resistance (fear of consciousness), a reaction to the insecurity I felt about getting intimate with my own dark side (and with my analyst). In my writing, it was similar. Every time I tried to rewrite a passage or a section of the book that was overly academic, I discovered that the reason I had lapsed into academic jargon was that I didn't really know what I was talking about. I hadn't fully worked out all the details and implications of whatever theory I was trying to explain, so I felt insecure about the explanation and tried to hide that insecurity under a cloak of big words. This, too, was a fear of consciousness, an insecurity about getting intimate with my own ideas and communicating with full clarity of awareness. To work out all the details and implications of my theories, I had to fully experience and integrate the conflicting emotions that charged my theorizing: what the ideas meant to me personally; why some felt so important, others so objectionable; and how they all applied to and grew out of my own experience. (For instance, I could not write usefully about the dehumanizing materialism of our quick-fix society until I understood it through experiencing the dehumanizing materialism of my own quick-fix repetition compulsion.) Once I had done that, it came naturally and easily to express even the most complex ideas in the plain language of personal experience.

Two drafts of the book were not enough to accomplish this, however, and it turned out that one editor wasn't enough either. Pam felt that the second draft was much improved, but still too heavy on abstract philosophizing. She knew the philosophy was important to me, though, and didn't trust her own impatience with it, so she called in Beena, who likes philosophy, and asked her for a second opinion on the manuscript. Having the benefit of two top-notch editors independently critiquing my manuscript was an extraordinary blessing. Pam and Beena tended to agree on which sections needed work, but where Pam was impatient to get past the philosophy, Beena wanted to understand it better. The detailed comments, personal associations, and pointed questions she wrote in the margins gave me validation. Beena was reacting just as I hoped my readers would, with enthusiastic curiosity, trying to apply my ideas to her own self-reflection. At the same time, her questions also helped me understand Pam's impatience. Both were reacting to the fact that my thinking was still fuzzy in crucial places. I had skipped over necessary steps in my reasoning and left the reader to fill in the gaps. So Pam's impatience and Beena's questions were really sending me the same message: I wasn't being fair to the reader. It was my book and I should fill in the gaps myself.

Filling in the Gaps with the Repetition Compulsion

I don't need to tell you—because you've read the book and can tell for yourself—that even after writing three more full drafts over the next three years, I still haven't completely filled in all the gaps. But I can tell you that what I *have* been able to fill in is almost entirely the result of my deepening experience and understanding of the repetition compulsion.

When I first started writing the book, and even while writing the first two drafts, I would never have guessed how important the repetition compulsion was to become in my understanding of human nature. I thought that, by using the principle of complementarity, I had already arrived at an integrated philosophy of the soul. But I hadn't. I was still so passionately opposed to a one-sided biological approach that I tended to go to the other extreme and insist on explaining everything psychologically. I truly underestimated the importance of biology and brain chemistry in human motivation; although I prescribed plenty of medication, I wasn't always comfortable prescribing it. It was only through my evolving ideas about the repetition compulsion that I finally did develop what feels to me like a true integration.

At first, I thought of the repetition compulsion only clinically, as the need to reenact an unconscious childhood scenario. Then I realized how important it was for the scientific validation of psychotherapy—as a repeated pattern of observable behavior that can be confirmed through the inner observations of transference and countertransference emotions in the psychotherapeutic process. Then, in trying to explain how Freud got the idea of Thanatos from his observations of the repetition compulsion I was struck by its conservative, stabilizing function and recognized this as the swimming-pool tendency in human nature. The repetition compulsion was the part of the soul that actually fit Freud's constancy principle and his early model of the psyche as a reflex "apparatus." It was a complex neurological reflex par excellence—an organized pattern of emotion and behavior that is triggered by anxiety as automatically as if it were triggered by one of Wilder Penfield's electrodes. That got me thinking about the repetition compulsion as the source of our addictive behaviors, our I–It motivations, and the dehumanizing materialism of modern culture generally. It also tied in with the Eastern concept of karma—an egoistic attachment to negative emotional patterns of the past.[8]

In this way it gradually dawned on me—but only crystallized during the third major rewrite of the book—that the repetition compulsion was the key I had been looking for to an integration of neurobiology with the psychology of inner conflict. As an enduring pattern of psychological experience *encoded in the brain,* it incorporates all the influences that biological psychiatrists consider important: genes, temperament, hormones, chemical imbalances, brain injury, and the like. At the same time it organizes all the important psychological influences on motivation: traumatic experience, unconscious fantasy, and inner conflict (the raw affective impulses of the *It*, the emotional reactions and personality patterns of the ego, and the family values and societal standards of the superego, as learned under the observing aegis of the *I that stands above*). Recognizing the importance of the repetition compulsion helped me finally accept how important biology really is in psychiatry, without detracting from the primacy of the psychological perspective.

In practice this meant that in thinking about a patient with a manic-depressive psychosis, for instance, I could continue to understand his symptom as a product of inner conflict and expect that, eventually, resolving that conflict would make him less vulnerable to a recurrence of his symptom. But I could also better appreciate how a Medical Model psychiatrist could see the problem as purely biological. The manic symptom was essentially a supercharged repetition compulsion that, once triggered by anxiety, was like a runaway biological train that only medication could slow down. Someone else with a different biology could have had the same conflict, the same anxiety, and even the same unconscious scenario without getting so sick over it.

Not that I had ever been slow to prescribe lithium at the first sign of a patient's hypomanic episode, but before understanding the repetition compulsion I had never felt quite right about doing it, as if it represented a failure of psychotherapy. For my own symptom, too, I had originally had misgivings about using medication, feeling that psychoanalysis *should* be enough to take care of it. Once I began to appreciate the biological power of the repetition compulsion, however, I didn't hesitate to take a half milligram of Klonopin before giving a lecture.

The Repetition Compulsion and the Quest

In convincing me how important the biological perspective is for psychiatry, the repetition compulsion also helped me appreciate the importance of the spiritual. As a biological drive, the repetition compulsion is limited by the biological need for homeostasis. It embodies the swimming-pool motivations of the Flesh—materialistic, hedonistic, egoistic, and intrinsically amoral—in pursuit of the stabilizing comforts of the quick fix: instant gratification, instant rewards, instant retribution, instant relief, easy rationalization, and always the path of least resistance. If that were all there was to life, I would never have needed to have a panic attack.

In other words, the repetition compulsion does a pretty good job of integrating the body, brain, and mind, but it is missing the crucial element of the spirit. It lacks the self-reflective, moral consciousness of the *I that stands above,* the higher consciousness that makes us—or rather allows us to become—fully human. Without this higher consciousness, the repetition compulsion may provide a sense of excitement—via the drama of its unconscious scenario—but it cannot give meaning or purpose to our lives. It may provide energy for the quest, but it cannot provide the motivation or the direction. My own story is a good illustration. Without the intervention of my higher consciousness, I never could have renewed my unfinished psychotherapeutic process or rediscovered my calling as a teacher. Instead I would have continued happily preaching to the choir while sowing discord in the congregation, polarizing my world into good guys and bad guys, insulting the people I thought I wanted to convince, living off the tremendous energy of my repetition compulsion but never seeking to harness that energy toward any higher purpose.

Comments from Beena and Pam

Perhaps you could hear a hint of speechifying in that last section. It's there, but I didn't catch it until Beena and Pam alerted me that the section needed more work. "We need to see the leap of faith to the loving, compassionate Elio from the more combative, arrogant one more clearly," Beena wrote in the margin. "How do you make this a touchstone for the reader? How does your experience teach us how to listen to our own souls?" Pam, as usual, was more blunt: "Show how your life changed post-realization."

Once again, my editors' red pencils pointed to an area where my speechifying was covering up fuzzy thinking. In fact, my transition from the egoistic passions of my repetition compulsion to the higher values of my quest was not quite so dramatically black-to-white, unconscious-to-conscious, as I have been suggesting. My higher consciousness was present in the background all along, presiding over the working through of my repetition compulsion so that I could become conscious of my unconscious scenario. Reenacting my scenario was like putting bananas in my ears: a way of provoking my higher consciousness to pay attention by relentlessly refusing to listen to it. That relentless refusal to listen—embodied in that mindless compulsion to repeat— is what mystic philosopher G. I. Gurdjieff was talking about when he said that our ordinary life is that of an unconscious machine and our ordinary state of consciousness is really a form of sleep.[9]

When you consider how long it took me to wake up—that is, to consciously experience inner conflict over my enactment tendency—even after years of analysis *prior* to the panic attack, you might be tempted to take this as evidence of the inefficacy of dynamic psychotherapy. On the contrary, it is evidence of the stability of the human personality and is par for the course for human nature. In fact, the most consistent and perhaps the most remarkable observation I have made in my years of practicing intensive psychotherapy is how incredibly difficult it is, and how long it takes, for people to change—to gain conscious awareness of and some degree of freedom from the compulsion of their automatic personality patterns. The relentless unconsciousness of these patterns does, I believe, reflect the raw biological force of the repetition compulsion in human nature. In fact, biologically speaking, the whole swimming-pool point of the repetition compulsion–personality is *to avoid consciousness altogether.* For, as Adam and Eve discovered, consciousness is the most powerfully destabilizing force in the world.

From Reaction to Recognition; From Passion to Compassion

The flip side of Adam and Eve's discovery—and the overall message of this book—is that *consciousness is also the most powerfully humanizing force in the world.* It directs our inward journey from the place where *It* was to the place where *I* become. Without it, we are merely biological puppets, controlled by the strings of DNA and brain wiring. With it, we can achieve the full richness of human being, burdened with the knowledge of good and evil and blessed with the freedom to choose between them.

Which brings me to the substance of Beena's and Pam's questions. I've been describing my own inward journey as a deep qualitative change from the dehumanizing passion of my repetition compulsion to the humanizing compassion of my higher consciousness. But how did I—and how can you— actually make this change? Was it really a permanent transformation? You might easily be skeptical. After all, beyond the fact that I have written this book, I haven't provided any other evidence that my life has changed as a result of the more integrated self-awareness I've acquired in the ten years since my panic attack. In fact, I've shown and admitted that even today, in writing this chapter, I still tend to get carried away by my repetition compulsion. And you should have seen me six weeks ago! That was when Beena and Pam pulled the rug out from under me, by sending what I thought was the final copyedited manuscript for my review and informing me that, to do justice to such a wonderful book, I really needed to rewrite this last chapter! And because we were on such a tight schedule, could I possibly get it done in the next week?

Perhaps you will get the flavor of my reaction when I tell you that it gave vivid new meaning to the concepts of transference and resistance. I went slightly ballistic. My repetition compulsion kicked into high gear as I registered my self-righteous protest, defending the honor of the chapter just as it was—in the form I had already written, rewritten, and grown attached to it. Yet even as I was groaning over their outrageous request, I knew that Pam and Beena had a point. As it stood then, the last chapter was written entirely in the somewhat speechifying style of the opening section, "Author's Message." Pam and Beena wanted it to be more personal, something that would leave the reader with a vivid sense of how healing the soul applies to *you*—why you should care about becoming conscious. What an obviously good idea!

Nevertheless, I spent the next few weeks arguing with Pam and Beena, resisting every suggestion they made. I explained that their idea would make sense if I could think of a good personal story around which to organize the chapter, but I wasn't sure I had any good stories left to tell, and even if I did, it would take me at least a month to rewrite the chapter. Meanwhile, between irritated phone calls and E-mails to Pam and Beena, I was complaining to any friend who would listen about the unfair pressure they were putting me under. At the same time, I was trying to tune in each day to my creative inner channel for any ideas that might emerge for a good story.

Things came to a head rather quickly when I decided to try writing about my panic attack and E-mailed a preliminary version of the story to Pam and Beena for their reactions. When the next morning arrived and I hadn't received any feedback, I dashed off the following urgent message:

Please. I'm hanging out to dry over here. . . . You've pushed me into a whirl-wind romance with this thing and I'm ready to marry it today but not if I have to divorce myself from it tomorrow. So tell me you like it or tell me you hate it but tell me something.

It didn't help my insecurity when Beena responded at the end of that day with an equivocal message about "going in the right direction but we need to think about how well it is integrated with what has gone before." I was annoyed and immediately fired back:

> I'm surprised to hear you say you're not sure how well it is integrated with the book up to that point. I think it crystallizes EVERYTHING I've been saying in the book up to that point. There isn't even a ghost of a question, doubt, or insecurity about that in my mind.

I was still annoyed when I woke up the next morning and reread this abrupt response to Beena's last message. "Whoops!" I thought, and quickly sent another response—"On second thought"—explaining that I could now see what she meant. The connection between my story and the rest of the book was "vividly clear in my own mind," I wrote, "and once I articulate it I'm pretty sure it will be ah-hah obvious, but I haven't yet nailed that 'obvious' articulation."

Meanwhile, however, Beena had been so upset by my previous E-mail that she hadn't slept at all the night before. She responded to my "On second thought" message by saying that she was tremendously relieved to get it, but realized nevertheless that she had been so upset for the last few weeks that she needed to clear the air:

> It seemed to me as if I could no longer communicate with you, as if I was failing in a way I hadn't all these years that we've been working together. . . . Somehow, now, at this late stage, I was beginning to feel peripheral, as if nothing I said could make a difference anymore. . . . So, thank you for acknowledging that I may have a point even if you don't ultimately agree with me.

Initially I was shocked to think that I could have upset Beena so much, but when I talked to her on the phone I quickly understood that over the preceding weeks she had taken my assorted expressions of irritation and annoy-

ance much more personally than I had meant them. That evening I sent another E-mail:

> Thinking over our conversation and the state of mind I have been in since
> my first flash of irritation at the copy edits, I realize that I have thoughtlessly
> made you the brunt of the very tendency of arrogant egoism that my story is
> about. Even though only a small portion of my frustration was really at you,
> I vented it all in your direction without bothering to think how you might
> interpret it and feel about it. That was wrong and it is proof positive that I
> really am still an ass. . . . I hope you will not think too badly of me now that
> you have been the victim of my dark side. I feel honored that you care so
> much about the book and have put so much of yourself into it. . . . I think
> of the book as having two behind-the-scenes co-authors without whom I
> couldn't have done it at all or would have done it very very badly. One is my
> analyst. The other is you.

That night I set my alarm for 3:45 a.m., eager to get back to work on my
story. But now it was my turn to have trouble getting to sleep. When I finally
did fall asleep, it wasn't for long. At 3 a.m. I woke up with a start from the following dream:

> *It was late and my wife, Dianne, and I had just fallen asleep when the doorbell*
> *rang. I stumbled downstairs to find five of my son's high school buddies crowding*
> *in at the door. This is a wonderful group of guys and I am always glad to see them*
> *when they come to hang out in our TV room, as they did many times during high*
> *school and again during college vacations. But this time I was annoyed. "You*
> *guys should get your schedules straight," I said curtly. "Greg's still up at college."*
> *I then turned around and went back to bed. But Dianne was no longer in the*
> *bed, and I couldn't get back to sleep because there was a loud noise of laughing*
> *and talking coming from the TV room. I went back downstairs and was greeted*
> *by Greg's buddies with their typical happy boisterous enthusiasm. "Hey Mr. Frat-*
> *taroli! How's it going, big guy!" they called out as if everything was normal. Now*
> *I was getting seriously irritated and it only got worse when I went looking for Di-*
> *anne and found her in the kitchen making sandwiches for the boys. "What are*
> *you doing!" I yelled. "Do you want these guys to keep us awake all night?!!" "It's*
> *no problem," she said calmly. "They're Greg's friends." That did it. I snapped. I*

went stomping into the TV room and read those boys the riot act. "How dare you storm in here, wake us up out of a sound sleep, and then expect us to make a party for you! That's the most selfish, childish thing I've ever heard of. Get out of my house right now!" They bowed their heads and, without another word, went slinking out of the house. Instantly I was filled with the most gut-wrenching remorse. I was horrified at what I had done. I had shamed the boys, but I was the one who really deserved to be shamed. "I love those kids," I thought, "and now they're afraid of me and they're never going to come back again. I've ruined everything!"

At that point, I woke up and went quickly from feeling damned to feeling blessed—blessed to have had such an integrating dream, blessed to have such a wonderful wife who makes me sandwiches and keeps me honest, blessed to have two wonderful children who have incredibly good taste in their friends, and blessed to have two wonderful editors who believed in me and in themselves enough to make me keep doing it until I got it right. I wrote to Beena that my dream "pretty much confirmed . . . you being the innocent victim of my self-indulgent egoistic anger."

> Although the dream was not about you or the book—it was prompted mainly by another EM I got last nite from my daughter asking me at the last minute to change our travel plans to Boston tomorrow to arrive at a time that was not so convenient (of course, like a good disguised dream, it was not overtly about my daughter either)—the two situations were so parallel that it was amazing. A perfectly reasonable though poorly timed request from someone I care about to do a last minute change of plans which in the end would actually be good for me, but I react with childish anger because it is inconvenient. I guess the good news is that I don't need to have a panic attack or go back into analysis to see what I have been doing. . . . I have indeed met the enemy and he is me!!

The Royal Road to the Golden Rule: A Dream About Waking Up

Every character in a dream represents a part of the dreamer. The happy, boisterous boys were me and so was the outraged boisterous man. Together they represent the good and evil energy of my repetition compulsion—my Ariel and my Caliban. Dianne represented my loving, compassionate self, my inner Miranda.

Through this dream I became for the first time fully conscious of the emotions that had generated my panic attack. I consciously, intentionally, humiliated the boys in the dream just as I had unconsciously wanted to humiliate Glen. I was outraged and at the same time envious over the boys' easy sense of entitlement just as I was unconsciously outraged and envious over Glen's prestige and his easy commanding presence on stage. My shame was the shame of my panic attack, but in the dream I could feel and understand how I deserved to be shamed—for willfully, arrogantly, childishly hurting people I loved—whereas in the panic attack I was shamed by a chemical imbalance that seemed to erupt within me for no apparent reason.

How odd to be more fully conscious in a dream than in waking life! How odd to have trouble falling asleep and then dream about having trouble staying asleep! It's as if my dream was a commentary by Gurdjieff reminding me that the consciousness of the repetition compulsion is a kind of sleeping state—the complacent state of having bananas in your ears and not thinking there is anything strange about it. Who are those guys who so rudely insist on waking me up when I would rather sleep?

The boys waking me up in the dream stand for Pam and Beena waking me up from the speechifying sleep of the book's last chapter (and from my complacency about it) and insisting that I get the bananas out of my ears and get real with myself and my readers. But the boys also stand for my children waking me up (as they have done often and well), insisting that I let go of my own childish sense of entitlement and grow up to become a better father to them. And finally, the boys stand for me—the irrepressible drive of my own repetition compulsion—waking myself up to the shameful but also joyful knowledge of good and evil. The contrast between Dianne presiding in the kitchen making sandwiches and me stomping around the house yelling represents the inner conflict between the compassionate, loving consciousness of my *I that stands above* and the arrogant pride of my repetition compulsion.

So That's Healing the Soul?

Initially, I had reservations about telling the story of my E-mail exchange with Beena and my dream. In the course of resolving our miscommunication, and even more when I woke from the dream, I could feel how much I had grown through my psychotherapeutic process. But I wasn't at all sure that a reader would be able to tell, or could relate to my experience in the way that Pam and Beena were hoping. Pam and Beena felt differently. They assured me that *they* could relate to my experience and they thought that the interchange with Beena together with the dream illustrated the value of healing the soul very well. "I felt so pleased after we talked, Elio," Beena said. "I thought, 'That was so easy! Why can't all misunderstandings be resolved like that. Why can't all communication be so clear?' "

Still, to appreciate how my experience might apply to your own life, I'm sure you could use a little more explanation. The idea is that by becoming more conscious, you become a better person—more loving and compassionate, less caught up in the addictive pursuit of egoistic satisfactions. But what does that mean really and how does it happen? Being more conscious does not mean that the repetition compulsion disappears, or even that it becomes impossible to fall into it unconsciously—as I did with Beena for several weeks. It does mean that it becomes more difficult to fall into it without having at least an inkling of what you're doing, so that when you do fall into it, your reactions tend to be less extreme, and you recover more quickly. Even though I was somewhat polemical at the beginning of this chapter, for instance, my polemic was far less strident than it had been in earlier versions of the chapter. Even when I was mindlessly lashing out in annoyance at having to rewrite the chapter—and unwittingly hurting Beena's feelings in the process—I wasn't really angry *at her,* nor did I lose sight of the fact that she was my friend. When I did briefly get angry at her I recognized quickly that I had been unfair, and when I learned that she had been upset for weeks before that, I understood immediately how I had hurt her.

So is that what I mean by healing the soul? Is that a permanent transformation of my personality? In a word, yes. But it may not be exactly what you would have expected. I believe I have experienced a permanent transformation, but I am not a new person. I haven't lost the capacity to be an ass and been transformed into a saint. Rather, I am no longer trapped in the *compulsion* to be an ass and therefore I have easier access to the saintly qualities I've always had—and that we all have when we are at our best. To put it differently, I am not so attached to my speechifying I–It passion and can more quickly recover my compassionate I–Thou awareness. Under stress, I still have an automatic tendency to slip the bananas back into my ears and fall into the "sleep mode" of my repetition compulsion. But if you stop me at any point and say, "Hey buddy, why do you have bananas in your ears?" I will quickly take them out, say, "I'm sorry, I was sleepwalking," and then be able to have a real conversation with you.

What feels permanent is a shift in the *emphasis* of my personality tendencies from reaction to recognition, from passion to compassion, from Caliban or Ariel to Miranda. If *I* am a harmony of my *It,* my ego–repetition compulsion/superego, my *I that stands above,* and the world of other people, then *I* have modulated to a new key. All the notes are still there, but the balance of the chords is different. And how did this new harmony happen? There were several factors: first, the healing, thorn-in-my-psyche, consciousness-raising action of my symptom; second, the disciplined practice of listening to the soul, which over time transformed the unconscious affect of the symptom into the conscious emotion and feeling of conflicting desires; third, the intense psychotherapeutic process through which that new consciousness gradually emerged.

Of course, when we talk about transformation, we tend to imagine it in terms of a conversion experience—the sudden joy of an epiphany. Pam and Beena had an E-mail exchange about this that grew out of a kind of group epiphany they had shared with me in a conference call. At the time of the call I had written the story of my panic attack and had just had my own little epiphany through my dream, but it was only in that conference call that I finally grokked Pam and Beena's vision for the chapter. They saw that my experience of writing and rewriting the chapter with them was a wonderful illustration of the very thing I was trying to write about: the transformative healing power of consciousness. Because I was better able to listen to them and they were in turn better able to listen to me, that call became a true meeting of minds. I think this is evident from the following highly illuminating E-mail exchange, which I insist on publishing whether they like it or not:

BEENA: The idea of permanent transformation is really a smaller swinging back-and-forth each time . . . which goes back to the reaction/recognition-of-reaction thing I had pointed out earlier to Elio. One's awareness could end with the emotional reaction, or one could use it to reveal something deeper, to "stop and pay attention." It is the difference between having bananas in one's ears, and being aware, listening. It is desirable to be constantly aware, finely attuned to one's consciousness because it affects one's quality of life, and life-affirming experience. . . .

An author's emotional reaction to an editor's suggestion is understandable, but not necessarily the most aware one. It's like a grain of sand around which only the author can build, create a nacreous luminescent whole. It's an irritation, as a grain of sand is to an oyster, but out of it comes this other whole, this new thing. It's having the inner resources to allow that grain of sand in to access one's own creativity . . . involving a receptivity that could be likened to listening to one's inner consciousness, and, ultimately, to one's soul. . . .

How is there the kind of epiphany—the baseball game at the beginning of the book—from which one can grow? Do you have the epiphany because you are more finely aware, because you've been listening? Are there breakthroughs of the self-transforming kind that there aren't when you're not listening?

PAM: So what we are saying is that there *is* a "permanent transformation" that grows out of the pendulum swinging of the repetition compulsion—the pendulum that swings in ever-narrower arcs, but continues to swing (i.e., we *do* regress, but not as far as we used to)—but that only after it happens again and again can the gate swing open and the NEW THING (the insight, the creative spark, in Elio's case, the "new story" of the panic attack/writing story) spring forth. It is the difference between being an editor and being a writer—an editor can continue to point out the ways in which the pendulum swings back and forth, can show the ways one gets "stuck," but only a writer can come up with the NEW IDEA, the NEW STORY—as a result of the prodding offered by the editor.

As you said, it is the irritation of the grain of sand . . . which in the end creates a pearl unseen before (a new thing). So what Elio has to do for us is show us how he went from exercising the repetition compulsion in the writing of the chapter/book to saying, "Eureka! I see what you mean—and it requires a whole new story (e.g., the panic attack)." Something DOES happen that is a transforming moment, in which we DO see things "with new eyes" and therefore create something new (the Miranda vision?) . . .

I can summarize and gloss this exchange by saying that healing the soul is not a conversion experience that happens in a single transforming "Eureka!" moment—though such moments are memorable parts of the experience— but it is, rather, a gradual progression, an evolving process, like the formation of a pearl. There are certainly epiphanies along the way, but those epiphanies are as much the result of the healing process as the cause. You can't have an epiphany if you aren't receptively listening and you can't be receptively listening unless you've already begun to learn how to take the bananas out of your ears. Much of that learning-and-growing process happens without "ah-ha" moments, through the painful, arduous, repetitive labor of working through. And that labor is never complete. The repetition compulsion is relentless and there is always more working through to be done.

Here is an E-mail to Pam and Beena describing a moment when I felt the sudden epiphany and the endless burden simultaneously:

So I started writing at about 4:30 a.m. By 8:30 I was getting that familiar feeling of creative excitement where you can sense how everything (in the book and possibly in the universe) is falling into place but you don't know exactly how that's going to happen and you know it has to happen through your agency and that feels like an impossible task which leaves you in a state of intense creative enthusiasm weighted down by an almost-as-intense sense of ennui.

So I stepped into the shower and a stream of consciousness which led to the thought, "Now I know why Michelangelo never finished his prisoners. It was too damn much work!" Which then led to, "Oh yeah, prisoners trying to get out of the marble, becoming conscious in an unconscious (materialis- tic) world; the human spirit emerging out of the endless struggle with the physical passions of the repetition compulsion, the last chapter as it should be emerging out of the last chapter that I have been so deeply embedded in (and karmically attached to) for so many years."

Now see what you've done!!!!!!

The Answer You Seek Is Within Yourself

A friend of mine who practices and teaches Tibetan Buddhism once ex- plained to me that there are two schools of thought about enlightenment.

One is that we can achieve it only through many lifetimes of suffering and many years of disciplined practice. The other is that we are already enlightened, and can recognize it at any moment if we only stop and pay attention. My understanding of the psychotherapeutic process turned out to be very similar to my friend's understanding of the Buddha's path: it takes many years of suffering and disciplined practice—and a whole lot of working through—to get to the point where it becomes easy and natural to stop and pay attention.

In practice, this means that *you always have within you the resources necessary to solve the problems that confront you.* Healing the soul means becoming able to access those inner resources easily and at will. My experience with patients is a good example. I have always had a deep capacity for empathy. From the very start of my training as a psychotherapist—even when I had bananas in my ears in every other arena of my life—when in the office I was always able to establish a healing I–Thou connection with my patients. The problem was, I could never do it with every patient, and I couldn't do it with *any* patient all of the time. But as I grew through my own psychotherapeutic process, I found that I could maintain an I–Thou connection much more of the time, with a greater number of my patients. When I am at my best now, my capacity for empathy is no deeper than it has ever been, but it is broader, and I am at my best more often.

I think of this in terms of everyone having a personal "in-group" and "out-group." Your in-group is everyone you genuinely love (at least some of the time) with the I–Thou attitude of the golden rule. Your out-group is everyone against whom you have an instinctive prejudice: the bad guys of your unconscious scenario. Healing the soul—making the unconscious conscious—means transforming your out-group into your in-group, expanding the range of people with whom you can empathize and whom you can recognize as part of your extended family. That, in the end, was probably the most important message of my dream. My failure in the dream was treating the boys as outsiders, not recognizing them as members of my family. Generalizing, I would say that the failure of our society—the problem with our dehumanizing quick-fix culture—is that in our collective addiction to the goals of the repetition compulsion, we treat far too many people as outsiders and fail to recognize our membership in a common family.

Consciousness, Fate, and Moral Responsibility

So the real importance of being conscious is that it allows us to become better people. It opens us to love and a genuine sense of community with our fellow human beings. It inspires us to live in accord with our higher values, and to recognize and change the patterns of suffering we inflict (on ourselves as well as others) through the unreflective enactment of our repetition compulsions. By generating anxiety, shame, and guilt in reaction to the dehumanizing urgency of our repetition compulsion, consciousness gives us the knowledge of good and evil that makes us human and helps us grow.

If, as Heraclitus said, "A man's character is his fate"—that is, if our fate is largely determined by the habitual tendencies of our repetition compulsion–personality—then the power of consciousness is that it allows us to change our fate. In our awareness of anxiety, shame, and guilt about our actions and impulses, we have what Kierkegaard called "the possibility of possibility": the possibility of having a free choice and the moral responsibility that comes with it. In that sense, *the fear of consciousness is ultimately a fear of moral responsibility*, because if we own our anxiety, shame, and guilt, and allow ourselves to have full consciousness of the emotions that motivate our behavior, then we will inevitably recognize the full weight of our responsibility for that behavior.

Oedipus Is Us

The story of my panic attack is really the story of Oedipus. As Sophocles portrays him, Oedipus's problem was that in his hubris he felt no anxiety. He had no hesitation at all about killing *anyone* who dared to get in his way and no shame or guilt about it afterward. He thus unwittingly killed his father not because it was fated by the Delphic oracle, but because it was fated by his character. Had he properly understood the message of the oracle, he would have tried a different approach to changing his fate. Instead of running away from his father to minimize the risk of killing him, he would have resolved to treat every man as a father and eliminate the risk entirely by *choosing never to kill anyone at all!* He might then have felt an inner signal of anxiety and guilt at his first impulse to slaughter the arrogant, contemptuous stranger who blocked his path to Thebes, and in that moment he might have become conscious of his own arrogant contemptuousness.

Which brings me back to Freud. In making the Oedipus complex his central metaphor for inner conflict, Freud, I believe, wanted to spell out a moral lesson that Sophocles only implies: that each of us is the unconscious author of our own fate, and has the possibility of changing our fate by making the unconscious conscious. If we apply the power of conscious attention–Needleman's "way of the physician"–in the psychotherapeutic process, we can feel and become responsible for the conflicting passions embodied in our repetition compulsion, consciously integrate them into a more harmonious, less driven, personality, and thus become the better selves we have it in us to be.

This is exactly the message of my dream. By becoming conscious I become a better person. If I remember to treat all people as compassionately as I aspire to treat my wife and children, then I will feel anxiety *before* I attack or shame anyone and will recognize that, in their patient kindness and their impatient contempt, in their joyous, boisterous enthusiasm and their arrogant, selfish entitlement, all God's children are really just like me.

Notes

1. A Brief Introduction to the Soul

1. T. M. Luhrmann, *Of Two Minds: The Growing Disorder in American Psychiatry* (New York: Alfred A. Knopf, 2000), p. 20.

2. Eric Kandel, "A New Intellectual Framework for Psychiatry," *American Journal of Psychiatry* 155, no. 4 (Apr. 1998); John Searle, "The Mystery of Consciousness," *New York Review of Books*, Nov. 2, 1995, p. 60; Francis Crick, *The Astonishing Hypothesis: The Scientific Search for the Soul* (New York: Simon & Schuster, 1994), p. 3; Antonio Damasio: *Descartes' Error* (New York: G. P. Putnam's Sons, 1994), p. 251; Lewis Judd, from a speech as reported in a Sandoz Pharmaceuticals newsletter for psychiatrists, *Peer to Peer*, vol. 2 (summer 1990), p. 10; and David Satcher, from an interview on the Newshour with Jim Lehrer, Dec. 13, 1999, discussing his just released, first-ever surgeon general's report on mental health.

3. *Webster's New International Dictionary*, third ed., defines materialism as "a doctrine, theory or principle according to which physical matter is the only reality and the reality through which all being and processes and phenomena can be explained." *Scientific materialism* involves the additional, quite erroneous, belief that materialism is the only philosophy that is consistent with the evidence of modern science.

4. To refute it, you have to *prove*—not simply assume—that brain processes actually do cause consciousness. In Chapter 15 I will propose a thought experiment to demonstrate that this is impossible in principle: that no matter how far neuroscience advances, it will never be able to prove that brain processes cause consciousness.

5. In a recent *Psychiatric Times* article ("Meeting Advances Surgeon General's Recommendation on Children's Mental Health," 17, no. 7, July 2000) Arline Kaplan reported that "Although children and adolescents receive many of the traditional treatments for mental disorders, much of the research on psychosocial and pharmacologic treatments has been conducted on adults, with results extrapolated to children. . . . For most prescribed medications, including psychotropics, there are no studies of safety and efficacy for children and adolescents. 'Depending on the specific medication, evidence may be lacking for short-term or, most commonly, for long-term safety and efficacy,' the surgeon general's report said. '. . . [T]he combined effectiveness of pharmacological and psychosocial treatments . . . is seldom studied.' "

6. S. Son and J. Kirchner, "Depression in Children and Adolescents," *American Family Physician,* Nov. 15, 2000; and B. Geller, D. Reising, et al., "Critical Review of Tricyclic Antidepressant Use in Children and Adolescents," *Journal of the American Academy of Child and Adolescent Psychiatry* 38, no. 5 (May 1999), pp. 513–16.

7. J. Bieferman, R. Thisted, et al., "Estimation of the Association Between Desipramine and the Risk for Sudden Death in 5- to 14-Year-Old Children," *Journal of Clinical Psychiatry* 1, no. 56 (1995), pp. 87–93.

8. In a recent *JAMA* editorial ("Psychotropic Drug Use in Very Young Children," 283, no. 8, Feb. 23, 2000) Dr. Joseph T. Coyle wrote that "there is no empirical evidence to support psychotropic drug treatment in very young children and . . . there are valid concerns that such treatment could have deleterious effects on the developing brain." A *Time* magazine article from May 31, 1999 ("Escaping from the Darkness," 153, no. 21) reported on "[t]he lack of science about the effects of these drugs on childhood development," quoting Peter Kramer: " 'Anyone who thinks about this problem is worried about what it means to substantially change neurotransmission in a developing brain. We don't know if these kids would compensate on their own over time and if by giving them these medicines we are interfering with that compensatory mechanism.' "

9. Karl Stark (*Inquirer* staff writer), "Medication of Children Is Surging . . ." *The Philadelphia Inquirer,* Jan. 18, 1998; and K. Minde, "The Use of Psychotropic Medications in Preschoolers: Some Recent Developments," *Canadian Journal of Psychiatry* 43 (1998), pp. 571–75.

10. Sharon Begley, "Is Everybody Crazy?" *Newsweek,* Jan. 26, 1998, pp. 50–55; and Jerry Adler, "My Brain Made Me Do It," p. 56. Both articles were prompted by the 1997 book *Shadow Syndromes,* by John Ratey and Catherine Johnson.

11. Peter Kramer, *Listening to Prozac* (New York: Viking, 1993), p. xv.

12. Ibid., p. 195.

13. Unless otherwise stated, all definitions in this book are from *Webster's New International Dictionary,* third ed.

14. René Descartes, "Discourse on the Method of Rightly Conduction the Reason," In E. S. Haldane and G. R. T. Ross, trans., *Philosophical Works of Descartes,* vol. 1 (New York: Dover Publications, 1955), p. 92.

15. Damasio, *Descartes' Error.*

16. In fact, Descartes did ultimately recognize and try to correct this weakness in his philosophy. His last work, *The Passions of the Soul,* focused entirely on the emotions.

17. Bruno Bettelheim, *Freud and Man's Soul* (New York: Alfred A. Knopf, 1982).

18. All biblical quotes are from the New Revised Standard Version.

2. The Technocrat and the Cowboy

1. Throughout this book, the direct quotes from therapy sessions, while faithful to the sense of what transpired, are not verbatim transcriptions. Furthermore, I have disguised or changed aspects of Bill's story, and of the other clinical stories in the book, as much as I believed necessary to preserve the confidentiality of all involved.

2. If you reread the last two paragraphs, you will notice that my attempt to reflect on my feelings—I wasn't aware of liking or disliking Bill, but only of dread—didn't last

long. I drifted away from my own feelings to my sense of Bill's emotional disconnected-ness, then to his attitude and style of communicating, then to generalizations about trust in the relationship between patient and psychiatrist, and finally so far from my feelings about Bill that I am now getting ready to write about another patient altogether. This di-gression does happen to fit my narrative purposes, but it also reflects what actually hap-pened whenever I tried to focus on my anxiety about Bill (and what happens generally when people try to focus on their uncomfortable feelings). Without realizing it, I would tend to lose focus and begin to distance myself from what was making me uneasy.

3. It may indeed be cheaper for the insurance company, but not for the patient, and not for society. The long-term consequences of a quick-fix pharmacological approach to psychological crisis include mistrust, noncompliance, repeated relapses, sick days and loss of productivity at work, more long-term disability, more street people, and more sui-cides. In addition, inadequate treatment for psychiatric conditions leads to *higher* medi-cal costs because of an increased incidence and duration of physical illnesses. These points are well documented in a collection of articles on the cost-effectiveness of long-term dynamic psychotherapy in the 1997 supplement to *Psychoanalytic Inquiry.* See es-pecially Susan Lazar's overview article and her article on depression (pp. 4–16 and 51–57), the data from Germany presented by Rüdiger Dossmann et al. (pp. 74–86), and the review of increased medical costs in the article by Norman Doidge (pp. 140–43).

4. According to commitment law in our state, a person can be committed only if he has taken some overtly dangerous action against himself or another in the preceding thirty days (which Bill had now spent in hospitals).

5. This loss of concern for the individual is, of course, not unique to psychiatry. It is to some degree inherent in the tendency within all medical specialties toward subspe-cialization that encourages and validates a narrow focus on an organ system rather than a person.

6. The *DSM* is periodically revised. I started out my psychiatric residency under *DSM-II,* and have seen the *DSM-III* and the *DSM-IIIR* (revised third edition) come and go. The current version is *DSM-IV.*

7. The patient would thus have eight 45-minute sessions with a psychiatrist (or two) each week. At that time (1980) the standard of care for inpatient psychiatry was five forty-five-minute psychiatric visits per week for a minimum of four weeks. Today the standard for care is no more than five minutes a day for no more than a week.

3. An Introduction to the Psychotherapeutic Process

1. Martin Buber, "The William Alanson White Memorial Lectures, Fourth Series," *Psychiatry* 20 (1957), pp. 95–129. Buber's idea is close to Abraham Maslow's concept of *self-actualization,* except that Maslow tends to locate the forces opposing the process in society, whereas Buber, like Freud, sees them as intrinsic to human nature.

4. A Lecture to Young Psychiatrists

1. William Styron, *Darkness Visible: A Memoir of Madness* (New York: Random House, 1990).

5. The Swimming Pool and the Quest

1. Bettelheim was director of the Orthogenic School from the mid-1940s until the early 1970s. He reported on the work of the school in four books: *Love Is Not Enough, Truants from Life, The Empty Fortress,* and *A Home for the Heart.*

2. Alfred Flarsheim, "Treatability," in P. Giovacchini, ed., *Tactics and Techniques in Psychoanalytic Therapy* (New York: Science House, 1972); George Schaller, *The Year of the Gorilla* (Chicago: University of Chicago Press, 1964).

3. Bruno Bettelheim, *A Home for the Heart* (Chicago: University of Chicago Press, 1985), p. 425.

4. The term *perennial philosophy* goes back to the Renaissance and refers to the common theme in all great religious/philosophical traditions. Socrates' philosophy of Eros in Plato's *Symposium* is the most familiar example in Western philosophy.

5. As elaborated first in *Childhood and Society* (New York: Norton, 1950), and later in *Identity and the Life Cycle* (Psychological Issues Monograph, New York: International Universities Press, 1959) and *Insight and Responsibility* (New York: Norton, 1964).

6. The End Is in the Beginning: A Tribute to Bruno Bettelheim

1. Bruno Bettelheim, "Training the Child Care Worker," *American Journal of Orthopsychiatry* 36 (1966), p. 705.

2. Martin Buber, "The William Alanson White Memorial Lectures, Fourth Series." *Psychiatry* 20 (1957), p. 110.

7. Two Kinds of Truth: The Principle of Complementarity

1. This is not such an esoteric, mystical idea as it may sound at first. Most of us are familiar with the fact that great scientists like Newton, Einstein, and Bohr have been inspired to an I–Thou, quasi-religious attitude of awe and humility toward the universe they observe. What Bohr did was simply to take this I–Thou experience out of the realm of religion and try to explain its scientific basis.

2. Quoted in Ronald W. Clark, *Einstein: The Life and Times* (New York: World Publishing Company, 1999), p. 345.

8. A Science of Subjectivity: Complementarity and Consciousness

1. Joseph Glenmullen, *Prozac Backlash* (New York: Simon & Schuster, 2000), pp. 189–90, 236–37.

2. Peter Kramer asserts that medication changes personality in ways that make patients feel "like a new person" or "more like myself." This is not what I mean by "becoming more fully oneself" through a psychotherapeutic process. In the first case—when patients say they feel "like a new person"—the medication has shifted their brain state in a way that allows them to experience a side of themselves that was always there but that they are not used to feeling. In the second case—when patients say "I feel more like myself"—what they generally mean is "more like my *familiar* self." The medication has helped them achieve the swimming-pool goal of restoring the stability of their old interpersonal patterns. Becoming more fully oneself, in contrast, requires recognizing, feeling, and integrating *unfamiliar* parts of oneself—making the unconscious conscious—in a process of growth through the quest.

3. Frederick Crews, "The Revenge of the Repressed," *New York Review of Books*, Nov. 17, 1994.

4. Psychoanalyst Howard Shevrin, for example, has done extensive controlled laboratory research that supports the concept of repression, and has published it in numerous journals dating as far back as 1967. Shevrin presented a summary of his research in a plenary address to the American Psychoanalytic Association on Dec. 17, 1993. This address was later published in the *Journal of the American Psychoanalytic Association* no. 43, 4 (1995).

5. In his published case reports, Freud tends to be selectively attentive to the evidence that confirms his theory and does not always give his patients room to discover something in themselves that might disconfirm or qualify his theory. He tends to use his theory to infer what is going on unconsciously in his patient, and then tells the patient about it as if it were fact, instead of waiting for it (or something else) to become conscious through the natural evolution of the psychotherapeutic process.

6. Werner Heisenberg, "The Representation of Nature in Contemporary Physics," *Daedalus* 87 (1958).

7. Niels Bohr, *Essays 1958–1962 on Atomic Physics and Human Knowledge* (New York: John Wiley & Sons, 1958), p. 77.

8. "[U]nambiguous communication of physical evidence demands that the experimental arrangement as well as the recording of the observations be expressed in common language." Niels Bohr, *Essays 1958–1962 on Atomic Physics and Human Knowledge* (New York: John Wiley & Sons, 1963), p. 91.

9. Bohr, *Atomic Physics and Human Knowledge*, p. 12.

10. Edward O. Wilson, *Consilience: The Unity of Knowledge* (New York: Alfred A. Knopf, 1998).

11. Objective tests can determine what percentage of the time a *typical* patient will have a medication response versus a placebo response, but they cannot determine what kind of response a *particular* patient is actually having.

12. To put it more precisely: Just as an atomic object appears as an impression on a photographic plate, registering as a wave or particle depending on the experimental

framework, so a patient's transference emotion appears as a countertransference impression on the consciousness of the therapist, registering as a subjective emotional reaction to the patient or an objective observation of the patient's pattern depending on the therapist's frame of mind—his degree of detachment from the transference projection of the moment. A complete scientific description of a psychotherapeutic process would have to correlate an objective theoretical explanation of the patient's pattern (the analogue to the mathematical description in atomic physics) with a detailed account of the therapist's subjective countertransference "impressions." To be unambiguous, it should also describe the therapist's "conceptual framework"—the basic assumptions in which his theoretical explanation is grounded.

9. Anxiety and the Spirit of Questioning

1. Full psychoanalysis is not necessary, or even appropriate for everyone. Most of the psychotherapy I do is once or twice a week and I have found this to be very effective in most situations. However, for certain patients and certain problems, the increased frequency of four to five times per week is important. It facilitates the intensification of the transference, allowing the patient to recreate in the therapy the very problem he or she needs help with (which you will see as Mary's story unfolds). Moreover, it provides a setting in which the patient can learn from the transference (make the unconscious conscious) more easily than he or she could do in other relationships and other therapeutic settings. The issue is whether the therapy is a place where the patient can talk about his or her life outside of therapy and develop transference along the way or whether the patient's life (at least an important part of it) is happening *in* therapy, through the transference relationship.

There is currently a debate among psychoanalysts about whether three sessions a week can be as effective as four or five in facilitating working with the transference. There is general consensus, however, that fewer than three times a week is not enough for this specialized but important purpose. There are therapists who treat patients once a week and call it psychoanalysis, but they have typically not had the kind of training recommended by our established psychoanalytic training institutes and so have never learned to work with patients four or five times a week. Of course, the therapy they do once a week may be very helpful but it isn't psychoanalysis.

2. This theory of *affective resonance* was first proposed by Sylvan Tomkins in Volume 1 of his *Affect, Imagery, Consciousness* (New York: Springer, 1962). Tomkins wrote: "It is only when the joy of the other activates joy in the self, fear of the other activates fear within, distress of the other activates distress within, anger of the other activates anger within, excitement of the other activates one's own excitement that we may speak of an animal as a social animal" (pp. 296–97). Psychoanalyst Michael Basch describes this kind of affective resonance as a biological instinct that shapes the relationship between infant and mother, and that forms the basis for the adult experience of empathy ("Empathic Understanding: A Review of the Concept and Some Theoretical Considerations," *Journal of the American Psychoanalytic Association* 13 [1983], pp. 171–87.) Psychiatrist Donald Nathanson points out that there also needs to be some mechanism whereby the infant learns to block affective resonance—tune out the affective signals coming from

mother—as part of the normal process of learning to distinguish what is inside from what is outside. ("The Empathic Wall and the Ecology of Affect," *Psychoanalytic Study of the Child* 41 [1986], pp. 171–87.)

3. Friedrich Nietzsche, *Beyond Good and Evil*, trans. Walter Kaufmann (1886; reprint, New York: Vintage, 1996), p. 24.

10. Introspection and Putting It into Words

1. Peter Kramer does discuss how early traumatic experiences can change brain chemistry and so lead to symptoms and personality problems. But he views these as chemical imbalances and *not* as expressions of inner conflict.

11. Resistance and Transference

1. Of course, this research does involve interpretations of infant behavior, which still depend on unconfirmable (however plausible) inferences. In the end, we have no choice but to consult our own instinctive, intuitive, empathy for what an infant's experience must be like. For those interested in further reading on this topic, a good place to start is Robert Karen's *Becoming Attached: First Relationships and How They Shape Our Capacity to Love* (Oxford: Oxford University Press, 1998). Particularly interesting is Karen's account of Melanie Klein's theory of development, in which he describes what love and hate must be like for an infant who cannot yet distinguish mother as a separate person. Also recommended—for its fascinating discussion of research on the perceptual world of the infant, and what makes an infant smile—is T.G.R. Bower's *Human Development* (San Francisco: W. H. Freeman, 1979).

2. This is not to say that old, unremembered traumas are irrelevant, or that they were not terribly damaging to the psyche of the growing child, or that it is not sometimes helpful when clear memories of such traumas emerge in the course of psychotherapy. But the traumas are not the whole story. When people who are traumatized become mentally ill, it is because the traumatic wound has activated or aggravated some inner conflict in them, arousing anxiety-provoking unconscious emotions (the nature of which varies depending both on the person and the trauma) to the point that they are no longer manageable through ordinary defense mechanisms.

3. This was the point, which comes in many analyses, when the transference manifestations seem to become more concentrated and more pervasive, whether focused in a symptom, as in Mary's case, or in an emotional preoccupation with the analyst. This is referred to as the establishment of *transference neurosis,* meaning that the original neurotic conflict that the patient came into treatment with is now concentrated in the transference relationship with the analyst.

12. But Isn't Psychoanalysis Supposed to Be About Sex?

1. Wilfred Bion, *Attention and Interpretation* (New York: Basic Books, 1970), p. 42.

2. The term *sadomasochistic* implies that sadism and masochism are two sides of one coin. The pleasurable satisfaction of controlling (manipulating) or humiliating the other person is overt in sadism, covert in masochism. For more on this topic, I highly recommend the writings of Robert Stoller, especially his book *Sexual Excitement* (New York: Pantheon Books, 1979).

3. This awareness, I believe, is a universal human experience that is the basis for the common etymological origin of the words "whole," "heal," and "holy."

13. Respect the Symptom

1. Of course, it may be that some psychiatric symptoms are indeed genetic defects and have not yet shown signs of becoming extinct only because evolutionary changes take too long to be noticeable over the course of recorded human history. But we don't really know how fast human evolution happens. What we do know is more consistent with the idea that symptoms are evolutionary advantages than that they are evolutionary mistakes.

2. Further evidence that depression may protect against suicide came in a January 1999 report by the *Psychiatric Times*—"China's Suicide Patterns Challenge Depression Theory"—that the suicide rate in China is two to three times higher than in the United States while their rate of depression is three to five times lower. Perhaps if the Chinese could more easily become "biologically" depressed they would not be killing themselves in such high numbers.

3. Many readers will recognize that, though psychoanalytic, this is not the traditional Freudian interpretation of Hamlet's dilemma. I presented it in much more detail in a 1990 article for the *International Journal of Psycho-Analysis*, entitled "A New Look at *Hamlet*: Aesthetic Response and Shakespeare's Meaning."

4. Although Plato's tripartite soul has sometimes been interpreted as a synthesis of body, mind, and spirit, Plato himself considered all three levels of desire in the soul—even the apparently physical level of appetite—to be quite distinct from the body and its humors. On the other hand, as he described in the *Symposium*, he did consider the soul to be rooted in the body—as a growing tree is rooted in the earth—and he thought of the soul's desire as evolving from the physical level of appetite to the spiritual level of philosophy as a person matured.

5. Harris Dienstfrey, *Where the Mind Meets the Body* (New York: HarperCollins, 1991), p. xv.

6. Even when we know what neurotransmitter system they act on, we have no idea why or how that works to change the patient's mental state.

14. Freud's Theory of the Soul: From the Swimming Pool to the Quest

1. Sigmund Freud, "The Resistances to Psychoanalysis," *Standard Edition*, vol. 19 (London: Hogarth Press, 1961), pp. 213–22.

2. I mention Freud's anxiety here not merely as a theoretical inference based on Bloom's literary theory. In fact Freud suffered during just these years of the 1890s from a well-documented anxiety neurosis. A good case can be made—though this is not the place to do it—that Freud's two theories of neurosis reflected not only a philosophical ambivalence but a more private personal ambivalence about how to understand his own anxiety symptoms. Of course, this takes nothing away from the validity of his theorizing. Every scientific theory, like every work of art, can in principle be linked psychologically to the private neurotic concerns of its creator.

3. "[T]he accumulation of excitation [libido] is felt as unpleasure and . . . sets the apparatus in action with a view to repeating the experience of satisfaction, which involved a diminution of excitation and was felt as pleasure. A current of this kind in the apparatus, starting from unpleasure and aiming at pleasure, we have termed a 'wish'; and we have asserted that only a wish is able to set the apparatus in motion and that the course of the excitation in it is automatically regulated by feelings of pleasure and unpleasure." *Interpretation of Dreams* (London: Hogarth Press, 1953), p. 598

4. Robert Waelder, "The Principle of Multiple Function," in S. Guttman, ed., *Psychoanalysis: Observation, Theory, Application. Selected Papers of Robert Waelder* (New York: International Universities Press, 1976), pp. 68–83.

5. Similarly, in a 1965 monograph, Waelder wrote: "The ability to step back and take a look at oneself from an imaginary observation point—the self-consciousness or the transcendence of one's self as it has been called by philosophers . . .—is the essence of the superego function." *Psychoanalytic Avenues to Art* (New York: International Universities Press), p. 59.

6. Freud based this theory on Darwin's hypothesis of the "primal horde."

7. For Freud, the idea that "the aim of all life is death" had negative, pessimistic connotations quite different from what it has in Eastern religions, where it seems to combine the meanings of both Eros and Thanatos. As the *Oxford English Dictionary* defines it, for instance, nirvana is not only "the extinction of individual existence . . . or the extinction of all desires and passions" (akin to Thanatos) but also "absorption into the supreme spirit . . . and attainment of perfect beautitude" (more like Eros). Similarly, the *American Heritage Dictionary* defines *nirvana* as "an ideal condition of rest, harmony, stability, or joy." For Freud, rest and stability belong to Thanatos. Harmony and joy belong to Eros.

8. Sigmund Freud, "Why War?" originally published in 1932. *Standard Edition*, vol. 22 (London: Hogarth Press, 1964), p. 209.

9. These quotes are taken from the 1920 monograph in which Freud first introduced the concepts of Eros and the death instinct: "Beyond the Pleasure Principle," *Standard Edition*, vol. 18 (London: Hogarth Press, 1955), p. 38.

15. Integrating the Swimming Pool Within the Quest: "Where *It* Was, There Shall *I* Become"

1. Sigmund Freud, "New Introductory Lectures, Lecture XXXI," *Standard Edition*, vol. 22 (London: Hogarth Press, 1964), p. 77.

2. Bohr delivered his first paper on the principle of complementarity at the International Congress of Physics in Como, Italy, in 1927. The paper was published in 1928 under the title "The Quantum Postulate and the Recent Development of Atomic Theory" (*Nature* 121, supplement, pp. 580–90).

3. Robert Waelder "The Principle of Multiple Function," in S. Guttman, ed., *Psychoanalysis: Observation, Theory, Application: Selected Papers of Rebert Waelder* (New York: International Universities Press, 1976), pp. 68–69. (In the quotes from this paper, I have substituted *It* for *id*, *I* for *ego*, and *I that stands above* for *superego*.)

4. Ibid., p. 69.

16. What Is the Soul?

1. Erich Fromm, *The Anatomy of Human Destructiveness* (New York: Holt, Rinehart and Winston, 1973), p. 357.

2. Autism used to be considered the most severe form of childhood schizophrenia. It is now generally thought of as a neurological disorder. In fact, it is probably both. Or there may be more than one disorder that looks like autism. But whatever the nature of autism, the experience I had with Laura speaks very clearly for itself.

3. Sigmund Freud, "On Narcissism: An Introduction," *Standard Edition*, vol. 14 (London: Hogarth Press, 1957), p. 95.

4. In fact, even when schizophrenic hallucinations take the form Freud described of ostensibly neutral self-observations, like "Now she's thinking of that again" or "Now he's going out," they are really a caricature of the genuine self-observing function, and are often spoken by the hallucinated voices in a very mocking tone of voice that makes them feel quite humiliating. Ultimately, they have the same effect on the person as the more overtly punitive, self-attacking hallucinations; they make it very difficult to live comfortably and spontaneously without paralyzing self-consciousness or fear of being judged or attacked. As such, they are the most vivid and obvious manifestation of the inner-directed self-punitive action of Thanatos.

5. James Carse, *Breakfast at the Victory: The Mysticism of Everyday Experience* (San Francisco: HarperCollins, 1994).

6. Gilbert Ryle, *The Concept of Mind*, 1949. Ironically, Ryle did not think of himself as a materialist but as a behaviorist. His point (which makes little sense to me) was that mind is neither an immaterial ghost nor a neurological machine but simply a publicly observable form of behavior.

7. Daniel Dennett, *Consciousness Explained* (Boston: Little, Brown and Company, 1991). The most accessible summary of Dennett's position is in a brief review of his book by John Searle, including a response to the review by Dennett and a counterresponse by

Searle, in Searle's *The Mystery of Consciousness* (New York: The New York Review of Books, 1997).

8. Gerald Edelman, *Bright Air, Brilliant Fire: On the Matter of the Mind* (New York: Basic Books, 1992).

9. John Searle, *The Mystery of Consciousness* (New York: *The New York Review of Books*, 1997), pp. 17–18.

10. Rupert Sheldrake, quoted in the roundtable discussion from the PBS television series *A Glorious Accident*. It is probably not an accident that, when the series was published in book form (New York: W. H. Freeman, 1997), the last two sentences of Sheldrake's quote—which most directly challenge the materialistic assumptions of the evolutionary model, and implies an appreciation of Bohr's principle of complementarity—were edited out.

11. Wilder Penfield, *The Mystery of the Mind* (Princeton, New Jersey: Princeton University Press, 1975), pp. 55 and 76.

12. Of course Penfield also pointed out that it is possible to turn off consciousness completely by electrical means. In fact that's what happens to an epileptic patient when he loses consciousness in a seizure, or to all of us when we go to sleep. There is a center in the upper brain stem—the reticular activating system—that supports consciousness when its neurons are firing and deactivates consciousness when they are inhibited. But the firing of those neurons does not *cause* consciousness, any more than oxygen causes life. It is only a necessary but not sufficient condition for consciousness, just as oxygen is a necessary but not sufficient condition for life.

13. See, for instance, the passage from Descartes's *Principles of Philosophy* on p. 30 of David Rosenthal's anthology, *The Nature of Mind* (New York: Oxford University Press, 1991). Another translation of this passage can be found in Haldane and Ross, trans., *Philosophical Works of Descartes*, vol. 1 (New York: Dover Publications, 1955), p. 222.

14. René Descartes, *The Passions of the Soul*, in Haldane and Ross, trans., *Philosophical Works of Descartes*, vol. 1, pp. 329–99.

15. Ibid., p. 398. Descartes's book is dedicated primarily to cataloguing the "passions" of the soul, and refers to "actions of the soul" only briefly, on p. 340, and again—as "interior emotions" of the soul—on p. 398. Nevertheless, Descartes assigns the actions of the soul a higher status than its passions, stating "that our good and our harm depend mainly on the interior emotions which are only excited in the soul by the soul itself" (p. 398). (For clarification, an *interior* emotion is one that arises from within, as an action of the soul, as opposed to an emotion generated *externally* by movements of the body–brain acting on the soul.)

16. Carl Jung drew the same sort of distinction between emotion and feeling, viewing emotion as an experience connected to the body and feeling as a nonphysiological "*rational* function." "Feeling informs you through its feeling-tones of the values of things," he wrote. "Feeling tells you . . . what a thing is worth to you." (First Tavistock Lecture of 1935, reprinted in *The Symbolic Life: Collected Works of C. G. Jung*, vol. 18 [Princeton, New Jersey: Princeton University Press, 1976], p. 13.)

17. From "The Principle of Multiple Function," in S. Guttman, ed., *Psychoanalysis: Observation, Theory, Application: Selected Papers of Robert Waelder* (New York: International Universities Press, 1976), p. 73.

17. What Are We Really Hearing When We Listen to Prozac?

1. For further details about how and why managed care has coerced primary care physicians to become the primary prescribers of psychiatric medications and to avoid referrals to psychiatrists, see Joseph Glenmullen, *Prozac Backlash* (New York: Simon & Schuster, 2000), pp. 217–23.

2. I will have much more to say about these shifting brain states toward the end of this chapter.

3. This happens so commonly with Prozac and other serotonergic antidepressants that it has become popularly known as "Prozac poop-out," described memorably in Lauren Slater's *Prozac Diary* (New York: Random House, 1998). Psychiatrist Joseph Glenmullen has suggested that this wearing off of antidepressant effectiveness may be inevitable—a result of the fact that the antidepressant actually *causes* a chemical imbalance, and thereby stimulates the neurons to compensate over time in a way that counteracts the imbalance (and with it the antidepressant effect). Glenmullen calls this compensatory neuronal reaction "Prozac backlash" (in the book of the same name cited previously), but it happens in one way or another with any antidepressant.

4. Joseph Glenmullen is the only other psychiatrist I know of who has written about the emotional blunting produced by serotonin boosters (*Prozac Backlash*, p.84), but he understands this blunting more from a Medical Model than a Psychotherapeutic Model perspective—not as a suppression of inner conflict, but merely as an unwanted biological side effect of the medication.

5. Of course, Phyllis never felt that she had been transformed in any way. Rather, she felt that she didn't *deserve* to feel so much "better than well" because it was selfish. That reactivated her need to go back to serving others to compensate for her selfishness, and that in turn re-activated her depression.

6. Actually there are three basic ego states. The third is the state of "quiet alertness" in which exploring the world and learning take place.

7. On p. 18, for instance, Kramer writes that, "Tess had existed in one mental state for twenty or thirty years; she then briefly felt different on medication. Now that the old mental state was threatening to re-emerge—the one she had experienced almost all her adult life—her response was 'I am not myself.' "

8. Although Kramer asserts (p. 287) that "traditional psychodynamic psychotherapy" is his "usual approach to patients," this is decidedly not the case with the patients he discusses in *Listening to Prozac*. His reports of his work with Gail (pp. 92–95), Sonia (pp. 237–39, 242–43), Sally (pp. 144–48), Tess (pp. 1–21, 33–37), Allison (pp. 204–8, 216–17), and Julia (pp. 22–41) deal only with medication management. In the case of Tess, he specifies that the visits were fifteen minutes long. The period of time he worked with these patients is not always specified, but for Tess his report covers less than two years; for Sally a year and a half; for Julia less than a year; for Allison less than six months. Kramer does report (p. 292) that, "The patients I medicate with Prozac tend first to have undergone extensive course of psychotherapy," and many of the patients he discusses continued to see a psychologist or social worker for psychotherapy during the period in which he was medicating them. But there is no information about a psychotherapeutic process in any of his reports.

18. Repetition, Reflection, and the Search for Meaning

1. Jacob Needleman, *The Way of the Physician* (San Francisco: Harper&Row, 1985, p.142).

2. This problem goes back even before the advent of managed care in the 1990s, Needleman wrote in 1985 that "the practice of the art of medicine has now developed into what is called 'the delivery of health-care.' Health-care is a commodity and falls under, as it were, the laws of 'Caesar.'" (*The Way of the Physician*, p. 136)

3. The essay won honorable mention in the contest and the *Psychiatric Times* published it in their November 1987 issue, p. 35ff.

4. Where Freud believed that dreams are generated from the unconscious as disguised expressions of repressed wishes, McCarley and Hobson claimed, based on their research, that the dream state is generated by random electrical impulses—from brain stem nerve cells—that are inherently devoid of psychological meaning. They argued that the bizarreness and apparent illogic of dreams (which for Freud held a disguised meaning) are merely byproducts of this meaningless neurological randomness, and therefore that *all dreams must be inherently random and meaningless.* To refute this specious reasoning, I pointed out that the waking state too had long ago been proved to be activated and sustained by random electrical impulses from brain stem neurons. By McCarley and Hobson's logic then, all waking mental activity, *including their own theory,* must be a byproduct of neurological randomness and therefore inherently meaningless.

5. Grünbaum's argument against psychoanalysis is that a patient's introspective knowledge about his own state of mind is irretrievably distorted by suggestion—i.e., by the patient's assumptions and concerns about what is acceptable to the analyst. Here is my response from my closing statement at the debate:

"[S]imply by drawing the distinction between veridical and distorted introspective knowledge, Grünbaum suggests that the distinction can be made, by some unspecified persons if not by analytic patients . . . For instance, I suspect that if I were to ask [Grünbaum] now whether he still believes his argument against Freud is valid, he would say 'yes.' If I then asked him whether that 'yes' reflected accurate introspective knowledge of his state of mind or a concern about what the audience would expect him to say, I take it he would feel capable of telling the difference. But consider the circumstances. He is engaged in a debate before a large audience, hoping to convince them that his point of view is more cogent than that of his opponents. It would hardly be conducive to this goal if he answered 'no.' It would adversely affect the audience's opinion of him and his argument, and could even end up being reported, to his embarrassment, in print somewhere. I take it that, in spite of these circumstances, Dr. Grünbaum would remain confident that he can tell the difference between his genuine personal experience and a false compliance with the expectations of his listeners. If I then asked him, 'Do you think it possible that your 'yes' could be subtly influenced by concerns about the audience's attitudes without your being aware of it?' I take it he would . . . have a sense of the kind of subtle self-examination that would be necessary to answer such a question. I'm here to tell him that every one of my analytic patients feels the same way. The hypothetical questions I just posed to Dr. Grünbaum are the kinds of questions I and all analysts ask our patients, who, like Dr. Grünbaum, are both capable of and vitally interested in distinguishing between accurate introspective awareness and suggestion . . .

"The influence of suggestion . . . is a universal phenomenon of human interaction . . . There is no communication which is not potentially influenced by the speaker's assumptions and concerns about the disposition of his listeners. Even . . . reports of experiments in the objective sciences are vulnerable to both intentional and unintentional distortions because of concerns about the attitudes of department chairmen, journal referees, the Nobel prize committee, not to mention parents, spouses and children. Psychoanalysis is uniquely capable of eliminating such distortions from its data. It makes a virtue of necessity by making the inevitable distortions that occur the focus of intensive scrutiny. To this end it is designed specifically to be a setting in which there are no real adverse consequences for saying what one really thinks and feels. This puts a frame around the fantasied adverse consequences so that they can be recognized as transference. Recognizing his distorted awareness for what it is then frees the patient to become aware of the undistorted facts of his inner experience. Suggestion is not the enemy of the truth psychoanalysis seeks to understand. It is a central part of the truth psychoanalysis seeks to understand."

6. *Psychiatric Times*, April 1992: Ronald Pies, "Splitting the Discipline of Psychiatry: Modern Manichaean" (pp. 13–14); Elio Frattaroli, "Disordered Brain Does Not Create Disordered Mind" (pp. 15–17).

7. Burness Morre and Bernard Fine, eds., *Psychoanalytic Terms & Concepts* (New Haven: Yale University Press, 1990), p. 210.

8. The connection between the repetition compulsion and karma will perhaps be clearer from the following passage, taken from *The Tibetan Yogas of Dream and Sleep* by Tenzin Wangyal Rinpoche (Ithaca, N.Y.: Snow Lion Publications, 1998), p. 27:

As long as we identify with the grasping and aversion of the moving mind, we produce the negative emotions that are born in the gap between what is and what we want. Actions generated from these emotions, which include nearly all actions taken in our ordinary lives, leave karmic traces.

Karma means action. Karmic traces are the results of actions, which remain in the mental consciousness and influence our future. We can partially understand karmic traces if we think of them as what in the West are called tendencies in the unconscious. They are inclinations, patterns of internal and external behavior, ingrained reactions, habitual conceptualizations. They dictate our emotional reactions to situations and our intellectual understandings as well as our characteristic emotional habits and intellectual rigidities. They create and condition every response we normally have to every element of our experience.

9. As reported by P. D. Ouspensky, *In Search of the Miraculous* (New York: Harcourt, Brace & World, 1949), chapters 1 and 8.

Index